A Professional Professoriate

VANDERBILT ISSUES IN HIGHER EDUCATION is a timely series that focuses on the three core functions of higher education: teaching, research, and service. Interdisciplinary in nature, it concentrates not only on how these core functions are carried out in colleges and universities but also on the contributions they make to larger issues of social and economic development, as well as the various organizational, political, psychological, and social forces that influence their fulfillment and evolution.

A Professional Professoriate

Unionization, Bureaucratization, and the AAUP

PHILO A. HUTCHESON

Vanderbilt University Press
Nashville

First Edition 2000

04 03 02 01 00   5 4 3 2 1

Library of Congress Cataloging-in-Publication Data

Hutcheson, Philo A., 1951–
A professional professoriate : unionization, bureaucratization,
and the AAUP / Philo Hutcheson.
p. cm. — (Vanderbilt issues in higher education)
Includes bibliographical references and index.
ISBN 0-8265-1323-9 (cloth)
ISBN 0-8265-1348-4 (pbk.)
1. American Association of University Professors—History.
2. College teachers' unions—United States—History.
3. Collective bargaining—College teachers—United States—History.
I. Title. II. Series.
LB2335.865.U6 H88 1999
331.88'1137812'0973—dc21
99-6509

Published by Vanderbilt University Press
Printed in the United States of America

To Alyssa

CONTENTS

Preface   viii

Introduction: Professionalism, Bureaucratization,
and the AAUP   1

Chapter 1. The AAUP from 1946 to 1958:
McCarthyism and Reconstruction Efforts   22

Chapter 2. A Revitalized AAUP, 1958 to 1964   43

Chapter 3. Custodians of the Interests of Higher
Education, or Employees?   65

Chapter 4. The AAUP and Unionization,
1966 to 1971   97

Chapter 5. To Hedge Our Bets: The Uneasy Balance
 of Professionalism and Unionization, 1971 to 1976   136

Chapter 6. "More": 1976 to the Early 1990s   173

Notes   188
Bibliography   258
Index   293

PREFACE

In a sense this work began in 1969, when I entered college and encountered professors on a firsthand basis. Then in the winter of my first year I was appointed a student representative to the college faculty, and thereafter I served on several student-faculty committees. After college I entered college administration and worked closely with faculty members, first in admissions and then in academic advising, for nearly twenty years. Throughout that time I found professors to be fascinating, and I found governance and administration issues to be equally fascinating. Many a colleague still cringes when I announce that I enjoy faculty meetings and have since the first one I attended in 1970. The expressions of professional concern, juxtaposed against or nestled within administrative goals, find or omit voice in extraordinary ways at faculty meetings.

I do not intend to suggest in this book that professors are simply experiencing a deprofessionalization. While on a daily basis I recognize the encroachments of bureaucracy, with central goals of efficiency and hierarchy, at the same time I recognize how professors continuously develop higher expectations about their levels of performance especially in research yet also in organizational participation and teaching, thus increasing professional expectations and behavior. I do not argue that this is a labor market issue, although certainly the labor market of the 1970s and 1980s was a key factor in pushing up the levels of faculty credentials. Instead I look at how professors view themselves as professionals and as members of bureaucracies: these are conditions that vary tremendously across types of institutions as well as across individual institutions. Nevertheless there are powerful similarities for all professors, more so as the professoriate in preparation and work developed in the 1980s and 1990s. As a historian, of sorts, I am compelled to ask, "Well, how did we get here?" What elements of our occupations and our organizations arose at what times, so that now we find ourselves dashing from class to library to meeting to office, where we answer dozens or more of E-mail messages, some of which lead us back to class, renewing the process. I hope the question, as well as the answer, proves satisfactory.

Many people have contributed to this work, and I wish to thank as many as my memory allows. First, thanks to Ben Lane and Shirley Hilger, who respectively got me started in faculty affairs and administration. Also, to Larry Breitborde, Jerry Gustafson, and Harry Davis (Beloit College professors past and present) as well as John Lind (former Beloit administrator), whose early support as I sought and then began to earn, albeit slowly, the doctorate was a critical factor. Second, to my fellow students and the faculty of the former University of Chicago Department of Education, where I learned that no answer is better than the question and no question is good enough. Third, to the Furlan family, whose love and support through some very trying times kept me moving forward. Fourth, to the many faculty, administrators, and students at Hamline University who appreciated my efforts especially Scott Pratt, Carole Brown, Steve Bjork, Matt Olson, Sal Landers, Chantell Kadin, Jodie Knutsen, Janet Meyer, and Serena Erickson. Fifth, to the many colleagues in the study of higher education whose appreciation (or perhaps tolerance) of my interests and research furthered my professional development in many ways: Les Goodchild, Sheila Slaughter, Bill Tierney, Barbara Townsend, Jim Hearn, John Braxton, Clif Conrad, Estela Bensimon, Yvonna Lincoln, Julie Neururer, Katherine Reynolds, Jana Nidiffer, Linda Eisenmann (to those two: E-mail colleagues extraordinaire!), Roger Geiger, Chris Maitland, and many more whom I should name. It is an odd assortment, but that befits the study of higher education. And thanks to the higher education editors who thought my work was worth publishing. Sixth, the faculty and especially the students of the higher education doctoral program at Georgia State University, who were patient and curious, a wonderful combination for scholarship. And to Parker Blount, department chair, and Ron Henry, provost, who wanted me to get tenure. Seventh, Charles Backus and Maggy Shannon of Vanderbilt University Press, who waited for me, with remarkable patience, to complete this manuscript. Eighth, to my friends. Through thick and thin, and all my sarcasm, you have been there (and Babette go Cubs!). Ninth, to my parents, who have always valued my education regardless of the costs and asked that I think. Tenth, to Harold Wechlser. His encyclopedic knowledge is exceeded only by his theoretical grasp, and when students refer to me as Dr. Citation, I know I have made a small step toward honoring an extraordinary scholar. He put me on this topic in our last meeting as professor-advisee, and I am deeply indebted. Finally, and most of all, to my wife, Alyssa, my daughter, Monica, and my son, Thomas. You make me cry with joy.

Of course, all of the above and those whom I have failed to mention are responsible for the strengths of this work. I hold only myself accountable for the errors and omissions.

Finally, a word on generalizibility, a word that nags the positivists and threatens the postpositivists. As a historian I find often that I lie between those two epistemological terrains, and so I feel free to talk about generalization. When I have talked about this work with colleagues and friends, I have often sensed or even heard an unanticipated identification. It does seem to me that many occupations have found themselves moving between professional ideals and bureaucratic goals. For professors, however, it is no small irony that Frederick Winslow Taylor's biographer surmised that Taylor first developed his initial sense of the imperative of efficiency in a mathematics class at Phillips Exeter Academy.*

And thus, with a footnote, I begin.

*Robert Kanigel, *The One Best Way: Frederick Winslow Taylor and the Enigma of Efficiency* (New York: Viking Penguin, 1997), 215.

A Professional Professoriate

INTRODUCTION

Professionalism, Bureaucratization, and the AAUP

From the late 1940s to the mid-1970s, U.S. higher education underwent a series of changes that historians of higher education view as among the most substantial of any period in this country. Numerous studies have documented the shifts in institutions and students from the late 1940s to the mid-1970s. These shifts have persisted, in varying degrees, and continue to command the attention of scholars. Although the professoriate underwent shifts as well, there has been no historical examination of those changes in the occupation's numbers, structure, and composition or of the consequences of those changes. Thus this book addresses both a critical higher education issue, changes in the structure and nature of the professoriate, and a critical period, from the mid-1940s to the mid-1970s, with specific considerations of the ensuing developments in the 1980s and the 1990s.

The tension between professionalism and bureaucratic demands is a recurring theme in discussions about, and examinations of, the professoriate. The American Association of University Professors (AAUP) provides an important focal point for understanding the professoriate and that tension. The AAUP, as the only national association solely for college and university professors and their occupational interests (beyond disciplinary associations), reflects the professoriate in substantial ways. Such issues as academic freedom and tenure, participation in college and university governance, and salaries have been constant AAUP concerns. Thus the nature of the occupation finds expression in AAUP actions and reports; as a national organization struggling to find ways to represent the nation's professoriate, the association found that increasingly bureaucratized employment procedures posed substantial challenges to its goal of professionalism. The AAUP explicitly identified itself with professional associations such as the American Medical Association well into the 1960s. Yet by 1976 it was also firmly committed to faculty collective bargaining, a legal relation clearly assigning the role of bureaucratic employee to the professor. This book offers a

1

detailed examination of the AAUP in its search for ways to sustain professionalism and address the fundamental changes in the nature of the professoriate in the post–World War II era, illustrating the tension between professionalism and bureaucratization.

In 1914 a committee of faculty members issued a call to organize a national association of professors, the American Association of University Professors. The committee members made clear the purposes of this new organization, intending "to maintain and advance the standards and ideals of the profession," viewing their role as "custodians of the interests of higher education." These standards and ideals were clearly within the concept of a profession; the organizing committee referred specifically to the American Medical Association and the American Bar Association.[1] Over forty years later, members at the 1957 AAUP Annual Meeting offered changes to the wording of the organization's constitution to reflect an additional goal, the advancement of material interests. A member moved from the floor to amend the proposed revision of Article I—Purpose of the Constitution by adding "economic welfare" to the phrase "to advance the standards and ideals of the profession."[2] Another member amended the proposed amendment with the deletion of "economic," and the members at the annual meeting approved the phrase "to advance the standards, ideals, and welfare of the profession."[3] With this revision of the Constitution, the AAUP goals began to shift. Rather than broadly advancing the standards and ideals of a profession serving as the custodian of the interests of higher education, the AAUP had added a specific interest in the material conditions of the profession, conditions that recognized professors as employees. Association activities have increasingly reflected the goals of professional ideals and economic welfare since the mid-1950s.

The Professoriate and Professionalism

A variety of definitions of professionalism have appeared in the literature on occupations. In one case the study of professors themselves led a scholar to conclusions about the characteristics of a profession and hence of professionalism. Logan Wilson concluded as a result of studying professors at research universities that there were specific characteristics of professionalism; he drew a careful distinction between all college and university teachers and professors at "central or major universities . . . such as Harvard, Chicago, Columbia, California, Wisconsin, and others that rank high in the universe of learning."[4] Wilson suggested six criteria as the framework for a profession:

1. Prolonged and specialized training based upon a systematized intellectual tradition that rarely can be acquired through mere apprenticeship.

2. Rigorous standards of licensure, fulfillment of which often confers upon the functionary a degree or title signifying specialized competence.
3. Application of techniques of such intricacy that competency tests cannot be deduced upon any simple continuum scale, nor can supervision be more than loosely applied.
4. Absence of precise contractual terms of work, which otherwise imply a calculated limitation of output and an exploitative attitude toward productivity.
5. A limitation upon the self-interest of the practitioner, and a careful insulation of professional considerations from extraneous matters, such as private opinions, economic interest, and class position.
6. Certain positive obligations to the profession and its clientele.[5]

Three characteristics are immediately apparent in Wilson's list (which he acknowledges as rarely applying completely to any occupation). First, there is an antibureaucratic theme. Max Weber discussed the ideal type of the bureaucracy specifically in terms of economic efficiency, and Wilson established criteria for professions that are explicitly contrary to output and economic interest.[6] Second, and somewhat implicit, the profession is exclusive, a pattern that Wilson briefly mentions.[7] Finally, it is the Ph.D. that represents expertise, a degree offered and most valued at research universities, and participation in governance is illustrative of the professional's desire for autonomy through control of the workplace

During the 1960s and the 1970s some sociologists debated the meaning of professions. In one case a scholar, Harold L. Wilensky, argued that greater knowledge in the general population meant not only skepticism about the certainties of professional judgments but also a greater willingness to use professional services. In response Marie Haug argued in 1974 that a process of deprofessionalization was occurring as clients acquired greater access to specialized knowledge. She evidenced concern about the construct of profession, suggesting that it was an Anglo-Saxon, Western industrial-capitalist concept. She also argued that "The deprofessionalization of everyone would usher in the age of the client as consumer, a consumer who is expected to question, compare, and treat all advice with a skeptical ear."[8]

Yet the idea of the professor as professional continued to hold sway. Donald Light's 1974 examination of the professoriate as an occupation with three separate but interrelated forms continues to be a productive framework for understanding the professional components of the professorial career. His work advances and refines Logan Wilson's analyses while acknowledging the complexities of the professoriate. For example, Light critiques Talcott Parson's formulation of the academic profession as one that simply establishes an ideal in the research university. Instead Light argues that there are three types of occupations in the professoriate: the faculty, the scholarly profession, and the academic profession. A profession exhibits five characteristics:

1. It has exclusive powers to recruit and train new members as it sees fit.
2. It has exclusive powers to judge who is qualified.
3. It is responsible for regulating the quality of professional work.
4. It has high social prestige.
5. It is grounded in an esoteric and complex body of knowledge.[9]

Faculty members are teachers at colleges and universities. Members of a scholarly profession are those people, not all necessarily employed at colleges and universities, "whose core activity is the advancement of knowledge." At the intersection of the faculty and a scholarly profession is an academic profession, an occupational category that is actually composed of several professions, each of them one of the disciplines. Light suggests that it is not clear whether or not the faculty is a profession, although he points out that it evidences occupational activity clearly distinct from scholarship. His major concern about the consideration of the faculty as a profession rests on the evaluation of teaching; since faculty members are not influential evaluators of teachers, they do not regulate the quality of the work in the occupation.[10] Light echoes the antibureaucratic and exclusive nature of professions.

Logan Wilson wrote a second book, *American Academics: Then and Now,* published in 1979, in which he indicated that most of his 1942 conclusions about the academic profession were still appropriate. Some shifts, such as the spread of research across many institutions and slightly more diverse social backgrounds among graduate students, were evident, but overall Wilson contended that the problems of the professor were much the same in the 1970s as they were in the 1940s.[11] Burton R. Clark wrote of the different worlds of the academic profession in 1987, locating professionalism according to such characteristics as disciplinary identity.[12]

Thus the sociological definitions of profession, in the context of the professoriate, focus on expert (disciplinary) knowledge resulting from advanced education, autonomy from contractual standards of technical work, control of appointment and promotion, ethics, and social prestige. For the sake of this inquiry, professionalization is the process of a profession, that is, how an individual or an occupational group achieves professional status. And professionalism is the act of being professional as either an individual or as a group.

Questions regarding professionalism and the professoriate have important historical considerations as well as sociological implications. Scholars continue to reassess the chronological beginnings of the professional career of the professor, attempting to specify at what point in time professors indeed started to become professionals in their own right in the United States, rather than participants in a broader occupational category of ministry and teaching. Martin Finkelstein has argued that the professionalization process began in the late 1700s; a more recent examination by John D. Burton suggested that the process began in the late 1600s. Both Finkelstein and Burton agree on the nature of professionalization, as professors began to enter college teaching as a lifetime career and increasingly taught in specialized areas, even in the era of the classical curriculum.[13] One conclusion is clear: elements of professionalization are deeply rooted in the academic career. Furthermore, as another historian has found, the exclusive nature of the profession has social characteristics. The meritocracy, the intellectual tradition and intricate techniques suggested by Wilson, has particularistic interpretations. James D. Anderson examined the attempt of an official of the Roswenwald Fund to convince colleges and universities in the late 1940s that there were many well-qualified African-American scholars. Despite a list of 150 such candidates, college and university presidents claimed that they would select African-American scholars but none was available.[14]

Yet whether those elements are rooted in the same manner now, or were in the 1970s, as they were in the 1940s may not be so evident as Logan Wilson argued. In some ways the literature on the academic profession qua profession is all too brief in its review of faculty unionization, a process that necessarily places the professor in the position of bureaucratic employee.[15] Wilson offered only a few pages of analysis on unionization in his 1979 work, concluding, "Many others [in the professoriate] . . . are unwilling to barter away what they deem to be their intellectual birthright as professionals for a dubious mess of pottage as trade unionists." Clark argued that unionization occurred mostly among professors at community colleges and teachers colleges while institutions with established traditions of collegiality and faculty senates had little need for such activity.[16] How bureaucratization of the college and university has progressed in the twentieth century, and especially in the post–World War II period, is illustrative of the boundaries of professionalization of the professoriate.

The Professoriate and Bureaucratization

As Richard Hofstadter has argued, the earliest organizational forms of higher education in the colonies differed from the northern European forms. The latter were characterized by faculty control of institutions while the early colleges in the United States were administrative entities, led by presidents selected by governing boards with legal charters for the operation of the institutions. These colleges remained small throughout the 1600s, 1700s, and 1800s; as late as 1909 only six universities had enrollments exceeding 5,000 students.[17]

Yet the Gilded Age would bring a period of enormous growth to U.S. higher education, especially in terms of the functions of higher education, enrollments, and eventually the size of administrations. Thorstein Veblen would caustically remark on the "captains of erudition" while presidents such as Charles Franklin Thwing and Charles W. Eliot produced articles and even books on the topic of administration.[18] One consequence of this growth was bureaucratization.

Max Weber's analysis of bureaucracies provides the central conception of that form for this book. Weber argued that bureaucratization was at its ideal the most economically efficient method of organizing a social group. The bureaucratic organization is a means of assuring clients that judgments are based on technical criteria rather than personal ones and that all members of the organization participate in hierarchical relationships of authority. While bureaucratic employees can develop areas of expertise that allow some autonomy, they nevertheless work within the boundaries of specific technical rules and under contract to the organization.[19] The organizational goal of efficiency also had specific U.S. educational manifestations, as exemplified by the work of Frederick Winslow Taylor. According to his biographer, Taylor "helped instill in us the fierce, unholy obsession with time, order, productivity, and efficiency that marks our age," which he first learned in school. Taylor's emphasis on productivity and efficiency began in the late 1800s and early 1900s as colleges and universities began to embrace bureaucracy.[20] The characteristics of professionalization, especially autonomy, expertise, and the lack of specified work rules, are in obvious contrast to bureaucratization.

Thus, as the AAUP was forming, higher education at large was developing in ways contrary to the association's conception of how the professor and higher education ought to operate. The first few decades of AAUP activity illustrate the organization's continuous interest in professionalism as well as its engagement with bureaucratic operations.

The AAUP and Professionalism

Early leaders of the American Association of University Professors, professors explicitly in search of professional identity, spoke directly about professionalism.

They made it clear that professors were not employees and that unionization was not an appropriate activity. The organizing committee for the association was explicit in its intent to form a professional association, stating in its 1914 call to organize:

> Believing that a society, comparable to the American Bar Association and the American Medical Association in kindred professions, could be of substantial service to the ends for which universities exist, members of the faculties of a number of institutions have undertaken to bring about the formation of a national Association of University Professors.[21]

The 1914 call to organize the American Association of University Professors led to the organization's first meeting in 1915. Those charter members established organizational goals, expecting the AAUP

> . . . to facilitate a more effective cooperation among the members of the profession in the discharge of their special responsibilities as custodians of the interests of higher education and research in America; to promote a more general and methodical discussion of problems relating to education in higher institutions of learning; to create means for the authoritative expression of the public opinion of college and university teachers; to make collective action possible; and to maintain and advance the standards and ideals of the profession.[22]

The charter members of the AAUP established the organizational structure at the first annual meeting. The association had a council, consisting of thirty members elected at large, and several committees assigned to address different issues. What became the best known of the committees, Committee A, addressed issues of academic freedom and tenure and investigated alleged violations of academic freedom and tenure. Executive officers of the association included the president and eventually the general secretary, the former elected in single-nominee elections (until 1974, as reviewed in chapter 6) and the latter appointed by the council. Local forms of the association, while not initially specified, became chapters at individual colleges and universities and state or regional conferences.[23] Organizational activity, such as the reform of academic freedom practices, originated at the national level. The AAUP addressed many concerns in its early years, the most pressing of which was academic freedom.

The AAUP and Academic Freedom

The first external activity of the AAUP was an investigation of alleged academic freedom violations at the University of Utah, where the president had dismissed two associate professors and two instructors.[24] Arthur O. Lovejoy, a charter member, read by happenstance an editorial in the *New York Evening Post* concerning the recent events at the University of Utah. He concluded that an AAUP investigation would serve the dismissed professors and the association—the former by coming to their aid at a time when no mechanisms existed for the protection of their rights, the latter by establishing publicly AAUP concern for academic freedom.[25] Lovejoy went to Utah in the spring of 1915 (his trip financed by a personal contribution from John Dewey, AAUP president) and interviewed the university president and the dismissed professors as well as trustees and other professors involved in the case. When he had all the available evidence, he wrote a comprehensive report, which was the first publication of the AAUP.[26]

The first investigation set the precedent for the association, as reform of academic freedom and tenure practices became the predominant concern of the AAUP. Only one of the dismissed professors was qualified for membership in the association, so Lovejoy's investigation at the University of Utah would not recruit new members among the dismissed. Nor did the report or the association urge their reinstatement; rather both urged the implementation of institutional procedures for protecting academic freedom and tenure practices.[27] The primary focus of the AAUP in regard to this and future reports of academic freedom and tenure violations was the reform of institutional practices and procedures. This investigation also established nearly the full range of AAUP methods for judging alleged academic freedom violations. The association representatives would negotiate with all of the parties involved (including dismissed professors not qualified for AAUP membership, administrators, and trustees), and the association would publish all of the evidence.

The second academic freedom case established the full range of methods. It was an investigation of a University of Colorado professor's accusation that the university president had violated academic freedom when he refused to renew the professor's contract. The AAUP investigating committee concluded in the published report that the president had not violated any principles of academic freedom.[28] The association was willing to promote academic freedom and to advance the position of such freedom for professors, yet it was also willing to publish the statement that a professor's accusation of an academic freedom violation was incorrect. Not only the investigations but also the principles and practical proposals on academic freedom written by AAUP members accepted the condition that presidents and trustees were not guilty just because a professor had accused them. The initial AAUP members voted to approve the first association policy statement, on academic freedom, which included the goal "to protect college executives and governing boards against unjust charges of infringement of academic freedom, or of arbitrary and dictatorial conduct."[29] AAUP leaders and members viewed their role as custodians of the interests of higher education, not as simply representatives of professorial interests.

The first AAUP report on the principles of academic freedom and academic tenure, the "General Declaration of Principles and Practical Proposals," was approved by the members in attendance at the second annual meeting in 1916.[30] The report also served as the basis for a 1925 conference on academic freedom attended by representatives of nine higher education associations, ranging from the AAUP and the American Council on Education (ACE) to the American Association of University Women. They adopted a code of academic freedom, the 1925 Conference Statement on Academic Freedom and Tenure, which has been ever since the basis for academic freedom and tenure conceptions in U.S. higher education, and they developed it by consensus.[31] The AAUP approach to problems in higher education was negotiation with administrators and trustees (or their representatives) in investigations by Committee A on Academic Freedom and in the development of a national statement on academic freedom.

The association recognized by 1930 that it needed a method to inform professors, administrators, trustees, students, and even the general public when colleges and universities failed to meet the standards of academic freedom and tenure. While redress for the individual professor was not an organizational goal, the AAUP wanted to illustrate the worst cases. In 1931 association members agreed to publish a list of those institutions, a list eventually named in 1938 as the "censured" colleges and universities.[32] This method of highlighting the most intransigent administrations and governing boards continues today.

The first AAUP censure of a college or university after World War II was the result of association investigations led by General Secretary Ralph E. Himstead during the war years. In 1946 the council censured the Board of Regents of the University of Texas because it had dismissed Harold P. Rainey, the university president, for his repeated support of academic freedom and tenure.[33] At this point the AAUP reached the widest breadth of its attempts to reform institutional practices of academic freedom and tenure in its response to the dismissal of an administrator. The regents did not fire Rainey for reasons of academic freedom but because he, as an administrator, had attempted to protect such principles.[34] This censure establishes a maximum level of reform activity in that the AAUP took action on behalf of a university president.

AAUP activity in academic freedom from 1915 to the mid-1940s exemplified the organization's interest in serving as the custodian of higher education. Professors were professionals, using expert judgment to address institutional concerns and exhibiting an ethic of service that incorporated presidential and trustee comprehension as a means to understanding a problematic situation. During this same period the AAUP also examined issues of salaries and institutional governance, and in these areas the association again evidenced expert judgment and an ethic of service.

The AAUP, Economic Interests and Faculty Participation in Governance

The AAUP began to protect and advance professors' economic interests in 1916, when it started negotiations with representatives of the Carnegie Foundation for the Advancement of Teaching to determine the future of the rapidly decreasing pension fund for professors at selected colleges and universities. The association published reports of the meetings and correspondence between its representatives and Carnegie president Henry S. Pritchett, and its efforts were on behalf of all professors who were eligible for the fund's benefits.[35] In economic matters as in academic freedom cases, the association used negotiation and full publication of the evidence to advance the interests of members and nonmembers.

In 1937 the AAUP issued its first major report on the economic status of the professoriate, *Depression, Recovery and Higher Education.* The authors of the book examined the effects of the Great Depression on professors and higher education; despite their conclusion that the effects were severe in terms of staffing, salaries, and benefits, their tone was moderate. While the Great Depression had an obviously serious effect on extraordinary numbers of people, AAUP leaders chose an accommodating stance. For example, in the final section on the effects on instructors and assistant professors—who felt the brunt of staff and salary cuts according to the report—the authors stated, "The depression raises the question of whether or not adequate consideration has been given to the men and women of lowest rank. There is much to suggest that it has not."[36] The passive voice (who gave the consideration?) suggests that even in extremely negative conditions for professors, the association was accommodating to administrators and trustee, those who typically gave consideration to questions of faculty staffing and salaries.

In 1920 Committee T on the Place and Function of Faculties in University Government and Administration issued the results of the first AAUP survey of faculty participation in institutional governance. On the basis of information from seventy elite colleges and universities, the committee report concluded that extensive faculty participation was rare in several areas. They recommended that colleges and universities implement procedures for increased faculty participation, and subsequent Committee T reports in the 1920s and 1930s reiterated that recommendation.[37] The AAUP, however, did not implement the recommendation through the negotiation of a policy statement, as it had done in the case of academic freedom and tenure.

Academic freedom, economic issues, and faculty participation in governance formed an important set of issues for the AAUP. The three concerns address professionalism and bureaucratization. Academic freedom protects the development of expert knowledge and faculty participation in governance advances professorial control of the institution. Economic issues address the material interests of institutionally employed professors. These three concerns form a focal point for this work, highlighting how the AAUP engaged the broad topics of professionalism and bureaucratization.

AAUP Leadership and Membership

The association changed its membership criteria in 1919, approving a reduction of the required length of service from ten to three years.[38] That decision represented a change of vision of many founders who were still active in the AAUP, including the president, Arthur O. Lovejoy. The founders had used ten years as a membership requirement because of the presumed relationship between the length of service and scientific productivity; the 1919 members instituted the change in order to open the association to a wider range of professors.[39] Regardless of the change in membership, association leadership was dominated by well-established professors in the arts and sciences or professional fields at research-oriented universities as indicated by table 1. Many of the AAUP committee chairs were from similar backgrounds. In this regard, throughout this book references to AAUP leaders will typically indicate their discipline or field of study and their institution, establishing the patterns of leaders' disciplinary and institutional experiences and the differences in those experiences as the association leadership slowly changed in the late 1960s and early 1970s.

TABLE 1

AAUP PRESIDENTS FROM 1915 TO 1946 BY DISCIPLINE, INSTITUTION, AND EXPERIENCE

Year(s) of Presidency	Presidency	Discipline	Employing Institution	First Year Teaching
1915–1916	John Dewey	Philosophy	Columbia	1884
1916–1917	J. H. Wigmore	Law	Northwestern	1887
1917–1918	Frank Thilly	Philosophy	Cornell	1891
1918–1919	J. M. Coulter	Botany	Chicago	1874
1919–1920	Arthur O. Lovejoy	Philosophy	Johns Hopkins	1899
1920	Edward Capps*	Classics	Princeton	1887
1920–1921	Vernon A. Kellogg	Astronomy	Stanford	1890
1921–1922	E. R. A. Seligman	Pol. Science	Columbia	1885
1922–1924	J. V. Denney	English	Ohio State	1891
1924–1926	A. O. Leuschner	Astronomy	California	1890
1926–1928	W. T. Semple	Classics	Cincinnati	1900
1928–1930	Henry Crew	Physics	Northwestern	1887
1930–1932	W. B. Munro	Government	Harvard	1901
1932–1934	W. W. Cook	Law	Johns Hopkins	1895
1934–1936	S. A. Mitchell	Astronomy	Virginia	(1916)
1936–1938	A. J. Carlson	Physiology	Chicago	1905
1938–1940	Mark H. Ingraham	Mathematics	Wisconsin	1919
1940–1942	Frederick S. Deibler	Economics	Northwestern	1904
1942–1944	William T. Laprade	History	Duke	1909
1944–1946	Quincy Wright	Int'l Law	Chicago	1916

SOURCES: The disciplines and employing institutions from 1916 to 1942 are from "The Presidency of the Association," *Bulletin of the A.A.U.P.* 28 (February 1942): 5. Years of entry for all except Leuschner, Semple, Mitchell, and Ingraham are from *The National Cyclopedia of American Biography.* Years of entry for Leuschner and Semple are from *Who Was Who in America* (St. Louis: Von Hoffman Press, 1968, 4: 847 and 1960, 3: 514, respectively), for Mitchell from "List of Members," *Bulletin of the A.A.U.P.* 2 (March 1916): 43 (he presumably began teaching before 1916), and for Ingraham from "Supplementary Material on Nominees," *Bulletin of the A.A.U.P.* 23 (December 1937): 658. All data from 1940 to 1946 except for Frederick Deibler's year of entry are from the reports of the nominating committees as published in the *AAUP Bulletin* in the autumn of the year before election. Deibler's year of entry is identified in *Who Was Who In America* (St. Louis: Von Hoffman Press, 1968) 4: 241.

* Edward Capps resigned to become U.S. ambassador to Greece. Vernon A. Kellogg replaced him, moving up from his position as vice-president of the association. "General Announcement," *Bulletin of the A.A.U.P.* 6 (May 1920): 3.

While the membership base may have broadened (suggesting a possible broadening of membership concerns), the association leadership maintained the organizational emphasis on academic freedom and tenure. The negotiations for the 1925 Conference Statement were noted above, and in the 1930s the AAUP negotiated a revision of the statement with representatives of the Association of American Colleges (AAC), resulting in the 1940 Statement of Principles on Academic Freedom and Tenure. In the case of each statement the AAUP secured its endorsement by a wide range of education associations.[40]

The AAUP appointed its first full-time general secretary, Ralph E. Himstead, in 1935. He was influential in the negotiations between the AAUP and the AAC in the revision of the 1925 Conference Statement, insisting upon "the most controversial" aspect of the changes, implementation of the maximum acceptable probationary period for professors in tenure-track positions. He was also, as one of his critics admits, "an unflinching antagonist of academic dictators and an ardent protagonist of faculty government."[41]

In 1939 the AAUP broadened its membership criteria again when the delegates at the annual meeting voted to admit professors from junior colleges and to remove the required years of service. Although the Committee O on Organization and Policy report as approved by the members at the annual meeting noted that only professors at junior colleges with "adequate standards" were to be admitted, the AAUP admitted junior college professors regardless of institutional standards.[42] Association membership now officially included professors at all types of U.S. colleges and universities, excluding those at proprietary schools and at technical institutes offering two years or less of instruction.[43]

For over thirty years the AAUP repeatedly portrayed its work as advancing the interests of the academic profession and higher education, and it rarely attempted to achieve any public redress for unjustly dismissed professors. The predominant organizational objective of the AAUP was the reform of practices and procedures of academic freedom and tenure. The attempts at reform went so far as the previously mentioned censure of the Board of Regents of the University of Texas in 1946 for its dismissal of the university president.

By 1946 the professoriate's activities in the United States encompassed a broad range from teaching remedial subjects at two-year colleges to conducting basic research at universities that granted the doctorate.[44] Professors were more or less equally divided between public and private institutions, and 93 percent taught at institutions that offered at least the bachelor's degree.[45] A small number of private research universities and an even smaller number of public research universities were the primary sources of new professors entering the professoriate.[46]

Professors at research universities clearly considered themselves to be professionals, as noted in the title of Logan Wilson's fundamental work on research-university professors, *The Academic Man: A Study in the Sociology of a Profession* and his choice of universities to study. By the 1940s professors' control of their work, as professionals, was a prominent characteristic of the ideal professor, and they could achieve that control through full participation in institutional decisions.

The AAUP and Unionization

Despite the intentions of the organizers and charter members to establish a professional association, external observers of the association, from college and university presidents to newspaper editors, said it was a trade union. AAUP elected and staff leaders denied consistently any affiliation with unions and based association programs on negotiations with administrators and trustees.[47] In the late 1930s association leaders repeatedly addressed the question of whether the AAUP was a professional association or a union, apparently in at least partial response to the suggestion by members that the AAUP consider union activity. In the February 1938 *Bulletin of the A.A.U.P.* former general secretary H. W. Tyler stated:

> The Association is not a "Professors Union." The epithet, many times thoughtlessly rather than ignorantly applied, might be fitting if the Association had devoted itself to protecting the economic rights and increasing the monetary rewards of its own members, or perhaps of restricting their performance.[48]

Not only Tyler but also other members of the association commented on the AAUP and how it was not a union.[49] The comments also reveal some pressures within the professoriate for unionization.

The American Federation of Teachers (AFT) was an ardent promoter of faculty unionization. The AFT began as a loosely organized group of teachers' locals in the early twentieth century, focusing on "winning concrete advances for the welfare of classroom teachers."[50] The AFT organized college faculty locals early in its history; its first university local was at Howard University in November 1918. At another early local at the University of Illinois, its first president told the *Christian Science Monitor* that reasons for its organization included "lack of democratic procedures for faculty members and the general dissatisfaction with salaries."[51] There was not much growth in the numbers of these locals, however, until the 1930s and again in the 1960s. Although the 1960s movement among AFT locals was different from the movements of previous decades, Jeanette Ann Lester identifies four major AFT principles from 1916 to 1966. They were the promotion of higher salaries and benefits as measures of professionalism, action toward securing a greater voice for faculties, a stand for academic freedom, and an emphasis on the professor as an employee. Lester also reports that the AFT placed greater emphasis on action than on reports and thus had a disproportionate influence in the collective bargaining movement among professors.[52]

Unionization is therefore a representation of an employee group's interests in such matters as economic benefits, influence and control of organizational affairs, and, in the case of the professoriate, academic freedom. AFT activity in faculty unionization began in the 1960s at public two-year institutions, which often still had strong ties to school systems, systems characterized by bureaucratic forms of authority. As the National Education Association began to enter into faculty collective bargaining in the mid-1960s (and the AAUP, in much slower fashion), unionization spread to public four-year campuses and systems, organizations also heavily bureaucratized.

The AAUP entered unionization in a much less direct manner than the AFT or the National Education Association (NEA). While its first approval of faculty collective bargaining was tentative, its reaction to administrative intransigence in arenas other than unionization was more definite. In April 1967 the faculty at the Catholic University of America conducted a strike in response to the administration's refusal to grant tenure to the Reverend Charles Curran, closing the institution for three days. Bertram H. Davis, general secretary of the American Association of University Professors, commented on that action:

> And when our professional dignity and decency are outraged by a flagrant violation of our most fundamental principles, and it becomes necessary to storm one of the citadels of the unredeemed, let us bear in mind that our militance is only an expedient, unnatural to us at best and adopted only for an extreme occasion.[53]

Buried in the elegance of this language is a basic tension between professionalism and bureaucratic employment in the professoriate. Professionals will not want to strike, disrupting service to clients (i.e., students), but employees may encounter unacceptable management behavior. This tension became increasingly apparent in the post–World War II period, and it represents a substantial change in the professoriate. The AAUP reflected that tension in its movement into faculty unionization.

The literature on the association's decision to pursue collective bargaining is relatively brief and for the most part leaves the questions of professionalism and bureaucratization unanswered. Edward Jackson studied junior college professors' involvement in the AAUP and concluded, "Although some past Council members, including past AAUP Presidents and Vice-Presidents, apparently attribute the Association's movement in the direction of collective bargaining to pressure from community/junior college faculty, the limited extent and nature of such faculty in the affairs of the AAUP makes this proposition unlikely."[54] George Strauss determined in his 1965 comparison of AAUP behavior with trade unionism that the association's emphasis on academic freedom and tenure and its lack of adversarial relationships with administrators and trustees precluded consideration of the AAUP as a trade union.[55] Finally two other authors examine the AAUP as an association based on professors' interests in working conditions, using the same content analysis of AAUP presidential addresses to examine the AAUP both as a professional association and as a union. They suggest that the association moved into collective bargaining because its emphasis on professionalism did not provide professors with enough power.[56] That analysis illustrates part of the problem of bureaucratization although it does not offer explanation as to the consequences of the AAUP decision to enter collective bargaining or explain the tension between professionalism and bureaucratization.

Professors, Professionalization, and Unionization

Thus one view of professionalism and bureaucratization in the professoriate might suggest, as Wilson, Light, and Clark have, that in essence two occupations exist, one composed of the academic professions, the other of unionized faculties. Although such a distinction ignores to some degree the complexity of argument that Clark brings to bear on the nature of the professoriate, it is how all three scholars organize their arguments. And the distinction serves as a way of understanding labor market activity as well as career performance and aspirations. Two other sociologists, however, reveal that another view of the professoriate, as an occupation with considerable variation but nevertheless overall characterized by a tension between professionalism and bureaucratization, is a more encompassing construction. Jencks and Riesman argued in their 1968 book, *The Academic Revolution,* that faculty power had achieved primacy on campuses. Yet in retrospect, and in somewhat hidden terms, David Riesman stated a dozen years later that social movements are most likely to falter at their most powerful moment, as was the case of the apparent victory of faculty power in the late 1960s.[57] This conclusion is not only one concerning social movements but also one that confirms the power of bureaucratization. As Laurence Veysey noted, the bureaucratization of the university—and specifically the research university—began in the late 1800s: "The second stage of administrative growth began during the early nineties; it has never stopped."[58] Institutions such as Columbia University and the University of Chicago began to develop managerial staffs, and other institutions quickly followed suit. At the same time, as several scholars including Veysey have argued, professors were becoming increasingly professionalized although the process itself, slow in development, had begun decades or even centuries earlier.[59] Thus the professoriate shares two critical occupational characteristics: its members typically experience some form of professionalization, and they find employment at academic institutions that often use bureaucratic forms of organization.

Furthermore a historical analysis of professions highlights the importance of the changes in the professoriate in the post–World War II era. Bruce Kimball argues that the changes in professions are marked by "episodic shifts in cultural ideals, architectonics, and the status and authority" of professions.[60] As Kimball argues, although in terms of professors in the late nineteenth and not the late twentieth century, our specific use of rhetoric, the academic profession, evidences a shift in the meaning from the learned professions of the late 1800s and early 1990s.[61]

As increasing numbers and proportions of professors found employment at public two-year and four-year colleges in the 1950s and 1960s, bureaucratic conditions became more important to the AAUP and more characteristic of the professorial experience. Yet at the same time the professor as researcher, practicing a particular form of professionalism, continued to be an ideal. By the mid-1970s it was clear that some faculties, particularly those at research universities and selective liberal arts colleges, would not enter into unionization while other faculties, especially those at public two-year and four-year colleges, had chosen or would soon choose collective bargaining. (There were, of course, also regional differences since such areas as the southern states generally had legislation that made unionization very difficult.)[62] Nevertheless the apparent resolution of the tension between professionalism and bureaucracy, effected by the mid-1970s, was in fact an uneasy balance reflecting occupational conditions far more complex than just the apparent differences between professions and unions. (As will be noted in chapter 4, concerning the rise of faculty unionization, professions and unions share goals, including control of working conditions.) Since the 1970s scholarship (i.e., evidence of expertise and a key characteristic of traditional conceptions of professionalism) has continued to be of primary importance to professors.[63] Doctoral education demands more rigorous expressions of scholarship, as does the tenure process. Yet professors have lost autonomy, another key characteristic of traditional conceptions of professionalism. Institutions at all levels of higher education require (ironically) more scholarship, evidence of effective teaching, and involvement in the bureaucratic operations through such devices as committees and task forces.[64]

In this sense a historical investigation raises questions that a sociological one might not. As John R. Thelin suggests, historians have benefited from sociologists' inquiries about higher education and their use of "concepts and themes which constituted an escape route from the formula of linear chronicles associated with the house histories.'" Thelin also suggests that sociologists were interested in how historical methods allow the exploration of "all the closets and corners of complex institutions."[65] This book seeks to integrate the historian's familiarity with organizational records with sociological concepts about both professionalism and bureaucratization. Thus the apparent insularity of research universities' faculties to issues of bureaucratization becomes a question rather than a theme, as does the importance of research, and autonomy, among professors at two-year and four-year colleges.[66] Whatever the efforts to storm the citadels of the unredeemed, while faculty members face continued pressure to address professional demands, they face increased pressure to respond to bureaucratic concerns.

Methods and Organization

There are several sociological studies of professionalism and the professoriate, those noted in the preceding review as well as others.[67] Those investigations serve as one foundation for questions about professionalism (and, at times, bureaucratization), as will the several surveys of the professoriate that have scholars and researchers have conducted in the post–World War II period. Of special importance concerning the latter are the Carnegie surveys of 1969, 1975, 1984, and 1988 and the reports issued from those surveys, as well as federal surveys, particularly the one completed in 1993.[68] In addition, federal data on professors and higher education in general, from 1946 to the 1990s, will be used in examination of changes in the professoriate and colleges and universities. The discussion about faculty responses to questions about professionalization and bureaucratization using Carnegie and federal information is only a discussion and not an attempt to provide analysis of responses; national databases on faculty are flawed.[69] The databases provide opportunity for some generalization but not precise and specific longitudinal comparisons.

18

Yet this is a historical investigation, and however helpful examinations re-constructed as longitudinal dimensions may be, the purpose of this study is not to investigate the themes of professionalism and bureaucratization as sep-arate occupational issues over time. Rather questions of how professors and institutions, as groups and subgroups, responded to pressures to be profes-sional and to act bureaucratically form the focus of this book. Thus historical records, with their inconvenient facts and irregularities, form the basis of the inquiry. Such public documents as organizational journals—the *AAUP Bulletin* (now *Academe*)—for example, offer expression of how professors viewed them-selves in the context of profession and bureaucracy. For many years the *AAUP Bulletin* reported association business in a relatively forthright manner. At the foundation of historical method, however, lies documentary research and (in recent years) oral history interviews. Thus archival records of the AAUP pro-vide critical insight into the statements and arguments of professors regarding their place in higher education; these records are nearly complete until the early 1970s, when the association stopped transcribing annual and council meetings. In addition oral history interviews with AAUP leaders of the 1960s and 1970s give historical voice to the investigation.

As suggested by the discussion of methods, each chapter employs both so-ciological and historical principles to develop an understanding of the prob-lem. The second chapter examines the immediate post–World War II era. That period brought first a sense of hope for higher education (as noted, for example, in the Truman Commission report) and then a developing sense of apprehension (as documented by Lazarsfeld and Thielens) to the professori-ate.[70] Attacks on professors at all types of institutions proved largely successful during McCarthyism; nevertheless instances of resistance based on the direct representation of faculty interests began in this period, even within the highly traditional AAUP. As institutions began to offer higher levels of degrees and to hire more professors, the nature of the professoriate itself began to change. The third chapter focuses on the late 1950s and the early 1960s, a period of substantial growth and remarkable support for the professoriate. Almost upon the end of the McCarthyism attacks, professors encountered national encour-agement and support as the society hurriedly responded to *Sputnik*. Professors became important for the goal of national development, and both salaries and the number of professors increased rapidly. The AAUP also enjoyed unprece-dented growth. Much of the growth, however, occurred among professors at new institutions, particularly public two-year and four-year colleges; associa-tion goals of professionalism did not adequately address the employment con-ditions which many new members explicitly faced. Chapter 4 offers an examination of faculty collective bargaining. In one sense enabling laws and bureaucratized universities appear to explain the rapid rise of faculty collective bargaining from the middle to late 1960s. Yet faculty members are also agents on their own, and who the faculty is—or, more accurately, who the faculties are—is an important factor in examining the rise of collective bargaining. Chapter 5 focuses on the AAUP and its experience in collective bargaining from 1966 to 1971. (This work does not discuss the complexities of AAUP involvement in bargaining, including the problems of the industrial model of unionization and the subtleties of opposition to the process throughout the years following its adoption by the association).[71] Initially the AAUP forbade collective bargaining among its chapters unless there was express consent from the national elected and appointed leaders. In the late 1960s, however, the association began in its policy statements to encourage collective bargaining and offered an ambiguous approval of faculty participation in strikes. Chapter 6 discusses the association's decision to begin direct involvement in faculty unionization. In 1972 the AAUP developed guidelines that encouraged the selective development of collective bargaining activity. The hesitancy and support evident in "selective development" reveal the developing tension between professionalism and bureaucracy. Association leaders hesitated to commit fully to collective bargaining, in part because of their own professional ideals; at the same time they recognized the highly bureaucratic conditions that had emerged at many public two-year and four-year colleges. This chapter also details changes in faculty preparation, appointment, and employment, including changes in the social composition of the professoriate. During the early 1970s colleges and universities slowly began to appoint women and people of color in increasing numbers to faculty positions. In addition the academic labor market began to shift from one of demand to one of supply. How these changes affected, and did not affect, higher education is an important component of the tension between professionalism and bureaucratization. Examination of these changes also offer additional and powerful explanations for the rise of unionism and the faculty place in the bureaucracy. The sixth chapter also uses the AAUP as means to explain the uneasy balance of professionalism and bureaucracy that developed in the 1970s. Following its confirmation of collective bargaining, the AAUP moved through a process of accommodating both its professional and union goals—evidenced in a curious way by its letterhead, with association officials listed on the left-hand margin and collective bargaining officials listed on the right-hand margin. The 1974–1976 president effected an uneasy balance between the two sets of goals in his presidential address, reflecting the professoriate's own uneasy balance.

The final chapter argues that the issues of professionalism and unionism in the professoriate (as illustrated in the AAUP) lead to an understanding of the professorial dilemma. Attempts to characterize professors simply as professionals fail to encompass important occupational characteristics and working conditions. Yet attempts to identify professors as bureaucratic employees ignore the complex demands of professionalism, including expertise, control of working conditions through governance arrangements, and at least partial autonomy. As of the mid-1970s professors faced a dilemma of professional and bureaucratic demands, a dilemma that continues unabated today.

The professor's ambiguous role is an important part of understanding the development of higher education after World War II. It is a period marked by growth, by struggles to understand and accommodate new populations, and by the largesse of the 1960s and the financial strains that began in the early 1970s. For professors the post–World War II period is a time when opportunities for advancement have grown and shrunk at remarkable rates. It is also a period when professional autonomy and expertise clashed with bureaucratic expectations in ways unforeseen in the decades prior to World War II. This tension may have been best expressed, ironically, given his union background, by Samuel Gompers when asked what unions wanted: "More." Both faculties and institutions have come to ask more of professors, at a cost not yet determined. This book endeavors to begin to define those costs by asking how professors responded to pressures to be professionals within a bureaucratic organization.

Chapter 1

THE AAUP FROM 1946 TO 1958

McCarthyism and Reconstruction Efforts

The federal government acted immediately upon the end of World War II to address the country's educational needs. The first of these efforts was the massive G.I. Bill of Rights program, enacted into law in 1944. As a result of the G.I. Bill approximately one-third of U.S. World War II veterans entered colleges and universities.[1] The second reflected the sentiments of the egalitarian nature of the G.I. Bill; the President's Commission on Higher Education stated in its 1947 report, "It is obvious, then, that free and universal access to education, in terms of the interest, ability, and need of the student, must be a major goal in American education." The commission noted later in its report that according to results of the Army General Classification Test, "the most inclusive testing program ever conducted, that even with the present inflexibility of college curricula, a minimum of 49 percent of the college-age population of this country has the ability to complete at least the first two years of college work, and at least 32 percent has the ability to complete additional years of higher education."[2] The third effort, however, focused on a very different aspect of higher education, its research capabilities. In 1945 Vannevar Bush, who was then director of the Office of Scientific Research and Development, submitted to President Roosevelt his report, *Science, the Endless Frontier,* in which Bush urged the nation to invest heavily in basic research. That report is generally regarded as the basis for the establishment of the National Science Foundation, an institution at the vanguard of massive federal financial support of research.[3] Both universal access and high-quality basic research were important national goals following World War II. Both of these goals also had consequences for higher education and the professoriate.

The federal government, through both unprecedented levels of funding and the issuance of policy reports, created a context of institutional growth and an emphasis on research. In view of higher education's commitment to enrollment growth and the long-standing tradition of scholarship, it would not suffice to ascribe the reasons for bureaucratization and professionalization to the federal government. Nevertheless its substantial commitment to the uses of higher education provided a powerful set of contributing factors.

Enrollment in higher education increased from 2,078,095 in the fall of 1946 to 2,446,693 in the fall of 1955.[4] The enrollment of first-time students in the fall of 1946 was relatively large compared to following years, the result of the G.I. Bill. There were 696,419 first-time students in 1946, compared to 592,846 in 1947, and in ensuing years the number stayed below the 1947 level until 1954, when there were 624,910 first-time students.[5]

The growth in the number of professors appears to have surpassed the growth in the number of students. In 1945–1946 there were 125,811 college instructors, and in November 1955 there were 197,791 college instructors.[6] During the late 1940s the supply of potential professors did not meet the demand. It was a time "when standards were relatively low for entering college teaching, a high proportion of young people entered college teaching with only master's degree credentials or were content to remain ABDs."[7] Nevertheless colleges and universities typically appointed new professors in accordance with the institutions' levels of prestige. The major study of the academic labor market in the mid-1950s reported that the type and prestige of the employing institution, the level (master's degree or higher) and prestige of the professor's education, and the professor's discipline, age, and rank all proved to be powerful factors in the academic labor market.[8] Institutions at the top of the academic hierarchy continued to attract new professors with doctorates. Graduate-level research, the demonstration of expertise, continued to be of primary importance to highly influential and prestigious institutions. To a substantial degree in the first decade after World War II, there continued to be a dual labor market for professors, one focused on securing instructors for burgeoning enrollments and one for institutions emphasizing research expertise. Yet labor market issues were of minimal importance in those years; instead the serious and sustained attacks on professors during the era of McCarthyism attracted the most attention.

The AAUP from 1946 to 1955: Oligarchy and McCarthyism

In the decade following the end of World War II the AAUP confronted two obstacles that restrained its activities. One was internal, the presence of a singularly powerful and relatively unresponsive general secretary and a compliant elected leadership. The other was external, the continuous and often virulent attacks upon professors and the professoriate typically led by Senator Joseph P. McCarthy, allied legislators, and business people. The eventual responses of the AAUP elected leadership and the membership to the association's silence established an organizational framework that would eventually facilitate direct representation of professors' working interests.

Three internal factors apparently combined to create the organizational silence in alleged academic freedom violations. First, General Secretary Himstead was not a competent administrator; he did not delegate the detailed and lengthy tasks of correspondence and investigation in alleged academic freedom violations.[9] Furthermore, "he was timorous when it came to any opposition to Senator [Joseph] McCarthy and the actions of universities in that period of Communist hysteria," and he told the council several times that if the AAUP opposed McCarthy and anti-Communism, the association "would just disintegrate."[10] Second, the association had not operated completely during World War II. Only the council met from 1942 to 1946, and after the war the organization and the members and leaders had to turn from the national focus on the war back to association programs.[11] Third, most of the charter members, those professors who had shared the vision of a national professional association, were by reason of age or death no longer participating in the AAUP.[12]

Himstead handled most of the association's correspondence and affairs by 1946. Loya Metzger argues that Himstead dominated the association and was vague regarding the work of the staff.[13] It appears that Himstead did not respond to much of the association correspondence and affairs because of the burden of those activities as well as his picayune attention to details and his desire to maintain control of the association.[14] An early example of the burden and attention to detail appears in an October 1947 letter to *Bulletin* readers. Himstead wrote that the staff was back to two professional members despite a net increase of 8,000 members in the past two years.[15] Equally troublesome was the upcoming and unexpected move of the Central Office, and Himstead implored readers to be patient with slow responses to inquiries.[16] As he continued, his sense of his central importance to the organization and his attention to details appeared:

> In the nature of the case we must be the judge of what constitutes "first things." In determining the parts of our work that are to be given priority, the paramount consideration is the welfare of the

profession. Another very important consideration is the quality of our work. We must never sacrifice quality for quantity.[17]

Despite his concerns about organizational demands, Himstead's reports on association activities indicated a healthy organization. In the Winter 1950 issue of the *Bulletin* he reviewed the AAUP's growth in membership and financial resources since 1936. The association had experienced consistent growth in its membership, from 12,713 members in 1936 to 39,092 as of January 1950. From 1938 to 1949 the AAUP had enjoyed surpluses each year, and its reserve fund showed steady growth since 1937.[18] Yet Himstead concluded his report by reminding AAUP members that the staff was the same size as it had been in 1937.[19] There was only one addition to the AAUP staff from 1947 to 1955: Warren Middleton was appointed staff associate in February 1952.[20] With the addition of Middleton there was one staff member for every 13,746 AAUP active members.[21]

In the middle and late 1940s Himstead was the AAUP's primary force not only in such areas as academic freedom but also in studies of the economic status of the profession and faculty participation in college and university government. In fact he identified himself, perhaps unwittingly, as such. In the investigation of the alleged academic freedom violations at the University of Texas, Himstead used the first-person singular pronoun, an extremely unusual occurrence in AAUP reports.[22] In 1947 the council gave Himstead five hundred dollars to assemble data on faculty salaries. He met with representatives of the AAC, American Council on Education (ACE), and the United States Office of Education and reported that he had regular discussions with the chair and the executive secretary of the President's Commission on Higher Education, again using the first-person singular pronoun.[23] In January 1948 Himstead handled a Committee T survey of faculty participation in governance at forty institutions, sending out duplicates of the 1939–1940 survey to those institutions' chapters.[24]

Following the censure of the University of Texas, the AAUP began a period of inaction, especially in the area of investigations of alleged violations of academic freedom. The only noticeable association work in the area was the result of extensive negotiations between the AAUP and the AAC, which began in 1943, to develop the Statement of Principles on Academic Retirement. The negotiations ended in 1950, and both the AAC and the AAUP endorsed the statement in 1951.[25] The association did not publish any investigations of alleged violations of academic freedom and tenure from the summer of 1949 until the spring of 1956.[26] The exceptional nature of

national and local attention to professors in this period accentuated the consequences of AAUP inactivity.

From the late 1940s to the mid-1950s the profession was under attack,
often the subject of vituperative charges against its members' loyalty to the nation and the society. Senator Joseph P. McCarthy is the foremost example of
the attacks on the professoriate, but requirements such as loyalty oaths for
faculties or trustees' condemnations of irreligious professors went far beyond
McCarthy's work in the U.S. Senate.[27] The attacks came from a variety of
sources—state as well as federal investigating committees (from both the legislative and executive branches), local business people, newspaper editors and
columnists, and even a "professional" anti-Communist network.[28] The attacks
on professors also ranged from coast to coast at public and private colleges
and universities.[29] Professors felt vulnerable and scared during this time. Even
in professors' most valued professional activity—the review of peers for appointment, promotion, and dismissal—the fear took hold. Trustees, administrators, and even professors often refused to support attacked professors, and
many professors alerted administrators and faculties to the alleged undesir-
ability of their attacked peers.[30] Very often these attacks on professors constituted violations of the principles of academic freedom. The attacks persisted
until the mid-1950s, when U.S. Senate witnesses began to challenge successfully McCarthy's undocumented claims of Communist conspiracies, thereby
generally discrediting the attacks.

Even in the case of the 1950 attempt of the Board of Regents of the
University of California to require a loyalty oath of faculty members, a case
which generated national publicity and support for California faculty members from professors all over the nation, the AAUP did not report its investigation until 1956.[31] The University of California AAUP chapter members
emphasized the need for an investigation, even going so far as to fly to
Washington, D.C., to discuss the situation with AAUP staff members. Although two AAUP members investigated the situation in the spring of 1951
and sent their final report to the Central Office in December 1951, the report (even in partial format) remained hidden from public review until the
spring of 1956.[32]

As Lazarsfeld and Thielens show, the academic profession itself was thoroughly afraid of attacks on professors.[33] Himstead reinforced that fear by claim-
ing that any AAUP response to the anti-Communist attacks would "paralyze
the Association."[34] He was a major factor in the paralysis of the predominant
program of the association, the work of Committee A. It is important to remember, however, that there was also a national elected leadership that

acquiesced to a considerable degree as Himstead slowed the organization, thus constituting the other major factor.

From 1946 to 1955 there was the beginning of a transition in the AAUP institutional experience of association presidents. The last president who was a charter member, Frederick Deibler at Northwestern University, served from 1940 to 1942.[35] AAUP presidents after Deibler had joined the association increasingly, if irregularly, in later years of the organization—ranging in this period from 1923 to 1930. Only one president, Edward Kirkland (history, Bowdoin College), who served from 1946 to 1948, had been chair of Committee A, and only one other had been a member of Committee A, William Britton (law, University of Illinois, AAUP president from 1954 to 1956).[36] These presidents began their experience with the AAUP after the organizational membership standards had changed and organizational activity had broadened beyond the initial work of Committees A, P (on Pensions), and T. They also had limited direct experience with the association's predominant program, the protection of academic freedom and tenure, suggesting a gap between AAUP goals and leadership experience.

More problematic, however, was the composition and activity of Committee A. Its leadership and membership were static from 1946 to 1955. There were only two chairs of the committee from 1946 to 1954. The first, George Pope Shannon, served as chair in 1946 and 1947.[37] William Laprade, former AAUP president, was chair of the committee from 1948 until 1954.[38] Committee members tended to come from elite colleges and universities where academic freedom problems were less likely to occur, and there was little change of membership from 1946 to 1954.[39] The Committee A annual reports, while indicating the receipt of complaints from professors and often noting the informal negotiations resulting in resolved cases, were general in their approach; they did not name specific institutions. Despite repeated insistence upon adherence to academic freedom and tenure principles and practices with such phrases as "teachers and scholars cannot afford to be silent when danger threatens," the committee's formal investigative practices were at a standstill.[40] Although Loya Metzger, and to a lesser degree Ellen Schrecker, focus blame for AAUP inactivity on Himstead, Committee A inactivity indicates that elected leaders must share the blame.[41] At the least Committee A leaders and members paralyzed by Himstead's arguments allowed hundreds of professors' cases to remain in the files. The "timid" professors of the nation whom Schrecker questions were well represented on Committee A of the AAUP. Laprade suggested in his final report as chair of Committee A that only the Central Office staff was in the proper, central place for the conduct of

Committee A affairs. Nevertheless he chose to support Himstead *despite* Central Office inactivity, in his final report and in his nine-year presence as chair of Committee A.[42]

Nor was the AAUP Council active from 1946 to 1955, with only one *Bulletin* report of activity, its 1946 censure of the governing board at the University of Texas. Annual meeting reports typically noted that the council had met, but there were no statements concerning council activity, and other reports indicate that local leaders pushed the council into action.[43] In general, as was the case with Committee A, council members came from elite colleges and universities.[44] The sense of the profession, even under attack from external forces, from the AAUP perspective derived from professors at institutions that were less likely to experience such attacks.

AAUP Activity and Salaries and Governance

AAUP interest in salaries and governance continued at about the same level from 1946 to 1955 as had existed prior to World War II. The 1946 *Bulletin* carried two articles on the deteriorating state of professors' salaries. Himstead introduced the two articles and wrote that the association "has never been as specific or as vigorous as the significance of the subject warrants."[45] Later that year the members at the annual meeting passed resolutions urging national and chapter studies of salaries and research by Committee Z ("A Symposium on the Economic Status of the Profession") on salary problems and the study of faculties' role in college and university government.[46] In 1948 the Harvard University chapter issued another Committee Z report, this one the result of a survey of 119 colleges and universities, indicating that since 1939 the nation's cost of living had risen faster than professors' salaries or tuition charges.[47]

In the Summer 1948 issue of the *Bulletin,* Himstead announced that the newly revitalized national Committee Z was preparing a study of forty-six colleges and universities. Among the committee's first recommendations were the establishment of annual salary surveys and the addition of a staff member to the national office to assist the study of faculty salaries.[48] The Summer 1948 issue also included an article on professors' salaries that identified a critical problem. A study of 21 percent of U.S. colleges and universities found that there was no agreement about an appropriate salary scale.[49] Without that consensus faculties and the AAUP would obviously have difficulty convincing administrations and governing boards as to appropriate levels of salaries, even within the context of professional standards. Committee Z offered an extensive report in the Winter 1953–1954 *Bulletin* and stated:

The most striking conclusion evidenced by the comparison of all the salary data now collected by the Committee is that instructional salaries have not, since 1939–40, kept pace with living costs, with improvements in the incomes of other professions, or with the per capita growth of the national income.[50]

Yet, as the committee indicated, its data were from institutions with "good practices with respect to instructional salaries and related matters."[51] Those practices were apparently unlikely to have parallels at many other institutions.

In 1948 Committee T issued a report on its study of forty colleges and universities that the association had surveyed in 1939–1940; twenty of them had shown the lowest rates of faculty participation in government and twenty the highest rates of participation. Thirty of the institutions responded, and the Committee T report concluded that there was no trend in faculty participation in college and university government nor any evidence of more participation among faculties. The report suggested that professors should have more participation in college and university government.[52]

Committee T announced in 1953 its continued research into faculty participation in college and university government, finding that there was some increase in administrations' consultations with faculties.[53] A spring 1955 report compared current faculty participation in college and university government with such participation in 1939 and concluded:

The implication which the data force upon us is that the general picture, so far as faculty participation in the selection of institutional policies is concerned, is somewhat better; in some spots it is a little worse, but in other spots it is very much better. A slow but pervasive shift toward more consultation of the faculty by the administration is evidently in process.[54]

Only one group that had worsened was specifically identified, six small liberal arts colleges. The committee noted, however, some improved groups. They were the "'less democratic'" state universities of 1939, teachers colleges that "were conspicuously autocratic" in 1939, women's colleges, and, to a lesser degree, five private research universities. One group of institutions, engineering colleges, changed very little in faculty participation.[55]

Committee T suggested in its 1955 report that the association pursue the possibility of a joint statement with the Association of American Colleges, one similar to the 1966 Statement on Academic Freedom. And it asked that the committee serve in continuous form, rather than in its previous "periodic efforts."[56] Issues of professional influence at colleges and universities seemed slightly improved in the mid-1950s despite McCarthyism, and Committee T members wanted a procedural statement about professional participation in university governance.

Members' interests in salaries and governance went beyond the national work of Committees T and Z, as local activity increased in the AAUP. In the Southeast and Ohio there was some membership activity, including annual meetings. In the Southeast concerns about economic status "always occupied a prominent place in the meetings."[57] Ohio members were particularly concerned about academic freedom and also considered in detail faculty participation in government.[58]

Whatever the interests of AAUP leaders and members, they could do very little about those interests in operational terms as long as the Central Office under Himstead remained inactive and the council and Committee A were acquiescent. Members at the local and regional levels appeared to have generated much of the protest against national AAUP inactivity. The details of the actions indicate substantial interest in the association's capacity and failure to act as a custodian of the interests of higher education.

The Collapse of the Oligarchy

By 1953 the University of Minnesota chapter was sufficiently disturbed by the inactivity of the national AAUP that it sent a delegate, Werner Levi (political science), to the annual meeting to attend to the chapter's complaints.[59] At that meeting the concern of members and leaders about Himstead reached a peak "when exceedingly bitter and well-documented complaints were loudly voiced."[60] In opposition the "national office 'steam-rolled its wishes and almost succeeded in a machine-like domination of the Chicago meetings.'" Levi reported back to his Minnesota colleagues that a fellow group of "'rebels'" had "forced a vote instructing the national headquarters to take action on the grievances" of the members, grievances that focused on Committee A inactivity.[61] The council responded by reactivating Committee O on Organization and Policy and instructed the chairman and members to examine Central Office operations and communications with members and chapters.[62]

The *Bulletin* report of the 1953 Annual Meeting included an unusual "Addendum" written by Himstead in which he offered rebuttals to the objections raised at the annual meeting. As concerned the lack of communication between the Central Office and chapters and state conferences he indicated that he had repeatedly requested reports of their meetings for publication in the *Bulletin* but had received none. Although he had received thirty-seven invitations to attend chapter or state conference meetings in 1952–1953, he had refused them all because of office demands. These two rebuttals appear to be accurate, given the previous publication of "Association News" and the small size of the association staff. On the issue of alleged violations of academic freedom, however, Himstead was at once evasive and excessively blunt. He wrote that at times the Central Office did not respond to inquiries about academic freedom cases because the situations were under investigation and thus were confidential; he offered no explanation for those cases not under investigation. He then proceeded to offer two provocative, albeit accurate, statements. He indicated that chapter involvement in academic freedom cases made the investigative process more difficult and was also in violation of the AAUP Constitution.[63] At a time when he had a choice between inclusive and exclusive behavior toward local activities, he chose the latter. He concluded his "Addendum" with a review of the demands on the AAUP staff, suggesting that in the past year the Central Office received one hundred thousand communications (telephone calls, letters, telegrams) of which twenty thousand could be handled only by professional staff members.[64] He argued again that the staff was too small and the financial resources were too limited for the demands on the association.[65]

Himstead avoided Committee O meetings, canceling three appointments with it scheduled for the fall of 1953, until members met with him in February 1954. The committee reported to the council that the Central Office should be reorganized with "specifically designated" associate secretaries for academic freedom and for chapters and membership. The council responded with an approval in principle, a secret-ballot expression of confidence in Himstead, and the appointment of a two-member subcommittee for further investigation. The subcommittee's report "seemed to exonerate Himstead's management," suggesting that the professional staff be increased by two members and that the association increase dues, and it "termed the need for these moves urgent." Although Himstead liked the report, he submitted his resignation as general secretary to the council before the 1954 Annual Meeting, requesting to be retained as *Bulletin* editor. His letter noted that he had lost the members' confidence; Loya Metzger suggests that he was trying to generate sympathy.[66]

While the national leaders were providing a weak defense of Himstead, members at the local level were planning a change. Werner Levi organized a regional meeting of AAUP members, contacting many officers at "first-rank institutions" who were concerned about the association's current operations. Thirty-nine members from twenty-one institutions attended the meeting, and they agreed on the importance of greater regional activity and decided to begin drafting a formal protest.[67] The first section of the protest statement addressed national AAUP operations in the area of academic freedom, especially its "failure to act," to communicate with chapters on its actions, and to reinstate censured institutions without "excessive delay." The second section criticized the lack of usable information in the *Bulletin,* while the third spoke to the Central Office's inefficiency and concentration of power. The statement's recommendations included establishing a national academic freedom defense fund and appointing a full-time academic freedom investigator in the Central Office. The AAUP members drafting the protest agreed to circulate it among chapters in the region, make any changes necessary, and then send a final version to the Central Office.[68]

In February 1954 the University of Minnesota chapter hosted the second regional meeting. By that time members at Minnesota had evidence of national inactivity in the area of academic freedom as the result of their contacts with colleagues at the University of Nevada, where a difficult case had developed. This information, in combination with the standing dissatisfaction with the national organization, generated discussion that suggested local activity supplementing national activity. The AAUP members at the meeting reviewed several topics, including development of local public relations programs to inform professors and the public about academic freedom issues, forming a regional academic freedom defense panel, and "plans for acting whenever a need might be unmet by the national organization." In addition they examined the annual meeting and the procedures "blocking full discussion of criticisms of the national office." They instructed Professor Levi to ask if the motions of the 1953 Annual Meeting had any results in order to focus attention on the members' grievances.[69]

The members at the 1954 Annual Meeting were even angrier than those at the 1953 meeting. Levi reported:

> "There was strong tension between sections of the audience and Secretaries Himstead and Shannon, which at times deteriorated into almost personal insults. At one point Mr. Himstead was shouted down and on another occasion several members of the Council felt obliged to speak against Mr. Himstead."[70]

Nor did Himstead enjoy the same organizational control that he had somewhat effected at the 1953 Annual Meeting. He objected to the appointment of two new staff members (although he himself had noted the inadequate size of the AAUP staff), stating that he could not train them quickly in the "delicate work" of the association. The council overrode his objection and authorized the appointments. When Himstead opposed the rescheduling of discussion on his report, members reminded him that he had been instructed in 1953 to schedule more time for the general secretary's report.[71] George Pope Shannon, associate secretary of the AAUP, attempted to defend Himstead, but the members at the annual meeting would not countenance supporters either. Shannon read letters from members as an attempt to illustrate the diverse demands on the Central Office and was accused of trying to filibuster.[72]

The council voted at the 1954 Annual Meeting to accept Himstead's resignation, effective 1 February 1955.[73] He fought the council action, including arranging his appointment to the search committee and suggesting in an interview with the committee's choice, Ralph F. Fuchs, that AAUP finances were too uncertain for a strong future. In August 1954 Himstead suffered a heart attack, and subsequent illness forced him to miss the 1955 Annual Meeting; at that meeting the council announced his retirement from the general secretaryship.[74]

Yet Himstead continued to fight his removal and refused to announce the appointment of Ralph F. Fuchs as general secretary "despite direct instruction from the president of the Association to do so."[75] On 8 June 1955 Himstead collapsed at his desk, stricken by a cerebral hemorrhage. The news release that he had written for Fuchs' appointment lay on his desk. Himstead died the next day, and following his death Fuchs assumed the general secretaryship.[76] In the same period Himstead and McCarthyism ended as obstacles to AAUP activity.

Revitalizing the Association, 1955 to 1958

Ralph F. Fuchs had considerable local and national AAUP experience; the association appointed as general secretary an experienced member with disciplinary distinction in law at a time when the organization needed strong and inclusive executive leadership.[77] When Fuchs began his new position, he saw several important association tasks, two of which were to address the backlog of academic freedom cases and to meet the demand for other types of association activity. In regard to the latter, he wanted to develop "an expanded and more diversified program of activities, involving widespread membership participation and enhanced Association influence in a broad range of professional matters."[78] The council supported Fuchs, approving in March 1955 the appointment of two more staff members and directing Committee A to prepare short reports on the academic freedom cases at University of California and University of Washington, two cases from the late 1940s and early 1950s.[79]

The two current AAUP staff members also supported Fuchs' goals, and in the summer of 1955 they completed several important tasks to give the association "a smooth transition."[80]

Within months of Fuchs's appointment he was effecting a rapid increase in association activity. Most important, Fuchs accelerated the removal of the backlog of Committee A cases by appointing a special committee to report on alleged violations since 1948 that involved anti-Communism.[81] The membership of the committee was announced in the Autumn 1955 *Bulletin* with the accompanying statements that the committee had been authorized by the council's written vote and would report to Committee A, the council, and the annual meeting. Fuchs also coordinated activities with the AAUP Council and AAUP President Britton in California.[82]

The presentation and approval of the report, "Academic Freedom and Tenure in the Quest for National Security," at the 1956 Annual Meeting allowed the AAUP to clear most of its backlog of academic freedom cases and thus move ahead with its business. As the Special Committee explained, the association accomplished a great deal by addressing the troubling issue of academic freedom and national security:

> The Association has not, however, expressed itself publicly on these particular situations. The insistence that it do so is widespread among its members; and this committee believes that, at the present hour in national and world affairs, we may gain much by announcing the Association's position in reference to these situations, and by stating anew, in the present context, the principles upon which the Association relies.[83]

The committee's report discussed the context of the actions of administrations and boards of trustees during the McCarthy era, noting the "growing realization of the Communist strategy of infiltration." The report accepted "unhesitatingly the application to colleges and universities of needed safeguards against the misuse of specially classified information important for military security" in the case of persons with access to that information.[84] The committee also included "conspiracy against the government," established by evidence and reviewed under due process, as a specific justification for the removal of a professor. The 1940 Statement on Principles refers only to incompetence in teaching or scholarship and to moral turpitude as causes for dismissal, and it was published in the pages preceding the Special Committee's report; the Special Committee placed additional limitations on academic freedom. The committee also narrowed professors' personal freedom in its interpretation of the use of the Fifth Amendment, arguing that professors had the duty to reveal information about their teaching to their institutions.[85] The Special Committee even offered criticism, albeit light, of faculties and faculty committees, indicating for example that the faculty at Kansas State Teachers College at Emporia "may not have realized that academic freedom is the right of every teacher."[86] The committee exercised considerable caution in its report in response to the still powerful anti-Communism sentiments; the report also reflected, however, AAUP commitment to the interests of higher education and professors as opposed to only the interests of professors.

The AAUP report appeared to be immediately successful, as the report and censures received widespread public notice, perhaps the most the AAUP has ever received. Many national and local newspapers carried editorials on the AAUP action, and college and university educators responded as well.[87] The AAUP had resumed in full its predominant program, with some exceptional internal procedures, and had suggested institutional and professorial practices, and the nation had taken notice.

The Special Committee report also allowed the organization to develop programs in other areas of interest to faculty members since it demonstrated that the AAUP could effectively respond to issues of academic freedom and tenure. As part of that development, the association needed to examine its capacities and its members' interests.

The Committee O on Organization and Policy report at the 1956 Annual Meeting assessed the state of the association. It noted that the staff had three full-time members (the most in years because of previous illnesses) and that by June 1956 there would be five full-time staff members. Other staff members were already working with representatives from the Commission on Academic Freedom and Tenure of the Association of American Colleges to develop procedural standards in dismissals. The national leadership had "either reconstituted entirely or created" six committees, including Committee A.[88]

The council further formalized association structure and operations when in October 1956 it approved a new committee structure that included descriptions of each committee.[89] The three most extensive descriptions were of Committees A, T, and Z; Committees T and Z were the only two of the thirteen described that had subcommittees. In addition Committee A had district panels with members to assist Committee A work in their geographic regions.[90] This attention to issues of governance and economic status, as well as to local interest in the work of Committee A, indicated that the AAUP was ready to return to its perceived role and perhaps to expand upon it.

The expansion of association activity following the Special Committee's report on academic freedom indicates the extent to which the organization was committed to revitalizing its efforts and to addressing a broader range of professional issues. Both the elected and staff leaders were moving the association toward changes in policies and practices, yet it was an activism of professionals. In the Spring 1956 *Bulletin* the association reprinted the 1938 statement on the nature of the AAUP by then–general secretary H. W. Tyler, in which he argued that the association was not a union.[91] George Pope Shannon, the *Bulletin* editor, added a note to the reprint indicating that the letter was published "because of its relevance to continuing or recurrent problems of the Association."[92] AAUP national leaders remained careful in their activism. The first major step in the association's commitment to expansion was the development of a thorough national graded survey of professors' salaries.

The Economic Interests of AAUP Members

Members, chapters, and state and regional conferences urged the national AAUP to focus on the economic status of the profession during this reconstruction period. For example, the Committee O analyses revealed a strong occupational interest among some members:

> Another group of responses can be understood only as conscious or unconscious pressure for a shift toward a pattern of organization and performance more largely protective of the immediate interests, economic and other, of the members of the academic profession. The Committee is aware of the fact that circumstances have, over the years, forced our Association, as they have similar professional groups, to assume a greater degree of responsibility for the security of the individual member. It may well be, as some members insist, that the social context in which higher education now functions is such as to require of us both a more aggressive and protective policy in the area in which we have traditionally operated and an extension of such policy into other areas once thought not to be within the limits of our concern.[93]

The committee recommended careful examination of potentially appropriate changes in "traditional policies and practices" in order to achieve traditional association goals given the current circumstances.[94]

National attention to the economic status of the profession also occurred at the 1957 Annual Meeting when members changed the AAUP Constitution, adding the word "welfare" to the phrase "to advance the standards and ideals of the profession" following the initial amendment to add "economic welfare."[95] Members at the 1957 Annual Meeting also approved a resolution on economic status:

> The Meeting further resolves that the Association be requested to establish as immediate objectives the discovery of tactical ways and means of securing proper salary levels throughout the country and the implementation of these ways and means at national and local levels, and that the Council report to the Forty-Fourth Annual Meeting on the progress achieved in this program.[96]

Members wanted the AAUP to achieve as quickly as possible the new constitutional goal of advancing the welfare of the profession.

There was also increased interest in association examination of faculty salaries at the local level. In April 1957 delegates from the chapter at American University wrote a letter to the Central Office suggesting that the AAUP should work to make adherence to national salary minima a criterion for accreditation.[97] Later that year the chair of the District of Columbia Conference sent a proposal to the presidents of state and regional conferences and chapters as well as council members suggesting "we must initiate a *National Campaign to make Economic Welfare a Major Objective of the AAUP*."[98] The Illinois Conference passed a resolution in support of the proposal in October 1957.[99]

The District of Columbia proposal examined the welfare of the profession beyond economic status. The first recommendation of the proposal emphasized faculty participation in college and university government because problems of economic status or academic freedom and tenure were "symptoms [rather] than the real disease." The proposal suggested using full-time staff members (instead of professors volunteering their time and energy) to implement the recommendations, including the use of a professional public relations person. Despite the assertive nature of the statement, the District of Columbia proposal stated that even "hard-minded and unabashed assertion of our national importance" should model the assertion of such importance by members of the medical and legal professions.[100] Although the District of Columbia and Illinois Conferences wanted AAUP activism, those leaders saw themselves in the same context as that of the national leaders: members of a profession analogous to the professions of medicine and law.

The enthusiasm and concerns in the AAUP paralleled national sentiment increasingly favorable toward higher education. In 1957, shortly after the attacks on the professoriate subsided, the Union of Soviet Socialist Republics launched *Sputnik*. One of the immediate responses in the United States was to identify the importance of education in achieving superiority in the technological and scientific race for space. President Eisenhower suggested expanding the work of the National Science Foundation and implementing the National Defense Education Act; the United States Congress agreed, and by 1958 the federal government began to spend even greater sums of money on scientific and technological research and on financial assistance for students.[101] President Eisenhower's Commission on Education Beyond the High School affirmed the national importance of professors in its *Second Report*. The commission recommended "the goal of doubling the average level [of professors' salaries] within five to ten years, and with particular attention to increasing the spread between the bottom and the top of each institution's salary structure."[102]

In 1958 Committee Z began a remarkable program to address members' concerns about their low salaries and benefits. Fritz Machlup of the committee and members of a subcommittee of Committee Z proposed that the AAUP grade the academic salary scales of United States colleges and universities.[103] Machlup noted that chapters and conferences had increasingly demanded "greater activity on the part of the Council, the national committees, and the Washington office in promoting the material welfare of the members of the profession."[104] He stated that the purposes could be construed as "to safeguard the standards of the profession and the quality of higher education; or, in the most mundane terms, to raise faculty salaries as quickly as possible." Machlup and Committee Z had considered numerous proposals for means to raise salaries, including "the employment of 'skilled organizers' and of 'high-caliber public-relations experts.'" Machlup and the committee felt, however, that most of the proposals were "impractical or inappropriate" and that some "would create ill-will and antagonism toward the profession." With the skilled use of econometrics and data from about four hundred colleges and universities, Machlup developed a scale, with grades A through F. Each grade was for a minimum salary for each rank, professor to full-time instructor. The proposal suggested that the scales first be used to grade 1957–1958 salary reports, and its spring 1958 publication allowed ample time for association discussion and implementation.[105]

The salary scales were moderate ones, as the lowest grades were less than the salaries of teachers at urban public secondary schools.[106] Nevertheless Committee Z was clearly intent upon improving salaries since the top grade did *not* include any salaries at any colleges or universities. The committee established a goal for top salaries that was above current practice "to accelerate the adjustment of salary scales to the realities of the market for highly qualified academic personnel."[107]

Despite the activity to improve faculty salaries, association leaders maintained their insistence that the AAUP met professional ideals. Helen C. White (English, University of Wisconsin), 1956–1958 AAUP president, reminded members at the 1958 Annual Meeting of the nature of academic freedom:

> We must be ready to explain again and again that academic freedom is not a matter of personal indulgence, not a self-interested union privilege, but the basic premise of the job which we have to do—that we are asking academic freedom not to exploit impulse or escape scrutiny for efficiency, but to do the work we have to for society.[108]

Association activity to promote better salaries did not mean that the AAUP would lose its professional face and become a union.

AAUP Ideals of Academic Freedom, AAUP Standards of Membership

Whatever the programmatic efforts in the area of faculty salaries, Committee A and academic freedom remained the primary professional program of the AAUP. Yet even in that arena the association evidenced forms of activism. And, while the organization had a pro forma membership process that modeled professional standards, it was readying to change that process.

At the 1958 Annual Meeting the association awarded its first Alexander Meiklejohn Award to the president and the trustees of the University of New Hampshire "for their 'significant contribution to academic freedom during the year.'"[109] The monies, and apparently even the conception of this award, came from outside the AAUP. In 1957 alumni and former professors of the Experimental College of the University of Wisconsin offered a three-thousand-dollar fund to the AAUP for an annual award in Meiklejohn's name, which the council accepted.[110] The AAUP had a new method for the advancement of academic freedom in the Meiklejohn Award.

Association efforts in 1958 to advance and protect academic freedom and tenure extended beyond censure and award. The members at the 1958 Annual Meeting, upon recommendation of the council, endorsed the Statement on Procedural Standards in Faculty Dismissal Proceedings as developed by representatives of the AAUP and the AAC.[111] The statement was detailed in its attempt to ensure due process, indicating that

> . . . formal proceedings should be commenced by a communication addressed to the faculty members by the president of the institution, informing the faculty member of the statement formulated [by the president and a faculty committee, concerning

particular grounds for dismissal], and informing him that, if he so requests, a hearing to determine whether he should be removed from his faculty position on the grounds stated will be conducted by a faculty committee at a specified time and place.[112]

The statement furthered faculty participation, peer review, in a college's or university's consideration of dismissing a professor, through a carefully articulated series of steps. This statement went beyond principles of academic freedom and tenure and addressed the issue of faculty participation in college or university operations, identifying specific practices. Such participation not only furthered the professional goals of the association, securing influence if not control of working conditions, it also furthered bureaucratic procedures.

Local and national leaders also wanted to simplify the membership application process, and in 1958 the council voted to discontinue "publishing in the *AAUP Bulletin* the names of nominees for membership." Council members instructed Committee F on Membership and Committee O on Organization and Policy "to formulate a constitutional amendment establishing a system of membership by application to supersede the present system of membership by nomination."[113] Bertram H. Davis, staff associate, was in charge of membership at that time, and he identified the length and cost of the lists of nominees in the *Bulletin* as two of the three primary factors in the council decision. The third was:

> In part because the chapters objected; it took too long to get people in. They wanted to have somebody who had sent in his dues, . . ., [to] become active in the chapter right away. The waiting period was an inconvenience, and there wasn't much need for it. It seemed fine when the Association was starting—you had to be a full professor, it was far more of an elite organization. But it had outworn its usefulness, and I don't think anyone seriously regretted that we scrapped that.[114]

The public face of the association as an elite group requiring nomination for membership changed to a professors' association requiring a simple application for membership.

Getting members in quickly also meant that the association was also able to increase membership quickly, which was important because membership declined during this time. As of 1 January 1955 the AAUP had 42,144 active members (those allowed to vote at annual meetings and in elections), 39,748 of whom were at colleges and universities.[115] One percent was composed of professors at public and private two-year colleges, 30 percent was at public four-year colleges, 15 percent at private universities, and 10 percent at private colleges. Under one-half of the membership was at institutions from which the AAUP tradition-ally drew its leaders; 6 percent at selective private colleges, 7 percent at selective private universities, and 28 percent at public research and state flagship universi-ties.[116] By 1 January 1959 the association had 38,347 active members of whom 36,631 were at colleges and universities.[117] In contrast the number of college in-structors nationally increased from 197,791 in November 1955 to 226,536 in 1957–1958.[118]

In a critical policy area, academic freedom, and a central organizational char-acteristic, membership, the association was evidencing some ambiguity in regard to professional ideals and standards. Bureaucratic procedures were having an im-pact on AAUP activities in terms of academic freedom, and the association was evidencing less concern about standards of membership.

Summary

The period from the spring of 1955 to the spring of 1958 was a very busy one for the AAUP following the organizational lull from the mid-1940s to 1955. Committee A and members at the annual meeting broke the tremendous back-log of academic freedom and tenure cases. Committee O and members at the annual meetings examined the Constitution and structure of the association and approved changes considered necessary "to advance the standards, ideals, and welfare of the profession." Committee Z began the implementation of grading salary scales at colleges and universities. The staff size increased to five members, one for every 7,669 active members.[119]

Committee structure among and within association committees changed in this period. The AAUP expanded the number of standing committees as prepa-ration for addressing membership concerns and problems of higher education and the professoriate. By the end of 1958 there were thirteen standing commit-tees, including committees on association investments, professorial ethics, and college and university accreditation, compared with apparently only four (A, O, T, Z) in 1955.[120] The AAUP leaders revived the committee structure, its basic organization for decision making and policy creation, from 1955 to 1958.

The completion of reconstruction of the association, however, needed the as-surance of continuous executive staff leadership. In April 1957 General Secretary Fuchs announced that he had decided to return to teaching law at Indiana University.[121] Fuchs had done the association a tremendous service, leading the revitalization of AAUP. He identified the importance of attracting new members and leaders to the association (two of whom, Clark Byse and Ralph S. Brown, Jr., would become presidents) and providing broader and greater opportunities for involvement in the organization.[122] He also saw the need to act upon many issues facing professors and had begun the organizational process of addressing those issues. The council selected Robert Carr, one of the AAUP vice-presidents, to succeed Fuchs as general secretary.[123] The transition from Ralph Fuchs to Robert Carr was apparently a smooth one, perhaps in part because they worked together in the Central Office during June 1957.[124]

Yet Carr stayed in the position less than a year. He announced his resignation in the June 1958 *Bulletin,* stating that his decision was "a step taken in accordance with the agreement by which I assumed the office." Although there was no mention of such an agreement in any of the *Bulletin* announcements about Carr's appointment, the brevity of his stay apparently had no impact on the association's operations. The council appointed William P. Fidler, who had joined the AAUP staff in 1956, as general secretary—with his "acceptance of the post . . . not restricted as to time."[125] The AAUP was now strong enough to continue through some rapid changes at the senior administrative level.

Association activity ranged from quietude to considerable efforts at reconstruction in the period from 1946 to 1958. Himstead and national elected leaders had allowed the AAUP to remain inactive on issues of academic freedom, the organization's predominant program. The strong reaction of chapter and conference leaders to oligarchy and McCarthyism as they rapidly addressed the organizational inactivity proved that the AAUP could act. The national leaders' implementation of new programs and organizational structure proved their commitment to an active organization and to effecting the suggestions of chapter and conference leaders. In fact the reinvigorated association could move toward more active and expansive application of membership and leadership solutions to the problems of higher education and the professoriate. The association had just effected one of those solutions, the Committee Z salary grading scale, and the coming years would prove to be ones of further expansion and activism.

Although the AAUP had begun to change its membership criteria, both within the AAUP and nationally college professors tended to be members of the academic profession as defined by Logan Wilson. Professors continued to teach mostly at four-year institutions in the mid-1950s.[126] Those teaching at two-year colleges tended to have backgrounds different from those at four-year institutions; more than 64 percent of the teaching staffs at seventy-six institutions surveyed in 1957 had taught at elementary or secondary schools.[127] Yet professors recognized some of the problems they faced. In 1957 Logan Wilson described professors as apparently "restive" about their working conditions, salaries, promotion policies, and the problem of arbitrary college and university administrations.[128] The AAUP had begun to address those issues, and the late 1950s and early 1960s would bring further expansion.

Chapter 2

A Revitalized AAUP, 1958 to 1964

The years immediately following the reconstruction efforts were critical ones for the association. The leaders and members had spent the mid-1950s developing policies, programs, and organizational structure to further the interests of the academic profession. Yet AAUP membership had lost ground at a time when the size of the academic profession was increasing, and the AAUP had no assurance that it was indeed moving in the right direction. The late 1950s and early 1960s would prove whether or not the decisions of the mid-1950s sufficiently reflected the needs and interests of the academic profession.

The new general secretary was well-suited to the position. William P. Fidler had both administrative experience within the AAUP and a long professorial career, most recently at the University of Alabama. He was most experienced at the AAUP national level in the work of Committee A.[1] One of his association staff colleagues, Bertram H. Davis, later described him as "thoroughly Southern" and "strongly anti-segregationist."[2] The transition from Carr to Fidler seems to have been a smooth one, a transition perhaps eased by Fidler's day-to-day experience with the administrative affairs of the association.

The association certainly appeared to be moving in the right direction. Fidler noted in his spring 1959 report, "We are pleased to report that all indications point to a continuing growth of the Association in 1959, with resulting revenue sufficient to support an expanded program." Instead of the estimated deficit for 1958 the AAUP had a surplus because of increased dues income, lower Washington office staff salaries, and lower council travel expenditures. Within the Washington office the expansion included two additional staff members to assist Committee Z. Fidler added, "Present plans call for expansion of activity in the areas of Committee B on Professional Ethics; Committee C on College and University Teaching, Research, and Publication; Committee H on the History of the Association; and Committee T on Faculty-

Administration Relationships."[3] Expansion and activism continued to focus on professional characteristics of the professoriate, yet included development of programs related to the representation of professors' material interests.

By this time the AAUP had a standard operating procedure for establishing policy. Everyone in the association from nonparticipatory local members to Washington office staff members had the opportunity to evaluate a proposed policy over several years and through two or more draft statements published in the *Bulletin*. The AAUP Council was the structural focal point for the initial and continuing considerations of proposed policies. It consisted of the general secretary (the senior staff official), the treasurer (appointed), and thirty-six elected members: the president, the two vice-presidents, the three latest living former presidents, and thirty members elected at large.[4] Typically the council approved a committee's suggestion to investigate a potentially appropriate policy; the approval resulted in a standing or special committee presenting a series of reports for comment and concluded with the council's tentative approval of policy and the recommendation that the annual meeting delegates approve the proposed policy. The procedure for developing the statement on academic freedom for students serves as an excellent example of this process. From 1960 to 1964 discussion of the statement drafts was within the association, from 1966 to 1968 Committee S negotiated with external groups, and in 1968 the delegates at the annual meeting approved the statement as association policy.[5] Members and leaders reviewed the statement and were able to offer suggested changes prior to its approval by the council or the members at the annual meeting.

Several committees began to address their responsibilities during this period, allowing the AAUP to consider the impact of these areas through the process of publication and, when appropriate, policy approval. Two of the most important committees, Committees Z and T, further developed their work in the late 1950s and early 1960s, addressing issues raised by members and negotiating with administrators and representatives of organizations composed primarily of administrators.

The Welfare of the Profession: Committee Z Reports and Activity

Member pressure to address the economic welfare of the profession, as well as long-term association interest in the topic, began to have substantial public results at the end of the 1950s. Committee Z reported the first results of its expanded survey in 1959 and in that report clarified the program:

> It is intended to create in the governing board, the legislators, the benefactors, alumni, and others concerned with the welfare of an

institution an increased sense of urgency in these matters. The program is designed to reveal whether the salary scale of their university or college is unduly low relative to the scales maintained by
"rival" institutions. Where this deficiency is found to exist, those
in authority will know that the situation has been called to public
attention and will face a frank challenge.[6]

The association was deliberately calling attention to economic disparities at
the institutional level in the hopes of improving professors' salaries.

The committee received 282 usable reports from the association's 584
chapters, representing approximately 55,000 professors and a sufficient number to trust the data's validity.[7] The distribution of responses by five reported
types of institutions was 38.5 percent of the chapters at two-year colleges,
42.4 percent of those at professional schools, 44.9 percent at teachers colleges, 48.5 percent at liberal arts colleges, and 62 percent at universities.[8] The
strong returns for a first-time survey are surprising not only in the numbers
and percentages themselves but also for the level of cooperation among administrations that had to furnish the data, especially since some institutions'
salary scales were likely to receive low grades. In fact the first institution in
the list of chapters following the report of Committee Z was the University of
Alabama, with a minimum salary grade of "F" and an average salary grade of
"E."[9] Only three institutions—Harvard, Princeton, and Yale Universities—
had minimum salary grades of "A," and only six had minimum salary grades
of "B" (Amherst College, New York School of Social Work and Teachers
College, which were both affiliated with Columbia University, Swarthmore
College, the United States Naval Postgraduate School, and Wayne State
University).[10] Despite the disappointing distribution of salaries according to
AAUP measurement, administrators cooperated with the survey.

As Committee Z pursued its salary scale grading reports, the AAUP began
to receive comments, and those from college and university presidents in response to the 1959 report were most promising for the future success of the
survey. Excerpted comments indicated that presidents welcomed having specific information to present to legislatures and boards of trustees.[11]

Committee Z reported in the spring of 1960 that 332 institutions had
submitted salary data.[12] One hundred nine institutions that had not participated in 1958–1959 did so in 1959–1960; sixty-six institutions participated
in 1958–1959 but not in 1959–1960.[13] For 214 institutions that reported
salary data in 1958–1959 and 1959–1960 the committee was able to provide year-to-year changes. On the one hand more than eighty colleges showed

improvements in either their minimum-compensation or average-compensation scales; only eight showed reductions in either of the scales. On the other hand over one-half of the reporting institutions had no change in the minimum or average-compensation scales.

The committee also addressed the issue of annual increases in the graded scales to account both for inflation and the need for relatively higher salaries for professors.[14] Committee Z had proposed in 1958 that the scales be adjusted upward to achieve "the general objective of the gradual realignment of academic salaries" and to counter increases in the national income levels or inflation.[15] Machlup and the committee members reviewed the 1959–1960 data and decided to revise the tables to focus progress on the proposed doubling of professors' average salaries from 1957 by either 1962 or 1967 according to the recommendation of the President's Commission on Education Beyond High School.[16] The committee stated that there was "the urgency of restoring the profession to an appropriate relative economic status in our society."[17]

Committee Z reviewed the purpose of the salary grading scales in its 1961 report and explained, "The point of this story is that the salary program was never intended as a club to be used for purposes of intimidation."[18] The committee also explained why the program was a cooperative venture:

> The reason for this, of course, stems from the unique attitude of the academic profession, which refuses to consider itself to be composed of "employees" of educational institutions. Indeed, we are more likely to take the position that we *are* the institution, and that the role of its administration is exactly what the term implies—to carry out the task of administering a faculty's operations.[19]

While some administrators might disagree with the assignment of such a narrow role, they knew that Committee Z was helping them, in effect advancing the interests of higher education. College and university administrators still occasionally informed committee members that they used the salary survey in raising funds for professors' salaries although in other cases administrators were resistant to the survey.[20] Finally, in 1960–1961, Committee Z efforts went outside the AAUP for the first time, as it collected data "from a small number of relatively arbitrarily selected institutions."[21] The AAUP expansion in economic concerns was beginning to develop true national proportions, both in negotiation and in operation.

Representatives of the AAUP and the AAC met in November 1961 as planned to discuss further the salary survey.[22] Committee Z members were pleased by the meeting, and one result in part was the "very welcome increase in the number of reporting institutions."[23] In 1961–1962 there were 588 institutions that participated in the survey, compared to 482 institutions in the 1960–1961 survey.[24] The growth rate of the salary survey surpassed that of U.S. colleges and universities; in 1960–1961 24 percent of the nation's colleges and universities participated in the survey and in 1961–1962 28 percent participated.[25]

Although Committee Z reported that relatively satisfactory progress for faculty compensation in 1961–1962, it also indicated "a number of serious problems." The two "most underpaid groups" were professors at "the least affluent institutions" and those at upper ranks at "outstanding universities" whose national or international prominence was not matched by income. Southern institutions, teachers colleges, and church-related institutions paid low salaries, and public universities fell further behind private universities. Despite the levels of increase nationally, Committee Z suggested "deriving guarded satisfaction" from the results of the 1961–1962 survey.[26]

The number of institutions participating in the salary survey increased again in 1962–1963, to 667 institutions or 32 percent of all colleges and universities.[27] Compensation levels continued to increase but in addition "a number of disturbing developments" appeared in the 1962–1963 survey. The problems noted in the 1961–1962 report persisted, and there was "a marked drop in the percentage rate of increase in faculty salaries," the rate of "increase differential" among ranks narrowed (full professors' purchasing power continued to be a significant concern), and there was apparently "a reduction of differentials within ranks" at many institutions. The drop in the percentage rate of increase compared poorly with the 1961–1962 rate and was far from the rate necessary "to achieve the widely proposed doubling goal."[28] As a result of the old and new problems, Committee Z offered a somber thought about its report:

> Above all, it reminds us that if there is a slackening of the dedicated efforts which have been expended by administrations and faculties, and by those who provide the required resources, the secular improvement in academic incomes may falter before really satisfactory compensation levels are achieved.[29]

Although survey participation was increasing, levels of salaries were not achieving the national goals, and Committee Z was reporting the problem in increasingly direct terms.

Committee Z announced at the Fall 1963 Council Meeting that it would discontinue the biennial survey of forty-one colleges and universities. The self-grading survey served some of the same purposes, and the committee would maintain longitudinal comparisons by providing appropriate information in the salary survey reports.[30] The AAUP had completed one transition in its reconstruction, from a survey of general use to professors and administrators to a survey providing professors and administrators with widespread, specific, institutional comparisons. The salary survey was not Committee Z's only effort in the area of professors' material interests. The Subcommittee on Taxes had tried for several years to convince the Internal Revenue Service that professors' research expenses were deductible. Following AAUP submission of legal briefs and subsequent meetings with representatives of the IRS, in December 1963 the IRS issued a ruling that recognized the deductibility of professors' research expenses.[31] Such efforts show increased association willingness to represent directly professors' material interests.

The 1963–1964 salary survey report began on a negative note, contrasting with the neutral or positive introductions of previous years: "The most important conclusion to be drawn from this year's data is that the rate of growth of both salaries and compensations is extremely disappointing."[32] Committee members were also disappointed by the fact that for the first time there were two consecutive years of poor performance.[33] The probable reason was not particularly comforting in the eyes of the committee members, as they reasoned, "An examination of relevant information classified by type of control of the institutions indicates that the performance of the public institutions fell shockingly short of that achieved by the private colleges and universities over a two-year period."[34] The committee's strong reaction continued into its conclusion:

> But if earlier figures offered cause for concern, this year's data must be considered with alarm; for what had the appearance of a limited if chronic malaise has apparently burst into full crisis. We can only urge all those who are directly concerned—students' parents, legislators, administrators, and faculties—to act quickly before the damage to public education really becomes too difficult for ready repair.[35]

Years of acceptable performance in professors' salaries had quickly turned into an unsettling situation.

Throughout the late 1950s and the early 1960s the AAUP successfully conducted annual surveys of professors' salary ranges. Despite the apparent sensitivity of such information, particularly in faculties' opportunities to compare directly their institutions' salary scales to those at other institutions, increasing proportions of colleges and universities participated in the survey. The results of the survey, however, were not encouraging for AAUP leaders or members.

Shared Authority: Committee T Reports and Activity

In 1958 Committee T began to develop a tentative revision of a statement of principles on faculty-administration relationships that had been first present-ed in 1937.[36] The committee's 1958 report stated:

> The current statement, although unobjectionable, is brief, incom-plete, and expressed in very general terms. The reformulation and amplification of this statement is being attempted in the hope of producing a set of standards with regard to faculty participation in university government similar to the standards developed by Committee A over the years concerning academic freedom and tenure matters. What seems important is an understanding con-cerning the philosophical basis for educational administration, rather than insistence upon any particular set of standards.[37]

The committee was also considering investigations of, and reports on, specific situations, something it had already begun to do. The committee members published extracts from a report of a 1957–1958 investigation as an appendix to the 1958 interim report; neither the institution nor the individuals involved were identified. Committee members were concerned about the potential vol-ume of work with investigations and did not want to make a decision about such methods until more was known about how much work might develop.[38]

The first official investigation by Committee T occurred in the spring of 1959, at the request of an AAUP chapter.[39] Members of Committee T con-cluded that the investigation was a "successful experiment" and decided at the committee's January 1960 meeting that it would authorize investigations with the expectation of publication of the reports in the *Bulletin*.[40] The committee considered the criteria for investigations in view of the criteria for Committee A investigations and reported,

> The violation of an individual's academic freedom or tenure has implications for an entire faculty. But an individual's complaint cannot by itself support a presumption that faculty-administration relationships may have deteriorated sufficiently to justify the asso-ciation's investigation, nor can it assure the cooperation necessary in an investigation so comprehensive. The committee concluded

that it could consider authorizing an investigation only if the request came from a responsible group, such as a faculty as a whole, an association chapter, a faculty senate or its executive committee, or a group of senior faculty members.[41]

The AAUP conception of faculty participation in institutional governance thus differed at this time from the association conception of protecting the principle of academic freedom and tenure. Only a collective voice could justify investigation into complaints about governance, and that collective voice would have to meet a criterion of responsible, executive, or senior status. Committee T moved toward a more activist position in faculties' participation in government and administration, yet it was a position aligned with senior professors, not entire faculties.

Staff member Louis Joughin reported for Committee T at the November 1959 Council Meeting that the committee was preparing two reports, "The Role of the Faculty—Statement of Principles" and "Faculty Authority and Responsibility—Problems and Practices." Professor Ian Campbell (geology, California Institute of Technology), a member of the council and Committee T, reported the results of a Committee T investigation. He stated that the investigating committee had given suggestions to the institution's president and faculty and was to send copies of its report to the chair of Committee T and the presidents of the college and its AAUP chapter. The council then discussed a number of complaints about faculty-administration relationships and approved "a thorough investigation" concerning one of the complaints.[42]

At its April 1960 meeting the council approved Committee T's tentative statement of principles of faculty participation in college and university government.[43] The statement was published in the June 1960 *Bulletin* with the request that chapters and individuals comment on the statement. Its preamble noted the legal power of boards of trustees, the size of U.S. colleges and universities, and the need for more administrators, as well as the "gradual professionalization" of professors, including the development of their qualifications for responsible participation in governance. As a consequence of those three characteristics, the de jure characteristics of higher education governance had generally changed to a "functional sharing of powers" among faculties, administrators, and boards. Since there was "doubt and disagreement over respective spheres of action" among and within institutions, the committee proposed specific principles in five areas. They were faculty representation in the administration and on the governing board, major responsibility for educational and research policy, "a direct role by the faculty" in budget decisions, "active faculty participation" in "appointments, promotions, and dismissals of academic personnel," and the election of department heads by department members as well as "meaningful participation by the faculty through its elected representatives" in the hiring and firing of deans, presidents, and other academic administrators. The committee also suggested, "Board members, administrators, and faculty members should share the task of maintaining institutional relations with the public."[44] Committee T expressed a broad view of faculty authority and influence in college and university government for all types of higher education institutions.

The gradual professionalization of faculties and faculty participation in college and university government was a complex issue for the AAUP in the early 1960s, and part of the AAUP response was the investigation of practices at individual institutions. In the March 1961 *Bulletin* two Committee T reports named the institutions under investigation: Monmouth College (New Jersey) and the School of Medicine at the University of Miami (Florida).[45] The members at the 1961 Annual Meeting responded to both the Committee T statement and the institutional investigations. They instructed Committee T to discuss the statement "with appropriate representatives of college and university administrations" with the goal of approving the final draft at the 1962 Annual Meeting. They also passed two motions on the reports, instructing Committee T to report again at the 1962 Annual Meeting about improvements in faculty-administration relationships at each institution. The motion concerning the University of Miami noted that the AAUP was encouraged by progress there, but the motion for Monmouth College noted only the willingness of the Board of Trustees to consult with professors in improving the situation.[46] Members at the 1961 Annual Meeting sustained Committee T activism.

Committee T efforts apparently had an impact on college and university administrators beyond the immediate and individual sense of the investigative reports. At the Fall 1961 Council Meeting Fidler reported that presidents and deans were requesting advice from the Washington office in areas of Committee T concern as well as those of Committee A concern. Fidler indicated that "in most cases the problems are resolved in substantial accord with the advice which the Washington Office staff has given."[47] An AAUP staff member reported for Committee T at that council meeting, stating that the committee would meet soon to discuss association chapters' comments about the draft statement. While the majority of the chapters responding supported the draft statement, concerns remained. They included "the needs and problems presented by the large variety of institutions in higher education," problems with faculty involvement "in administrative areas, particularly in relation to budgeting," and "discouraging mere *pro forma* adherence to general statements of principles." Following the next revision of the statement the committee members hoped to consult with representatives of the AAC.[48]

Committee T met in December 1961 and revised the draft statement; that version was published in the March 1962 *Bulletin* as well as circulated among chapters. In addition the committee met with "eleven selected representatives of administrations" at the end of March 1962 to discuss the statement. As a result of that meeting Committee T changed parts of the draft.[49] Association activism in faculty governance in the early 1960s continued the AAUP tradition of negotiating with administrations.

John Dawson (law, Harvard University), the new chair of Committee T, reported to the members at the 1962 Annual Meeting that the committee had observed some progress in Monmouth College faculty-administration relationships (primarily because of the efforts of a new president) and at the University of Miami (although a number of administrative vacancies had slowed the process). Dawson also noted that the committee had overseen a consultation with professors and administrators at Fairleigh Dickinson University, which had been founded as a junior college in 1942 but had since grown to a four-year institution with three campuses and 16,000 students. The Committee T discussion on investigations suggested that the "complex group of interconnected factors" precluded votes of censure by the annual meeting. Although published accounts, as in the case of Monmouth College and the University of Miami, might have "some general educational value and some deterrent effect," still "one cannot be sure that the institution itself will benefit." The committee concluded on this subject that published reports would be used only in extreme cases; it preferred the private mediation conducted by Washington office staff members. Private mediation appeared to work where situations had not "degenerated too far," although it presupposed "some willingness to receive suggestions within the particular institution." In public investigations of extreme cases, chapters would have the same role as they did in Committee A investigations: none. Finally, Committee T decided to present reports in the *Bulletin* of successful shared authority at ten institutions of various sizes and different control.[50]

Ralph Fuchs spoke to the matter of faculty participation in college and university government at the 1962 Annual Meeting. He accepted the complexities of the various structures of U.S. higher education and the problems created by those complexities. He then stated that in comparison with "the autocratically controlled small institutions" in place until the late 1800s, "the faculty of the typical modern college or university have gained, not lost, in authority." He referred to the 1955 Committee T report "which showed that in identical situations the role of the faculty in institutional government had expanded over a period of years."[51] Fuchs failed to note, however, as Committee T had in that 1955 report, that recent "expansion of the Association's membership may have brought into our latest study new chapters at institutions without much faculty consultation."[52] Despite the apparent optimism, Fuchs felt, "It does not follow that faculty authority is generally in a satisfactory state." He offered a tripartite solution: to welcome the "well-chosen administrator, stimulating the faculty and proposing measures to it"; to make sure that "faculty authority is clearly bestowed" and "faculty responsibility is clearly defined"; and to formulate "an articulated conception of the nature and status of the academic profession, related to its history and its contemporary function." Fuchs believed that Committee T was beginning to develop that conception. It would be based on studies of the nature of colleges and universities, "the legal relation of employment into which we are cast, and the tradition of individual professional responsibility which we share with such largely self-employed groups as the practitioners of medicine and law." He urged AAUP cooperation with national associations representing administrators and trustees in order to influence and concluded by reemphasizing the need for an "articulated conception."[53]

Committee T operations expanded further in the spring of 1963 when General Secretary Fidler announced at the annual meeting the decision to appoint advisers by geographic regions to assist both Committee A and Committee T. These advisers would relieve, at least in part, the burden on Washington office staff members by serving on "mediation and advisory" as well as investigating committees.[54] In addition Fidler reported at the April 1963 Council Meeting that Committee T and the ACE Commission on Administrative Affairs had met in New York to discuss the draft statement.[55] Committee T was achieving progress in its expanded operations and its development of an articulated conception.

Committee T was also sensitive to the demands of chapter members on the issues of faculty participation in governance. In the September 1963 *Bulletin* the committee printed, at the request of the members at the 1963 Annual Meeting, both its most recent version of the statement and an alternative proposed by the members of the Syracuse University chapter. The Syracuse chapter had previously offered alternatives in 1960, 1961, and 1962, and in 1962 chapter members had circulated copies to those in attendance at the annual meeting. This side-by-side comparison allowed readers to choose between the national committee's broad principles and the chapter's more specific statements. The Syracuse chapter's effort to "bring into clearer and sharper focus the proper scope of faculty participation in college and university government"" was a primary difference between the versions. For example, the Committee T draft indicated that faculties did not have to be involved with the preparation and administration of physical plant decisions. The Syracuse version contended that faculties needed to be involved fully in *all* budgetary matters. In evaluation of the differences John Dawson stated, "We do not conceive faculties, boards, and administrators as natural enemies," and he saw no reason to anticipate "hostile boards and administrators." The president of the Syracuse chapter wrote that a statement of principles should call for higher action than current practices and added, "Such statement should not even remotely suggest the possibility that the role of the faculty is in any sense subordinate to any other."[56] The institutional perspective of faculty, as expressed by the Syracuse chapter, was more specific and held higher expectations of faculty participation in college and university affairs.

Ralph S. Brown, Jr. (law, Yale University) reported to the 1964 Annual Meeting as the newly appointed chair of Committee T. He indicated that the situation at the University of Miami no longer required attention and that Committee T and the general secretary hoped the same would soon be true for Fairleigh Dickinson University. In the case of Monmouth College, Brown stated that, despite a decrease in complaints, "responsible information points to some faculty apathy" and Committee T felt another visit was appropriate.[57] The new chair continued the committee's activist direction. Brown also discussed the draft Statement of Principles and the reaction of chapters to that version as well as the alternative proposed by the Syracuse University chapter. He said that the "limited response" clearly favored the Committee T draft. Yet Committee T would use the Syracuse alternative in its negotiations with representatives of ACE because "it represents a substantial body of opinion within the Association that favors a rigorous expression of faculty primacy in central areas of college and university government."[58] The AAUP members favoring professorial control had gained an organizational voice, even if it were a small one.

Finally Ralph S. Brown explained that the negotiations with the ACE representatives had not progressed substantially because, as General Secretary Fidler had learned from his inquiries, "other commitments of officers" of ACE were responsible for their lack of response. ACE officers had assured Fidler that they were still interested in working on the draft statement. A member suggested from the floor that the annual meeting endorse the current draft, but President Machlup responded that such a move might be taken "as an act of bad faith" by ACE representatives since such adoption "might create the impression that Committee T had no scope for discussion and negotiation."[59] On the one hand the AAUP meant to present "a rigorous expression of faculty primacy." On the other hand the AAUP took care to avoid the appearance of confrontation with ACE.

The AAUP and Civil Liberties: Association Responses to Exclusion in Higher Education

In several areas relating to civil liberties, the AAUP became increasingly involved with the representation of professors and, in some cases, students. The rise of liberal political activity in the late 1950s and early 1960s, perhaps best illustrated by the civil rights movement, was reflected by the AAUP.

The association began expressing concern about legal conditions of students' freedom and national security in its opposition to the disclaimer affidavit requirement of the National Defense Education Act (which required that recipients sign a statement that they did not belong to organizations conspiring to overthrow the federal government). This extensive association activity began in November 1958 and ended in 1962; it involved chapter letters to members of the U.S. Congress, staff efforts to convince the leaders of other education associations to oppose the affidavit, and annual meeting resolutions opposing the requirement.[60] The AAUP was also concerned about states' actions toward professors' loyalties, and it paid special attention to a situation in Arkansas. The Arkansas state legislature passed a law in 1958 requiring professors at state-supported institutions to list their membership in all organizations. Five professors refused to submit their lists, and the AAUP went to great lengths to assist them, providing loans for living and travel expenses to all five. The association assisted two of the professors in securing new appointments and presented resum,s of the remaining three in the March 1960 *Bulletin*.[61]

The association also evidenced interest in racial issues in South Africa and the United States. AAUP opposition to apartheid began in 1957, when the members at the annual meeting adopted a resolution of concern, and the members at the 1958 and 1960 Annual Meetings passed resolutions protesting apartheid. In 1960 General Secretary Fidler coordinated efforts to assist South African professors, which included providing a fellowship to one professor who had resigned in protest and publishing background information in the *Bulletin* on several other South African professors to encourage possible employment in the United States.[62]

Also at the 1960 Annual Meeting the members in attendance passed two resolutions concerning civil rights in the United States.[63] In March 1962 President Fuchs testified by invitation before the U.S. House of

Representatives ad hoc subcommittee on integration in federally assisted education. Fuchs reviewed association activities in support of desegregation, including annual meeting resolutions, a then-upcoming study on desegregation and academic freedom by C. Vann Woodward, *Bulletin* articles, and academic freedom cases involving issues of race.[64] In 1963 Committee A appointed the Special Committee to Survey Conditions of Academic Freedom in Mississippi to report "about pressures on faculty members in Mississippi to force them to accept segregationist views."[65]

Staff appointments also reflected AAUP interest in civil liberties. In 1958 the association appointed Louis Joughin to the staff; he had been executive director of the American Civil Liberties Union Committee on Academic Freedom.[66] In 1964 the AAUP appointed as assistant counsel Charles Morgan, who had handled civil rights cases in Alabama.[67]

The association development of activities in the area of civil liberties had two consequences for the AAUP. First, the organization began to include new groups in its domain, recognizing specifically, for example, the issue of integrating black men and women into higher education. Second, the AAUP began to address governmental and legal activity. General Secretary Fidler, in fact, expressly noted that link at the November 1959 Council Meeting, stating, "When a person with legal training is added to the Washington Office staff, the Association's activities will be greatly expanded."[68] The expansion of AAUP interests also meant a subtle shift in association methods, with a concern for the legal conditions of the profession.

In fact the association initially expressed interest in legal conditions of higher education in the 1958 council decision to file a brief *amicus curiae* in the Barenblatt case on academic freedom.[69] Yet as one committee member, Ralph S. Brown, noted later, the Court's use of AAUP argument was a "Pyrrhic" victory; the Court's quotes were used to sustain a decision contrary to the association's arguments since the Court upheld Barenblatt's conviction for contempt of the U.S. Congress.[70] Fuchs suggested, however, in the conclusion to his *Bulletin* report on the decision that the result "can be a call to more effective action, rather than a ground of discouragement."[71] Even in defeat the association wanted to show optimism for further activity.

Academic Freedom and AAUP Activism

Even Committee A became more publicly activist in the late 1950s, publishing a 1959 report on institutions that had terminated professors' appointments late in the academic year. Staff Associate Bertram H. Davis had recommended to General Secretary Carr that the AAUP publish reports on the association's unsuccessful attempts to secure redress for professors subjected to late terminations. Davis suggested that the publication of the cases would gain the AAUP "greater influence in future negotiations" and would inform the profession as to what the AAUP was doing and what it believed about this issue.[72] The association had not been able to resolve four cases, and a brief statement of each case was published in the Spring issue of the *Bulletin.* The names of the institutions and individuals were not published in this report because it was the first of its kind; Staff Associate Davis noted, however, that "future reports will identify both institutions and individuals."[73]

David Fellman, reporting as chair of Committee A at the 1960 Annual Meeting, told association members that Committee A had decided "to take a much more active part in litigation" concerning academic freedom and tenure because of increased litigation, and the committee was increasingly interested in the issue of redress for individuals, and redress was more likely to entail litigation. The committee also decided to place greater attention on publicizing its codification of the 1940 Statement. Two statements reflecting that codification, "Association Procedures in Academic Freedom and Tenure Cases" and "Recommended Institutional Regulations on Academic Freedom and Tenure," were only available as mimeographed copies, and the committee hoped to have those statements published in the *Bulletin.*[74]

Yet Committee A sustained its traditional approach to academic freedom and tenure issues. Committee chair David Fellman argued at the Fall 1961 Council Meeting that "the best interests of higher education" were "served by the careful and thorough examination of the issues." He stated that cases involving "principles of general concern to the academic profession" were most likely to be selected for examination.[75] Although Committee A evidenced interest in redress for individuals, it continued to advance the principles of academic freedom and tenure. Even though the staff members negotiated the resolution of many complaints, Fellman suggested that publicizing only cases of principle was the most appropriate route.

Nevertheless the committee persisted in highlighting institutions that violated the standard of late notice, reporting eight cases of late notice in the December 1962 *Bulletin.*[76] And in the same issue the association began to publish advisory letters interpreting general policy on academic freedom and tenure, with identification of institutions and individuals removed. The publication of the letters served to publicize—albeit anonymously and only to a small degree—private AAUP mediation efforts.[77] Committee A also adopted a brief "Statement on the Standards for Notice of Nonreappointment" in 1963.[78] This statement clarified association policy on notice of nonreappointment and gave "the American academic community adequate notice" of association standards. The council approved the statement at its October 1963 meeting, and the members at the 1964 Annual Meeting also approved it.[79]

During this period of expansion and activism Committee A activities shifted relative to its traditional work. On the one hand it was specifying such areas as nonreappointment and late notice and evidencing some interest in individual redress. On the other hand it maintained its emphasis on national approaches to academic freedom issues.

Membership and Leadership Characteristics, 1959 to 1964

In 1959 Committee O and the council recommended changes in membership nomination and election that completed the transition from peer review to simple application. The proposed changes in the Constitution deleted both nomination for membership and the necessity of a membership committee voting on nominations; the general secretary simply needed to determine applicants' eligibility and to notify them of their acceptance.[80]

Membership drives continued throughout this period of expansion. In 1960 the AAUP decided to set a goal of doubling its membership within a decade, and its first report on membership for that year indicated that it would meet its annual goals and take a step closer to the ten-year goal.[81] In the same year the association addressed the issue of demand for professors as well as its need for members, "concentrating on recruitment of graduate students into college teaching, and into membership in the Association as well."[82] Membership drives in the early 1960s also acknowledged the rapid growth in the number and size of public colleges and universities. In 1962–1963 the association supported legislation concerned with improving professors' economic status and increasing participation in governance for faculties at public institutions in California, Minnesota, and Pennsylvania. These efforts were related specifically to a "substantial increase in membership in recent years and the establishment of many new chapters." Association staff members also identified professors at state colleges and universities without AAUP chapters and mailed to them "organizational materials and model chapter constitutions."[83] The AAUP was conducting vigorous membership campaigns among young professors and professors at public colleges and universities, and it was successful. From January 1959 to January 1965, the number of active members increased 63 percent from 38,347 to 61,259.[84] Nationally the number of college instructors during this period increased from 244,461 to an estimated 372,000, an increase of 52 percent.[85]

The distribution of membership by institutional type changed from 1940 to 1960, the last year when a full report of members' employing institutions was published in the *Bulletin*. The approval of junior college professors' membership eligibility resulted in increasing numbers of those faculty members in the association. By 1960 professors at 107 public and 30 private two-year colleges were AAUP members (1,360 colleges and universities had professors who were AAUP members by then).[86] In addition there was increased representation of professors at public four-year colleges. In 1940 professors at 168 public four-year colleges were AAUP members; by 1960 the number of such institutions represented by AAUP members had increased to 312.[87] In comparison, the number of those institutions nationally in 1939–1940 was 255 and in 1960 it was 342.[88] The association leaders, however, continued to be senior professors at elite colleges and universities as indicated by table 2.

Association concern about younger professors extended beyond simply their possible membership in the AAUP. At the April 1964 meeting of the council, Eveline Burns (economics, the Columbia University School of Social Work) stated that the AAUP had to deal with academics without tenure, "a piece of unfinished business that we should come to grips with."[89]

TABLE 2

AAUP PRESIDENTS FROM 1946 TO 1966 BY DISCIPLINE, INSTITUTIONS, AND EXPERIENCE

Year(s) of Presidency	Presidency	Discipline	Employing Institution	First Year Teaching
1946–1948	Edward C. Kirkland	History	Bowdoin College	1920
1948–1950	Ralph H. Lutz	History	Stanford	1911
1950–1952	Richard H. Shryock	History	Johns Hopkins	1921
1952–1954	Fred B. Millett	English	Wesleyan University	1916
1954–1956	William E. Britton	Law	Illinois	1916
1956–1958	Helen C. White	English	Wisconsin	1917
1958–1960	H. Bentley Glass	Biology	Johns Hopkins	1934
1960–1962	Ralph F. Fuchs	Law	Indiana	1927
1962–1964	Fritz Machlup	Economics	Princeton	1934
1946–1966	David Fellman	Pol. Science	Wisconsin	1934

SOURCES: All data for all of the presidents are from the reports of the nominating committees as published in the *AAUP Bulletin* in the autumn of the year before election.

At that same meeting Bertram H. Davis reported that Committees A, C (on College and University Teaching), and T were working on the nontenured problem.[90]

Davis gave additional recognition to nontenured professors in a *Bulletin* editorial when he quoted from "a key section" of the Committee T draft statement that urged active professorial participation in faculty members' appointments, promotions, and tenure decisions. The participation was important, he wrote, since, "To judge from the complaints of probationary teachers—and no complaints are more numerous—many institutions have failed to establish committees for these purposes, or to adopt acceptable procedures." Davis suggested that such participation would provide "a reasoned professional opinion on which a sound, and thus not easily disputed, decision can be based."[91] AAUP attention to professors' concerns was beginning to distinguish between those of tenured, senior professors and those of untenured, junior professors. The ability of those two groups to act within the college or university would in fact begin to take new dimensions for the association, as the question of faculty unionism returned.

Professors, Power, and the AAUP: Initial Speculation about Collective Bargaining

In the September 1962 *Bulletin,* Melvin Lurie, an economics professor at the University of Rhode Island, wrote on the AAUP, the AMA, and unions.[92] He offered a provocative conclusion:

> University professors are currently in an economic position that could, under effective unionism, result in a large increase in income over the next two decades. We could disguise our real goals by asking for and imposing higher standards on those desiring to enter the teaching profession. Clearly university professors will not accept all or perhaps any of the restrictionist union activities suggested here, but it seems appropriate to speculate on these policies and, in so doing, to realize the great differences between college teachers and the medical profession on the question of unionism.[93]

Lurie based part of his argument on a statement in an AAUP membership-recruitment brochure that likened the association to the ABA and the AMA; *Bulletin* Editor Bertram H. Davis noted that the phrase had since been deleted from that brochure.[94] The identification of the AAUP with the ABA and the AMA quietly changed to a lack of identification, apparently recognizing the cogency of Lurie's arguments, at least in regard to the differences between the academic and medical professions.

Israel Kugler, a social science professor at New York Community College of Applied Arts and Sciences, responded by letter to Lurie's article. Kugler stated that he was vice-president for Colleges of the United Federation of Teachers, Local 2 of the AFT, and that he had led the "union chapter" at New York Community College for ten years. He claimed that the chapter enrolled the majority of the professors at the community college and had gained on behalf of professors "legislative tenure, professional vacations in place of an eleven-month year, reductions in workload from a 21-hour standard, and greatly improved salaries." Most important was "the feeling that the staff has an organization on the campus that will secure redress of grievances and negotiate with the college administration and governing board." Professors at the institution had concluded that "the AAUP was *not* structurally or functionally equipped to deal with many of the problems confronting the faculty" and that their working conditions meant that they were "*employees.*" Although Kugler gave credit to the AAUP for such services as the salary survey, censure of administrators in violation of academic freedom, and resolutions on desegregation, it "did not serve as the on-campus power structure to channel the collective strength of the professional staff." Kugler urged the use of "the technique of collective bargaining," arguing that the AMA physicians were "largely *self-employed* establishing their own conditions for professional practice by setting fees." He also argued, "The existence of higher salaries in the few institutions that merit an 'A' rating and the higher policy-making powers granted a few faculties should not blind one to the reality that exists generally." He assured readers, "The union would jealously guard the excellence of their professional craft." He concluded by urging that the AAUP transform "itself into a union" and "shed the illusion that college teachers are not professional employees but professionals on appointment." Kugler wanted the association to "recognize the true nature of the power structure in American education."[95]

General Secretary Fidler attended a breakfast session of state and regional conferences at the 1964 Annual Meeting where there was "a singularly provocative discussion" on "the relationship between local and national AAUP functions." Two Kent State University professors described the discussion in a letter to the *Bulletin* editor, highlighting the image of the national AAUP as "genteel, impeccably objective, rather remote, and essentially reflective as opposed to an executive (action) body." The authors of the letter were concerned that the national AAUP tended "to view administration *and* faculty as litigants" while boards of trustees and administrations tended to view the AAUP, "in spite of ourselves, as a special interest group seeking to further the welfare of its membership." The national AAUP wanted to control investigations so that chapters would not "'prejudge'" (apparently Fidler's wording) and "press for actions which apparently threaten National's image." Consequently the national association was the only organizational level for addressing complaints, a structure that imposed "on the local a complementary character of gentility, but of passivity as well." The authors suggested that "floor actions" at annual meetings such as the motions to reverse Committee A recommendations made it clear that "the local chapters resent this role."[96] In general the authors wanted *a change of the national image, less, perhaps in the minds of others as in our own minds, to that of an action group dedicated without apology to serving the interests of its membership rather than standing in aloof judgement thereon.*[97] In more specific terms the authors wanted election to the council within districts rather than election on a nationwide basis since the latter method meant "giving weight to professional visibility as against local (AAUP) exposure and commitment." They also suggested insurance in support of protest resignations at censured institutions, indicating that although the AAUP had opposed organized strikes it had "informally encouraged *individual* 'strikes' in the form of *protest resignations.*"[98] The discussion began during the breakfast meeting when Fidler

> . . . noted that in New York City the AAUP may be facing competition from a "labor union" now seeking to represent the faculty of a New York college in negotiations with the administration. Are we faced, Fidler asked, with the need to revise our functioning to embrace aspirations and techniques commonly identified with unionism? He then partially answered his own question by lamenting any gravitation from our professional role as "officers" of our separate institutions to mere "employees" thereof. Obviously, for Fidler (and current AAUP officialdom) unionism is an odious concept.[99]

The AAUP leadership saw competition from the union movement and was asking what the competition meant for AAUP operations. In the case of General Secretary Fidler, he knew what the AAUP should be. There were local representatives, however, who did not agree with the general secretary.

Summary

From late 1958 to late 1964 the AAUP expanded the salary survey, and its efforts included both national conceptions of the ideal characteristics and the local conditions that professors experienced—the latter not necessarily concomitant with the ideals. Its expansion of interest in faculty participation in governance addressed not only the possibility of a national statement, achieved much as the association had achieved the 1940 Statement, but also the problems of local conditions as defined by the AAUP. In the work of Committee A the AAUP had begun to represent publicly individual professors in its review of cases of late notice of nonreappointment. The organization also developed substantially increased concern over legal and political conditions that professors (and students) faced. At the chapter and conference levels members were successful in gaining recognition from the national leaders.

During this time the association experienced tremendous membership growth. Staff size increased too, doubling from four members in December 1958 to eight in December 1964.[100] This in fact meant a slight increase in the ratio of staff members to active members, from one staff member for every 9,587 active members to one for every 7,657.[101] Yet the growth of membership, staff, and programs was not simply an organizational advantage. The burdens of office which General Secretary Himstead had claimed in defense of the backlog of AAUP activities were not so fully the result of his "strange pathology" or "personality" as Schrecker and Loya Metzger suggest.[102] In the spring of 1962 General Secretary Fidler presented his resignation, and President Ralph Fuchs reported at the Spring 1962 Council Meeting that "the situation which led Dr. Fidler to tender his resignation some weeks ago was simply one of excessive burden of work, which he felt on a personal basis he would be unable to continue to discharge to his own satisfaction."[103] Fuchs also stated, "As a past incumbent of that office I have been vividly aware of the problems confronting him and the office as the activities of the association have continuously expanded."[104] The Executive Committee and Fuchs decided to arrange a situation that allowed Fidler to continue as general secretary; their decision included redefinition of the position as one of "policy maker and guiding director of the work of the Association" and establishing a new position of deputy general secretary for "administrative functions."[105] The council approved voting status for the general secretary for his service on certain committees "of a critical nature," those being Committees A, I (on investments), J (on association publications), O, and T.[106] Bertram H. Davis, longtime staff associate and *Bulletin* editor, took the new position.[107] The AAUP was healthy enough to restructure a continuously burdensome position, that of general secretary, since it had sufficient staff members and competent and knowledgeable elected leadership.

The reconstruction had succeeded, yet its marks of success—expansion and activism—were leading it onto uncertain terrain. Committee A was considering the issue of redress for individuals, and Committees T and Z were examining conditions at individual institutions. AAUP expansion and activism in the area of representation of professors' interests was about to include examination of the issue of direct, de jure, representation: unionization.

Chapter 3

Custodians of the Interests of Higher Education, or Employees?

In the early and mid-1960s, the AAUP experienced considerable expansion of its membership and programs. The reconstruction of the post-McCarthy years appeared to be having benefits. Yet new institutions, new professors, and new AAUP members presented questions that the association had either not previously considered or had answered in brief. As Deputy General Secretary Bertram H. Davis noted in a 1961 editorial statement:

> The community college emerging from the public school system, the university sponsoring increased research, the transforming teacher-training institutions, the junior college attempting a four-year program and the liberal arts college a graduate school—these shifting grounds of American education, indicative of its vaulting complexity as it accommodates itself to the population rise and the space age, pose an unprecedented challenge for responsible faculty-administrative decision.[1]

Davis also saw that the complexities were leading to professorial activism, arguing, "As more and more of our faculties have come professionally of age, the demands upon administrators and trustees to accord them active roles in all phases of institutional governance have become more urgent."[2] In particular the AAUP wrestled with the question of faculty participation in college and university governance. Its first response was in accordance with traditional association responses, the emphasis upon negotiated practices. Yet it quickly looked at another response, one that it had considered in the past and dismissed: unionization.

Professorial Power and Activism in the Late 1950s and Early 1960s

In one of the most influential publications on higher education in the early 1960s, *The Uses of the University,* Clark Kerr remarked repeatedly on the strength of professors and faculties—their increasing sense of affluence, their rising status, and the increasing demand for their services.[3] The general mood of the professoriate from 1958 to the early 1960s appears to have been one of strong self-worth in the interest of the nation and the society.[4]

The federal and state governments responded positively to the substantial growth in higher education, providing tremendous support. Additionally professors increasingly found their labor market to be favorable.[5] Yet the stratification of the academic labor market continued, suggesting that there still existed an academic profession located primarily at research universities and a professoriate of faculty instructors. The major study of the academic labor market in this period, based on data from 1965, reported that the type and prestige of the employing institution, the level (master's degree or higher) and prestige of the professor's education, the geographic region of the employing institution and the professor, and the professor's discipline, age, and rank all proved to be powerful factors in the academic labor market.[6] Research universities and highly selective private colleges continued their tendency of appointing new professors with doctorates from research universities.

The early 1960s also mark the beginning of faculty unionization. Scholars tend to agree that some faculties at some times used informal collective bargaining with administrations or boards of trustees in U.S. higher education.[7] There are, however, some substantial differences between informal (de facto) and formal (de jure) methods of collective bargaining.

Informal, or de facto, collective bargaining is evident in the traditional faculty-administration relationships of governance. Two works from the late 1950s and early 1960s on college governance, by Dennison and by Corson, highlight the informal, yet often highly structured, ways that faculties and administrations worked to run their institutions.[8] In this manner faculty participation in such matters as budget development and implementation results from administrative decisions to involve the faculty to one degree or another. This form of faculty-administration relationship differs from Logan Wilson's analysis of the AAUP in that he emphasizes the association's ability to improve the "individual bargaining power" of its members.[9] Nevertheless the de facto form of collective bargaining is obviously characteristic of the forms of institutional governance that the AAUP favored, based on its professional ideals.

Formal, de jure, collective bargaining derives its authority from state or federal authorization. Governmental actions, particularly certain state legislative actions and President Kennedy's Executive Order 10988 (which authorized collective negotiations by federal employees beginning in 1962), constitute one of the three sets of major causes of faculty unionization. Those decisions required public employers to recognize the legal right of a group of public employees to organize and to represent all such employees in contract negotiations in exclusive representation; no other organization may represent the employees. In 1959 the Wisconsin state legislature passed the first state law permitting collective bargaining by municipalities and their employees. Although the law excluded the faculties at the public colleges and universities, it included teachers at locally controlled schools such as the two-year postsecondary technical institutions.[10] In 1970 the National Labor Relations Board ruled that it had responsibility for collective bargaining by employees of private colleges and universities, thereby extending the legal right of organization and representation to that sector.[11]

Another set of causes was the unsatisfactory governance relationships, accentuated by higher education's rapid growth and bureaucratization in the 1960s, between faculties and administrations, boards of trustees, and states' central administrations. Robert O. Berdahl studied the increasing distance between public institutions of higher education and states' central administrations and found that from 1940 to 1969 there was an extensive movement toward state coordinating boards that state legislators and executives expected to influence if not govern public colleges and universities.[12] Berdahl focused on institutional relationships with state governing apparatuses, but nevertheless there was no mention of any faculty influence of any type in his three chapters on planning, budget review, and program review. The exclusion speaks directly to the bureaucratization of higher education and to the consequences for the professoriate; key areas of institutional maintenance and development fell outside the purview of the faculty. Joseph W. Garbarino also identified a specific aspect of governance, the desire of "craft workers" to control their working conditions.[13] This desire is important because a substantial part of the association debate concerning collective bargaining focused on the control of working conditions by professionals and by employees.

The third set of causes was the presence of associations whose methods include collective bargaining. The AFT was established as a union in the early 1900s and has been the most militant national organization representing teachers. The NEA began its policy of organizing elementary and secondary schoolteachers for collective bargaining in 1962 and moved quickly to collective bargaining among faculties in higher education.[14] The AAUP was the last of the three organizations to approve collective bargaining.

Professors at two-year and four-year institutions often based their collective bargaining on the industrial trade union model, conducting negotiations with administrators and trustees with the understanding that their relationships with those groups were adversarial.[15] The professorial strike represents the most adversarial form of union behavior because it halts the fundamental function of a college or university: teaching students. The first union strike by professors occurred in September 1966 at Henry Ford Community College (where an AFT local represented the faculty) in Michigan.[16] The adversarial assumptions of collective bargaining advocates and participants indicate the difference between de facto and de jure bargaining, and the strike highlights the radical difference between the two types of interorganizational relations.

AFT efforts to organize teachers in the post–World War II period were largely unsuccessful until the early 1960s, when the United Federation of Teachers (UFT, an affiliate of the AFT and supported by the AFL-CIO) organized New York City schoolteachers, and succeeded in engaging in de jure collective bargaining with the Board of Education.[17] AFT success in organizing teachers in higher education for collective bargaining began at the boundary between secondary and higher education as the result of the enabling legislation passed by the Wisconsin state legislature. The AFT started to organize academic and vocational teachers at the Milwaukee Vocational School in the fall of 1962.[18] In May 1963 the Wisconsin Employment Relations Board ordered a two-part election for Milwaukee Vocational School teachers, the first part to allow the faculty to determine if it wanted an organization separate from the schoolteachers and the second to choose among the AFT Local 212, the Milwaukee Vocational and Adult Education Schools Education Association (the National Education Association affiliate), and no representation.[19] The teachers selected a separate organization and chose the AFT local as their representative. Following the election, Philip J. Blank, president of the AFT local, said that salaries would be among the first matters of negotiation.[20] Further AFT efforts in faculty unionization moved slowly as faculties at only a few community colleges selected AFT locals as bargaining agents. After the Milwaukee election, the next AFT victory occurred at Olympia College (Washington) in February 1964.[21]

The NEA evidenced no interest in teachers' or faculties' collective bargaining until the early 1960s. Increased numbers of male teachers who were more aggressive than their predecessors in calling for participation in school government, the increasingly bureaucratic school systems, and government approval of collective bargaining for public employees were among the factors contributing to the NEA move toward unionization.[22] Furthermore the urban schoolteachers in the NEA began to convince the organization in the late 1950s and early 1960s to address their concerns about participation in school government and teachers' salaries.[23]

AFT success also pressured the NEA, both in broad terms as with the UFT success in New York City as well as direct taunts. James A. Carey, president of the International Union of Electrical, Radio, and Machine Workers, bluntly told NEA members at their 1962 Annual Meeting that the AFT would work harder at organizing teachers with the help of the labor movement:

> And if I sound somewhat shocked because the charwomen in some high schools get a higher rate of pay than the high school teachers, *understand,* it comes from the heart. And if the charwomen in the high schools have more tenure in their jobs and more security than the high school teachers, to me it is a shocking disclosure of the method in which we pay our reward. Or if the charwomen of the schools have sense enough to band together and organize and negotiate contracts, and the teachers do not, I wonder sometimes who should have the degrees.[24]

The message from the AFT in New York City and in Carey's speech in combination with the urban members' activism "shocked the Association into action."[25] The NEA began immediately in 1962 to marshal its considerable resources for what it called "professional negotiation," a euphemism for collective bargaining by public employees.[26] With 1962 membership at 812,497, 1962 dues income at nearly $7,358,000, and sixty-nine national staff members plus many state staff members, the NEA's resources were far greater than those of the AFT or the AAUP.[27] The NEA moved quickly to attempt to represent professors, beginning with its local affiliate's participation in the collective bargaining election at the Milwaukee Vocational School in 1963.

Both the AFT and the NEA were using substantial resources to implement faculty collective bargaining as early as 1964. Their commitments—one historical, one nascent—contrasted with the AAUP emphasis on activism within the context of professionalism. All three organizations, however, recognized that professors were increasingly concerned about their material interests and their participation in governance.

The AAUP and "The Representation of Economic Interests"

At the October 1964 meeting of the Executive Committee, one agenda item was "The problem of Collective Bargaining."[28] During the council meeting that followed, AAUP President David Fellman instructed Deputy General Secretary Bertram H. Davis to plan and finance a conference on collective bargaining to be held in Washington, D.C., "at the earliest opportunity."[29] Davis reports that although such labor law experts as Sanford Kadish (law, University of California–Berkeley) were active in the AAUP:

> . . . it was very, very difficult to see just what collective bargaining would mean for higher education and for the AAUP, whose approach was totally different. All we could do was speculate and we didn't have enough knowledge to be able to speculate with any conviction. So this was discussed at length in the council meeting and it was decided we ought to get in experts from all over the country, as far as we could, on collective bargaining—people who had some experience with it.[30]

At that time the Executive Committee members were all professors in the arts and sciences or law, and all were at elite institutions, where unionization was not a faculty issue.[31] Nevertheless the AAUP leaders felt that they had to develop quickly an understanding of this new form of faculty representation:

> There was a sense of real urgency because the profession was growing so fast and everyone was aware, for example, that these enormous institutions like the City University of New York had tens and tens of thousands of students and many campuses; the faculty members were feeling more and more remote from the administrators. Inevitably they were going to take whatever strongest organization they could to try to combat, to counter their own weaknesses.[32]

Finally, the Washington office had received an inquiry from New York City professors about AAUP policy on collective bargaining. The Washington office response had been "we didn't have a position and perhaps we should."[33] Thus the AAUP's early consideration of faculty unionization developed from a need to know the movement as well as pressures from faculty activity at institutions.

The conference took place in late December 1964; the participants ranged from AAUP officers, committee chairs, and staff members to disciplinary experts on collective bargaining and professors experiencing the developing union movement in higher education.[34] The number of AAUP elected and appointed leaders and staff members at the conference was high; most AAUP conferences of this nature involved members of the relevant committee and an AAUP staff member (as well as the representatives of the other institutions or associations).[35] Both the disciplinary experts and those experiencing collective bargaining offered a clear message to the AAUP leaders and staff members: collective bargaining by faculties was beginning to develop at four-year institutions. William

McPherson, a professor of industrial relations at the University of Illinois and chair of Committee B, suggested that collective negotiations "will soon be a possibility at a group of important colleges."[36] The only administrator at the conference, President Martin Dworkis of the Borough of Manhattan Community College, suggested that the New York City situation was likely to set the pace for the rest of the country.[37]

Despite the clear message that collective bargaining was coming to the professoriate, the nature of such bargaining was not clear. Some of the uncertainty over that nature concerned the issue of exclusive representation. Jack Barbash (economics, University of Wisconsin, and long-time AFT supporter) stated that it provided a clear advantage to those who held it while Clyde W. Summers (labor law, Yale University, and AFT and AAUP member) responded that multiple organizations were preferable because they competed to protect and advance professors' interests. Not even the question of the strike was clear; President Fellman asked if the strike was essential to collective bargaining, and Barbash responded that it was not but was one of the methods in the private sector.[38]

Fellman asked for advice as to what association leaders should do about collective bargaining, saying that he felt that such groups as the Legislative Conference (at the City University of New York) were not pursuing collective bargaining according to the industrial union model. He also argued that the best approach was to build collective bargaining into the institutional structure in accordance with the principles of the proposed AAUP Statement on Faculty Participation in College and University Government. Ralph S. Brown then spoke to the Committee T statement and the faculty's proper role of determining educational policies; Barbash responded that the statement did not adequately address grievance procedures and economic interests. He added that the association's "professional credentials are unimpeachable." If the AAUP issued a statement addressing all the relevant issues, that would help to remove a "middle-class snobbish attitude that a professional ought not to concern himself with the economic conditions under which he works."[39] Clark Byse, chair of Committee A, repeated Fellman's unanswered request for advice, asking whether the AAUP should have a policy on collective bargaining. Barbash suggested that the question of whether to pursue collective bargaining was "a matter for local determination" and that the AAUP would face factional disputes and "would find its professional objectivity and status impaired" if it issued a formal statement. Summers disagreed in part, saying that although the AAUP ought to oppose exclusive representation, it should consider getting its "snout in the tent" or else the union (the AFT) would preempt the situation.[40]

President Fellman then asked William McPherson for a summary. McPherson noted that according to the AAUP the exclusive representative was the faculty and opposition to exclusive representation was not antiunion but left the same "function and status" for unions as the AAUP held, that a request by a nonunion faculty body to be the exclusive representative would constitute "digging its own grave" and that the work of Committee T was vitally important. He concluded with a comparison of the strong relationships of the AFT and the NEA with their local affiliates and the weak relationship of the AAUP, despite recent efforts, with its chapters. He felt the AAUP needed to address that problem since those close relationships "proved very effective in operation."[41]

William P. Fidler then expressed concern about the current emphasis on public institutions since much of the association's strength and many of its leaders came from private institutions. He also noted that there was a basic policy question in the potential reallocation of resources. Louis Joughin asked the final question of the conference, addressing it to Barbash and Summers; he wondered if the eventual solution would be the development of a "well-conceived, properly organized, and powerful faculty unit within the organic structure of the faculty, with exclusive bargaining representation powers." Barbash replied that in public institutions there were also external questions such as lobbying; Summers basically agreed, adding that faculty members have the right to external representation on their behalf.[42] Neither of the collective bargaining experts were comfortable with the AAUP leaders' notion of an internal body of representation.

Following the conference the members of the Executive Committee met with the chairs of Committees A, B, and T (Clark Byse, William McPherson, Ralph S. Brown) and Washington office staff members and reached the following conclusions:

1. In a university, each faculty group should have access to those who make the decisions;
2. The rights of multiple faculties should be recognized;
3. If there is a dues check-off system, it should be granted to all interested groups;
4. Each faculty should be encouraged to establish its own organization;
5. The Association should give some attention to the so-called sub-faculty [part-time professors] which is denied rights that are granted to full-time faculty.[43]

The committee also decided that a policy statement was not currently necessary.[44]

The December 1964 conference provided the framework for AAUP understanding of the issue and thus for future AAUP consideration of collective bargaining. They had named the issue, representation of economic interests, accepting the admittedly euphemistic expression devised by Louis Joughin.[45] AAUP leaders who would become association presidents, Clark Byse and Ralph S. Brown, as well as future general secretary Bertram H. Davis, were at the conference. Even the chair and three members of the eventually formed Special Committee on Representation of Economic Interests were at the conference.[46] While association leaders were clearly opposed to exclusive representation, at least President Fellman (if not others) felt that collective bargaining *as separated from the industrial union model* was similar to AAUP principles of faculty participation in college and university government. Finally, they learned that collective bargaining was beginning to develop among professors, particularly those at public institutions.

AAUP members also expressed interest in collective bargaining. At the 1965 Annual Meeting a Northern Illinois University professor offered resolutions including a proposal that professors engage in negotiations with administrations and governing boards for "binding agreements" to establish salaries and benefits.[47] The members at the annual meeting did not endorse the resolutions, and President Fellman remarked at the council meeting afterward:

> If I may say so, I think this meeting will be long remembered—far more significant than any Annual Meeting I have ever attended. I think we have a very basic issue—I don't think it was met head on but the members were perfectly aware of what was going on. I think the great issue of the convention was not the Arizona [academic freedom] case, difficult as it may have been. I think it was whether we should convert into a trade union. In a sense, I don't think we are at a parting of the ways. The decisive vote was the vote which rejected so decisively the proposals of the Northern Illinois Chapter—I thought that was the high point of the meeting and not the Arizona case.[48]

Although Fellman saw some similarity between collective bargaining and AAUP principles of college and university government, he was opposed to association involvement in bargaining.

At the council meeting during the 1965 Annual Meeting, Fellman reviewed the December 1964 conference and presented a summary of the Executive

Committee's discussion of the advantages and disadvantages of collective bargaining. His summary included the decision that a policy statement was not necessary at this time. Louis Joughin added a report on a letter sent by Clark Byse to the chancellor of the City University of New York (CUNY) that "expressed particularly the Association's unwillingness to recognize a particular bargaining agency." Joughin stated that the five thousand faculty members at CUNY were likely to take the Executive Committee's position of 22 December 1964. He also referred to a 15 September letter from Ralph Fuchs concerning the relevance of collective bargaining to the work of Committees T and Z.[49] Byse stated that he thought the "St. John's [University, New York] people are bargaining" and asked, "Is this a Committee T question?"[50] William P. Fidler responded that the association had sent consultants, including Ralph S. Brown, to St. John's University and collective bargaining was likely to be a question for Committee T.[51] William McPherson and John Dawson suggested that the association consider the question of the strike, and Robert Bierstedt (sociology, New York University) stated, "It seems to me if we strike we are striking against ourselves," and "various Council members agreed."[52] President Fellman then directed the discussion to a consideration of a policy statement, saying:

> I see no reason for the staff not to try their hand at a policy statement. If the staff can find the time and if the Council will study the statement it may be that a statement would emerge that would be free of the implications that concern many . . . I think our position is that we would not suggest to a chapter becoming a union but would suggest to a chapter acting as a union . . . . We bring pressure on the administration and I suppose this in a sense is collective bargaining.[53]

He added, "We have not even said we took a position that they could not strike. It may be that professors will have to be inventive in pressuring for bargaining."[54]

Ralph Fuchs suggested that the association formulate a policy statement, and Fellman asked if the staff should prepare a tentative formulation. Clark Byse responded that it might be wise to send out copies of his letter to the CUNY chancellor and to publish articles in the *Bulletin,* adding "I would like to hear American Federation of Teacher arguments." He concluded, "I don't think we should consider formulating position on collective bargaining in the Council," to which Fellman replied, "I was placing the initial responsibility on the Washington Office staff."[55] After William McPherson pointed out that an article in the *Bulletin* should present the advantages and disadvantages rather than a position, President Fellman closed the discussion.[56]

The AAUP leaders faced a situation for which the association had no policy statement although previous leaders had expressed opposition to the idea of trade union activities conducted in the name of the AAUP as well as to the external identification of the AAUP as a trade union. Yet the December 1964 conference suggested similarities between some forms of collective bargaining and association activities. It alerted association leaders to the fact that the AFT was making progress in its attempts to bring collective bargaining to the professoriate, particularly among two of the largest faculties in the nation (at CUNY and the California State Colleges). Council members' discussion of the issue reminded them that *some* younger members of the AAUP at the local level were sympathetic to professorial militancy and impatient with association programs and procedures. Two of the association's central leaders, President David Fellman and former general secretary Ralph Fuchs, felt that the AAUP should address the problem of collective bargaining with a consideration of a policy statement. Both of them appeared to favor internal representation of a faculty, and both felt that association programs developed in the late 1950s sought to achieve such representation. At this point no association leader appeared to be enthusiastic about engaging in collective bargaining. The professor as professional continued to be the conception of the occupation for the AAUP leadership. As the 1960s progressed, however, the AAUP leadership faced further challenges to the ideal of the professor as a professional, and one event, the dismissal of thirty-one professors at St. John's University, highlighted association limitations in the face of administrative intransigence.

St. John's University, 1963 to 1966: An Intransigent Hierarchy and the AAUP

The Washington office initially learned about "strained relations between the faculty and the administration" at St. John's University in 1963. A group of St. John's professors had organized an AAUP chapter, but the administration refused to recognize the chapter and would not allow it to use university facilities. General Secretary Fidler began to negotiate with the administration to gain recognition; at that time the United Federation of College Teachers (UFCT, an AFT affiliate) organized a union local at the university. Eventually the administration chose to recognize the AAUP chapter but not the UFCT local.[57] The tension between the administration and members of the faculty continued, however, to grow, and General Secretary Fidler would eventually report, "Seldom in its history has the Association devoted such a great proportion of resources to a situation involving a single institution."[58]

In October 1965 the Board of Trustees at St. John's expressed support for the 1966 Statement on Academic Freedom and Tenure, and by early December both AAUP chapter members and St. John's administrators were focused on developing a university senate.[59] AAUP staff members helped to organize a 16 December meeting for St. John's professors and administrators to discuss various proposals for a senate. On 15 December, however, the special counsel to St. John's Board of Trustees telephoned the AAUP Washington office, informing the association that the university had sent termination notices to thirty-one faculty members. Twenty-one of the faculty members were "summarily separated from their classroom duties." All of those professors would receive their salaries until the end of their contractual periods, which in some cases extended to 30 June 1967.[60] The university eventually explained that all of the professors had engaged in "organized opposition amounting to a rebellion." The opposition included "libelous and slanderous statements in literature and placards," and faculty participation in "unauthorized demonstrations in cafeterias and elsewhere on campus." (The Committee A investigation found no evidence of rebellion, and only three instances of opposition as described by the administration itself.)[61] Fidler immediately sent a telegram to President Cahill at St. John's opposing the summary dismissals, especially in view of the board's recent support for the 1940 Statement, and the AAUP canceled the meeting to discuss a university senate.[62]

Deputy General Secretary Davis, assisted at times by Fidler, made several telephone calls to St. John's professors and administrators and was eventually able to arrange a 21 December meeting at the AAUP's Washington office with association staff members and representatives of the St. John's AAUP chapter and administration. At that meeting Fidler told the St. John's administrators that the dismissals constituted "a most serious violation of academic freedom and tenure" and urged them to attempt to persuade the Board of Trustees "to rescind all improper terminations immediately." A university administrator responded that he would present Fidler's views to the Board of Trustees at its meeting on the next day. The board replied to Fidler by telegram in the evening of 22 December, announcing the formation of a university senate, "the highest legislative body of the University, subject only to the Board of Trustees." The board also stated in the telegram that it had no intention of reconsidering its decision to dismiss the thirty-one professors.[63] On 29 December, Fidler, Davis, Associate Secretary and Counsel Herman Orentlicher, and Clark Byse (chair of Committee A, AAUP presidential nominee, and a law professor at Harvard University) met with seven trustees of St. John's in New York City. During this two-hour discussion the AAUP representatives made it clear that the termination notices were "*summary dismissals.*"[64]

The next day Fidler invited chapter and conference officers in the New York City area to an ad hoc conference; national leaders at the meeting included Clark Byse, Ralph S. Brown, Clyde W. Summers, and Staff Associate Paul Fenlon (whose responsibilities included working with the Special Committee on Representation of Economic Interests).[65] Fidler and Byse presented outlines of AAUP activity in regard to the St. John's situation, and Fidler announced an action unprecedented in association history, that "a firm of attorneys would be retained by the Washington office to advise chapter officers and the dismissed teachers, and funds would be made available to the St. John's Chapter of the AAUP for incidental expenses in its efforts to assist faculty members."[66] Then the conference participants debated for hours a possible motion concerning the St. John's situation. The eventual motion approved by the conference addressed several topics, including a possible faculty strike called by the United Federation of College Teachers, stating that neither refusal to cross a picket line nor refusal to teach a dismissed colleague's classes were breaches of professional ethics.[67] Although the issue of a faculty strike had arisen, the ad hoc conference participants went no further than to sustain individual integrity in consideration of participation in a strike.

The St. John's AAUP chapter president called a meeting of the chapter for 2 January 1966 at which the attorneys retained by the AAUP answered questions "as to faculty rights and obligations raised by the union's threatened strike." The university opened for classes on 4 January, and press reports indicated that about two hundred pickets were at the gates of St. John's two campuses. On 6 January, Fidler, upon authority of Byse as chair of Committee A and of the Executive Committee, issued a press release that addressed faculty participation in a strike.[68] The beginning of the release stated:

> The American Association of University Professors has never looked upon the strike as an appropriate mechanism for resolving academic controversies or violations of academic principles and standards. Regardless of an immediate situation it is in the best long-run interests of the institution and the academic community to use approaches and procedures developed by that community to meet its own objectives and needs. Accordingly, the Association does not endorse a strike against an academic institution.[69]

Yet, similar to the motion of the ad hoc conference, the press release also stated:

> In their roles as teachers, faculty members have a primary responsi-
> bility to their students. Accordingly, if a strike is called, the individ-
> ual faculty member must carefully weigh this responsibility to his
> students in reaching his decision whether or not to respect a picket
> line set up by his colleagues. In a continuing and flagrant situation,
> a refusal by individual faculty members to cross picket lines main-
> tained by colleagues, when their refusal is based upon personal dic-
> tates of conscience and their intimate familiarity with the facts,
> should not be considered a violation of professional ethics.[70]

An individual professor, by reason of conscience and knowledge, could respect
a strike, but neither individual professors not groups of professors could conduct strikes. The AAUP leaders rested upon the conception of the professor as
professional in response to the UFCT strike but were ambiguous about the professor's participation in strikes.

Association involvement in the St. John's affair continued well into 1966.
Throughout January AAUP staff members and attorneys continued to meet
with St. John's chapter officers. At the end of the month an ad hoc Committee
A investigating committee went to the university.[71] The investigating committee spent three days interviewing administrators and professors and concluded in its report that the administration and Board of Trustees had conducted
actions "seriously violative of professional academic standards" and of the
1940 Statement.[72] Other AAUP committees also addressed the events at St.
John's in 1966. Ralph S. Brown reported for Committee T at the 1966 Annual
Meeting that the committee had recommended "a more extensive investigation" of the situation and was forming an investigating committee.[73] In the
September 1966 *Bulletin,* Committee D on Accrediting of Colleges and
Universities reported its communications with the Commission on Institutions
of Higher Education of the Middle States Association of Colleges and
Secondary Schools. The commission had written to presidents of member institutions following its inquiry into conditions at St. John's, concluding that
the president and trustees were "acting responsibly and in good faith."[74]
Committee D wrote a letter of protest that the commission had provided a
"definition of responsible governance as simply a matter of uncoerced action,
or deliberate determination by the trustees, whether or not that action constitutes a reprehensible and unprecedented violation of academic freedom."[75]
The chair of Committee D, Joseph M. Conant (classics, Emory University),
indicated in his *Bulletin* report that the chair of the commission disagreed with
the committee's interpretation and that the committee and the commission
continued to correspond.[76]

General Secretary Fidler reported at the 1966 Annual Meeting that 182 members and 155 chapters had responded to the crisis at St. John's by contributing over $9,000 to the newly established St. John's Emergency Aid Fund. The monies were being used to provide interest-free loans, repayable at any time, to the dismissed professors.[77] He also reported association expenses in the St. John's crisis, estimating that the situation had cost the AAUP about $18,000 dollars; the 1966 AAUP budget for Committee A was $10,500, for Committee Z $13,000.[78] The AAUP had expended tremendous resources in its attempts to negotiate with the administration and the Board of Trustees at St. John's University, but the administration and the board refused to negotiate about the summary dismissals, which the AAUP deemed to be blatant violations of principles of academic freedom and tenure. Given that the board had announced support for the 1940 Statement not only before the dismissals but also in the spring of 1966, St. John's University in this period presents a remarkable example of administrative and governing board intransigence.[79] They would accept the principles of academic freedom and tenure as and when they cared to do so; they clearly saw themselves as the managers of the university, and the professors as employees to be dismissed at will; conceptions of the professor as professional did not enter into their decisions.

Expansion and Assessment

However much the association was apparently poised on the edge of collective bargaining, in the mid-1960s the AAUP had even more urgent affairs. Elected leaders and staff members were busy trying to cope with the extraordinary level of activity resulting from organizational expansion. The association was also readying itself for the celebration of its fiftieth anniversary, much of which involved a self-survey. Finally, the dismissal of the professors at St. John's University consumed association time and effort. All of these activities, especially the events at St. John's University, form the immediate context for the initial consideration of collective bargaining policy in the AAUP.

At the October 1964 Council Meeting, Bertram H. Davis reported increases "in both volume and scope" of the work of the Washington office staff in recent years.[80] He indicated that staff members were handling Committee A complaints at ninety-seven institutions and added:

> Much increased activity has occurred in other areas of the Association's program: a number of Committee T complaints are being studied; more institutions are participating in the salary survey and are requesting special advice on economic matters; and five

of the Association's standing committees are at work on statements
of principles for the guidance of the profession.[81]

The wide-ranging concerns of the professoriate, and hence the AAUP, meant
that to address those concerns required immense effort.

In the mid-1960s Committee A concerns continued to move beyond the reform of principles and procedures of academic freedom and tenure to more
nearly direct representation. Bertram H. Davis discussed grievance procedures
in his editorial notes in the March 1965 *Bulletin* issue. He indicated that they
provided "a needed safeguard" for the professor and added, "It is gratifying to
note that more and more colleges and universities are incorporating grievance
procedures into their regulations."[82] Davis appeared optimistic about institutions' willingness to establish due process for professors, clearly an area of advancement of professors' interests in their working conditions. The association
also continued its reports on late notice cases, publishing nine statements on
such situations in the March 1965 *Bulletin* issue.[83] Committee A discussed the
problem of effective censure at its April 1965 meeting and decided to appoint
the a special committee to examine further the issue. Committee A knew that
the self-survey report and members attending the 1965 Annual Meeting were
to address that topic, yet it decided not to "await either action" but rather to
"attack the problem of how to improve censure with more than all deliberate
speed."[84] Even Committee A appeared to move in an activist direction under
the direction of its chair, Clark Byse.

Nevertheless Committee A remained a center of professionalism. Its 1966
report established, apparently unintentionally, the association's sense of the
professor as professional. Both Princeton University and the American
University of Beirut had not awarded tenure to professors, and at both institutions those professors had served well past the seven years suggested by
the 1940 Statement. Committee A investigating committees reported the
result of their work to Committee A, and they concluded that there was no
violation of academic freedom and tenure at Princeton while the American
University of Beirut had violated principles of academic freedom and tenure.
Princeton was absolved because the faculty had established the procedures
for protecting academic freedom and tenure and had followed those procedures, even though the probationary period was greater than seven years. In
the case of the American University of Beirut, Committee A found that the
institution was in violation of academic freedom and tenure because the
president had not renewed the professor's contract.[85] Professors had the
prerogative to decide about their colleagues, but administrators did not;

professionals, not bureaucratic employees, held such responsibility to review their peers.

Committee Z participated in the self-survey mood of the AAUP in its 1965 report, considering it time to review recent accomplishments. The committee indicated that the information on absolute gains in salaries was positive but warned, "After all, poverty is a relative matter, and we must yet ask whether, with all this progress, we have managed to hold our own with the rest of society." The report presented a table of occupations with their income gains from 1949 to 1959 and projected gains to 1969. The committee concluded that professors' economic position had fallen relative to the full range of occupations, from recreation and group workers at the bottom to professional athletes at the top. The committee predicted that professors' income would not reach the doubling goal and the next decade's rate of increase in salaries was "unlikely to exceed the disappointing rate of growth of academic incomes" from 1949 to 1959.[86]

Ralph S. Brown reported to the 1965 Annual Meeting as chair of Committee T that the committee was negotiating another draft of the college and university government statement not only with representatives of ACE but also with representatives of the Association of Governing Boards of Universities and Colleges. He reviewed the situations at three institutions and then discussed the situation at St. John's.[87] Later in 1965 Brown reported to the council that Committee T negotiations with representatives of ACE and the Association of Governing Boards of Colleges and Universities thus far had had little result. He also indicated that Committee T representatives had visited a number of colleges and universities recently and had made recommendations to those institutions.[88]

The major AAUP committees were still expanding their work. That expansion increasingly addressed material interests and faculty authority, yet remained grounded in professional ideals. The Self-Survey Committee reflected the expansion of AAUP activities in its 1965 report to the membership. The committee's lengthy report, 108 pages, was mailed to the members as nearly all of a special issue of the *Bulletin* in May 1965.[89] The Self-Survey Committee members were particularly impressed by the association's activities of the past decade and its potential for continued expansion. The report highlighted the efforts of both Committee A and Committee T.[90] The professoriate's major problem, however, was inadequate salaries and benefits, and committee members wrote, "The most serious crisis that has confronted the academic profession since the war, apart from the attacks on academic freedom during the McCarthy era, was in the realm of economics." They concluded that Committee Z's salary grading program was influential, the reports being perhaps "the most avidly read by presidents and professors alike" of all the AAUP reports.[91]

The committee also reminded readers:

> The coming era in higher education is already showing features markedly different from those of the college and university world in which the older members of the Association grew up. If the Association expects to play an effective role in this new era, it should not allow itself to be taken by surprise; nor can it assume that the future into which we are moving is already determined without benefit of our effort and counsel.[92]

The committee was ambiguous in its consideration of possible future programs, reflecting both the past and the pressures of the present. It produced an eight-page statement on academic responsibility and insisted that the association address the issue, including the review of charges of unprofessional conduct among its own members.[93] In further echo of the charter members' concern for service as custodians of higher education, the committee suggested that the AAUP consider using tribunals to examine alleged violations of academic freedom and tenure. These tribunals, composed of representatives of administrators' organizations as well as of the AAUP, would offer judgements that "would obviously have greater weight throughout the academic world than a judgement pronounced by an organization which is often regarded as only an advocate for one of the interested parties."[94]

Yet the Self-Survey Committee also offered support for collective bargaining. It stated that in

> . . . the broad sense of structured, collective discussion of issues and policy, and the use of the available channels of influence about these issues, officers and committees of chapters and conferences of the Association are often involved in "collective bargaining" with administrative officers and even with governing boards and legislative bodies. Many AAUP chapters provide reasonably effective organized group representation of the economic status of faculty members.[95]

The committee observed that the industrial model of collective bargaining was too "limited and rigid" and that even the term "collective bargaining" should "be avoided altogether." Nevertheless the committee acknowledged the possibility of local situations where a group would be designated as a collective bargaining unit by the faculty and "a chapter or conference of the Association might be so designated, in preference to some less representative or desirable agency."

The committee continued with a restrictive view of the responsibilities and conduct of an AAUP collective bargaining unit. The unit would discuss only matters best discussed through "such direct negotiations," conduct itself in a fully professional manner "with full recognition of the high degree of community of interests" at the institution and without "any threat of ultimate sanctions," and insist upon faculty participation in other institutional areas of government.[96]

Despite the ambiguity of the Self-Survey Committee in its attention to the role of the professor as professional and as employee, it had a specific sense of the role of the association in regard to the professoriate, arguing, "It is hardly an exaggeration to say that members of the Association throughout its history have been the elite of the academic world; but such a statement should be made here only with the intention of adding that the proper role of the elite is to guide judgement and to set standards of performance."[97] For the future the committee recommended:

> It is the performance of this larger role as "custodians of the interests of higher education and research" that we now recommend to the Association as the aim around which our energies should be organized in the future. We must continue to emphasize the importance of academic freedom, as the vital center of our program; but we should couple with it an increasing emphasis upon academic responsibility, as has been advocated at length in the previous pages of this report.[98]

The committee was confident that the AAUP was best equipped to lead the way for the continued development of the academic profession.

William P. Fidler reported to the council at its October 1965 meeting that the Executive Committee had considered the recommendations of the Self-Survey Committee. As a result of that consideration four AAUP staff members were working specifically with the conferences, there was more use of staff members in assisting Committees A and T, and the Washington office had begun planning for a regional office in San Francisco. He also announced the formation of the Special Committee on Representation of Economic Interests.[99]

The AAUP took seriously its self-study mood and suggestions; it also was serious in its increased activism. By 1966 the AAUP was committed to a broad range of programs based on professional ideals. Walter P. Metzger compared the programs concerning economic status and faculty governance to academic freedom in his fiftieth anniversary address at the 1965 Annual Meeting: "Moreover, as the recent efforts of Committee Z and Committee T make clear, there was no reason why the other subject areas could not be rationalized given the requisite energy and will."[100] The association membership record was also strong. From 1946 to the end of 1965 the number of active members grew (albeit with some drops in the middle and late 1950s) from 20,671 to 68,900.[101] By the mid-1960s the AAUP was confident of its ability to advance the ideals and welfare of the profession. Yet it also faced immediate obstacles, such as the cautions of Committee Z about doubling salaries, Committee T attempts to move negotiations with representatives of ACE, and the intransigent administration and governing board of St. John's University. It also had to address the question of faculty collective bargaining.

Initial Consideration of Collective Bargaining Policy in the AAUP, 1965 to 1966

In addition to internal questions about faculty unions, the AAUP faced some external pressures in regard to bureaucratization. David G. Brown's 1965 survey of the academic labor market highlights the marked importance of professors' relationships with administrators at colleges and universities. In response to his question about reasons for leaving unacceptable jobs, professors were more than twice as likely to indicate that the administration and administrators were not competent than any other reason including poor research facilities and opportunities, excessive teaching hours, and low salaries.[102]

Nevertheless faculty members were not embracing collective bargaining. AFT successes in organizing professors for representation in higher education in the early and middle 1960s moved slowly as faculties at a few community colleges selected AFT locals as bargaining agents. After the Milwaukee election the next AFT victory occurred at Olympia College (Washington) in February 1964, followed by election victories at Highland Park Community College (Michigan) in October 1965 and at Henry Ford Community College (Michigan) in December 1965.[103] The AFT moved toward organizing four-year faculties in the mid-1960s, particularly in New York and California. According to a writer for the *New Republic,* the UFT in New York City pressured the New York City Board of Higher Education to negotiate with a group of 250 laboratory assistants and technicians beginning in 1965.[104] UFT leaders felt that their success in establishing a contract for that group "would open the way" to collective bargaining contracts at City Colleges of New York.[105] In February 1965 the *Los Angeles Times* reported that the AFT had announced a pledge of $100,000 from the AFL-CIO to organize professors at the California State Colleges.[106] The AFT employed at least one full-time organizer, a former assistant professor of economics, in California and from 1965 to February 1967, California AFT membership among state college professors grew from 350 to 1,300 (there were approximately 9,500 professors at California State Colleges).[107]

Scholars have reported that the AFT local at the United States Merchant Marine Academy was the first local that successfully represented college-level teachers at a four-year institution. Yet in February 1965 the AFT chartered Local 1570, University Employed Graduate Students, at the University of California–Berkeley.[108] The local was composed primarily of teaching assistants and achieved a number of bargaining victories during 1965, including reduced teaching loads in some departments.[109] When negotiations for teaching assistants in sociology became unsatisfactory in the spring of 1965, the AFT local responded with a picket line. Although it is not clear whether that adversarial tactic was successful, the article's author noted, "In almost all cases where meetings with union committees took place new lines of communication were set up, and in many workplaces grievances were settled."[110] There are no further documented descriptions of this AFT local; it may have been short-lived, but it enjoyed some small successes. Graduate students at a research-oriented university were the first university teachers to organize a union local. The effects of bureaucratization were clear at a research university, at least among the graduate students.

In the spring of 1966 the AFT announced its decision to address, as a national organization, the possibility of faculty unionization.[111] The AFT held its national conference on that topic in April 1966 in Chicago, and AFT leaders who attended the conference told the delegates that "the name of the game was power" and professors did not have power.[112] The AFT wanted to secure satisfactory working conditions for college and university professors through the acquisition and use of power. It was also committing resources to achieve its goal; while professors might be showing hesitancy about unionization, the AFT was determined to try to organize them.

The academic labor market seemed to favor the AFT efforts. During the mid-1960s the supply of potential professors did not meet the demand.[113] The middle 1960s was a time "when standards were relatively low for entering college teaching, a high proportion of young people entered college teaching with only master's degree credentials or were content to remain ABDs."[114] Much of the growth in demand occurred at public institutions. From 1963–1964 to 1966–1967, professors at public institutions increased from 57.8 to 62 percent of all professors. A substantial amount of that growth occurred at public two-year colleges. In 1963–1964 9.3 percent of all professors taught at two-year institutions, and in 1966–1967 11.4 percent taught at those colleges.[115] The traditional centers of professionalism were giving way to additional forms of college and university teaching, both in terms of professors' preparation and institutional settings. The advanced knowledge and expertise of professors at elite institutions did not necessarily obtain in the conduct of those institutions, and the expected shared governance of the elite college and university was being replaced by state bureaucratic systems.

The association leadership first presented the issue of collective bargaining to the membership in the September 1965 *Bulletin*. Ralph S. Brown's report on the December 1964 conference noted the association's opposition to conducting trade union activities and reviewed the major issues of exclusive representation, appropriate sanctions, and internal representation of faculty interests. He pointed out that some methods of collective bargaining might be appropriate for the AAUP and that an ad hoc committee was going to address the issue. He also stated that the AAUP could coexist peacefully with "seemingly rival organizations" and that "both practical considerations and the nature of higher education militate against recognition of any form of exclusive representation." Brown wrote that those who attended the conference tended to support the latter two propositions and concluded that, as a hypothesis, an effectively organized faculty might make external representation unnecessary.[116] Traditional AAUP conceptions of the faculty as the professional representative continued to influence association thinking about collective bargaining.

As the association leaders were presenting the issue of collective bargaining in the *Bulletin* they were forming the ad hoc committee, the Special Committee on Representation of Economic Interests (REI). General Secretary Fidler appointed the committee with the approval of President Fellman and began with the chair, Clyde W. Summers; he chose committee members from among those who attended the December 1964 conference and from members of Committees T and Z.[117] Only one of the committee members, however, was from the association leadership, William McPherson.

Clyde W. Summers had been active in the AAUP only at the local level, particularly at the University of Toledo in 1946–1947. At the same time he also organized the AFT local at the university. The two groups focused on lobbying the mayor of Toledo for more money for the city-supported university and to allow more faculty self-governance. "We in effect . . . coordinated the AAUP and the union so that we had the leaders in the union [who] were also the leaders in the AAUP, some of the leaders." In addition Summers was also on the faculty representation committee at Toledo and later at the University of Buffalo, where it dealt with the entire administration. He states, "So I had this sort of three-way experience of the union, the faculty senate, and the AAUP. From my viewpoint, I didn't see any difference."[118]

That viewpoint was evident immediately after his appointment; on 25 October 1965 Paul Fenlon (the AAUP staff member assigned to the Special Committee) sent a memorandum to council members with several excerpts from a 14 October letter written by Summers. Summers wrote, "'As a tentative policy pending discussion by our committee I would favor the AAUP taking the position that there should not be an exclusive representative chosen either for the purposes of negotiating an agreement or handling grievances in institutions of higher education.'"[119] Instead he felt that colleges and universities needed to establish grievance procedures and faculty grievance committees and that administrations should meet with faculty representatives.[120] Summers recognized, however, that what should be done and what the AAUP faced in terms of enabling legislation and regulations could be mutually exclusive, and thus he also suggested:

> "If a university determines to select an exclusive representative contrary to our recommendations then I believe we have no choice but to compete for that position, . . . committing ourselves in such a situation to perform all of the functions which any of the organizations would normally expect to perform."[121]

He hoped to preserve the rights of individual professors by maintaining "the right of the individual to choose which, if any, organization should aid him in presenting his case." Fenlon's excerpts concluded with Summers' observation that his views might not be shared by "all or even a majority of the proposed committee."[122]

The other members of the Special Committee were Jack Barbash, Valerie A. Earle (government, Georgetown University), J. Bailey Harvey, Forest G. Hill (economics, University of Texas), William McPherson, and William Patty (psychology, Los Angeles City College).[123] As noted earlier, Jack Barbash was an adamant supporter of the AFT. He had been featured on the front cover of *American Teacher Magazine* (published by the AFT), and his book *Union Philosophy and the Professional* had been advertised on the back cover of *American Teacher Magazine* as a work that told "why professionals need a union."[124] There is no evidence that Barbash had any involvement in the AAUP prior to his appointment to the Special Committee. Valerie A. Earle had been on the Georgetown University AAUP chapter committees on rank and tenure (1957–1958) and the academic senate (1960–1962); she was a member of the council and Committee T at the time of her appointment to the Special Committee.[125] J. Bailey Harvey was president-elect of the City College of New York AAUP chapter at the time of the December 1964 conference; there is no record of any other involvement in the AAUP as of November 1965.[126] Forest Hill was a member of Committee T when he was appointed to the Special Committee.[127] William McPherson served in several positions at the University of Illinois AAUP chapter, including president in 1957–1959, and he was a council member from 1961 to 1964; he was also a member of the Industrial Relations Research Association and the National Academy of Arbitrators and had prepared a background paper for the December 1964 conference. At the time of his appointment he was chair of Committee B on Professional Ethics.[128] William Patty had been AAUP chapter president (1949–1951, 1955–1956, and 1962–1963) at Los Angeles City College, a two-year institution, a member of the governing board of the AAUP Southern California Conference, and chair of the Conference's Committee T. He was also a member of the AFT and the California Federation of Teachers (an AFT state affiliate). Prior to his position at Los Angeles City College he was a lecturer employed by the New York City Board of Higher Education. Patty was nominated for election to the council in 1964, but his opponent was elected to the office.[129] None of the Special Committee members had served on Committee A; in terms of institutional and association experiences, the REI Committee did not particularly represent the professional ideals of the AAUP.

Paul Fenlon reported at the council meeting of October 1965 that the Special Committee was scheduled to meet on 19 and 20 November and asked council members for suggestions on AAUP positions relative to collective bargaining, "especially *exclusive* representation." Fenlon received several suggestions in the ensuing and extensive discussion. Fenlon noted that the Washington office had recently received two inquiries on the matter of exclusive representation.[130] The association was ready to consider the troubling and somewhat pressing issue of AAUP policy on collective bargaining by faculties.

It is not clear from association records whether the Special Committee met in the fall of 1965. Clyde W. Summers recalls, however, that at the 11 and 12 March 1966 meeting of the Special Committee its members developed the policy statement on representation of economic interests. He reports that on March 11 the members "worked out a draft" and "I thought we were going to have a unanimous report."[131] On March 12, however, Paul Fenlon raised adamant objections to the proposed statement. Summers states that

> . . . we thought we had it all worked out, it seemed to me one night, and then when I came in the next morning with this draft, all of a sudden he started articulating complete opposition to the

whole affair. And it was a very unpleasant situation because you know we thought we had worked out our differences, we thought we had worked it all out.[132]

Despite Fenlon's sudden rejection of the draft, Summers was able to convince committee members to stay with the version they had agreed upon the night before.[133] A month and a half before the Spring 1966 Council Meeting the Special Committee on Representation of Economic Interests presented its proposed policy statement on collective bargaining.

The procedures for establishing collective bargaining policy in the AAUP exhibited characteristics considerably different from the long-term consensus process of other policy developments. The first step, assigning a committee, followed standard operating procedure. From that point, however, noticeable changes occurred in the procedure. The *Bulletin* did not present a draft of the committee's report prior to the council's consideration of the issue, instead publishing the report as well as the council's consideration and approval as faits accomplis. Furthermore the committee presented its final report to the council a month and a half before the meeting when the council voted to approve the interim and conditional policy.[134]

The AAUP archives include extensive files on virtually all council and annual meetings from 1957 to 1971, often with full transcriptions of the discussions at those meetings (thereafter the archives contain mostly minutes of the meetings). But the archives do not include a file on the May 1966 Council Meeting and the council's discussion of approval of an interim, proscriptive collective bargaining policy. While virtually all of the AAUP leaders interviewed for this study recall a discussion often characterized as bitter, none offers specific recollections of what reasons were argued or who favored or opposed any form of collective bargaining by AAUP groups.[135] Although this work cannot examine the meeting and discussion with the desired detail, it can establish the reasons for the approval and identify some of the proponents and opponents.

The beginning of the *Bulletin* report of the approval states that the council adopted the following as council policy:

> The Association should oppose the extension of the principle of exclusive representation to faculty members in institutions of higher education and should therefore recommend legislation which would require public institutions to establish adequate internal structures of faculty participation in the government of the institution.[136]

Beyond the suggested opposition to exclusive representation, however, the council approved conditions for AAUP involvement in collective bargaining:

> If these conditions [of effective faculty voice and adequate protection and promotion of faculty economic interests] are not met, and a faculty feels compelled to seek representation through an outside organization, the Association believes itself, by virtue of its principles, programs, experience and broad membership to be best qualified to act as representative of the faculty in institutions of higher education.[137]

The statement assigned responsibility for determining such involvement to the general secretary, William P. Fidler.[138] Both the changes in the standard operating procedure—particularly the council approval of policy without the recommendation that the annual meeting also approve the statement—and the rapidity of the consideration and approval without presentation to the membership were substantial differences from the consideration and approval of other AAUP policies.

Although the timing of the review of the REI Statement exhibited characteristics different from the long-term consensus of other policy developments, the structure of the procedure remained standard. The committee was the primary source of policy development, as the Self-Survey Committee had found.[139] While council approval of new or revised policies was not pro forma, it repeatedly approved the substance, if not all, of policy reports of committees.

Recent AAUP discussions, such as the December 1964 conference and the 1965 Annual Meeting, were reminders that faculties were engaging in unionization, and support for some limited form of participation in collective bargaining was evident in various AAUP reports and constituencies. In addition, as Clark Byse had stated in a council meeting, there was reason to believe that the chapter at St. John's University was pursuing a form of collective bargaining. The council also had an immediate sense of AFT activity (and potential for success) because of several letters from C. M. Larsen, professor of mathematics at San Jose State College (California), just before the May 1966 meeting. Larsen was also president of the AAUP chapter at San Jose State College, an institution where the AFT was as strong as anywhere in the California system.[140] Larsen wrote several strongly worded letters to AAUP leaders in the spring of 1966; although he did not urge specific council action, he felt that the AAUP could "ill afford an overly cautious approach to the challenge which the AFT presents to the AAUP in California."[141] Paul Fenlon summarized some of Larsen's communications in an 13 April 1966 memorandum to the Special Committee, with copies to the members of the council and presidential nominee Clark Byse. The San Jose State College AAUP chapter had voted on a chapter Executive Committee statement supporting nonexclusive representation with a statewide faculty senate to work with the Board of Trustees on budget items. Thirty-five members favored such representation, twenty-one opposed it, and eleven supported no statement. Fenlon noted the March 1966 position of the Council of the Association of California State College Professors that local and statewide senates should have broad authority but an elected agent should be involved in budget matters.[142] Larsen's arguments were urgent and persistent, his evidence on concerted AFT activity among California State College faculties was extensive, and his evaluation of union interest among professors at California State Colleges included the state organization of those professors as well as AFT support.

AAUP members' interest in collective bargaining was again evident at the 1966 Annual Meeting, when Israel Kugler and Allen Weaver (Northern Illinois University) each presented resolutions from the floor concerning bargaining. Kugler wanted a merger with the AFT, but the members at the annual meeting responded by approving a substitute motion asking that the council consider "devising means of more effective cooperation with other national and state organizations which embrace college and university teachers as such."[143] Weaver's resolution suggested that chapters could enter into binding agreements on contracts with administrations, governing boards, or governments; the members at the annual meeting did not approve his proposal.[144] While Weaver's proposal indicates only individual support for collective bargaining, the members' response to Kugler's proposal—providing a substitution rather than completely rejecting it—suggests some appreciation for his goals.

There were also the intransigent and peremptory administrations and boards of trustees. Twenty-seven of the thirty 1966 council members were professors during the McCarthy era and had seen, often at their employing institutions, professors' lack of capacity for contesting the decisions of administrators or trustees.[145] Clark Byse, Ralph S. Brown, and Bertram H. Davis all became active in the national affairs of the AAUP during the mid-1950s, when the primary problem was addressing the backlog of academic freedom cases resulting from attacks of McCarthy followers.[146] Bertram H. Davis in fact came to the AAUP because of the peremptory behavior of the president at Dickinson College, who refused to renew Davis's contract despite the recommendation of Davis's departmental chair and demonstrations by students in support of Davis. Davis stated later, "I saw no reason to stay where I clearly wasn't wanted, and there was a position available with AAUP."[147] In 1973 he told a reporter from the *Chronicle of Higher Education* that he favored "'chapters having the opportunity to go into collective bargaining' since 1965."[148] Committee A and Committee T investigations repeatedly revealed administrators' and trustees' lack of regard for due process and professors' judgement. Finally the events at St. John's University were an organizationally compelling reminder of the de jure power of boards of trustees. Bureaucratic actions of colleges and universities, however contrary to the professional ideals of the AAUP, were a reality for many AAUP leaders.

Nor did anyone in the AAUP leadership know what collective bargaining would be like; they were obviously unclear as to even its nature in higher education.[149] An author of a very early article on the issue, Tracy H. Ferguson, notes the need to understand the "new and evolving concepts" in the field and pleads repeatedly for "central information."[150] No more than twenty-two faculties, all at two-year public colleges (a sector with limited AAUP membership and involvement), had elected collective bargaining agents by May 1966.[151] In fact the AAUP's leading authority on professors' collective bargaining, Clyde W. Summers, mistakenly identified both of the Michigan community college faculties as having selected the AFT for exclusive representation when actually one faculty had selected the AFT, the other the NEA.[152] Any interim policy would allow the association to explore the potentialities of unionization without committing it to a specific course of action.

The published reports of the committee and the council's approval were followed by unprecedented supporting and dissenting arguments on the issue. Clyde W. Summers wrote the statement of support; his major argument concerned the problem of exclusive representation in collective bargaining agreements. The association's history of negotiated representation of professors, the professionalism of the AAUP, was threatened by exclusive representation. His report also covered the movements for collective bargaining elections at the City University of New York and the California State Colleges.[153] At the time of the 1966 vote the AAUP faced the possibility that two of the largest groups of faculties in the country (at City University of New York and the California State Colleges) would no longer have strong reasons for AAUP membership and that individual faculties throughout the country (such as those at the two Michigan community colleges) would also choose exclusive representation. Summers also emphasized one other aspect of the proposed policy, its limited nature. It was an interim policy for special and explicit conditions, to be followed only when an AAUP chapter found institutional government seriously restricting faculty participation. A chapter elected as representative could neither call nor support a strike, nor could it require AAUP membership of professors represented by the chapter.[154] Thus it was not unionization as such, or even the increasingly bureaucratic nature of higher education, that provided the center of the arguments for the interim policy; it was exclusivity of unionization and the traditions of the association.

The dissenting statement, written by council members Robert Bierstadt and Fritz Machlup, was unique. No other policy statement had been published in the *Bulletin* with an accompanying "vigorous dissent." Their objection was based on principle: professors were professionals rather than employees, and the operation of a college or university was "one of shared responsibility." Bierstadt and Machlup concluded that an approval of collective bargaining as an AAUP method would mean that association members would become employees and by contravening the association's principles and policies "would fundamentally alter the nature of the Association."[155]

William P. Fidler was another leader who opposed AAUP participation in collective bargaining. In his report to the 1965 Annual Meeting he stated that the AAUP would "probably have to determine what position it will take in response to what might be called this 'era of ultimatum,'" including professors' "threatened strikes or boycotts."[156] He spoke clearly to the professional, negotiating, conception of the AAUP:

> In every situation we rely upon action of some kind to accomplish our purpose. But *action* is a cunning word. None of us would wish to achieve an aim merely because we can find the power to achieve by power what is accessible through other professional means at our disposal.[157]

General Secretary Fidler saw the professor as a professional, with traditional principles of reason and negotiation as the ways to fulfill the conception. His opposition reflects, of course, the argument of Bierstedt and Machlup.

His opposition to AAUP involvement in collective bargaining is also clear in a memorandum from Associate Secretary Winston Ehrmann to Fidler in the spring of 1966. Ehrmann wrote that he had listened to Fidler's "troubled expression of concern that certain members of the Association were pushing it toward the union approach by insisting upon the Association engaging in collective bargaining." Ehrmann and Fidler agreed that the AAUP should remain as it was since the argument that it could approve collective bargaining in exceptional situations was a "grievous error." Ehrmann argued that faculty members would claim exceptional circumstances or create such conditions to justify collective bargaining.[158]

Two days before the council vote, AAUP President David Fellman stated in his address to the annual meeting:

> Of course we defend the right of professors to join a trade union if they so desire, and we are strongly opposed to the imposition upon them of reprisals of any sort for so doing. Nevertheless, our Association is not a trade union, it is not part of the trade union movement, and it does not seek that identification with organized labor which trade union status would imply.[159]

Despite David Fellman's understanding that there were similarities between collective bargaining and association goals for faculty participation in governance, he was clearly opposed to AAUP involvement in trade union activity.

Clark Byse, 1966–1968 AAUP president, stated that despite the arguments against chapters as collective bargaining agents, "Other Council members felt that the Association should not flatly close the door to any role in the exclusive bargaining process."[160] Those members thought that the AAUP could be a professional association and permit instances of exclusive representation, so that a "fund of experience might be developed which would enable the Association to reach an informed decision concerning its role in collective bargaining. Accordingly, they argued for a 'compromise' solution."[161] Some comments by Ralph S. Brown in 1969 also confirm a purposeful compromise solution, when he stated at a council meeting that the council could maintain flexibility on another policy, faculty participation in strikes, "if we could do as we did with REI, at the original go-round . . . ; if we would do as we did with the first one, note the Council endorsement and then explain to the Annual Meeting."[162] This approach gave the AAUP a needed policy statement at one level, allowing staff members to respond to inquiries about association views on collective bargaining while the leadership could use findings from future events to adjust or withdraw the policy with little association debate.

The council approval of the REI Statement had procedural and substantive characteristics. The Special Committee had followed standard operating procedures. There were some parallels between the goals of shared authority and collective bargaining, and there was some general support within the association and the council itself. Also there was a strong possibility of increased faculty collective bargaining. Faculties were beginning to use collective bargaining, there were some immediate pressures as Charles Larsen urgently noted, and the AAUP leaders had recent and direct experience with an absolutely intransigent administration. Finally, no one at that council meeting could define the nature or direction of faculty collective bargaining, and the AAUP believed itself to be the most capable of representing professors. The quick approval of the interim, proscriptive, and conditional statement indicates a political compromise in the face of uncertainty.

Other association activities in 1966 suggested that the "requisite will and energy" might be sufficient to accomplish the goals of professor as professional, justifying a compromise approach to unionization. The 1966 Committee A report indicated that faculties rather than presidents were the institutional members who should determine renewal of appointments. Committees Z and T reported movement along the lines of preferred professional activity. The 1966 Committee Z report began with the statement, "For the first time since the inception of Committee Z's annual survey, faculty compensations have risen at the annual rate sufficient to achieve a doubling over a decade." Furthermore the number of participating institutions continued to increase; 905 colleges and universities sent reports in 1965–1966, representing 40 percent of all colleges and universities.[163] Although the report concluded on a cautionary note, reminding professors that it would be challenging to sustain the increases, the good news was clear.[164] The Committee Z also addressed professors' salaries at public two-year colleges that did not have academic ranks, publishing the report in the December 1966 *Bulletin* issue, continuing the association expansion of activities in regard to new institutions and their professors.[165]

Ralph S. Brown reported noticeable advances in negotiations with representatives of ACE and the Association of Governing Boards (AGB) at the 1966 Annual Meeting, and he hoped that Committee T would be able to present the statement on college and university government to the 1967 Annual Meeting for endorsement. Committee T continued to monitor the situations at individual institutions, assisting faculties in developing professional standards in their negotiations with administrations. Brown concluded that although the committee could not "make men out of mice," it could assist "those faculty men and women who are willing to accept a responsible role in the government of modern higher education."[166]

Committee T negotiations with representatives of ACE and AGB proved successful in the fall of 1966. In October the Board of Directors of the American Council on Education commended the Statement on Government of Colleges and Universities to its members, and in November the Executive Committee of the Association of Governing Boards commended the statement to its member boards.[167] The AAUP Council also approved the statement at the fall meeting and recommended that members at the 1967 Annual Meeting approve it.[168] Two reports on institutional governance in the December 1966 *Bulletin* reaffirmed the tone of the 1966 Statement. One suggested that shared governance could be successful given a supportive university president and board and a faculty committed to participation and "a great expenditure of time."[169] The other argued that if the administration took over functions, it was because of the faculty, based on two reasons, timidity or else reluctance "to undertake the long meetings and hours of committee work which are the usual means by which a faculty laboriously exercises its powers."[170] The AAUP directed a clear message: full participation in college and university government required the support of the administration and governing board and a full commitment on the part of the faculty.

Yet collective bargaining opposition would soon lose a key figure. William P. Fidler announced his resignation at the Fall 1966 Council Meeting. He noted that he suffered from hypertension and spoke succinctly about the burdens of his position, "I was not especially attracted to the charms of executive authority prior to assuming the post of general secretary, and after more than eight years of struggling with one of the toughest assignments in higher education, my fondness for being the overseer of all AAUP activity has not increased."[171]

Fidler requested to be assigned other responsibilities as a member of the Washington office staff. Fidler had notified David Fellman and Clark Byse in January 1966 that he wished to relinquish the general secretaryship; Clark Byse had appointed a subcommittee to recommend a successor.[172] Who would actually test the new interim collective bargaining policy, as mandated by the REI Statement, had yet to be selected.

The wording of the interim policy on representation of economic interests reflected the organization's uncertainty about professionalism and unionization. The statement began with the clear policy that the AAUP opposed exclusive representation and continued with an emphasis on association preference for shared authority. Still, the council recognized that association attempts to correct inadequate provisions might not suffice, and the policy stated the necessary conditions for a chapter to consider collective bargaining—inadequate faculty voice and promotion of economic interests.

The chance the AAUP had taken in approving the interim policy on representation of economic interests, however, had yet to be tested. As quickly as the next year the association would have the opportunity to evaluate the strength of the REI Statement. To what extent AAUP members were custodians of the interests of higher education, and to what extent they were employees, would begin to become clearer in the next few years.

Chapter 4

THE AAUP AND UNIONIZATION,
1966 TO 1971

In the middle and late 1960s, both the AFT and the NEA were able to
organize college faculties with the AFT proving to be more successful during that time. The AFT, through Local 1640 of the United Federation of
College Teachers (UFCT), first secured exclusive representation on behalf of
a faculty at a four-year institution at the United States Merchant Marine
Academy in September 1966.[1] By the end of 1966 AFT locals were exclusive
collective bargaining agents for faculties at five two-year colleges and one four-
year college. AFT efforts to establish legal collective bargaining at two-year
and four-year institutions accelerated following its success at the U. S.
Merchant Marine Academy. Although California had no enabling legislation
for public employees to bargain in the mid-1960s, the AFT was able to organize a mock election at San Francisco State College in October 1966.
Professors there approved the concept of collective bargaining by a wide margin, 313 approving and 139 disapproving. Yet, in the following agent-selec-
tion election, the AFT lost to the Association of California State College
Professors with 239 choosing the AFT and 351 choosing the California association.[2]

By the end of 1969 there were twenty-one faculties at two-year colleges
and two at four-year colleges with elected AFT collective bargaining representatives as well as the faculties at the nineteen two-year and four-year colleges
of the City University of New York (formerly the City Colleges of New York).[3]
AFT efforts to organize graduate students also gained momentum in the late
1960s and early 1970s. In 1967 teaching assistants at three public research
and flagship universities organized into units in order to attempt collective

bargaining with the universities' administrations.[4] Assistants at the University of California–Berkeley, the University of California–Los Angeles, and the University of Wisconsin–Madison organized AFT locals; the local at Berkeley had between 400 and 500 of the 1,200 teaching assistants there as members while the local at Los Angeles had between 100 and 150 of the 800 assistants there as members.[5] Graduate students at public research and flagship universities were willing to organize specifically into union locals in order to gain better working conditions in response to the bureaucratic setting. As the AFT director of the Department of Colleges and Universities stated at a late 1960s conference on collective bargaining, "What we do, of course, is identify the conflict and exploit it."[6]

Early NEA successes in organizing professors were among faculties at public two-year colleges in Michigan. Ensuing elections of NEA representatives continued to be at public two-year colleges until 1969, when the faculties at Central Michigan University and the six New Jersey State Colleges elected NEA collective bargaining representatives.[7]

By 1967 a task force of the American Association for Higher Education (AAHE) was reporting that the main sources of professors' widespread discontent were the obstacles to their participation in college and university government and in establishing policies as well as the decreased local control of public institutions because of the establishment of statewide systems. The task force members also stated that salaries contributed to the discontent but were secondary to problems of institutional governance.[8] The task force argued that although professionalism was often a "polite fiction" on many campuses, there was still demand for "the full prerogatives of professionalism" such as participation in college and university government.[9]

The AAHE report also indicated that the main centers of discontent were public two-year and new or emerging (from teachers' colleges to public universities) four-year institutions of higher education. The task force members noted that they had found most instances of administrative dominance or primacy at two-year colleges and new or emerging universities. In response to these types of problems the AAHE task force suggested that faculty members in fact had the right to organize for collective bargaining and to strike.[10] Characteristics of bureaucracy, including administrative hierarchy with professors treated as employees, were often evident at public two-year and four-year colleges.

Yet faculties at those institutions were also developing professional characteristics and goals. Professors at two-year institutions were beginning to exhibit characteristics different from those even of a few years before. While they were still primarily engaged in teaching, with their only research activity likely to be focused on improving teaching, the institutions themselves were separating from the school district administrations.[11] Consequently there was an apparent "trend toward the strengthening of faculty influence upon policy-making," a trend also due to "a generally more aggressive teaching profession."[12] A 1967–1968 survey showed a decrease in school-teaching experience among two-year college professors; one-third had taught at elementary or secondary schools, compared to 64 percent in 1957.[13] E. Alden Dunham suggested in a late 1960s review of fourteen public colleges that faculties at such institutions were clearly restive, jealous of university faculties' salaries, workloads, and research opportunities and "concerned . . . about their role in policy determination."[14]

In contrast to the AAHE report suggesting administrative dominance, Christopher Jencks and David Riesman went so far as to suggest in 1968 (and again in 1969) the existence of an "academic imperium" of professors essentially in control of universities and university colleges and indicated that university colleges were models for the future.[15] The ideal of the professor as professional was clearly predominant in the middle and late 1960s. Labor market conditions in the late 1960s tended to reflect that ideal. The major study of the academic labor market in this period, based on data from the 1960s and early 1970s, reports divisions by prestige, gender, and discipline.[16] As was the case in earlier studies of the academic labor market, research universities and elite liberal arts colleges tended to appoint professors with doctorates, sustaining the ideal.

Faculty sentiment about participation in university affairs remained uneasy at the end of the decade. In the 1969 Carnegie Commission on Higher Education and American Council on Education survey of U.S. professors, only 38.3 percent of professors at all institutions (two-year and four-year) rated the campus-senate effectiveness as excellent or good. Only one item received a lower rate of approval, availability of research funds, and even faculty salaries had a higher rate of approval, 46.6 percent.[17] The developments of the middle and late 1960s suggest a widening gap between the academic profession and the administration, and the AAUP responded cautiously to these developments.

"Thus Did Collective Bargaining Come to the AAUP"

The association's first efforts in response to collective bargaining essentially reflected the interim policy. As the association gave further consideration to the challenges of the bureaucratized college and university and the subsequent faculty response, in many cases, of unionization, it began to specify what the AAUP was willing to do.

In April 1966 the AAUP received an invitation to work with its chapters at the California State Colleges in exploring the issue of exclusive representation; the negotiations began in August of that year and continued through February 1967.[18] Louis Joughin, Clyde W. Summers, Charles M. Larsen, and William P. Fidler went to California to work with those faculties and their representatives.[19] They negotiated with faculties, administrations, and the chair of the Board of Trustees of the California State Colleges, promoting the application of shared responsibility as expressed in the 1966 Statement on College and University Government. In contrast AFT representatives called for the election of an exclusive representative. The faculties voted in May 1967 to select "no agent," and in October of that year the Board of Trustees passed a resolution favoring the development of institutional governance based on the Statement on College and University Government.[20] In its first formal attempt to address unionization, the AAUP successfully promoted the implementation of shared responsibility rather than collective bargaining. That success, however, was soon countered by an unusual chain of events at a small two-year college in Illinois.

In February 1967 the faculty at Belleville College (Illinois) voted to have the AAUP chapter serve as its exclusive representative. Until that election AFT Local 434 had represented the Belleville faculty as well as the district schoolteachers in informal negotiations with the school board. The AFT Local was on the ballot, but the AAUP chapter received thirty-two votes and the union only two votes of the thirty-eight cast. AAUP President Byse interpreted the election result as an indication of the faculty's desire to be identified with higher education and not as an extension of the high school. He anticipated that the faculty and board at Belleville College would continue to use informal negotiations in the AAUP tradition.[21]

Despite the Representation of Economic Interests Statement, which made clear that the general secretary had to approve chapter involvement in collective bargaining, Belleville chapter members did not contact the Washington office, or any elected AAUP leaders, until after the election, when they realized that they did not know what their next step should be.[22] Clark Byse summarized the Belleville situation:

> Thus, did collective bargaining come to the AAUP—in Belleville, Illinois, without the knowledge, encouragement, or consent of the General Secretary or the officers or Council of the AAUP. Indeed,

had a request been made to the General Secretary, I know not what the answer would have been.[23]

He also offered his opinion: "I cannot say I am displeased with the development."[24]

The AAUP did not disavow the actions of the chapter at Belleville although there was no mention of the chapter's selection in the *Bulletin* until 1970.[25] In fact, in late September 1967 Staff Associate Charles Larsen, who was newly appointed, and General Secretary Davis went to Belleville because the chapter had reached an impasse and was unsure as to its next steps and appropriate sanctions it could use against the administration. Larsen and Davis went to resolve the impasse and succeeded in doing so.[26] In its first involvement with chapter union activity, national staff members were able to use negotiations to achieve a satisfactory agreement between a faculty and a governing board at a public two-year college and to avoid the use of sanctions.

In another local event the AAUP chapter at Indiana University voted in March 1967 on the question of association involvement in collective bargaining. One hundred sixteen members favored retention of the association's traditional character and function without collective bargaining. One hundred twelve members favored either an interim policy of collective bargaining to promote faculty participation in institutional government (seventy-nine supported this form of involvement) or the active AAUP use of collective bargaining, seeking to become an agent whenever possible.[27] Even among professors at a state flagship university in a fairly conservative state, there was a nearly equal division of opinion on the appropriateness of AAUP involvement in collective bargaining.

AAUP President Clark Byse analyzed collective bargaining and the AAUP in a July 1967 memorandum distributed to the council and in an address he gave at a Danforth Foundation workshop in 1967. Although he considered the REI Statement to be sound, he told the council that he thought the policy would be inadequate for three groups of institutions. Two of the three groups were composed of institutions with no tradition of governance, one of those exemplified by two-year colleges and emerging institutions and the other by institutions where despite strong AAUP efforts the faculty could not attain a proper role. The third group was composed of institutions with a structure for faculty participation in governance, but where the faculty felt that collective bargaining would be more satisfactory.[28] Byse saw two AAUP options. It could continue its current course, which would not lead to shared authority at these institutions and would likely result in a decrease in AAUP membership. Or it could change association structure, continuing national affairs and allowing state or local AAUP affiliates in collective bargaining. He recognized, however, a basic problem with affiliate involvement in collective bargaining, "I believe that many of our members, particularly those in institutions which would not be participating in collective bargaining, would be unwilling to pay the amount of dues that would be necessary to provide the services that collective bargaining requires." He suggested that he was not arguing for collective bargaining but was advocating immediate review.[29]

He cited the arguments of Robert Bierstedt and Fritz Machlup as well as those of Israel Kugler, but he found no comfort in their what he viewed as their extreme approaches. He reviewed faculty collective bargaining efforts in California, Illinois, Michigan, and New York and indicated they were occurring in faculties at public two-year and four-year colleges, the U.S. Merchant Marine Academy, and institutions such as the Fashion Institute of Technology (New York). He anticipated further developments, for example, at the City University of New York and the State University of New York as the result of the New York Taylor Act (enabling legislation for New York state employees). Although he worried about the possibility of professors' collective bargaining leading "inevitably to the indiscriminate use of the sanctions of trade unionism," he recognized also the recalcitrant administrations and governing boards "so out of step with decent practices and policies that extreme measures are justified." Byse suggested that he was "somewhat open and flexible" about collective bargaining and indicated again a preference for a decentralized AAUP with state conferences empowered (by staff resources as well as organizational autonomy) to experiment in the area of direct representation.[30] The AAUP president was well informed about bureaucratized colleges and universities as well as faculty unionization.

Collective bargaining was one of the topics at the fall 1967 meeting of the council although the discussion and council action focused on AAUP interpretations of unionism and shared governance. Council member Daniel Adler (psychology, San Francisco State College) reviewed the recent developments in California, and the council adopted a resolution commending the Board of Trustees of the California State Colleges for adopting the Statement on Government of Colleges and Universities. Associate General Secretary Joughin reported on the activity in New York concerning collective bargaining.[31] Despite the discussion about collective bargaining, *Bulletin* reports continued to emphasize shared authority and not exclusive representation.[32] The leadership was willing to examine unionization, but the association chose a public emphasis on professionalism.

Despite apparent initial successes in the implementation of principles of professionalism in response to the unionization issue, faculty militancy would shortly confront the AAUP. Once again an administration and a governing board would prove to be intransigent in response to the institution's faculty. Successes in negotiation, whether in regard to collective bargaining or AAUP ideals of academic freedom and tenure, would diminish in the context of the dismissal of the Reverend Charles Curran.

Strike! The Reverend Charles Curran and the Catholic University of America

Even more than the 1965–1966 events at St. John's University, the 1967 decision of the administration and governing board at the Catholic University not to renew the contract of the Reverend Charles Curran exemplified intransigence in the face of the principles of academic freedom and procedures of academic tenure and due process. For the AAUP it would also highlight both the limits of its professional standards such as negotiation and the power of the faculty strike.

In October 1966 the faculty of the Graduate School of Sacred Theology at the Catholic University unanimously expressed confidence in Curran's teaching, and both that faculty and the Catholic University Academic Senate recommended his promotion to associate professor.[33] Reverend Curran was a well-known liberal who favored the "New Morality," which some traditionalists regarded as heresy.[34] In April 1967 the board of trustees dismissed Father Curran from his position.[35] Students and faculty members in the theology school immediately responded with a boycott, the faculty members resolving unanimously not to teach until the university reinstated Curran.[36] Professors leading the strike told reporters that they did not agree with Father Curran, yet they thought, as stated in the theology faculty resolution, that "The academic freedom and the security of every professor of this university is jeopardized."[37] The next day most professors at the university agreed with the theology faculty, voting 400 to 18 (out of 440 full-time faculty members) to join the strike. The university-wide strike continued until late April, when the board of trustees reinstated and promoted Father Curran.[38]

William P. Fidler and Bertram H. Davis, as the departing and incoming general secretaries, expressed different levels of support for the Catholic University strike in speeches at the 1967 Annual Meeting. In a statement reported as revised to stronger terms in response to the recent strike by Catholic University professors, Fidler did not condone the faculty strike although he noted that "public protest is not only in order, it may be the only way of gaining the attention of authorities."[39] Bertram H. Davis commented on such militancy in a different tone:

> And when our professional dignity and decency are outraged by a flagrant violation of our most fundamental principles, and it becomes necessary to storm one of the citadels of the unredeemed, let us bear in mind that our militance is only an expedient, unnatural to us at best and adopted only for an extreme occasion.[40]

Fidler spent much of his address encouraging his listeners to support shared authority in college and university governance. At one point he voiced opposition to unionism, "I remain highly skeptical of the benefits for an entire academic community to be derived from faculty selection of an outside organization to coordinate its efforts in bargaining organizations."[41] Davis, on the other hand, offered no comment on the efficacy of collective bargaining, reviewing instead with approximately equal attention the efforts of Committees A and T and the situation at the Catholic University.[42] His omission of opposition to representation of economic interests and his eloquence in support of the faculty strike—even as expedient—portray a new general secretary of very different mind than his predecessor although Davis's comments to the *Chronicle of Higher Education* shortly after his appointment indicated he too supported professionalism.[43] The strike at the Catholic University provided an example which according to Bertram H. Davis "clearly showed that there were occasions when the refusal of the faculty members to provide their services could be justified." He noted later, "The provocation was very real, and they were standing up for important principles."[44]

Israel Kugler raised the issue of faculty participation in strikes at the 1967 Annual Meeting, when he presented a resolution to endorse an ACLU statement that supported teachers' freedom to organize and right to strike.[45] Sanford H. Kadish (law, University of California–Berkeley), chair of Committee A, expressed concern that professors, administrators, and the press would assume that passage of the resolution indicated "the assertion of new and basic policy."[46] The issue of the right to strike became the focal point of a debate, and the delegates decided to place the question before Committee A as "the proper course to take for full examination of matters of policy."[47] A *Chronicle of Higher Education* reporter at the meeting indicated that "the Annual [Meeting] was made well aware, prior to its vote, that if it had chosen not to refer the resolution to the committee it would have had the opportunity to reject the resolution entirely. This it clearly did not want to do."[48] Members at the annual meetings seemed far more interested in pressing activism, even militancy, than did association leaders.

Prior to the annual meeting, Kadish had moved at the council meeting that it form an ad hoc committee to examine and report on faculty strikes.[49] The council approved the motion and established the Special Joint Committee on Representation, Bargaining, and Sanctions; consideration of the strike issue went to that committee rather than to Committee A as suggested at the annual meeting. The core of AAUP leadership, as well as Clyde W. Summers, composed the Special Committee: the president, the general secretary, and the chairs of Committees A, B, T, and Z. The chair of Committee B was John Christie (English, Vassar College), Ralph S. Brown (who served as chair of the Special Committee) was chair of Committee T, and William Baumol (economics, Princeton University) was chair of Committee Z.[50] According to Kadish a statement by the regents of the University of California threatening dismissal of professors who participated in strikes "had 'a great effect' on the AAUP leadership."[51] Brown's personal file on the development of the statement on strikes has two articles on the faculty and student strikes at the Catholic University, and the eventual published rationale for faculty participation in strikes cited the events also.[52] Fidler's and Davis's comments about the strike also establish the importance of this particular event. Governing boards at private and public institutions brought the issue of faculty strikes to the direct attention of AAUP leaders.

The development of the AAUP position on faculty participation in strikes was a critical event in the organization's movement toward faculty representation. The strike disrupts the university's fundamental functions, education and research. Following the first union strike at Henry Ford Community College in 1966, the first union strikes by professors at four-year institutions were in April 1968 at Chicago State and Northeastern Illinois Colleges (now universities). The AFT organized those strikes because the board of governors refused to allow collective bargaining elections.[53] More than any other behavior, the strike affirms the difference between shared governance and collective bargaining, between professionalism and the bureaucracy. Thus the following section offers a detailed examination of the association leaders' consideration and development of a policy on strikes.

The AAUP and the Faculty Strike: "Not to Say That It Should Never Be Done"

The Special Joint Committee on Bargaining, Sanctions, and Representation met in September 1967 following extensive correspondence among members concerning faculty participation in strikes. The committee drafted a statement at the meeting that it submitted to the council for discussion at its fall meeting.[54] The draft statement indicated AAUP preference for shared authority and responsibility, argued that there should be no legal restraints on faculty participation in strikes, and tried to move AAUP policy from "never" supporting faculty participation to "hardly ever" supporting such action.[55] The position of "hardly ever" was, not surprisingly, ambiguous:

> . . . on particular campuses there may arise situations involving extremely serious violations of academic freedom (of students as well as faculty) or of the principles of academic governance, in which there appears to be no scope for rational methods of discussion, persuasion, and conciliation. In such circumstances it is difficult not to sympathize with faculty members who are impelled to express their condemnation by withholding their services, either singly or in concert with others.[56]

While the draft statement did not mention strikes based on economic issues, the committee members were able to support strikes based on issues of academic freedom or governance albeit in remarkably circuitous phrasing.

Yet this statement was too specific for most of the Special Committee members. Ralph S. Brown wrote in a fall 1967 memorandum to the council that while all committee members probably agreed that the association needed a brief policy statement and additional analysis, he added, "At the same time, most of us think that there are aspects of the problem with respect to which experience furnishes so little guidance that we can not, and should not, attempt to, present a full rationale."[57] The council reviewed the draft statement at its October 1967 meeting. Brown described the discussion as useful, and it appears from a later memorandum that the major point of the discussion was a suggestion to include "a sentence or two of further explanation of the general inappropriateness of strikes."[58] Despite that hesitancy, the council evidenced no greater resistance to the suggestion of faculty participation in strikes, expecting the committee to continue its efforts.

In February 1968 Brown distributed to members of the Special Joint Committee a draft statement (the result of members' responses to a January 1968 draft statement), a draft memorandum to the council, a draft analysis of appropriate cause for faculty participation in strikes, and a copy of a 1 February 1968 letter from Sanford Kadish to Brown.[59] Brown wrote in his cover memorandum that the new draft differed only minimally from an early January version of the statement.[60] Kadish's letter suggested another set of four sentences of transition that provided reasons for diminishing "the legitimacy of the strike."[61] The February draft statement carried a new sentence relative to the 1967 draft:

> It should be assumed that faculty members will exercise their right to strike only if they believe that another component of the institution (or a controlling agency of government, such as a legislature or governor) is inflexibly bent on a course which undermines an essential element of the educational process.[62]

In addition the draft no longer included the expression of sympathy but simply noted that professors might feel impelled to withhold services in the face of flagrant violations of academic freedom or academic government.[63] Committee members were satisfied with the 23 February draft, and no one indicated a desire to accept Kadish's suggestion of diminishing the legitimacy of the strike.[64] The committee members also agreed to Ralph S. Brown's suggestion that they recommend to the council that it authorize publication of the statement and analysis in the *Bulletin* as well as presentation of the statement at the 1968 Annual Meeting so that chapters and members could respond to it.[65]

Brown presented the draft statement on strikes at the annual meeting in 1968, stating:

> This is new policy; this is not simply such a flexible operating mechanism like the REI Statement. It represents a shift in historic position, so the position of the Special Committee was that we didn't want to act on it.[66]

He explained further, "In this case I not only do not invite your action, I implore you not to act on it, because this is something the membership hasn't seen, and certainly in this case the membership in the chapter are entitled to have an opportunity to discuss this statement."[67] As discussion began he warned the members at the annual meeting, "This is a dangerous weapon, my friends."[68] Ten members spoke to the statement, with two offering conditional opposition and three (including Israel Kugler) offering support; the other five presented points of information.[69] Immediately thereafter President Byse closed discussion. Previously the association viewed its members, and professors in general, as custodians of higher education. While that responsibility was still very important to the AAUP, at the same time it had established professors as employees with the right to strike against management.[70]

The June 1968 issue of the *Bulletin* presented the Statement on Faculty Participation in Strikes, an accompanying analysis, and a paper presented by Sanford Kadish on the strike and the professoriate at a symposium at the University of Illinois School of Law.[71] Kadish voiced leadership's ambiguity about the strike in his paper. While he noted that a professor may "depart from the norms of academic propriety," most of his article presented evidence against professors' strikes.[72] He recognized his ambiguity and offered as explanation, "For to give reasons for not doing something is not to say that it should never be done, or that it may not be more defensible under some conditions than others."[73] The bureaucratized university with unionized professors might result in a faculty strike, but the AAUP leaders were manifestly uncertain about the wisdom of such action.

Committees T and Z: The Limits of Professionalism

The work of Committees T and Z progressed during the later 1960s, but the national AAUP leaders recognized that the committees were experiencing limitations. Professors were clearly not the sole custodians of the interests of higher education, and their economic welfare faced an uncertain if not dismal future.

Both the council and Committee T recommended that the members at the 1967 Annual Meeting endorse the Statement on College and University Government.[74] Ralph S. Brown (chair of Committee T) recognized in his recommendation for annual meeting endorsement that the nature of the joint statement meant that the AAUP could not modify it of its own accord, acknowledging that the 1940 Statement elicited some dissatisfaction among members for the same reason.[75] Brown cited two constraints resulting from the negotiations, shared responsibility rather than faculty responsibility for budget policies and shared rather than faculty responsibility for the institutional educational policies. He also indicated two advantages, faculty involvement in the determination of building programs and salary increases, and he argued that joint sponsorship outweighed any restrictions inherent in the statement. The members at the annual meeting endorsed the statement.[76]

The Committee T report also included two recommendations that members of both Committee T and the REI Committee had approved at a joint meeting in January 1967.[77] The first was the development and implementation of a survey of institutional practices that would include grading institutions. The second recommendation indicated AAUP leaders' continuing desire to have an active organization in professional affairs; it suggested that staff and other resources be expanded to assist those several colleges and universities that needed help in improving faculty participation in governance. Although there were severe limitations to such expansion according to General Secretary Davis, he had endorsed both recommendations.[78]

At the 1969 Annual Meeting, Otway Pardee (mathematics, Syracuse University) presented the results of the trial survey of faculty participation in college and university government.[79] The initial survey suggested that "the average faculty member exists in an environment where his participation is slightly better than *Consultation,*" hardly encouraging news.[80] Members approved a proposal to survey the levels of faculty participation in government at U.S. colleges and universities every three years.[81] In addition the members at the annual meeting requested a study of developing faculty accreditation of colleges and universities "as a proper recognition of the central place of faculty members in evaluating their academic community and as a guarantee of the standards vital to the academic profession and the Association."[82] The members at the 1969 Annual Meeting also expressed further interest in association support of faculty activity at two-year colleges. The chapter at Marshalltown Community College (Iowa) presented a proposal on faculty participation in governance at such institutions, requesting that the AAUP work with the American Association of Junior Colleges and regional accrediting groups to further the adoption of the 1966 Statement.[83] The AAUP expansion of interest concerning governance now included those faculties at two-year colleges.[84]

The council too was widening organizational relationships with professors at two-year colleges. At its fall 1969 meeting the council approved a recommendation that AAUP membership include professors regardless of whether they were instructors for liberal arts or technical-vocational programs.[85] AAUP membership now included professors at all types of institutions. While association leadership tended to come from elite institutions in the late 1960s, association membership and concerns continued to broaden. These new groups, with their newfound organizational voices, represented an expanded definition of the professoriate for the AAUP.

Committee Z published encouraging information in 1967; professors' annual salaries and benefits had risen substantially. Although the rate was not sufficient to achieve the goal of doubling salaries, the 1966–1967 results were "only the third time" since the salary survey began that the rate came close to that suggested goal. Nevertheless the committee concluded its report with caution, noting substandard compensation at several institutions and expressing concern that private institutions appeared to be "in a very serious financial siege."[86]

In 1968 Committee Z changed the focus of its report from analysis of professors' financial status to an analysis of the increasing financial difficulties facing colleges and universities, particularly private institutions.[87] The report offered the traditional AAUP conception of the academic profession as the reason for its new focus, "But we believe passionately that our profession is perhaps unique in its concern not only with its own interests, but also with those of the institutions of which we are so vital a part and those of the system of education as a whole."[88] The committee's report indicated that there was "the marked leveling off of compensation levels at the private colleges and universities."[89] The report concluded that costs of private higher education were likely to rise considerably and it did not make sense to simply hope for the necessary funds to address the rising costs.[90]

A former member of Committee Z presented concerns about public higher education in a December 1968 *Bulletin* article. He focused his analysis on the relationship between faculty compensation and full-time student equivalent figures at public and private institutions of higher education. He concluded that "the public sector still has a long way to go in this age of affluence in catching up to the private sector."[91] Analysis of faculty salaries in 1968 suggested that professors at private and public institutions had little reason to be satisfied with the financial prospects of higher education.

In 1969 William J. Baumol reported for Committee Z to the annual meeting that inflation was eroding professors' purchasing power. For its 1968–1969 report the committee analyzed faculty salaries in comparison to the consumer price index since 1939 (when the biennial survey began), and the analysis showed that despite some growth from the late 1940s to 1957 and real growth from 1957 to 1967, the rate of increase had slowed considerably. The report accentuated the concern in noting that elite institutions that had typically given the highest salaries were now just keeping abreast of the rate of inflation in their most recent faculty salary increases. These institutions included both private universities such as the University of Chicago and Harvard and Stanford Universities and public ones such as the Universities of Iowa and Michigan. At the other end of the scale there continued to be colleges and universities "whose teaching staffs are distressingly underpaid."[92] The end of the decade did not bring the achievement of doubling the salaries of U.S. professors.

Association members elected Ralph S. Brown to the presidency in 1968. His leadership experience included Committee A membership in the late 1950s and early 1960s although his predominant experience was with Committee T. He was also heavily involved in the American Civil Liberties Union, serving as a member of its Board of Directors since 1954.[93] His initial interest in the AAUP stemmed from a long-term project for a book, *Loyalty and Security,* and he became involved in association activities at the invitation of Ralph Fuchs.[94]

Brown began the October 1968 Council Meeting by noting "the bold program" that Clark Byse presented to the council in his first year as president. Brown admitted that he did not have a similar program but rather saw a "defensive and protective" AAUP. He indicated that despite the apparent vigor of the AAUP and its staff as well as the academic profession, there were obstacles. They included considerable public sentiment against rebelling students who were linked to professors, the attempts to politicize academic life—with threats from the Right and the Left—and students' strenuous objections to conservative professors. He suggested that contrary to the arguments of Jencks and Riesman in *The Academic Revolution,* there were "relatively few instances where the faculty exercises the breadth of power that the tripartite statement sets forth." Nor did he foresee any immediate improvement, suggesting that student demands for participation in governance would take some decisions away from faculties.[95] Students as well as administrators and governing boards were now affecting the nature of governance, threatening the breadth of faculty involvement in decision making.

He also identified a concern that "comes closer to the integrity and dimensions of AAUP as an organization," collective bargaining in "the industrial union model." He was particularly concerned about fatalism among administrators since a recent ACE survey had indicated that although 90 percent of those administrators surveyed responded that they did not like collective bargaining, 80 percent said it would be the standard operating procedure by 1980. President Brown felt that the AAUP had "to check the real push toward unionism on the industrial model."[96]

His concluding remarks reflect, however, a curious sense of vigor in comparison to his cautionary opening statement. He told the council, "I would say the old right is blasting us, the new left is flaying us, and the anti-intellectual center is sitting on us. Let us attack."[97]

Despite AAUP President Brown's vigor, the militance of professors in regard to their participation in college or university affairs had little to do with their interest in political militance. Ladd and Lipset found little relationship between professors' identification of general liberalism or conservatism on national politics and identification of attitudes on faculty governance.[98] Although the AAUP responded to such national events as the riots at the 1968 Democratic Convention in Chicago by moving its 1969 Annual Meeting to Minneapolis and sponsoring sessions at that meeting on the New Left, AAUP activism continued to focus on professors' working relationships with colleges and universities.[99] Whatever attacks the AAUP might mount, they would be on behalf of professors, separate from the militancy of the late 1960s.

Limits on association efforts in regard to professionalism continued to appear in administrative actions. Committee A published reports on cases of late notice at eleven colleges and universities in the December 1968 issue of the *Bulletin.*[100] The article presented two of the institutions, the University of Georgia and Southern University (Louisiana), as having repeatedly violated the Standards for Notice of Nonreappointment.[101] The committee also published a unilateral statement in 1968, the revised Recommended Institutional Regulations on Academic Freedom and Tenure. These regulations were AAUP interpretations of the policy of the 1940 Statement; even Committee A was displaying a willingness to represent unilaterally professors' occupational interests.[102] In view of state political activity, the committee's limited activism made sense. In 1969 the chair of the Special Committee on State Legislation Affecting Academic Freedom reported to the annual meeting that the variety of bills to curb academic freedom being introduced in state legislatures "boggles the mind."[103]

To some degree the association itself placed limits on its definition of professionalism. Members at the 1969 Annual Meeting endorsed the Statement on Professional Ethics developed by Committee B. Curiously the association divorced itself from direct responsibility for ethical conduct among professors:

> In the enforcement of ethical standards, the academic profession differs from those of law and medicine, whose associations act to assure the integrity of members engaged in private practice. In the academic profession the individual institution of higher learning provides this assurance and so should normally handle questions concerning propriety of conduct within its own framework by reference to a faculty group.[104]

The gap between the association and its counterparts in law and medicine continued to grow. From 1966 to 1969 whatever gains the association made in terms of the profession were apparently matched by limitations.

The Association Affirms Unionism: From Proscription to Prescription

In 1968 the association leaders revised the AAUP position on collective bargaining. In January 1968, Committee T approved a revised REI statement, and the council approved the revision in April 1968.[105] One major change in the statement was in the language of the guidelines for AAUP chapters considering collective bargaining. The language of the 1966 version was proscriptive, "Chapters of the Association should not seek to become the exclusive representative of the faculty without first obtaining the approval of the General Secretary. Normally approval will be granted only when the following conditions exist . . . ."[106] In contrast the 1968 version was prescriptive, "The initial decision to consider representative status, whether through a chapter or other agency of the Association . . ., should be made in consultation with the General Secretary, and should be the result of judgement about the following considerations. . . ."[107] The collective bargaining policy was beginning to enable rather than constrain chapters.

The developing association vision of the efficacy of faculty collective bargaining was clear in the 1968 version of the Policy on Representation of Economic Interests. The 1966 version expressed opposition to the "extension of the principle of exclusive representation" to faculties. In contrast the 1968 statement called attention to the "special characteristics of the academic community" and identified association opposition only to "legislation imposing upon faculty members in higher education the principle of exclusive representation derived from models of industrial collective bargaining."[108] Despite the opposition to industrial forms of collective bargaining, the 1968 statement changed the prohibition on strikes in the 1966 Statement to an allowance for "extraordinary circumstances" as written in the statement on faculty participation in strikes.[109] The members at the 1968 Annual Meeting concurred with the revised statement, and the statement in the June issue of the *Bulletin* included the notation that the statement "constitutes present Association policy."[110]

There continued to be, however, a level of organizational concern about professors as professionals among AAUP leaders. General Secretary Davis told members at the 1968 Annual Meeting:

> If I feel certain of anything . . . it is that the Association's view of the professional college and university teacher, and its program for him, will prevail in the future as it has in the past. For what characterizes the professional is both an attitude and a commitment to knowledge in depth, to self-examination, and to advancement of the milieu in which he carries on his work; and it is essentially the Association's professional attitude which has shaped its program and stimulated its success.[111]

The general secretary presented the association as supporting the conception of the professor as an individual professional with a de facto right to authority and responsibility. The association's traditional conception of the professor would prevail, rather than the conception of the professor as employee under contract.

At the October 1968 Council Meeting, Staff Associates Alfred Sumberg and Matthew Finkin gave extensive presentations about their activities in support of the REI Committee.[112] They noted their work, either jointly or singly, in Rhode Island, New Jersey, and New York, and highlighted the hearings at CUNY and the other unit-determination hearings at SUNY.[113] In general Sumberg and Finkin seemed to find considerable interest in mediation consistent with the 1966 Statement on College and University Government.[114] Yet in specific cases where faculties had elected bargaining agents, Bertram H. Davis indicated that the contracts were "by and large atrocious things," and Ralph S. Brown called them "deplorable episodes."[115] Davis also reported that the association's exclusive representative at Belleville College had been trying to implement a role for the faculty senate consistent with the 1966 Statement. He added, "It has not yet achieved for the faculty senate, which it got established, the role which ultimately we hoped that senate would have."[116] Association leaders were concerned that the AAUP conception of faculty collective bargaining, with the goal of implementing the 1966 Statement, did not obtain in indirect and direct AAUP collective bargaining activity.

Alfred Sumberg expressed a concern that penetrated to the core of the AAUP when he reviewed collective bargaining contracts in which "academic freedom has been defined as opposition of both *management* and *employees* to any discrimination because of race, color or creed or national origin."[117] Among elected leaders and staff members there was considerable concern that the primary program of the AAUP, issues of academic freedom, would be compromised by collective bargaining contracts with local interpretations quite different from association definitions. He indicated a need to educate public employment relations boards, legislatures, and labor relations boards as to the particular nature of higher education, especially since many legislatures thought about the civil service, *not* professors, when they passed enabling laws. Ralph S. Brown added that the AAUP should educate professors too because New York State's Taylor Act, based on an industrial relations model of unionism, had been drafted by Professor Taylor of the University of Pennsylvania.[118] As Brown summarized the current problem for the AAUP, "Collective bargaining on the industrial model is incompatible with the 1966 Statement, but we hope to wrench around where we have to in higher education to make it compatible." He concluded the discussion by recommending Bertram H. Davis's article on the AAUP "high-road" approach to collective bargaining in the

September 1968 issue of the *Bulletin* as the "best general propaganda" for the association.[119]

Davis's article was actually a response to an earlier article by an ACE staff member that was published in the *Educational Record*. Harry A. Marmion had argued that the AAUP, faced with a "vocal minority of union-oriented delegates," needed to go "where 'the action is.'"[120] Davis's response was first published in the Spring 1968 issue of the *Educational Record,* and he expressed surprise that a staff member of one of the organizations that helped write the 1966 Statement "would view the problems of institutional government in terms of a clinical remedy rather than a philosophical commitment."[121] Davis then maintained the argument of principle, suggesting that professionalism and action were not antithetical. As far as Davis was concerned, the AAUP had always been where the action was in such areas as academic freedom and tenure, faculty salaries, and the disclaimer affidavit requirement and at individual institutions.[122] Yet Marmion's locus of action, unionism, was seductive according to Davis. Without direct reference to the REI statement, Davis concluded his response:

> If collective bargaining techniques are to be employed, they should be directed, as the AAUP has stated, toward the establishment of those forms of institutional government that will permit faculty members to fulfill their role as institutional officers with primary responsibility for the institution's professional life. The organization which encourages them to seek anything less is selling both them and their institutions short.[123]

General Secretary Davis favored a model of unionism that held the 1966 Statement as its ultimate goal. The association was attempting to develop a particular form of bargaining, a combination of shared authority representative of the professor as a professional and the direct representation afforded through collective bargaining. This perspective is evident in William Leonard's report as chair of Committee T at the May 1969 Council Meeting. He indicated that it was important to assist chapters in collective bargaining efforts because of "a grave concern over the poor contracts that have been negotiated in a number of institutions by other external bodies and the serious economic and academic limitations that have resulted."[124]

Alfred Sumberg gave a report on representation of economic interests at that council meeting. He stated that there were two particular concerns for the AAUP, one being legislative changes in "rather mild laws" allowing conferences for negotiations and the other the changes in the rules and procedures of employment relations boards. In one instance the New Jersey Public Employment Relations Commission ruled that he could not speak at a campus with an upcoming collective bargaining election. Second, he reported that there was a movement toward collective bargaining among faculties at private colleges and universities and that among public institutions the number of collective bargaining units and agents was sharply increasing. The result was "we are now in the area of competing for the right to represent our own members."[125] He summarized the past AAUP approach to chapters facing representation elections:

> I must say that we have on the whole waited until our members or our chapters have come to us and said they wanted us to participate in an election. In some cases we have called them and asked them what their wishes are, but we have not taken the position thus far, and perhaps will not, of going to them and telling them they must participate, that this is their responsibility to participate in a forthcoming certification election.[126]

He added that when the AAUP received a request, it was ready to participate at all levels and the association had "the finest set of proposals to make" based on AAUP policy statements.[127]

Ralph S. Brown then asked for discussion about representation of economic interests, asking "if at this point people want to know where we are drifting in collective bargaining." As a result of the discussion about organizational drift and of William Leonard's comment that the REI subcommittee felt strongly that the REI Statement needed revision, Brown asked for a presentation at the Fall Council Meeting on the "theoretical and practical" aspects of the REI situation. He reminded the council that the paradox between the REI Statement and the 1966 Statement as well as the "dilemma" of organizational drift "does confront us."[128]

During this discussion about organizational drift a council member asked about competition from the NEA and the AFT. Sumberg replied that the AAUP faced competition from the NEA and its affiliates but not from the AFT. Matthew Finkin added that the NEA was working on organizing faculties at several four-year colleges and universities.[129] Later in the discussion the same council member asked how many institutions and professors were involved in collective bargaining. Again Sumberg responded, this time emphasizing that his numbers were estimates, that approximately forty-five institutions and twelve thousand or more professors were involved in such representation.[130]

As determined in 1968, the council reconsidered the statement of policy on strikes at its May 1969 meeting. Despite the request for comments from members and chapters, the AAUP leadership received only one letter. Brown said, "It has been received either with indifference or complete satisfaction; we don't know which."[131] Clark Byse suggested that the council approve the statement only as "Council policy" and wait a year to gain more from experience. He was especially interested in the situation at Cornell University, where students were carrying guns on campus as a political statement and in response professors were threatening to refuse to teach.[132] Brown agreed with the suggestion to wait and quickly assembled a quorum of the Special Joint Committee—Byse, Davis, and Kadish as well as himself—and it promptly recommended council endorsement and ensuing presentation to the members at the annual meeting. The council approved without dissent the motion to endorse and present.[133] Brown explained the new council position on the Statement on Faculty Participation in Strikes to the members at the annual meeting, stating, "It stands as operating policy."[134] Although he indicated that the members were free to do otherwise if they so desired, there was no discussion.[135]

Shortly thereafter a member stated that his chapter at New York University had determined that the REI Statement essentially said, "'don't do a damn thing unless somebody is breathing down your neck on this.'"[136] William Leonard replied that

> . . . the REI statement is not the present operating procedure of the Association. We are working with and, even in some cases, very actively encouraging Chapters to consider themselves to stand as possible collective bargaining units or represent economic interests . . . and academic interests of the faculty.[137]

The AAUP was not *telling* chapters to participate in collective bargaining, as Alfred Sumberg indicated at the council meeting. According, however, to the chair of Committee T (with his responsibility for the REI Subcommittee) the association was *encouraging* chapters to pursue such representation. In fact Leonard stated in his report to the annual meeting as chair of Committee T:

> As the result of chapter involvement with decisions on collective bargaining and the experience of the Association's staff during the past year, a more positive policy towards faculties which desire collective bargaining has emerged. It can be summarized thus: for those faculties which believe that shared authority through faculty

senates can be achieved, or for those faculties which believe collective bargaining to be essential and are willing to support viable
faculty senates or AAUP chapters as collective bargaining units, the
Association will provide full assistance.[138]

He made clear why the AAUP had progressed to such an understanding of its
role in collective bargaining when he continued:

The latter policy results from a grave concern over the poor contracts sometimes negotiated by other groups which have had serious economic and academic limitations. Where a faculty finds,
after evaluation, that it stands in an adversary relationship with its
administration, the Association believes that it is in a better position to negotiate a creative contract fully protective of faculty rights
than other organizations.[139]

When faculty-administration relationships reached an adversarial nature and
the ideals of the profession could not obtain, the AAUP was willing to seek
representation of faculties in such situations. While Leonard affirmed that the
goal of contract negotiations would be "the principle and practice of shared
authority," he also reported that the REI Subcommittee expected to produce
a "handbook on collective bargaining" to assist chapters facing unionization
questions.[140]

On 31 October 1969 the council approved another revision of the REI
policy.[141] The subcommittee that rewrote the REI Statement incorporated
some telling changes, and Associate Secretary Alfred Sumberg explained
those changes as being a more positive approach to "the realities of current
life in some parts of academe."[142] He spoke directly to one of those realities
in discussing a trip he made to Wisconsin, where he learned about possible
changes in the state's employment relations law. It was not clear whether
the changes

. . . would affect the nonclassified employees in Wisconsin. I apol-
ogize, Ralph [Brown], for using the term "employees," but, as I
am sometimes described as the business agent for the AAUP—as
Matt is sometimes described also—we sometimes run into these
terminology problems.[143]

In view of Machlup's and Bierstedt's objections to the 1966 REI Statement,
these were much more than terminology problems. The idea of the professor
as an employee limited the association's hopes for implementing professional
ideals. The AAUP leadership continued to grapple with the question of the

faculty's relation to the administration and the governing board. In this particular case staff members provided the most recent answer since Sumberg and Finkin drafted three versions of the revision.[144]

The revised statement reflected the association's newly achieved understanding of some developments in faculties' collective bargaining. While the 1969 version encouraged, again, legislation to assure shared governance, it did so within the context of successful collective bargaining:

> The Association recognizes the significant role which collective bargaining may play in bringing agreement between faculty and administration on economic and academic issues. Through the negotiation of a collective agreement, it may in some institutions be possible to create a proper environment for faculty and administration to carry out their respective functions and to provide for the eventual establishment of necessary instruments of shared authority.[145]

In comparison the 1968 revision had not acknowledged the capacity of collective bargaining to achieve agreement on "economic and academic issues," either through the instrument of the faculty senate or the AAUP chapter as bargaining agent.

Not all council members were comfortable with the suggested acknowledgment of current realities. William Baumol, despite his support for collective bargaining, argued:

> But [it] seems to me a gratuitous statement to say, the second sentence, for example, "Through the negotiation of a collective agreement, it may be possible to create a proper environment." Many of us really don't feel that way in general; in fact, we feel that this undermines the proper environment. Look, this statement is facing up to realities, but in facing up to realities I think we gain nothing by sort [of] coming along mechanically and saying, "oh, it has all sorts of virtues we never realized."[146]

Bertram H. Davis pointed out, however, that "chapters and conferences have been complaining that we are still backing into collective bargaining, we are going very grudgingly into it." As he saw it, the revision recognized the possible advantages of collective bargaining. Associate Secretary Daniel Adler supported Davis's assessment, stating that "we have not given up our basic ideology but, lacking power to pursue that method, we will also pursue the secondary one, or new-fangled ones, of collective bargaining."[147]

Council members also discussed the AAUP role in collective bargaining vis-à-vis other organizations, responding to a sentence in the statement about conditions of effective faculty voice not fully in place, the traditional reason for AAUP involvement. Council member Donald Koster (English, Adelphi University) noted Israel Kugler's attacks on the association for not engaging in vigorous representation of faculties and suggested that the AFT rather than the AAUP might be the best representative.[148] Carl Stevens objected by pointing out that labor organizations always made such comments and that the AAUP should state what it believed.[149] Yet Finkin, involved in day-to-day collective bargaining activities for the AAUP, responded, "And I hate to say there is some credence, in other words, to the statement of Kugler—although I'm glad he's not here and hearing me say it."[150] The council shortly thereafter voted to cut a proposed clause at the beginning of the sentence on conditions of effective participation that stated the association's preference for shared authority, returning the sense of the statement to the more direct phrasing of previous versions. It was, however, a split vote of 15 to 9, and Ralph S. Brown recalled that this was the first counted vote on the REI Statement. Nevertheless the vote to approve the revised statement passed without objection.[151]

The 1969 version also specified the association position on institutional autonomy and the special nature of the academic community, addressing the problem of public agencies' evaluating colleges and universities. The AAUP was increasingly concerned about the impact of collective bargaining laws on academic institutions' traditional principles of governance. In fact the revised statement had a new name that suggested expanded areas of concern, the Statement on Representation of Economic and Professional Interests.[152]

Ralph S. Brown questioned the suggestion in the REPI Statement that chapters and conferences attend to rigid state laws, asking why the statement emphasized those groups. Sumberg replied that the REI Committee "felt we had to give some greater responsibility to the chapters and conferences in the area of legislation concerning collective bargaining."[153] The increasing numbers of public institutions, and their faculties, meant that the AAUP had to address their particular conditions.

The *Bulletin* reported the council discussion of the revised statement as focusing on the association "role in collective bargaining."[154] For the first time the AAUP was using the phrase "collective bargaining" in discussion of its activities. In terms of organizational procedures and policies as well as its publication, the association had established a firm commitment to unionization. Furthermore, the development of an activist collective bargaining policy caused Committee T members to recommend that the association discontinue the

REI Committee and form a standing committee on collective bargaining. As Bertram H. Davis told the council:

> I supported this in the committee, primarily because I think it is important now that we give emphasis to our role in this area by making this a special, a standing committee of the Association rather than a subcommittee of Committee T. I think that there have been advantages in the last year or two in having the REI Committee as a subcommittee of Committee T, but I think its problems and the matters which it must consider are far beyond those of the usual subcommittee.[155]

He added that representation of economic interests had relationships not only to Committee T but also to Committees A and B. The motion to approve the new standing committee was passed without any opposing votes. The committee was later given the letter "N" and the name of Committee on Representation of Economic and Professional Interests.[156] The tension between professionalism and bureaucratization had reached the status of a standing committee for the AAUP, and the organization was now ready to implement collective bargaining.

State and regional activity grew in late 1969, and the activity included increased emphasis on organizational involvement in collective bargaining. At an association conference for the state and regional officers in December, Matthew Finkin summarized faculties' collective bargaining as most often the result of states' enabling legislation for public employees. He told the participants that bargaining was likely to occur at "two-year colleges where faculties tend to follow secondary school patterns rather than the professional approaches that characterize higher education, and other types of institutions where administrative autocracy, a history of faculty grievances, or severe pressure to protect economic gains, create a search for panaceas."[157] Bureaucratic demands, whether expressed in terms of two-year colleges or individual institutional patterns, focused professors on the possible benefits of unionization. Finkin also noted that the AAUP did not see a necessary conflict between collective bargaining and shared governance. Yet, according to Finkin, there were problems with collective bargaining since some inadequate contracts "bargained away academic freedom, crystallized management prerogatives, reduced faculty authority, and included terms to 'protect' the bargaining agent in the industrial, rather than academic, pattern."[158] In contrast Finkin described a "'creative contract' negotiated by a college faculty senate with AAUP assistance." The contract included AAUP principles on academic freedom and governance and produced economic benefits. He indicated that AAUP involvement in collective bargaining would promote association principles and bring "improved conditions to beleaguered faculties."[159]

Ralph S. Brown led much of the discussion during the conference's collective bargaining workshop and "took note of dilemmas and paradoxes raised by the collective bargaining issue." He suggested that the best AAUP solution would be "retaining its distinctive professional goals and developing a new pattern of collective bargaining attuned to the special requirements of professional life in higher education."[160] The AAUP movement to implement collective bargaining continued to specify a professional form of collective bargaining.

By the end of 1969 the AAUP had a prescriptive policy for collective bargaining and an operating policy for limited faculty participation in strikes. An association that had called for the broad implementation of the ideals of the academic profession had added adversarial methods to its operations. The previously unacceptable union methods of exclusive representation and strikes were now acceptable to the AAUP. These adversarial methods were contrary to one of the central characteristics of the AAUP conception of the professor as professional: shared responsibility in the college or university community. Despite the commitment of the 1969 collective bargaining policy and the vague sense of support for faculty strikes, the association leaders were uncertain about the effectiveness of either policy. The 1970s would bring both internal and external conditions that would force the association to specify its approach to faculty representation.

The newly established Committee N on Representation of Economic and Professional Interests had its first meeting in February 1970. Committee discussion included several subjects, ranging from collective bargaining developments at the State University of New York and the City University of New York to the possibility that the National Labor Relations Board would assume jurisdiction for bargaining in private higher education. While many previous collective bargaining discussions among AAUP leaders had covered such areas as activities at various institutions and the legal status of professors considering bargaining, the first Committee N meeting reflected a pragmatic concern about the AAUP conduct of collective bargaining. Other Committee N issues included areas of negotiation, the question of necessary legal and financial resources, collective bargaining and membership requirements, and the impact of the agency shop on academic freedom and finances, all of which were operational concerns.[161] The AAUP's national leaders' attention to the policies of collective bargaining and the faculty strike had dominated consideration of

AAUP involvement in exclusive representation. Committee N transformed that policy orientation to consideration of the day-to-day affairs of bargaining. More important, in April 1970, for the first time, the *Bulletin* carried a report of specific chapter bargaining agents in the council meeting report, indicating that the Belleville Area College chapter, the Rutgers University chapter, and the combined chapter/faculty association at St. John's University (New York) were agents.[162]

Membership in collective bargaining units was a pressing issue. During a discussion of dues at collective bargaining chapters, at the April 1970 council meeting, President Ralph S. Brown stated:

> I will remind the body that from the very beginning of our having an REI policy, we have occupied a high ground of principle, that is all very well. We had no collective bargaining representation contract anywhere. We announced firmly never, never, would we get people involved in an agency shop and compel them to pay dues, et cetera. But now, as you see, Matt Finkin is just one voice of practicality who sees all of that money there [in an agency shop]. It will be interesting to see what happens to principles in the next few years.[163]

This was apparently the first time that association leaders discussed the possible financial benefits of AAUP involvement in collective bargaining. The leadership also had to consider the fact that enabling legislation often required employee units beyond the parameters of AAUP membership, and at the same meeting the council approved consideration of changes in membership to include part-time professors and "non-faculty professional staff members."[164]

Associate Secretary Sumberg reported to the council about the February 1970 meeting of Committee N. He told council members that there was a "good deal of controversy within the Association" concerning the relationship between the agency shop and academic freedom since the AAUP had traditionally investigated complaints at any institution, but agency shops appeared to deny that possibility, as only the elected representative could negotiate with the administration. At the request of Committee A he had written a memorandum on the agency shop, and Committee A had considered it briefly at its October 1969 meeting. The committee had decided to continue discussing the topic.[165] Later in the discussion Sanford Kadish, chair of Committee A, spoke to the industrial parallels of closed and agency shops and indicated his own indecision on the topic. He stated, "At the moment I don't know where I ought to stand. I therefore don't know where Committee

A ought to stand at the moment."[166] Committee A concern about exclusive representation was now uncertain, in comparison to the bitter opposition expressed in 1966.

Council members asked several specific questions about bargaining during the council meeting. Ned Bowler (speech and drama, University of Colorado) wondered if the association was "moving fast enough and with enough energy," how real a threat the AFT and NEA posed, and whether there was consistency between shared authority and collective bargaining. Sumberg responded that each situation determined whether Committees T or N was the appropriate committee to address the situation, and that the energy problem was helped by volunteers in the AAUP tradition.[167] Finkin added later, "I tend to regard the NEA as stronger competition than the AFT," and Brown noted that the NEA was doing well among public institutions which had been teachers colleges.[168] AAUP staff member Richard Peairs suggested that the AAUP, AFT, and NEA were very civilized in their relations in Washington, D.C., but the situation was different elsewhere.[169]

In response to a question about AFT and NEA efforts among faculties at Pennsylvania state colleges and junior colleges and the AAUP budget, Bertram H. Davis replied that the association budget was limited—the CUNY loss and the SUNY effort would cost the association $100,000. While he did not know how much it would all cost, he estimated, "But if you add all this up and all the other demands which are likely to increase, I suppose, we won't be doing much else but supporting collective bargaining."[170] Finkin anticipated further increases in collective bargaining as faculties at state colleges pursued bargaining in order to protect their budgets, as in the case of the New Jersey State Colleges. He also provided an example of collective bargaining interest at a private institution, stating that AAUP members of the Syracuse University chapter had talked to him about planning for collective bargaining there in about two years.[171]

The issue of appropriate contracts arose again at this council meeting. Carl Stevens told fellow council members that if the 1940 and 1958 statements were negotiated, then collective bargaining would disappear. He added, "Our power is really in the content of agreements, whoever negotiates."[172] Brown agreed in part, replying:

> That's exactly our policy, but the question is who negotiates those agreements, if they are not us, unless we get a joint agreement. The thing here is exclusive. The guy who first gets in elbows everybody else out. My own feeling is that we ought to work along

the St. John's line, closing up to a faculty association so we are in there.[173]

Association leaders continued to see the AAUP as best suited to represent faculty interests based on its comprehension of the professional status of professors.

The association published the proposed changes in membership criteria in the December 1970 *Bulletin*. While the comments following the proposed amendments indicated that the new category of affiliate membership would not only assist collective bargaining efforts but also allow membership among professional staff members, the introduction to the proposed amendments was blunt. The change "grew out of a need to assist chapters seeking representative status where, as is sometimes the case, the unit to be represented includes professional staff generally rather than full-time faculty alone."[174] The AAUP was establishing organizational means in its movement toward exclusive representation by changing membership criteria.

Further support for collective bargaining came from local groups. At the 1970 Annual Meeting the Assembly of State and Regional Conferences passed a resolution stating that:

> ". . . collective bargaining, conducted under the guidelines and for the objectives outlined in the revised REPI Statement of October, 1969, offers one additional means by which faculty members, operating through local AAUP chapters or appropriate faculty bodies, may secure academic rights, increase economic benefits, and promote participation in the governance of their institutions."[175]

The assembly resolution reaffirmed the national commitment to unionization; at all levels of the AAUP, collective bargaining was an important and appropriate tool.

C. Addison Hickman (economics, Southern Illinois University), chair of Committee N, reported to the council at its October 1970 meeting. He noted "the increasing complexity of the legal picture with respect to state legislation affecting collective bargaining, and the growing involvement of the Association in the area."[176] He then asked Alfred Sumberg and Matthew Finkin to review AAUP efforts of the past year. Sumberg reviewed the National Labor Relations Board decision to extend its jurisdiction to private colleges and universities. He also indicated that five AAUP chapters were bargaining representatives and a sixth shared bargaining rights with a local faculty association.[177] The external environment continued to pressure the AAUP, as private institutions' faculties now had the right to bargain.

In the December 1970 issue of the *Bulletin,* General Secretary Davis ended a tradition begun in 1915. He wrote:

> It is a mistake to conclude, as many do, that the American Association of University Professors should model its policies after those of the American Bar Association or the American Medical Association. However estimable those associations may be, their policies have been adapted to the fact that members of the legal and medical professions are largely self-employed and deal directly with the public. Members of the academic profession of course are not self-employed, and it is their institutions rather than they which deal directly with the public.[178]

While Davis went on to defend vigorously the conception of professor as professional and AAUP concern about professional ethics, his statement was a clear indication that the association conception of itself had changed.

Matthew Finkin wrote an article published in a 1971 issue of the *Wisconsin Law Review* that was later published in the *AAUP Bulletin.*[179] Finkin stated that three national organizations—the AFT, the NEA, and the AAUP—were contending for representation at the local level. After looking at collective bargaining contracts at five institutions, he concluded, "Given the variables present in higher education, it does not necessarily follow that collective bargaining will have a negative impact on the exercise of the faculty's authority as a faculty."[180] While recognizing that faculties at "mature colleges and universities" were not yet bargaining, he presented a model of understanding that portrayed exclusive representation as satisfactorily implementing faculty authority.[181] By the early 1970s association staff members were answering the questions raised in the middle 1960s about the efficiency and efficacy of collective bargaining in relation to shared authority. The AAUP was still, however, trying to define the relationship of its professional activities to its union activities.

The AAUP and Professional Ideals: Uncertainty in Response to Representation

Yet the association was not fully convinced that faculty control of colleges and universities was appropriate. Members at the 1969 Annual Meeting had instructed Committee D on Accrediting of Colleges and Universities to examine the possibility of faculty accreditation of colleges and universities. The committee held several meetings with staff members from the regional accrediting associations and college administrators. In addition some of the committee members had served on accrediting teams, and AAUP staff members reported their involvement with accrediting associations. In regard to faculty accreditation, the committee stated:

> Faculty monopoly, perhaps even faculty *predominance,* at every level of the accrediting process would be, if not impossible to attain, inherently unwise. Clearly administrative expertise is essential to any inquiry and to any ultimate judgement of the total operation of an academic institution.[182]

Committee D members felt that the accreditation process would advance, through institutional self-reflection, the shared authority recommended in the 1966 Statement on Government of Colleges and Universities. They reaffirmed the "Role of the Faculty in the Accrediting of Colleges and Universities," a statement endorsed by members at the 1969 Annual Meeting which encouraged faculty participation in institutional accreditation and shared authority.[183]

Bertram H. Davis offered a thorough defense of the association's work on academic freedom and tenure in his report at the 1970 Annual Meeting. His analysis of the recent activities of the AAUP in that area "exploded one or two myths." He indicated that in the cases of published reports, the association response was often two and a half years after the request for an investigation. The AAUP, however, resolved most cases without investigation and report and often very quickly. These resolutions were far more indicative of AAUP efforts and successes.[184] In addition he argued that 90 percent of those cases dealt with untenured faculty members and that the AAUP was the only association to have "enforced any reasonable standards for notice of nonreappointment."[185]

Davis' defense of Committee A became a spirited apologia in a June 1970 *Bulletin* article. In "Principles and Cases: The Mediative Work of the AAUP," Davis argued that the association tended "to publicize its most significant failures," those cases at the institutions under consideration for censure. He reviewed staff efforts to negotiate cases, restating the example of the complaint resolved in fifteen minutes and the preponderance of nontenured professors whom the association assisted. He concluded by arguing that the AAUP insistence on principles for all professors "extended the Association's influence to institutions not only without AAUP chapters but, on occasion, without a single AAUP member."[186] As the custodian of higher education, the AAUP was still willing to work on behalf of any professor regardless of membership.

Davis again defended the association's work in academic freedom in his 1971 report to the annual meeting. This time he examined sixty-four cases (involving eighty-nine professors) resolved by staff members' efforts, noting their often quick resolution, the reappointment of more than a third of the professors whose institutions were not renewing their contracts, and financial settlements in eighteen cases. He pointed to the large proportion of non-tenured faculty members (sixty-six of the eighty-nine) and, perhaps for the first time in AAUP history, identified that in the seventy cases where he was able to identify gender, twenty-seven of the professors were women.[187] On the latter point he stated that "the need for our Committee W on the Status of Women in the Academic Profession is underscored."[188] In cases of academic freedom and tenure Davis continued to identify individual cases of success and redress. He was also expanding the AAUP definition of the professoriate in terms of gender.

The Committee Z report for 1969–1970 focused on public institutions' problems as a balance to earlier reports on the state of private institutions. For all institutions, however, the change in faculty compensation "was scandously small," and committee members feared even more severe changes. For public institutions recent budget cuts suggested that recent favorable trends were no longer applicable. According to Committee Z, redress would require "an enormous outlay of effort."[189]

At the 1970 Annual Meeting, Davis commended Committee T for its work, noting that institutional investigations could bring governing boards, administrations, and faculties closer to the recommendations of the 1966 Statement on Government of Colleges and Universities.[190] One of the Committee T investigating ad hoc committees reported the results of its investigation in the March 1971 issue of the *Bulletin*. Despite General Secretary Davis's hope that the investigations would bring institutions closer to the 1966 Statement, the report captured the problems involved with effecting reform. The ad hoc committee examined faculty participation in the decision of the Board of Trustees of Long Island University to sell the institution's Brooklyn Center.[191] The Board of Trustees made the decision without consulting or telling the faculty, and faculty members responded vigorously on and off the campuses.[192] The report suggested that part of the faculty's problem rested with the decentralized structure of the institution since some faculty members at each center were active but there was little such effort across the university. Nevertheless, the committee stated, "The Board of Trustees of Long Island University has insisted on unilaterally exercising its legal right to make decisions which profoundly affect the entire academic community."[193] Administrations and

governing boards continued to pursue their goals, well within legal prerogatives, as they excluded faculties from participation in decisions. The association could ask, following reasoned and judicious inquiry, for the reform of
institutional practices, and administrations and governing boards could exercise an intransigent response under the aegis of the law.

By December 1970 chapters and administrations at 970 institutions had
responded to a Committee T survey on faculty participation in governance,
and the report analyzed the responses, dividing faculty participation into five
levels: Determination, Joint Action, Consultation, Discussion, and None.[194]
Faculties on average enjoyed Determination in only one area, academic performance of students, and on average had no participation in decisions relative to individual faculty salaries and long-range budgetary planning.[195] The
subcommittee's overall conclusion was equally disheartening, "on the average,
faculty participation in college and university government in the United States
is viewed by faculties and administrations as being at the level of CONSUL-
TATION, a far cry from the ideals envisaged by the 1966 'Statement on
Government of Colleges and Universities.'"[196] While some institutions' replies
showed that those ideals could be achieved, "considerable change, however,
will be required to improve the general picture."[197] As support for collective
bargaining grew among national and conference leaders, methods such as promoting shared governance seemed less promising.

Committee A efforts now included straightforward assessments of association activity to achieve individual redress. Committee Z reports continued to
reflect the material losses of the professoriate that had begun in the middle of
the 1960s. The Committee T survey clearly indicated that shared authority
was not the norm for institutional governance. Although the association sustained its efforts in its traditional areas, many of the efforts were marked by
losses as well as gains. Against that backdrop, and in the face of increasing
pressures in faculty collective bargaining, the AAUP decided to examine itself.

The Pressures of Collective Bargaining, 1970–1971

General Secretary Davis reported the state of AAUP financial affairs at the
1971 Annual Meeting. The association sustained two large deficits in consecutive years and consequently postponed important projects. Collective bargaining added considerably to the association financial burden, and recent
activities in the area, such as the NLRB decision to address unionization at
private colleges and universities, meant that the AAUP had a problem that it
had to "resolve very quickly." Despite the AAUP tradition of advancing its
program in many ways,

> . . . in collective bargaining we are faced with precedents growing
> out of industrial practice and based upon laws never adopted with
> any thought that college and university faculties would be subject-
> ed to them. The question for us is not which road we will go down,
> but how we can advance our program as we have done for fifty-six
> years—in ways still universally applicable and, as I have already in-
> dicated, increasingly in demand—and at the same time advance it
> through collective bargaining, without either approach limiting or
> conflicting with the other.[198]

Davis told AAUP members that the council's solution was to appoint a spring
and summer study to determine what organization and structure would be
most appropriate.[199] Whereas the 1965 self-study resulted from the AAUP
need to review the general conditions of previous years on the occasion of its
fiftieth anniversary, the 1971 self-study resulted only from the pressures of
collective bargaining.

Davis reported to the council that both Committee N and the Executive
Committee had given unanimous approval to the study. He reviewed restructuring by the American Nurses Association, the League of Women
Voters, and the National Society of Professional Engineers (organizations
substantially different from the AMA and the ABA). He offered as reasons
for the study the problems of tax status, membership in collective bargaining units under the federal Landrum-Griffin Act, and the AAUP's own professional stance. He also enclosed two articles on collective bargaining by
faculties, Joseph Garbarino's "Precarious Professors: New Patterns of
Representation" and Dexter L. Hanley (president of Scranton University),
"Issues and Models for Collective Bargaining in Higher Education."[200]
Garbarino stated that the AAUP faced "inexorable momentum" toward collective bargaining, and Hanley recommended a professional negotiating team
as an alternative to collective bargaining, with the AAUP as a good selection.[201] The Executive Committee and the council were to review the study
and its recommendations in the summer and fall of 1971, with any proposed
changes to be presented at the 1972 Annual Meeting.[202] Davis also told the
council "that the heaviest new demands being made upon the Association's
resources are in the area of collective bargaining." He added that the association was responding more than ever before to questions concerning financial exigency and was experiencing large increases in academic freedom
and tenure cases. The increased demands meant that the AAUP was likely
to have another deficit.[203]

Ralph S. Brown, newly appointed chair of Committee N, emphasized to council members, at their April 1971 meeting, the importance of the NLRB decision on private institutions. He added that Committee N members were very worried about unit determinations but had recommended against the proposed membership criteria changes, preferring a system of local membership determination. The council decided that such consideration was appropriately directed to the summer study. Brown also raised the problem of agency shops with their required dues payments from all unit members; Committee N wanted to continue the AAUP policy of allowing individuals to object conscientiously to agency shops and thus not be forced to pay dues. The council agreed that the problem was complex and decided that further examination was necessary.[204]

Walter Adams (economics, Michigan State University) spoke to the council as chair of Committee T. He indicated that the committee's two primary issues were the relationship of collective bargaining to shared governance and how faculties responded to the serious fiscal problems in higher education.[205] He also reported to the members at the annual meeting, identifying those two concerns as two challenges on the committee's agenda. He made clear Committee T sentiment on representation, stating, "Committee T does not accept the view that collective bargaining and shared authority are antithetical." The Committee T comprehension of the issue derived from its examination of the contract negotiated recently at St. John's University (New York), in which the AAUP chapter and local faculty group had specifically incorporated the 1966 Statement into the contract.[206] Committee T now had an example at a four-year institution of shared governance through a collective bargaining contract.

Ralph S. Brown reported to the members at the 1971 Annual Meeting, arguing that the main reason for the professoriate's movement toward collective bargaining was succinctly voiced by "Samuel Gompers: more." In the last decade "most of us were getting more without having to be very militant about it." In the present, however, "it now seems clear that we have overdone the post-Sputnik acceleration of Ph.D. production, so that we are confronted with one of the most painful of economic phenomena, an increase in supply opposed by a shrinkage of demand."[207] He acknowledged:

> If all administrations attended properly to our policy pronouncements, there would be no need for this kind of pressure to obtain better conditions. But we know that there are autocratic and obtuse administrations, responsive only to pressure.[208]

Furthermore, state and federal legislation and statutes enabled collective bargaining, providing "another shield against oppression." Finally, national organizations could be more effective in this work than "purely home-grown negotiations" because of their "expertness and resources."[209]

Brown also suggested that the AAUP was gaining the experience it needed to understand collective bargaining. There were the successes at "Oakland, Rutgers, St. John's, and smaller institutions that are equally important testing grounds for us." There were also failures, most notably at the State University of New York, which exhibited recurring problems for the association.[210] State or federal agencies determined who would be in bargaining units, at times including "professional employees who were neither teachers nor researchers" while excluding departmental chairs. Although the AAUP had moved toward inclusion of professional employees as affiliate members, the affiliated membership would violate federal law and thus the Executive Committee and Committee N had decided to postpone action on that proposed change in membership criteria. Nevertheless Brown knew that some change would have to occur, and after apparently humorously suggesting that one attempt would be to change the organization's name to the "American Association of University Professionals," he reported the Committee N recommendation that faculty members and "professional appointees included in a collective bargaining unit" be eligible for AAUP membership in accordance with local practices. He acknowledged that the proposal "has no rationale except that it responds to what may be the realities of collective bargaining situations" and asked the members to contemplate whether it could be a principle for the association or should be rejected.[211]

Then Brown turned his attention to internal considerations. He noted the expense of collective bargaining and the fact that the REPI Statement opposed the agency shop because it required union membership. Regrettably that meant that bitter opponents who lost the certification election could choose not to pay union dues as well as those who simply did not want to pay dues. Committee N was trying to develop a policy that included "some form of conscientious objection." The Committee had asked Committee A members to examine the questions and received a "rather Delphic proposal" that stated that conscientious objection to an agency shop should be based on objection to any representation agreements. Brown pointed out, again apparently with humor (note the initials), that a professor could not claim exemption because his or her "conscience recoils from supporting representative A, that is AAUP, but would be soothed if the representative were N, that is NEA."[212]

Continuing his examination of internal matters, he reported that the chair of Committee Z had met with Committee N in January and Committee Z "feels some tremors of concern about the extent of cooperation it will receive in its salary survey if we take on more of an adversary position in bargaining situations."[213] More important, Committee A had already found at one institution that the administration, faced with an exclusive representative, would not allow an AAUP investigation of an alleged arbitrary dismissal. Brown quoted Garbarino, AFT college department head Richard Hixson, and President Hanley of the University of Scranton, who all wrote in one form or another that the AAUP could not function as "the cautious, sparing, judicious imposer of censure" *and* as "the energetic collective bargainer." He did not fully address that problem, noting rather that the continued goal of the AAUP would be to implement collective bargaining contracts that reflected the shared authority of the 1966 Statement. He reminded the members that the answers would likely come from the summer study.[214] And he highlighted the professional and material issues:

> We have only begun to think about the structures that will optimize both our preferred role as participants in the conduct of higher education and our needs to organize to protect our economic and related interests. New structures in academic life may be attended to by a restructuring of our Association.[215]

He added a personal aside:

> Unless we make our way very carefully, and at the same time boldly, through the currents of change, I think we are in considerable danger of losing our identity, both as a profession and as an organization uniquely representing that profession. As an organization, if we turn our back on the need for vigorous representation of many of our colleagues, we risk inanition if not extinction. But if, as an organization, we blindly accept the conventions and stereotypes of industrial bargaining, we are likely to become just another pressure group, motivated by little but self-interest of a very material sort.[216]

The solution was to merge new and traditional methods that "are appropriate to our professional aspirations" as much as possible since association members were "to a shocking extent prisoners of law" in collective bargaining efforts. He saw hope, concluding, "We can, I believe, forge better tools than the old implements of conventional collective bargaining."[217] His belief reflected his appointment as chair of Committee N; as Brown acknowledged later in an interview, he was chair in order "to give respectability to the collective bargaining wing."[218]

At the 1971 Annual Meeting, Davis announced the forthcoming retirement of William P. Fidler, who had for the past four years worked in the area of academic freedom and tenure. He planned to retire at the end of 1971.[219] A strong defender of the association's traditional means of advancing professors' interests was leaving the association at the time it was reconsidering those means.

The 1970–1971 Committee Z report was titled "At the Brink." The committee's longstanding despair was now seemingly justified, and it summarized the data, "The news this year, in brief, is worse!"[220] Both private and public institutions were facing fiscal crises, and the report stated, "Faculties bear with particular incidence the force of these general pressures." These pressures came about in part because of the nation's struggling economy. Despite President Nixon's attempts to correct the economy—such as instituting the Wage-Price Freeze in the late summer and fall of 1971—by the end of the 1971–1972 academic year, many colleges and universities were facing substantial financial problems. These problems were highlighted by reports by scholars such as Earl Cheit, in his *The New Depression in Higher Education,* who estimated that two-thirds of the colleges and universitites in the country were having serious financial problems. Committee Z was certain in its assessment of professors' economic status, indicating that "a troublesome decade is upon us." It suggested that hard choices would have to be made about salaries and teaching loads, teaching and research, and teaching undergraduate and graduate students.[221] It reviewed three possible modes of response. In the passive mode the faculty would tend "to acquiesce in the decisions made by other segments of the institution or by outside agencies." The second mode was that of shared authority. The third was collective bargaining, with its variations in "the nature of the issues bargained about, the nature of group representation, and the degree of militancy pursued." Committee Z recognized that choice of mode would be difficult and urged faculties to avoid choice by default. While the committee did not suggest to readers that "autocratic and obtuse administrations" might force faculties' choices, it did, however, state that faculties were "on the brink of crisis."[222] The Committee Z report accentuated the fact that professors were not getting more.

Ralph S. Brown reported in the September 1971 issue of the *Bulletin* that the National Labor Relations Board in April and May 1971 delivered rulings on part-time teachers and department chairs. The NLRB decided that part-time professors should be in bargaining units and that department chairs were supervisors, a decision that would likely serve as precedent for both the NLRB and state boards.[223] Despite a national AAUP petition and two chapter petitions asking the board to clarify these issues, the National Labor Relations Board was unwilling to accept the AAUP premise that "the existing standards and guides are quite inappropriate."[224] The developing federal position on faculty unionization was contrary to AAUP traditions and to the association's conception of who was a member of the academic profession.

Summary

The AFT and the NEA were forcing the union issue for the AAUP, and association members at the public and private institutions were developing collective bargaining. And at state and federal levels the governmental interpretations of who was a professor for the purpose of collecting bargaining and what was the professor's relationship to the college or university were moving the AAUP toward unknown terrain. Feeling apparently somewhat embattled, the AAUP leadership continued to pursue a cautious yet oddly determined development of collective bargaining. The association moved from proscription to prescription, and it sanctioned the faculty strike in restrictive terms. The rush of unionization in the early 1970s sustained the issue for the AAUP and led it to the self-study. The self-study, completed rapidly, would present the challenge of collective bargaining to the association leadership within the context of organizational, state, and federal conceptions and force a decision about the AAUP response to professionalism and unionization.

Chapter 5

TO HEDGE OUR BETS

The Uneasy Balance of Professionalism and Unionization, 1971 to 1976

The early and mid-1970s represented substantial shifts in the composition of the professoriate. By 1976 the professoriate was very different from its composition in 1946. Twenty-two percent of all professors taught at two-year institutions (compared to 7 percent in 1946) and 73 percent taught at public institutions (compared to 51 percent in 1946).[1] The professoriate was no longer simply at four-year institutions or evenly divided between public and private institutions. In addition the social composition of the professoriate began to change. In 1972, 23.6 percent of all instructional faculty were women; by 1976 the percentage had increased to 27.3 percent. Although comparative data on percentages of faculty of color are not available, one federal table indicates very few such professors in 1969: 3.7 percent of the professoriate was a person of color.[2]

The AFT, the NEA, and the AAUP in Collective Bargaining

The AFT organized many faculties during the early 1970s. By the end of 1972 it had agents representing thirty-seven faculties at two-year colleges, seven at four-year colleges, the nineteen faculties at City University of New York, and the faculties at the twenty-six four-year colleges and universities of the State University of New York. In addition an AFT local represented the teaching assistants at the University of Wisconsin–Madison.[3] By 1971 the NEA was completely involved in collective bargaining, forming a national, informal alliance with the American Federation of State, County, and Municipal Employees and the International Association of Fire Fighters, called the Coalition of Public Employees.[4] Although the NEA's operating structure did not resemble the decentralized operations of the AFT, staff assignments to local organizing efforts and strong state associations gave the NEA the capacity to respond to local needs.[5] By 1972 there were ninety-three NEA agents at two-year colleges and thirty-one at four-year institutions.[6]

Just as the scholarly literature on the AAUP, the AFT, and the NEA is sparse, so too is the literature comparing and contrasting the three organizations. In 1970 Martha A. Brown examined the three, concluding that the NEA was close to the AAUP in its view of the need for professional status for professors while the AFT was the militant organization.[7] Ladd and Lipset examined the three groups in 1973 using data from a 1969 Carnegie survey and a 1972 survey by the authors. AAUP membership was strongest at universities, NEA membership was strongest at four-year institutions, particularly those emphasizing teacher training, and the AFT membership was strongest at community colleges. Approximately 75 percent of the "major-college" professors belonging to one of the three organizations were in the AAUP. AAUP members tended to publish more scholarly articles and tended to be older than members of the AFT and NEA. In addition Ladd and Lipset cited two surveys at the local level (one in the Pennsylvania State College System and the other at Humboldt State College, California) that indicated similarities with their national data.[8] Finally, V. L. Lussier analyzed the relationships between the objectives of the three national associations and the collective bargaining contracts of their local agents. Lussier found a general lack of correlation between the national objectives and the local contracts in all three organizations.[9] In the early 1970s the AAUP faced consistent competition in organizing faculties, and as Ladd and Lipset indicate, it held a special place in the professoriate. The association was not certain, however, as to the specific role it should play in the academic profession, and the 1971 self-study helped the organization to specify policies and procedures.

The 1971 Self-Study: The Vigorous and Selective Development of Collective Bargaining

In October 1971 Bertram H. Davis sent a fifty-four-page confidential review of the summer study, written by the Executive Committee, to council members.[10] The Executive Committee had been unable to reach unanimity in response to the summer study after considering two structural models to accommodate collective bargaining. The internal departmental model had the support of six members including Ralph S. Brown and Davis. The other model was an external affiliate supported by AAUP President Sanford Kadish and two other members.[11]

The introduction to the working paper reviewed AAUP efforts in collective bargaining elections since 1966. It focused on membership changes, the costs of AAUP participation, the extent of AAUP involvement, and election results.[12] Overall, membership changes appeared to be negligible, and the report suggested that part of the membership problem might be unit determination since it raised the serious question of who constituted a faculty.[13] Generally the AAUP spent very little on individual elections although AAUP staff assistance in chapters' preparation and participation in collective bargaining elections ranged from light to heavy.[14] The introduction reported on AAUP successes and losses in thirteen instances. The AAUP succeeded in seven of those elections and lost in six, including the New Jersey State Colleges and SUNY votes. The association expected to be involved in upcoming elections at several individual institutions and in the Pennsylvania state system; included among the individual institutions were major state universities—Michigan State University and the Universities of Hawaii and Rhode Island. Furthermore expected elections at private institutions showed a shift from such schools as the Polytechnic Institute of Brooklyn and Pratt Institute to Temple University and the University of Detroit.[15]

The introduction offered no clear, specific results of AAUP involvement in collective bargaining elections. It did not disparage AAUP efforts in the area, often matching losses with "modest" or "still more modest" investments or with unit determinations that did not favor the AAUP membership.[16] The second section of the working paper in fact suggested that the AAUP still had the opportunity to implement its traditional policies through collective bargaining.

"Collective Bargaining as a Proposed Mode of Action" reviewed arguments opposing and favoring AAUP participation in bargaining. The opposition position included national and AAUP information, noting that nearly half of the professors included in the 1969 Carnegie survey responded that bargaining had no place on college and university campuses. It repeated the arguments that the association would lose its traditional values and did not have enough experience or personnel to be involved in bargaining. It added two recent arguments, that the AAUP would lose membership and could not finance bargaining activity. The report also stated that the AAUP had yet to win a contested election.[17] Proponents of association efforts at bargaining said that many of the opposing arguments rested on the assumption of the industrial model of unionization. They felt that the AAUP should be able to implement a "specialized bargaining model for higher education." Since the AFT and NEA were less zealous about academic freedom and tenure and shared authority, AAUP attempts to promote those goals at unionized campuses could be met with charges of illegal behavior. The association would face no such problem at campuses where its chapters served as exclusive representatives. Furthermore the survival of the AAUP was at issue, with a potential loss of membership as bargaining increased among faculties. There would be resentment among collective bargaining chapters if the association withdrew from the area and reversed its "gradually developed policy." Finally, the section returned to the argument that the AAUP's potential contribution to collective bargaining in higher education would be lost if the association chose to be on the sidelines.[18]

The third section of the paper reviewed the legal and organizational consequences of AAUP participation in collective bargaining. The Executive Committee agreed that the association needed either to pursue vigorously or to eschew collective bargaining. Only one Executive Committee member, Robert Webb, had voted against pursuing bargaining, so the assumption of the report was that the AAUP would "pursue collective bargaining vigorously."[19]

Much of the legal review suggested that the AAUP would have to answer questions about associate membership category and an appointed, rather than elected, treasurer and general secretary. It would also have to determine whether it wanted to maintain its 501(c)(3) IRS status or become a labor organization. The organizational review addressed budget considerations in terms of both fiscal resources and staff members. The first year annual budget was estimated at between $250,000 and $350,000 (a substantial increase over the current $100,000 to $150,000). Staffing the internal model would mean three staff members including an experienced director of collective bargaining and an attorney. Funding would come from the scheduled dues increase, cuts in other association activities, and shuffling staff assignments. The Executive Committee did not know if these shifts were possible and only offered them for consideration by the Washington office staff and the council.[20]

The organizational review then moved to consideration of the effects of an internal model. Under that form the AAUP would be subject to federal law, and the report acknowledged that those legal consequences were not to the association's benefit. Yet the internal model also seemed to offer the AAUP control over the results of its efforts in collective bargaining. In terms of AAUP principles, the proponents of the internal model wrote, "Pursuant to its constitutionally stated purposes and its traditions, our Association has a great interest in and, indeed, responsibility for which outcome of collective bargaining government comes to pass." They thought that collective bargaining should be an integral part of AAUP activities and not the "second-best solution" of an external affiliate.[21] Their summary continued a central argument of the past five years:

> All are agreed that we do not know what the future holds; and that we should try to hedge our bets while doing *something* in a firm and forceful way. This part of the Report, in conclusion, contends that the creation of a collective bargaining department now conveys a clear intention to see how far collective representation, guided from within the Association, can advance the goals of our Association. At the same time, it creates a base from which we can advance, or move back or laterally as circumstances require.[22]

They acknowledged that if the internal model did not work, the AAUP could eventually choose to change to the external affiliate. They argued that there was not enough AAUP collective bargaining activity to sustain an external affiliate and that an affiliate would not fulfill the potential of AAUP representation.[23]

The leaders advocating the external affiliate model presented four considerations. First, neither abandonment of collective bargaining nor organizational change into a labor union was currently desirable; collective bargaining *and* traditional AAUP activities were desirable. Second, "increasing tensions, conflicts, and pressures—both internal and external—mandate some sort of structural separation between these activities." Committees A and Z were likely to face problems in their work with unionized campuses, the former in view of exclusive representation, the latter in terms of cooperation with the salary survey. Relations with other groups (such as the AAC) would be "increasingly difficult and unlikely." Third, the AAUP would lose its identity as a professors' association as membership criteria changed and consequently the "profession would suffer a major loss." Finally, there was the difference between shared authority and collective bargaining's "polarity between employer and employee" with the "vigorous adversary assertion of self-interest on the part of both parties." The proponents of the external affiliate thought that the association's venture into collective bargaining should not only result in a model different from the industrial union one, but also in the explicit statement that there were separate professional and collective bargaining goals.[24]

The change would also occasion another major organizational problem. The external affiliate proponents argued that the association members were sharply divided on the issue of organizational involvement in collective bargaining. The external model provided an opportunity to retain members on both sides of the issue, albeit with some possible short-term losses due to the sharp change in policy.[25] The proponents of this model willingly acknowledged membership consequences of the pursuit of collective bargaining.

The working paper concluded with two dissenting reports, one by Robert Webb and the other by William Van Alstyne, chair of Committee A. Webb began by referring to the 1966 Statement by Robert Bierstedt and Fritz Machlup. He saw the AAUP as standing "for a high view of an academic *profession* and for a concept of the university as a community of scholars and not as a corporation that employs teachers." Van Alstyne wanted no change in the AAUP approach to collective bargaining. He anticipated a credibility problem in Committee A investigations as the AAUP became increasingly viewed as a self-interested union, membership loss among senior professors, and hostility on the part of other collective bargaining organizations.[26] His conclusion was sharply critical of the basic assumptions of the AAUP proponents of collective bargaining:

> First, my own impression is that most of our members are thoroughly unaware of the direct and extremely limited involvement of the AAUP in collective bargaining up to the present moment. Indeed, the very suggestion that we are already into it in some measure meets repeated expressions of surprise and puzzlement. Second, the statement is simply disingenuous. Members of the Council surely must recall how we have temporized from meeting to meeting, entertaining brief reports on the subject, feeling restless that sooner-or-later we would have to come to terms with the basic issue, but in the meantime simply feeling our way. We have never discussed the subject to the point of deliberating basic policy, and the "gradual development" merely over "the past several years" has been vague, desultory, and very much limited to in-house conversation and to *ad hoc* responses.[27]

Van Alstyne accurately summarized the post-1966 events but not those from 1964 to 1966, when the leaders struggled briefly yet bitterly with policy issues in collective bargaining.

The AAUP staff also responded to the Gorman report, and its members were split on the wisdom of pursuing collective bargaining. Alfred Sumberg sent a memorandum to council members urging the association to pursue vigorously collective bargaining. He asked if the AAUP could not "turn the talents of our profession towards the molding of collective bargaining into a unique form of academic self-government?"[28] In contrast Louis Joughin stated his opposition to collective bargaining efforts by the AAUP. In his memorandum to the council he argued that the association did not have enough money or staff expertise and recommended disengaging from bargaining.[29] Another staff member wrote a memorandum to Bertram H. Davis which he shared with the council, indicating vague support for collective bargaining.[30]

Bertram H. Davis sent to council members a memorandum signed by several staff members (including William P. Fidler) in which they stated that the best direction was not promoting collective bargaining but rather recognizing it as a means to advance AAUP policies and practices.[31] They cautioned the council that the Executive Committee suggestion of organizational economic benefits was not realistic given the competition and could jeopardize the current work of the association; the NEA reportedly had twenty-nine million dollars for collective bargaining efforts. Yet complete withdrawal from collective bargaining would be unfair to those chapters already involved; nor would withdrawal "satisfy the felt need of chapters willing and able to represent their faculties in collective bargaining." The staff members reminded the council that the AAUP image was not "the clenched fist or flexed bicep *[sic]* such as many faculty members consider desirable to confront board members and administrators who seem to them impervious to any argument but power." They were equally concerned about the pressure on the association's traditional methods and policies since no other organization was as committed to "advancing the 'standards, ideals, and welfare of the profession.'" Thus they thought a "receptive but not embracing approach . . . should help to mitigate the erosion of the Association's judicial position which a vigorous and affirmative engagement in collective bargaining seems to render inevitable." They were convinced that the judicial function was vital to the academic profession and that within collective bargaining the association had to push AAUP principles.[32]

Two Michigan Conference officers wrote to council members, stating "we must go into collective bargaining in a very big way and do it right, or withdraw from it and thereby ensure a drastic reduction in members, funds, and activities." They were convinced that in Michigan all public and some private institutions of higher education would soon unionize. They anticipated that if the association rejected collective bargaining, it would lose the Eastern Michigan and Wayne State Universities chapters and that the Oakland University faculty would very quickly choose another agent. They concluded by remarking that Walter Adams (the nominee for the AAUP presidency) shared their "view that the Association must move ahead in collective bargaining or else wither away."[33]

Committee N met about a month before the Fall 1971 Council Meeting, and its members unanimously opposed the external model of collective bargaining; all of them supported increasing association investment in bargaining.[34] Committee T members' preferences were just as clear, supporting further work on bargaining.[35] Committee A also considered collective bargaining just before the October Council Meeting, taking several votes to measure a number of ways of considering the issue. By a vote of 6 to 2 the committee members concluded that the AAUP should give advice to faculty members interested in collective bargaining, and by an 8 to 0 count they agreed that AAUP chapters already engaged in collective bargaining could continue to do so. By a 1 to 7 vote they rejected the proposal that the AAUP commit itself to collective bargaining. They summed up their feelings with an 8 to 0 vote that the role of the AAUP would depend on the legal and factual conditions of an institution; the association might advise and assist local AAUP leaders in forming a local association or by supporting another organization, but the AAUP neither nationally nor locally would "engage in collective bargaining." The general secretary would pass judgement on whether to support the local AAUP leaders and, if so, what type of support would be provided.[36] Thus Committees N and T felt that the internal model of AAUP collective bargaining was preferable while Committee A essentially opposed further association involvement in unionization.

The debate about the future of collective bargaining within the association involved not only an unusual amount of correspondence and preliminary votes but also, in contrast to the May 1966 decision, an extraordinary amount of time. For a full day the council considered the proposals and argued about which was most appropriate.[37] By this time council membership was substantially different from the council of May 1966. Only twelve members were at colleges or universities that traditionally had AAUP members; the remainder were at a range of institutions, from Alma College (Michigan) to Framingham State College (Massachusetts) to Queensborough Community College (New York).[38]

While the AAUP Archives available for viewing did not include a full transcript of the October 1971 Council Meeting, a partial transcription of remarks by Sanford Kadish suggests that the opposition tended to be uncertain rather than adamant. Overall Kadish favored the position suggested by Committee A because "the chances of gaining something substantial seem to me too small in view of the substantial risk of losing so much." The AAUP offered "a likely and valuable function in higher education, which could be carved out for the Association as it pulls out of collective bargaining." He said he was not dogmatic yet felt that ". . . you've got to come out somewhere on this, and this is the way I balance it after much soul-searching."[39] So Kadish supported the

Committee A proposal to withdraw both nationally and from the chapter locals. Yet he could not be certain, calling it "an awful bold step to rush to take, and I'm scared to death, I'm cold as I say it." He even noted that if the council decided that the Committee A proposal was too risky, he would understand.[40] A key opponent to AAUP involvement in collective bargaining was uncertain about his opposition.

The council members considered three alternative courses of action developed by a committee after the day of debate.[41] The next morning the committee presented the three alternatives to the council:

1. The Association will not, nationally or through its chapters, engage in collective bargaining (with an exception for chapters so engaged during 1971 and with assistance still permissible for chapters wishing to become engaged through other entities).
2. The Association will continue to provide advice and guidance to individual chapters which wish to become exclusive bargaining agent [sic] under the present "Policy on Representation of Economic and Professional Interests" (with national Association resources invested in these efforts not to be substantially in excess of present levels).
3. The Association will pursue collective bargaining as a major additional way of realizing the Association's goals in higher education, and will allocate such resources and staff as are necessary for the vigorous selective development of this activity beyond present levels.[42]

None of the alternatives proposed complete withdrawal from the effort. Council members began the consideration of the three alternatives with votes of preference. Thirteen voted for the first proposition, two for the second, and nineteen stated their preference for the third alternative. There was "some further discussion" followed by a motion to adopt the third proposal as the council's position. The motion carried on a vote of twenty-two to eleven. As with the 1966 council decision on the REI policy, the 1971 council decided to present a full examination of the supporting and opposing arguments in an ensuing issue of the *Bulletin*.[43]

The 1972 Annual Meeting Vote on Collective Bargaining

Usually the fall council meeting report was published in the following year's spring issue of the *Bulletin*. General Secretary Davis, however, reported the council's position on collective bargaining in the December 1971 *Bulletin*. His report detailed the council's consideration and action, another unusual step in the AAUP consideration of collective bargaining. He noted the extensive discussions, but his review of the council debate examined only the proponents' considerations. He acknowledged the restrictions of the position, including the fact that council members "were not calling upon the Association, even if it had the resources to do so, to furnish blanket support to all chapters which consider the possibility of gaining certification as the faculty's agent." The AAUP would pursue bargaining at an institution only if the chapter would probably attain representative status and association goals.[44] Davis evaluated the association's finances in terms of collective bargaining and suggested that as much as an additional $125,000 could be allocated to collective bargaining efforts if the AAUP succeeded in its request for optional dues payments 20 percent beyond the standard scale. He also reaffirmed the council and AAUP commitment to its traditions, suggesting collective bargaining would complement them. He urged all chapters and conferences to discuss the council's position and to submit their responses to him. He alerted readers to the fact that the March 1972 *Bulletin* would have a more thorough review of the debate and concluded that the members at the annual meeting would be asked to ratify the position on collective bargaining.[45]

The March 1972 review of the council position on collective bargaining rivaled the extensive documentation of the committee efforts in the 1915 development of the association's position on academic freedom and academic tenure, suggesting the extraordinary organizational shift inherent in the decision to pursue collective bargaining. It also paralleled the arguments presented in the 1966 article on the new policy statement on representation of economic interests.[46]

The review began with the council's position on collective bargaining. It then presented the development of collective bargaining policy as a successive set of efforts that began with Brown's article on the 1964 conference and the stated preference for "greater faculty participation in institutional government" to the increasingly supportive 1968 and 1969 statements. It briefly addressed three additional issues of policy—the agency shop, the strike, and unit determination—in each case with the suggestion that the association made an appropriate accommodation between traditional principles and the demands of current practice. The discussion of association involvement with bargaining agents ignored the 1966–1967 negotiations among the California State Colleges, examining instead AAUP activity with its chapters pursuing collective bargaining. The article suggested that collective bargaining agreements at

St. John's University (New York) and Oakland University achieved AAUP goals of including the 1940 and 1966 Statements.[47] The discussion of experience with bargaining agents also addressed the issue of association resources and suggested that expenditures apparently had the potential to decrease and perhaps even to become revenues.[48] As for membership, the article noted that as of yet the association did not have enough experience to predict the consequences of collective bargaining. The sense was that there had been "a few sharp gains and losses but, on the whole, membership figures have remained relatively stable."[49]

The second part of the article presented the arguments of opponents and proponents in the council debate, and the differences between adversarial relationships and shared authority received extended treatment. The article clarified that the REPI policy statement acknowledged that collective bargaining was likely only on certain campuses and the role of the agent was to promote the faculty senate. It appeared that association chapters had for the most part been able to achieve such a role.[50] Supporters of collective bargaining also offered a frank evaluation of the administration-faculty relations in higher education, indicating that adversarial relationships were evident to some extent on all campuses.[51]

Membership eligibility and unit determination raised the broader possibilities of the AAUP's becoming increasingly "subject to or affected by a number of federal and state provisions and their administrative implementation." There was no obvious solution, only the suggestion that risks might be minimal.[52] This section also established the potentially high cost of further development of collective bargaining. While some council members questioned the association's ability to finance bargaining activities, others argued that careful expenditures would not damage the traditional efforts of the association.[53]

The section concluded with a statement on the potential for AAUP success in bargaining, addressing bureaucratization and professionalism:

> Many faculty members expect collective bargaining arrangements to be adopted by more and more campuses, for different individual reasons, but with one overall reason: collective bargaining is seen as offering a rational and equitable means of distributing resources and of providing recourse for an aggrieved individual in an age when centers of authority and responsibility have become increasingly distant and impersonal, and increasingly unreachable through traditional academic channels.[54]

The commitment to professionalism, however, was not clear, and one traditional phrase of the association, "in the interests of higher education," is

absent from this conclusion. Distant centers of authority rather than professional responsibility now seemingly characterized higher education.

The third part of the article explicated the nature of the council's position
on collective bargaining. It noted that vigorous selective development required
staff officers' extensive evaluation of the likelihood of chapter success in an
election, based on conversations with chapter officers and other AAUP members.[55] Financing this vigorous and selective development required nearly doubling the 1971 expenditures on bargaining, from $120,000 to approximately
$220,000. The association expected to achieve the increase through mem-
bers' optional payments beyond the assessed dues and economies and cut-
backs in unnamed association activities that were not part of any "fundamental
programs."[56]

Finally, the council declared that without participation in collective bargaining, the victories that the association had won over the decades in its traditional areas of academic freedom, tenure, and nonrenewal of appointments
might well be lost. The AAUP had "the unique potential, indeed the responsibility, to achieve through its chapters a brand of collective bargaining conso-
nant with the best features of higher education." Only by participating would
the association be able to shape what occurred.[57]

The description and analysis of the council's position was followed by supporting and dissenting remarks. Carl Stevens presented supporting statements,
and Sanford Kadish, William Van Alstyne, and Robert Webb offered opposition. Stevens argued that whatever the association's organizational involvement
with unions, it would necessarily deal with them in its traditional development
of appropriate policies.[58] From the level of policy Stevens moved to chapters'
conduct of bargaining, suggesting,

> Experience has shown that faculty members frequently feel the
> need to get into collective bargaining in order to achieve (by re-
> sort to this legal route) *de facto* recognition—recognition, that is,
> of the rights of the faculty effectively to share in the making of
> those decisions which they regard as properly belonging to the do-
> main of their own professional responsibilities, interests, and com-
> petence.[59]

He recommended that faculties already having de facto recognition needed to
accept those faculties with little or no hope of achieving any recognition without the assistance of bargaining laws.[60]

Kadish, Van Alstyne, and Webb entitled their arguments "The Manifest
Unwisdom of the AAUP as a Collective Bargaining Agency: A Dissenting

View." They opened their dissent with a brief history of the AAUP's establishment and its early and continuous use of negotiation. Their hope was that the members at the annual meeting would reject the council proposal and choose the Committee A alternative of providing advice only to chapters wishing to pursue collective bargaining. They were deeply concerned that the association would not be able to inquire about academic freedom and tenure complaints where exclusive representatives were in place or were campaigning for election.[61] The final threat to historic functions was in association membership, with the likely inclusion of academic employees and the equally likely loss of members "in the senior and, frankly, 'academic' ranks."[62] Their conclusion was unequivocal:

> We cannot hope to have it both ways: to the extent that the AAUP succeeds as an academic association in maintaining its historic purpose to safeguard the overall integrity of higher education, it must fail in contested elections against competition by unions promising—and by being prepared to deliver—*more*. To the extent that the AAUP would "succeed" in converting itself into a tough-minded, hard-bargaining national labor union, however, it must inevitably fail in what it already does far better than anyone else is prepared or seemingly concerned to do.[63]

They were convinced that the loss of identity would mean that there would be no organization "to save the only values that make the material sacrifices of an academic profession worthwhile."[64]

The proposal for the AAUP to pursue vigorous selective development of collective bargaining generated a "spirited two-and-a-half-hour debate that no one really expected to change many minds" at the 1972 Annual Meeting. David Fellman voiced his objection to the argument that widespread collective bargaining among college and university faculties was inevitable, and Council Member C. Addison Hickman stated that he was opposed to the measure because of the possible harm to other AAUP programs. A delegate from West Chester State College (Pennsylvania) argued that the AAUP loss to the NEA in the fall 1971 certification election in the Pennsylvania State College system showed that the association probably could not handle collective bargaining.[65] Yet the spirited debate did not engage all of the opponents among the leadership. "So clear-cut was the prevailing sentiment here that several respected leaders of the association who disagreed with the majority view chose not to speak out at all," and one leader quoted anonymously said, "The results were a foregone conclusion."[66] There was very little sense of the caution of Donald J. Keck, the associate director of the NEA higher education division, who suggested that the AAUP was five to six years behind the NEA, which saw collective bargaining as power and not as "professional" negotiations. The members voted 373 to 54 to endorse the recommendation to pursue collective bargaining.[67]

The members then defeated a motion urging the Executive Committee and council to establish substantial increases in funding for collective bargaining but approved a motion urging the Executive Committee and council "to make the appropriate budgetary decisions to reflect the will of this convention on the issue of collective bargaining." The final action on representation at the annual meeting followed when Ralph S. Brown moved to amend the Constitution so that active membership included "Any professional appointee included in a collective representation unit with the faculty," which the members approved.[68] In order to help finance the new policy and the ongoing expansion of activities, the council and the members at the annual meeting in 1972 approved an increase of dues at the top end of the salary scale for professors. Previously those professors earning over $12,000 annually paid dues of $30; the new dues schedule added another tier for professors earning annual salaries over $15,000 whose dues would be $36.[69] As Kadish, Van Alstyne, and Webb had noted, these AAUP members were least likely to be supportive of AAUP efforts in collective bargaining.

Other areas of association activity seemed to confirm the division of opinion about association involvement in unionization. On the one hand the 1972 Committee Z report indicated that "we are forced, *for the fourth year in a row,* to report that the change in the economic status of the profession is worse than it was a year ago."[70] The academic year had not been a good one for the professoriate, beginning with President Nixon's wage and price freeze and ending with the poorest performance in the economic status since the annual survey began in 1957, and further decline appeared likely.[71] Professional approaches to increasing salaries were not having the desired effect. On the other hand Committee T members decided that collective bargaining questions included "NLRB's proclivity for reaching terribly strange and troublesome decisions" on unit determination and representation usurping governance prerogatives.[72]

Yet Committee T reflected general AAUP concern about representation of professors' interests in its work on the issue of financial exigency. Members assisted the Joint Committee on Financial Exigency in the development of procedures for colleges and universities to use, which Walter Adams stated had "already served to assist numerous institutions" facing financial difficulties.[73]

Other Committee T activities included the development of its statement, "The Role of the Faculty in Budgetary and Salary Matters," and its report, "Faculty Participation in the Selection and Retention of Administrators." Both the council at its May 1972 meeting and the members at the 1972 Annual Meeting approved the statement on budgetary and salary matters. It offered specific recommendations, beginning with a proposed "elected representative committee" to participate in decisions on "the overall allocation of institutional resources and the proportion to be devoted directly to the academic program." In the case of financial exigency the report recommended faculty participation in decisions at all levels, from the department to the entire institution. Furthermore those "whose work stands to be adversely affected should have full opportunity to be heard," suggesting individual professors' participation at the critical time when individual dismissals would occur. In the matter of faculty salaries, the report suggested that departments should recommend salaries.[74] The report on selection and retention of administrators recommended joint determination in both activities.[75] Committee T activity was continuing to specify areas of direct representation of professors' interests in their working conditions, beyond the activities of collective bargaining units.

In contrast to the dismal outlook of the Committee Z report and the ambiguity of the Committee T report, Ralph S. Brown presented a strong image of AAUP collective bargaining efforts in his 1972 Committee N report, titled "Increasing Vigor, Increasing Success." His report on representation elections of the past year was very encouraging, noting that NEA affiliates had won two elections, the AFT three, and the AAUP six; four elections were undecided at the time of his report because of challenged ballots. The AAUP seemed to be keeping abreast in "the fantastically fast-moving parade of events in collective bargaining in higher education" as it watched the NLRB and the merger of the NEA and AFT affiliates at CUNY. In Brown's eyes, "Clearly the vigor of local Association activity did not wait upon the action of the 1972 Annual Meeting."[76] He responded to a 1971 Annual Meeting charge concerning an inquiry into the SUNY and CUNY elections with aplomb: "One is tempted to conclude, and not flippantly, that we did not win because we did not get enough votes. This should now occur less often."[77] The chair of Committee N was confident about the association's future work in representation.

By June 1972 the association was actively pursuing collective bargaining, in policy and tactics, at the local and national levels. The transition was not yet complete, however, as the activities of the next four years made organizationally explicit the balance between traditional principles and exclusive representation.

AAUP Union Successes

Initially the movement into collective bargaining had more successes than failures. The association won bargaining elections while administrations continued to cooperate with Committees A and Z. Although Committee T struggled with issues of faculty participation in governance in the role of department chair, it also increased the expectation that professors participate in college and university government.

At the October 1972 Council Meeting, Bertram H. Davis announced the appointment of a new director of the association's collective bargaining program. He also noted that the AAC Board of Directors had suggested during the summer that because the AAUP was now involved in collective bargaining, AAC member institutions should give Committee Z only the information they wanted published. Yet the responses did not appear to be negative; Committee Z sent two thousand questionnaires in September, and by the October Council Meeting only eight administrations had indicated that they would not participate because of the May 1972 decision on bargaining.[78] The Committee A experience was only mildly negative. William Van Alstyne, reporting as chair, indicated too that there had been "no overall setback" resulting from the bargaining posture although there were occasions when administrations raised the issue of compatibility between the AAUP as an investigator and as a chapter seeking representation rights.[79]

In the December 1972 issue of the *Bulletin* the association published the "Statement on Collective Bargaining," which superseded the REPI Statement. This Committee N revision deleted the 1969 emphases on shared authority and enabling legislation while adding a far more supportive statement on AAUP involvement in representation.[80] The support for collective bargaining was similar to earlier statements in 1971 and 1972 by the association leadership and in the annual meeting proposal, combining traditional goals with bargaining:

> The longstanding programs of the Association are means to achieve a number of basic ends at colleges and universities: the enhancement of academic freedom and tenure; of due process; of sound academic government. Collective bargaining, properly used, is essentially another means to achieve these ends, and at the same time to strengthen the influence of the faculty in the distribution of an institution's economic resources.[81]

The association now stated in specific terms how its traditional programs could find expression in collective bargaining. Furthermore it had dropped the euphemism, representation of economic interests, now calling its efforts "collective bargaining." At the 1973 Annual Meeting, members approved the Statement on Collective Bargaining as well as some changes in the Constitution regarding constitutional officers in order to meet the requirements of federal law.[82] In policy and constitution the AAUP was organizationally adjusted to unionization.

By the spring of 1973 it appeared that the AAUP was moving in an appropriate direction. Carl Stevens reported for Committee N at the Spring 1973 Council Meeting and indicated that since the 1972 Annual Meeting the association had entered seventeen elections and won ten of them. AAUP chapters were bargaining agents at "eighteen four-year institutions and three two-year institutions, with an aggregate faculty in these bargaining units of over 8,000."[83] As far as Stevens was concerned, AAUP support for bargaining "had not been allowed to drain the Association's resources to the point of imperiling the effective functioning of its other ongoing programs."[84]

The national leaders were also investigating coordinated union efforts at the national level. General Secretary Davis told the council at its October 1973 meeting that he planned to "attend as an observer" the board meeting of the Coalition of American Public Employees in the coming month. CAPE membership included the American Federation of State, County, and Municipal Employees of the AFL-CIO, the International Association of Fire Fighters of the AFL-CIO, the National Education Association, and the National Association of Internal Revenue Employees.[85] Even as an observer, Davis by being present at that meeting represents a contrast to annual meeting decisions to revise or ignore Israel Kugler's requests for merger with the union.

Even given the minimally negative situation for Committee A, William Van Alstyne remained uncomfortable with the association's bargaining policy. At the October 1972 Council Meeting he moved for the establishment of a study group to examine the possible reorganization of Committee A and other standing committees. The council responded with unanimous approval.[86] Association leaders did not want to lose the traditional practices of the organization.

Reflections and Costs

Ralph S. Brown presented the recommendations of the Study Group on Association Structure at the October 1973 Council Meeting. The report suggested further study of AAUP members: "It would be helpful to know why members join the Association, continue as members, or drop out; to know which groups want to emphasize academic freedom protection, which want collective bargaining, or which would retain the current balance."[87] It also rec-ommended against transferring any AAUP "major activities to a new entity that would be expected to gain and retain a 501(c)(3) tax status."[88] Whatever the concern about members and unionism, the association came again to the conclusion that it would be best served by containing all activities within one organization.

The study group suggested that Committee A "review its work to see if it can make a better separation between issues of academic freedom, of tenure, of academic civil liberties, and of economic abuses that may have implications for freedom and tenure." Committee A also needed to evaluate the increasing application of censure and the possible consequent loss of credibility. One recommendation was to look for sanctions less severe than censure. The Study Group advised Committee N to maintain the distinctive AAUP approach in collective bargaining activities. It cautioned Committee N, "If the quality of our representation is no different from that of others, there is little reason for our seeking representative status."[89] Despite this apparent clarification of as-sociation activities in comparison to other organizations, the council was will-ing to allow chapter affiliation with other unions. Carl Stevens asked for approval of chapter affiliation with other organizations at the council's April 1974 meeting, and the council approved the procedure.[90]

In organizational procedures the association was slowly adjusting to its commitment to collective bargaining. Yet in the area of organizational finances it was not adjusting. The AAUP rapidly increased its commitment to collec-tive bargaining after the 1972 approval of vigorous selective development. The association spent about 12.5 percent of its 1971 budget (the first year for which complete program expenditures were published in the *Bulletin*) on col-lective bargaining and 29.8 percent on academic freedom and related areas. By 1974 it was spending a greater proportion of its budget on bargaining, 25.4 percent, than on academic freedom, 22.9 percent.[91] These changes indicate substantial shifts in the allocation of the organization's resources for the sup-port of programs.

Although expenditures were going up, revenue was not. In 1972 the asso-ciation experienced a precipitous decline in membership as 18,181 active members (21 percent) did not pay dues for the upcoming year, 1973. Since over 9,000 professors joined the AAUP in 1973, the net decline of active members was about 9,000.[92] Carl Stevens addressed the membership issue at the Spring 1973 Council Meeting, stating that there was "no unequivocal an-swer to the impact of collective bargaining on AAUP membership, since only short-run evidence" was thus far available and other issues could be affecting membership.[93] Despite his comments there were some membership changes directly related to collective bargaining. At the time of the 1972 approval the association had ten chapters serving as bargaining agents; by the 1974 Annual Meeting there were twenty-seven chapters representing their faculties. Twenty-four of those twenty-seven were at public or private four-year colleges or universities; the association was succeeding in its further development of collective bargaining at the institutional level.[94] Despite the institutional successes the AAUP lost some members because of collective bargaining. From January 1971 to January 1974, the AAUP lost 2,532 members at those institutions where faculties and academic employees had selected other organizations as their exclusive representatives and gained 1,938 new members at colleges and universities where association chapters had been selected as representatives, a net loss of 594 members.[95] As for members not engaged in collective bargaining, General Secretary Davis stated in his 1973 report that of the few members who indicated why they resigned or did not renew their membership, "a fairly large number have given that reason [opposition to collective bargaining] for their withdrawals."[96]

The decline in membership presented a major problem to the AAUP. The association could not fund collective bargaining as a "major additional way of realizing the Association's goals" based on the dues increase for 1973. AAUP income from dues in 1971 was just over $1,500,000, in 1973 it was approximately $1,750,000, and in 1974 it decreased slightly to $1,708,128.[97] Collective bargaining activities, however, became more costly, from approximately $197,000 in 1971 to $475,400 in 1974. Yet the increase in dues income from the same period was $205,190.[98] The dues increase was not completely funding further development of bargaining because of the membership decline. Collective bargaining was not a major additional method (as suggested in the 1971 council statement of approval) but rather a displacement of other activities in terms of association expenditures.

The report on selective development had suggested cutting unnamed association activities; the Committee T survey became one of those cuts in the spring of 1973.[99] Although traditional programs were cut, the AAUP leaders continued to pursue collective bargaining. Carl Stevens reported as chair of Committee N to the council at the October 1973 meeting, focusing on association successes. They included elections' results, staff members' involvement in collective bargaining, and the development of the "AAUP Primer on Collective Bargaining in Higher Education."[100] Yet Stevens was bothered by the fact that the committee was experiencing undue stringency, and he told the council that chapters needed more assistance than the budget allowed.[101]

Council members proceeded to discuss the possible expansion of vigorous, selective development and of the number of staff to support bargaining efforts, as well as increasing the Committee N budget. Stevens agreed to raise the issue of resources at the next meeting of the committee.[102] The Spring 1974 Council Meeting focused on how much to spend on collective bargaining. Carl Stevens asked the council for another $20,000 to support a collective bargaining chapter caucus and another staff member. As in the case of staffing for collective bargaining, despite the association's fiscal problems, the council voted to increase funding for collective bargaining although it only committed $5,000 dollars to the program.[103]

It became increasingly clear, however, that collective bargaining would not serve as the means to increase membership and revenue. Donald Cameron (speech communication, California State University, Northridge) reported as chair of Committee F at the 1974 Annual Meeting. He indicated that the association continued to suffer membership losses "at a rate which, unless stopped and reversed, will force severe limitations in the services that can be offered."[104] Membership declined in forty-eight of the states; only Delaware and Rhode Island showed increases, and the only institutions with increases were those where professors could deduct their membership fee from their paychecks and at institutions where the AAUP represented the faculty in collective bargaining.[105] Committee F and the association had no idea as to whether or not any of their membership recruitment techniques were effective. Committee members intended to review and research those procedures in the next several months and "would seek the counsel of experts in American higher education."[106] Cameron did not mention expanded bargaining activity as a source of potential members.

Throughout 1973 and 1974 Committee F and the association attempted to address the membership problem, approving an optional increase in dues as well as seeking ways to change membership criteria and changing the membership fiscal year.[107] Still, membership and membership dues income continued to fall. Although the *AAUP Bulletin* does not indicate the characteristics of the membership loss, and AAUP documents on membership were not available for review, a later Committee A analysis of the problem for a somewhat comparable period suggests that much of the loss occurred among professors at two groups of institutions. Matthew Finkin, the chair of Committee A in 1984, reported that AAUP membership at 30 research universities (none of which had bargaining units) declined by 22 percent from 1965 to 1975. Membership at twenty-nine selective private colleges also experienced a decline in a somewhat longer time period, 1960 to 1975, of 4.3 percent.[108] Two important sources of AAUP leaders, the elite universities and colleges, were in fact becoming a declining resource.

The organizational consequences of the AAUP implementation of collective bargaining were beginning to be clear by 1974. Although the association suffered membership and revenue losses, it would further its efforts in bargaining. Successes in elections and intransigent administrations both seemed to confirm the wisdom of selective vigorous development. Yet it was still unclear what the AAUP would be able to do in either professional or union activities, and the 1974 presidential election highlighted that challenge.

Leadership Changes in the AAUP, 1974

Prior to 1974 there had been only one contested presidential election in the AAUP. In 1936 the members at the annual meeting elected A. J. Carlson in an unprecedented nomination and ballot from the floor because the nominated candidate was a dean at Cornell University and therefore an administrator.[109] In 1973, however, the Nominating Committee report differed from all of its predecessors in that the committee selected, in accordance with the instructions from the members at the 1973 Annual Meeting, two candidates for each of the national offices (the presidency and vice-presidencies).[110]

The Nominating Committee presented two presidential nominees, Carl Stevens and Marx Wartofsky. Their backgrounds did not reflect traditional association activities. Stevens had served as a member and as chair of Committee N; he was also a member of the American Arbitration Association. Wartofsky's national AAUP experience was as a member of Committee D (1964–1967), the council (1970–1973), the Annual Meeting Resolutions Committee (1972, and chair in 1973), and chair of the Special Council Committee on Discrimination since 1973. Only Carl Stevens had any Committee A experience, having served as a member of an investigating committee in 1969.[111] Neither of the candidates had served on Committee T or Z.

In the winter of 1974 William Van Alstyne decided to enter the race, offering as the simple reason, "I think I can do a better job." While Van Alstyne stated he was not opposed to Stevens and Wartofsky, he made clear in some comments to the *Chronicle of Higher Education* that he wanted to unify the AAUP, now divided by the 1972 decision, and to reverse the recent membership decline. He was cautious about further organizational changes, indicating, "I fear that, in an effort to appear effective to people on the outside, we will generate spasms of innovation that are not well-considered."[112]

Wartofksy wanted an AAUP that made "even greater use of collective bargaining" and had "stronger state and local organizations."[113] He told the *Chronicle of Higher Education:*

> "The illusions of formal participation in decision-making, of the benign paternalism of administrations, and of sustained, even penurious, job security are fast being eroded by the effects of stringency . . . . The AAUP is not geared up for the present crisis."[114]

Carl Stevens preferred to occupy a position between Van Alstyne and Wartofsky. Although more of an advocate for collective bargaining than Van Alstyne, Stevens distanced himself from Wartofsky's view of the AAUP. He indicated, "Marx believes that the association can have an impact on the environment in which institutions of higher education operate." Stevens, however, did not "happen to believe that."[115]

William Van Alstyne won the 1974 presidential election, securing 7,084 votes to 4,832 for Stevens and 4,780 for Wartofsky.[116] Although the collective bargaining advocates received more votes than Van Alstyne, the three-candidate race gave Van Alstyne the victory. The results of the split race ensured continued voice and leadership for professionalism in the AAUP.

The reception of Walter Adams's presidential address at the 1974 Annual Meeting also reflected members' concern about AAUP traditions. His comments included discussion about the need for professors to become involved in political affairs in order to protect their interests.[117] For the members at the meeting, however, it was Adams's "defense of the tenure system, not his call for action, that was interrupted repeatedly by applause."[118] Adams also admitted failure although in a sarcastic tone, "Indeed, I must confess that two years ago—before I won election as the only candidate in a South Vietnam style referendum—things were going reasonably well. Now they are going badly, and I come before you without a record of success or even modest accomplishment."[119] Yet he placed blame on the environment, making no mention of the membership losses, deficits, and internal struggles the AAUP was experiencing.[120] He concluded:

> So now, as I leave you to your new President and such militancy as you can muster, let me close with the hope that in the battles which lie ahead you will not fall victim to confusion, intimidation, or division. You are heirs of a great tradition which holds that happiness is the fruit of freedom, and freedom the fruit of courage.[121]

He left a blunt and awkward challenge for the association, given the 1974 presidential election.

The presidency was not the only AAUP leadership position to experience change. Bertram H. Davis announced his resignation in the fall of 1973.[122] He gave his final report as general secretary at the 1974 Annual Meeting, offering his reflections on the past decade of association activity. Davis did not think, however, that the collective bargaining decision was "a naive and thus ill-fated attempt to have the best of two conflicting worlds."[123] Instead he viewed the current results as encouraging:

> If we have not had the best of both worlds, we have nonetheless conducted a professional program no less effective than in earlier years, and, particularly since the 1972 decision, we have moved steadily towards a leading position in higher education collective bargaining. And we have had considerable success in keeping these two worlds—the professional and the union—from opposing each other.[124]

He argued that the association had been able to overcome some of the earlier rigid labor board decisions, convincing those boards of the unique characteristics of the academic world. He also drew attention to the fact that other bargaining organizations were beginning to emphasize traditional AAUP principles.[125]

As for association efforts in traditional areas, he pointed first to the continuing success of the Committee Z survey.[126] He then moved to the issue of academic freedom and tenure, noting the association's work in resolving ninety-two cases since April 1973. Given the variety of institutions involved—public and private institutions, community colleges, medical colleges, a technical institute, a seminary, and a music conservatory—Davis concluded that the AAUP could influence any college or university. In the fifteen cases involving nontenured faculty members, all of the professors received tenure or appropriate settlements. Tenure was an especially important issue, especially as institutions attempted to impose tenure quotas or declare financial exigency. Four institutions attempted to use financial reasons to dismiss a total of 216 faculty members, and in all four cases the association's influence caused the notices of dismissal to be withdrawn. There was no question in Davis's mind that there was "no diminution of our role as a professional association, no blurring of our fundamental objective 'to advance the standards, ideals, and welfare of the profession.'"[127] Additionally the AAUP continued to publicize the redress it achieved for unjustly dismissed professors.

Davis concluded his address in a far different tone from that of Adams's comments. Rather than militancy and expediency, he asked the members to take the professional path:

> In the midst of the cynicism which seems to pervade so much of modern life, perhaps there is no greater distinction than to hold to principles and policies which are at once a check to abuses of power—including our own—and a guide to professional fulfillment. This has always been the distinction of our Association, and I believe that it remains its distinction today.[128]

Davis encouraged the association to maintain the delicate balance he had typically tried to effect between the expediency of storming the citadels and the implementation of the professional traditions of the AAUP.

In September 1974 the association announced the appointment of Joseph Duffey, who had a background considerably different from that of his predecessors, as the new general secretary. Duffey had some academic experience, most recently as a 1971 fellow of the John Kennedy School of Government and Institute of Politics at Harvard University. Most of his experience, however, was in politics. He had been very involved in the civil rights movement during the 1960s, in 1969 "he became the youngest national Chairman of Americans for Democratic Action," and in 1970 he ran in Connecticut for the U.S. Senate. In contrast Davis had continued his professorial interests even while general secretary, having written books on eighteenth-century literature during that time.[129] President Van Alstyne was quite aware of the differences between Davis and Duffey and made a point of Duffey's fit to the American Association of University Professors:

> Yet it is also interesting (and at once reassuring) that the recommendations commending Dr. Duffey for this position with the AAUP came most substantially from established scholars and, indeed, from the heads of other professional educational associations with whom we work cooperatively to bring to bear the Association's influence on federal policies.[130]

Whatever the reassurances, the AAUP appeared to be taking a different step in its executive leadership.

General Secretary Duffey quickly made clear to AAUP members that he supported association efforts in collective bargaining. In the December 1974 *Bulletin* he presented an historical analogy based on the Great Depression and the AAUP publication of *Depression, Recovery and Higher Education*. Duffey suggested that Professor Paul Douglas's 1938 call for "more energized and humane collective action" exemplified the "great need of the profession" in the 1970s.[131] Duffey stated that the AAUP was responding to that need in three areas. First, it sought to shape federal and state legislative activity. Second, it was formulating the principles and procedures for academic freedom and tenure, due process, and government. Finally, it was participating in collective bargaining, and Duffey maintained the theme of the AAUP as uniquely able to pursue faculty collective bargaining:

> We can be justly proud of the collective bargaining contracts ne-gotiated by our chapters at major colleges and universities. Our purpose is to shape the evolution of the new form of collective ac-tion so that it serves the best purposes of higher education.[132]

Yet his comments suffered from some exaggeration. As V. L. Lussier demon-strated, there was very little difference among the contracts of the three pre-dominant collective bargaining organizations in the early 1970s. Furthermore the AAUP chapters with collective bargaining contracts included only one in-stitution validly described as "major," that being Rutgers University.

On the one hand the AAUP had a president with decided interests in the traditional, professional interests of the association. On the other hand it had selected a general secretary with specific interests in collective bargaining. As new leadership characteristics began to emerge, so too did new membership characteristics.

New Voices in the Association

The collective bargaining decision also engaged new voices within the associa-tion, as well as new forms of expression. Chapters engaged in collective bar-gaining began to organize within the association in 1973, forming an informal caucus.[133] According to Ralph S. Brown it "just evolved following in the wake of the Assemblies," developing "on its own because people thought quite prop-erly Committee N wasn't activist enough."[134] The caucus received early atten-tion from national leadership, as Staff Associate Richard Spector sent "a series of memoranda" in 1973 and 1974 to its members concerning chapters' con-tracts.[135]

Women began to receive specific attention in the AAUP in the early 1970s. Alice S. Rossi (sociology, Goucher College) reported for Committee W in 1973. She noted important gains for women in the association, such as the council and annual meeting decisions to omit the generic use of "he" and "man" from AAUP policy documents. She also saw the need for the association to attend to important concerns for women in collective bargaining contracts.[136] One example of the possible advantages of collective bargaining for women occurred at an AAUP chapter serving as a union representative.

In the December 1973 *Bulletin* Georgina M. Smith described "the successful use of collective bargaining to remedy pay inequities against women professors at Rutgers University."[137] In fact Smith was enthusiastic about the potential of bargaining:

> With the new-found unity and determination now visible among women on and off campus, it is likely that faculty women will increasingly perceive the value of organization in the collective bargaining area as in all other political and social areas, and that bargaining agents will increasingly recognize their moral and legal obligation to represent the interests of their women members. Both developments, I hope, will see AAUP playing a major role.[138]

The association had found a point of particular application for new principles of representation, the equitable treatment of women. Furthermore it found that application at the Rutgers University chapter, which the AAUP leadership had noted as a model for collective bargaining.

The Committee Z report of 1974 was direct in its evaluation of the economic difficulties for all professors during the past year. Increases in compensation were actually larger than in recent years, but inflation had negated those increases.[139] More specifically the report noted the committee's work toward developing analyses of the differences between compensation for women and men in the professoriate. As directed by members at the 1973 Annual Meeting, committee members and staff members developed surveys to collect the appropriate data, and the committee hoped to "cast light on the status of special groups that may have suffered from inequities, particularly blacks and women."[140]

During the council and annual meetings in the spring of 1974 the association established a new award and a new fund which reflected changes in the professoriate and the AAUP. The widower and children of Beatrice Konheim, a second vice-president of the association who died in the fall of 1973, established a generous award for an AAUP chapter (or a state conference) for "distinctive achievement in advancing the Association's objectives in academic freedom, student rights and freedoms, the status of academic women, the elimination of discrimination against minorities, or the establishment of equal opportunity for members of college and university faculties."[141] The association now recognized the specific efforts of women and minorities.

The 1974 Committee Z report was also the first to examine faculties at predominantly black institutions on a separate basis. There was no clear pattern of compensation, with considerable differences between institutions that granted bachelor's degrees and graduate degrees; public and private institutions also exhibited differences.[142] Despite the lack of pattern for succinct analysis, the committee had taken a step forward in addressing egalitarian issues in economic status. The association also addressed historically black colleges and universities, forming Committee L on Predominantly Black Institutions in 1973. Donald Pierce (mathematics, Lincoln University, Pennsylvania) reported for the committee at the 1974 Annual Meeting.[143] He reviewed the development of formal AAUP organizational interest in predominantly black institutions from the 1969 inception of the Special Project for Developing Institutions to the eventual formation of Committee L. In order to gain a sense of how the AAUP might assist faculty members at predominantly black institutions, the committee organized a regional conference in Atlanta, Georgia. Professors at the conference expressed concern that recent desegregation requirements might dissipate the opportunities for professors and students that predominantly black institutions provided.[144] The committee also distributed a questionnaire at the conference, and the responses suggested that

> . . . faculty members feel that the AAUP is *becoming* more concerned with their individual professional welfare and with the welfare of their institutions. Faculty members indicated that collective bargaining could be a suitable way to provide more effective faculty participation in institutional affairs and improve academic governance within their colleges.[145]

Following his report, Pierce moved that the association provide continued support for the committee, and the members at the annual meeting approved the motion.[146] The AAUP was advancing the interests of a group relatively new to its ranks. That advancement was expressly linked to association involvement in collective bargaining.

In 1975 the council approved an expansion of the definition of academic freedom and discrimination in response to a proposal by the New Jersey Conference, and the members at the annual meeting concurred, passing a motion:

> The Association is committed to use its procedures and take measures, including censure, against colleges and universities practicing

any sort of discrimination contrary to AAUP policy, including discrimination on the basis of age, sex, physical handicap, race, color, religion, national origin, or marital status.[147]

Even the definition of academic freedom was taking a new face, reflecting concerns about discrimination.

At the same time members at two-year colleges reaffirmed the link between their activities and AAUP activities. Clay C. Shepard (speech, Central Oregon Community College), chair of Committee V on Junior and Community Colleges, spoke to the members at the 1975 Annual Meeting. Committee V encouraged the national association to "augment its collective bargaining capabilities" and state conferences to establish committees on two-year colleges. He presented observations on the tensions of the two-year institution, in that its close community ties could "imperil the institution's independence and academic freedom." Finally, he indicated that collective bargaining agreements at two-year colleges "must safeguard important Association principles."[148]

Groups previously underrepresented in association affairs were now receiving specific attention. To a degree, the exclusive nature of the AAUP was lessening.

Austerity and Optimism in the AAUP, 1974 to 1976

Militancy among students and professors had declined during the early 1970s. By 1975 public response to professors' militancy proved to be strong and typically negative, and professors were defending themselves to the public and questioning themselves privately.[149] Professors were also on the defensive on fiscal matters as their compensation after 1972–1973 tumbled in comparison to previous years and colleges and universities declared financial exigencies.[150] These conditions had a considerable impact on the AAUP.

In 1974 Committees A and T continued their long-term processes of specifying procedures of due process. The financial exigencies declared by colleges and universities led both committees to detailed responses. The 1940 Statement recognized that an institution could terminate a professor's appointment because of "a demonstrably *bona fide* financial exigency," and the Recommended Institutional Regulations added acceptable terminations because of program or department discontinuations "not mandated by financial exigency" and because of medical reasons.[151] Committee A prepared a revision of part of the "Recommended Institutional Regulations" approved for publication by the committee and the council in order to provide more specific recommendations for institutional practices.[152] The revision included the expectation that faculty committees would serve as bodies for appeal of the termination.[153] During 1974 and 1975 the committee reviewed Regulation 4 and the comments it received from association members and in October 1975 approved publication of its revision.[154] The revised version was far more specific than its predecessor, the former approximately two pages long in the *Bulletin,* the latter approximately a half-page in length.[155]

Committee T clarified the 1966 Statement's comments on appointment and retention of administrators. The December 1974 publication of the clarification emphasized that faculty participation in the selection of the president and academic deans was essential and that there should be significant involvement of the faculty when any principal administrative officers were to be dismissed. The council adopted this statement at its fall 1974 meeting.[156] Both Committee A and T continued to specify the practices and due process of their broad principles, offering additional technical, bureaucratic, specificity to association professional ideals.

Not only colleges and universities experienced financial problems during the middle of the 1970s. The AAUP's fiscal distress became most apparent in 1974 and 1975. President Van Alstyne announced to the council at its November 1974 meeting that the association should be optimistic despite its "austerity budget." He congratulated the chapters, conferences, and Washington office staff members for halting the two-year decline in membership, noted success in representation, and highlighted the association's effective work in the Bloomfield College case in response to the problems of financial exigency.[157] Nevertheless the association's financial situation was a primary issue for the council. Secretary-Treasurer Richard P. Adams reported that "many worthy activities have been slashed, some ruthlessly." Those activities were far-ranging, from the reduction of grants to conferences to the reduction of the size of the *Bulletin* to subleasing the association's conference room and adjacent offices.[158]

Some council members raised objections to the fact that collective bargaining efforts were not self-sustaining, but others argued that AAUP membership had increased by 78 percent at chapters with collective bargaining status and had declined by 43 percent at those where other organizations were the bargaining agents. Carl Stevens reported to the council that the level of bargaining continued and that the "agency shop and strike situations" were the most pressing issues. He also anticipated that although bargaining's impact on academic government appeared to be mostly favorable, it was time for Committees A, T, and Z to examine the situation.[159] When the council discussed the questions of funds for Committee Z for a survey of female professors' salaries and for Committee N activity, it concluded that "these items reflected policy decisions by the Association's Annual Meeting."[160] Neither Committee Z nor Committee N funds were to be reduced despite the austere budget.

President Van Alstyne and General Secretary Duffey presented encouraging reports at the June 1975 Council Meeting, noting that membership decline had apparently halted, 1974–1975 participation in the Committee Z survey was again greater than in previous years, and Committee Z had accomplished the Committee W request to include data on women faculty in the compensation survey. They also reported that the recent trend of increases in the number of censured institutions had halted and the staff had successfully mediated two-thirds of the academic freedom cases. Collective bargaining activities were succeeding too, as faculties recently elected AAUP exclusive representatives at Boston University, Western Michigan and Northern Michigan Universities, Union College, and the Universities of Hawaii and Washington.[161] They offered, however, sobering financial news: "While the Association has managed significant economies in its administrative expenditures, unanticipated demands in the collective bargaining area will require a deficit budget for the year rather the no-deficit budget authorized by the Council at its last meeting."[162] Although Van Alstyne and Duffey voiced optimism about the association's status including the vigorous, selective development of collective bargaining, fiscal reality still overshadowed AAUP accomplishments.

Stevens then asked for $5,000 to be allocated to the Collective Bargaining Caucus, to be spent "with the approval of the Caucus as well as the General Secretary." Since the expenditure was not an increase of costs for the 1975 budget, the council approved the request, with the additional statement that the next year's budget specifically reflect that item.[163] Finally, the council reviewed Committee N's recommendation that the 1975 budget for collective bargaining grants and subvention be increased "from $90,000 to $150,000." Secretary-Treasurer Adams told the council that the Executive Committee had developed a revised 1975 budget with a $30,000 deficit, with the extra dollars to be spent on collective bargaining. Adams opposed the revision because he felt the association's reserve could not sustain a deficit. President Van Alstyne responded that Committee N had already spent 90 percent of its allocation and added that "if the Council decided that the sustenance of collective bargaining activity for the year was of primary importance it would make certain a deficit of $30,000, if not a larger deficit." Following discussion of a proposal to meet the $30,000 deficit by dividing the amount between the association and collective bargaining chapters, the council decided to approve the deficit without the suggested division. The council also reviewed a more general proposal, made by Wilfred Kaplan (mathematics, University of Michigan), for the general secretary to create a plan for a supplemental fund for collective bargaining. source of the funds. Debate over the proposal focused on the source of the funds. Some council members argued against using general funds to create a special collective bargaining fund, and others suggested that members at unionized institutions should supply the funds. A council member offered an amendment to remove national dues as a source for the fund, but Van Alstyne "spoke against the amendment and expressed a wish to enlist the assistance of Commitee N and the Collective Bargaining Caucus in the preparation of these plans." By a vote of 18 to 8 the council approved a motion to develop a separate fund for collective bargaining.[164] Despite fiscal problems the council and President Van Alstyne accepted the need for greater funding of collective bargaining.

There were some indications that continued selective development of collective bargaining was worth the additional funds. Carl Stevens reported to the members at the 1975 Annual Meeting as chair of Committee N, indicating that there were many successes in collective bargaining in the past year.[165] Faculties selected AAUP chapters as exclusive representatives at eight institutions in 1974–1975: the University of Cincinnati, Western Michigan and Northern Michigan Universities, the University of Hawaii (in affiliation with an NEA unit), the University of Washington, Boston University, and Emerson and Union (New Jersey) Colleges. Stevens suggested that "the size and character of institutions whose faculties elected AAUP bargaining agents tended to confirm that the trend toward collective bargaining retains its vigor and that the AAUP will remain a vital force in shaping this trend."[166] He also noted that the units added several thousand members to the AAUP, "holding out the prospect of substantial membership gains attributable to the year's organizing activity."[167]

Association activities in collective bargaining were advancing beyond the election of chapters as exclusive representatives. In 1974–1975 the AAUP produced its *Primer on Collective Bargaining* and a subcommittee of Committee N published "State Bargaining Legislation-Report of the Subcommittee on State Collective Bargaining Legislation Affecting Higher Education." Matthew Finkin, AAUP general counsel, had written several articles on higher education and collective bargaining. Stevens stated that such efforts as well as AAUP staff involvement in state and federal collective bargaining policy decisions lawyers in unit-determination cases and other labor litigation had "begun to sensitize labor boards and the courts to the important issues which arise when higher education is injected into the context of the state and federal labor laws."[168] It appeared that the problems of external organizations controlling AAUP matters had begun to dissipate, as association influence succeeded with state and federal agencies.

AAUP collective bargaining members achieved formal organizational status in 1975. Carl Stevens saw the maturation of the Collective Bargaining Caucus, representatives of the thirty-four chapters now involved in collective bargaining, as a significant matter. The chair of the caucus was a member of Committee N, and the committee had recommended that the AAUP further integrate the caucus into the association's structure. While the integration would be gradual, Stevens viewed it as necessary so that "members who are participating in collective bargaining should have a voice in the determination of the Association's collective bargaining policy."[169]

Council members at the fall 1975 meeting approved by the narrow margin of seventeen to fifteen to seat the chair of the caucus on the council but could not reach an agreement to have the chair serve as an ex officio member of the Executive Committee.[170] The advocates of unionization, the view of the professor as an employee in a bureaucratized institution, had gained official standing in association governance.

Leonard Woodcock, president of the United Auto Workers, addressed the 1975 Annual Meeting.[171] His presence at the annual meeting exemplifies the association's commitment to collective bargaining. Israel Kugler had been the sole continuous voice of unionism in the 1960s, and now in the 1970s a leading union official was a speaker at the annual meeting. Woodcock told the AAUP members, not surprisingly, that professors had "to become more active in the economic planning of higher education."[172]

Yet the overall economic picture for professors was not encouraging. The Committee Z report bluntly stated its conclusion in its title, "Two Steps Backward."[173] Faculty members' purchasing power had in fact decreased by 4.2 percent from 1973–1974 to 1974–1975. Nor was the gender difference heartening; for the first time the committee was able to report the salaries of faculty men and women. The analyses showed that women's compensation was lower than men's "at all ranks."[174]

General Secretary Duffy confirmed his interest in collective bargaining when in the early summer of 1975 he held several talks with NEA Executive Secretary Terry Herndon and AFT President Albert Shanker. The talks focused on possible cooperation in such areas as assistance in negotiations, technical and budget considerations, legal action, and lobbying. The AFT and NEA representatives thought that the AAUP interest resulted from its financial troubles, but Duffy stated that the problem was under control and he was not interested in discussing a merger.[175] Duffy also attended meetings of the Coalition of American Public Employees (CAPE) in early 1975. He attended only as an observer, and there was no council consideration of affiliation with that group.[176]

The Committee F report at the June 1976 Council Meeting expressed ongoing AAUP concern about the size of its membership. An AAUP staff member addressed the council on behalf of the committee and asked for council concurrence on an unusual recruitment approach that would give the general secretary and the chair of Committee F the power "to conduct limited tests of different dues schedules with respect to the acquisition of new members." The council did not concur, responding instead by questioning such methods and suggesting instead membership booths at other organizations' conferences.[177] The AAUP continued to struggle with membership recruitment, uncertain about how to increase its size and dues income.

Members at the 1976 Annual Meeting voted to recognize formally the Collective Bargaining Caucus and to seat its chair on the council. They also approved the constitutional amendment for trusteeship of chapters. Nevertheless they rejected a proposal to investigate with representatives of the NEA possible affiliation for collective bargaining.[178] The NEA was interested in working with the AAUP rather than the AFT because of the latter's AFL-CIO affiliation, but members of Committee N pointed to the fact that the association's membership was composed only of people in higher education while NEA membership included schoolteachers.[179] The AAUP recognized the importance of collective bargaining as well as its singular contribution to the activity.

That singular contribution was evident in Stevens's Committee N report at the 1976 Annual Meeting. The committee had found that there had been little research on the impact of collective bargaining on academic government. Nevertheless within that limited research there was a clear indication that exclusive representation had not had an ill effect on academic government, and in fact some faculties were able "more appropriately to share authority."[180] A major objection of the AAUP opponents of further association bargaining activity did not appear to have much substance.

The Committee Z report for 1975–1976 presented a sense of limited optimism as indicated in its title, "Nearly Keeping Up."[181] The substance of the report, however, was not encouraging. Compensation for women faculty members showed no progress.[182] The report argued that the analyses of the economic conditions of the early and middle 1970s predicted continuing problems for the entire professoriate and stated, "These trends are ominous for the maintenance of the economic status of the academic profession."[183] Of particular concern in the long term were the issues of inflation and unemployment, financial troubles at private liberal arts colleges, and changes in the federal government's student loan programs. The committee offered no words of hope in its review of those problems.[184]

Despite considerable fiscal pressures and noticeable uneasiness among former and current AAUP members, the AAUP pursued vigorous and selective development of collective bargaining at the cost of traditional programs. The austerity of traditional programs, as well as of the conditions of higher education, did not outweigh the optimism of collective bargaining efforts.

In view of the considerable gains among faculty unions in the mid-1970s, the optimism appeared justified. By 1976 there were AFT agents representing 79 faculties at two-year colleges, fifty-three faculties at four-year colleges, the 19 faculties at the City University of New York, teaching assistants at the University of Wisconsin–Madison and the University of Michigan, and 2 faculties at professional schools (Antioch School of Law and the College of Osteopathic Medicine and Surgery in Iowa).[185] Although the AFT locals did not represent a large proportion of faculties among the 3,075 institutions of higher education in 1976, the size of the faculties at City University of New York and State University of New York meant that the Federation represented a disproportionately large number of professors. By the end of 1976 there were NEA union representatives for 142 faculties at two-year colleges, 56 faculties at four-year colleges, and 1 at a professional school (University of Dubuque Seminary in Iowa).[186] Of the three national groups involved in faculty collective bargaining, by the mid-1970s the NEA, with its substantial resources, clearly held the dominant position in number of faculties and number of professors. Thirteen years after the first collective bargaining election by a college faculty, nearly one-third of the professoriate was engaged in such representation.[187]

Faculties were increasingly willing to use the union strike in the early 1970s, including AAUP chapters. From 1971 to 1976 there were eighteen strikes at two-year colleges or two-year college systems, one strike by graduate assistants (at the University of Michigan), and five strikes at four-year colleges or four-year college systems. The AAUP chapter at Oakland University in Michigan conducted a strike in the fall of 1971, in 1975 the AAUP chapter at Rider College held a strike, and in 1976 the AAUP chapter at the University of Bridgeport conducted a strike. All but two of the strikes resulted in some gains for the faculty unions.[188] In terms of unionization and the strike, collective bargaining efforts in higher education were successful.

President Van Alstyne Strikes the Uneasy Balance

William Van Alstyne chose to offer a self-examination of the association in his 1976 presidential address. His speech represents the organizational compromise between the proponents of professionalism and unionization. Van Alstyne argued that to some degree the association mirrored the nation's economic problems in its membership losses, but he focused on two internal issues.[189] These were the 1972 decision to pursue collective bargaining and the dues increase necessary to fund the bargaining efforts. The January 1973 dues increase resulted in only a one-year surplus of $83,000, immediately followed by a deficit in 1974 of $62,000. In Van Alstyne's view, by 1974 the AAUP faced "a vision of uncertainty."[190] Thus, he stated, "In 1974, I believed the challenge to this Association was, therefore, that the center be made to hold, that things not be allowed to fall apart, and that not here, within the AAUP of John Dewey and Arthur Lovejoy, would the 'ceremony of innocence' be drowned." Now, however, he argued that the AAUP was currently "more effective in more ways than at any time in its history."[191] Whatever the hardships of the AAUP, Van Alstyne was determined to portray success.

He reviewed the association's recent extensive efforts in the courts, with the establishment of the Legal Defense Fund and the considerable attention to the Bloomfield College case. As the result of AAUP efforts in the latter instance, the New Jersey Court of Appeals had decided that colleges and universities could not simply declare financial exigency but in fact had to prove the extraordinary financial stress they claimed. Despite earlier Pyrrhic victories within the courts, now the AAUP could point to the fact that the U.S. Supreme Court "uniquely distinguished this Association by singling out the professional recommendations of Committee A for colleges and universities to consider for adoption."[192]

As for collective bargaining, Van Alstyne identified two concerns for the AAUP. One was that the association did not simply imitate other bargaining organizations. The other was that the association not be reticent about its involvement in bargaining. He stated unequivocally on the latter point, "We have not been half-hearted, and we have in fact made it a resounding success." By 1976 the association had committed 31 percent of its budget to collective bargaining, and the activity was "by far the single largest program component of the entire AAUP." Committee N recently found that there were fifty four-year public and fifty private institutions with faculty unions. Of those one hundred colleges and universities, the AAUP represented thirty, the NEA represented twenty-seven, and the AFT had representatives at twenty of the institutions.[193] The bargaining efforts were expensive, and Van

Alstyne suggested that the association needed about six years before its bargaining expenditures would realize a rate of return which matched its investment. The AAUP was already seeing progress in that area, with an anticipated increase from 1976 to 1977 of 4,000 members as the result of collective bargaining chapters. He presented a subsidy ratio of program expenditure to members and dues, of 3-to-1 in 1972, which was only 1.3–to-1 in 1976.[194]

More important than the membership and dollar figures was the general sense of accomplishment:

> Moreover, not only do the most current surveys confirm that a substantial plurality of faculty favoring collective bargaining within their own institutions clearly prefer the AAUP for its professionalism, contrary to impressions elsewhere it is also true that the *AAUP collective bargaining affiliates have done fully as well in behalf of their faculties as any other agent even when only purely economic gains are considered.*[195]

The association was also succeeding where the 1971–1972 proponents had argued it would:

> The presence of the Association in collective bargaining has also brought with it the flattery of widespread imitation: not only do our own agreements reflect the enforceable contractualizing of the 1940 Statement and related AAUP standards, but the other associations and unions have now reached the point where negotiation for recognition of AAUP standards is commonplace throughout collective bargaining in higher education.[196]

Van Alstyne's comments presented a sharp contrast to his objections of 1971 and 1972.

He then proceeded to review the successes of Committee Z, testimony before the U.S. Congress, work on copyright and tax-related concerns, and "elimination of sex-based annuity tables," a position with which federal courts continued to agree.[197] He noted that the AAUP was the first to respond among national organizations to disclosures of "covert use of faculty members" by the Central Intelligence Agency. Finally, the association was also responding at all levels to the "disregard of academic civil liberties" by the Federal Bureau of Investigation.[198] He concluded his address by stating that the association's strength rested in "its diversity of means and services in a single organization of undiluted membership in higher education, and a unity of purpose to the values of higher learning."[199] His centrist posture suggested that the very compromises to which he objected in 1971 and 1972 now seemingly gave the AAUP its power. Van Alstyne did not choose to highlight any recent successes by Committee A, placing any comment on that program within the context of efforts in de jure representation such as the use of the courts or collective bargaining. His omission, especially as the former chair of Committee A and the opponent of collective bargaining based on its assumed negative impact on Committee A efforts, established the uneasy balance between professionalism and unionization in the AAUP.

Summary

From 1971 to 1976 the AAUP experienced the development of a balance between its methods for institutional reform and those for faculty representation. The broadening base of association members and even some leaders confirmed the organization's need to represent faculty members. The previously predominant program of Committee A was now one of two primary programs, and the AAUP would use either negotiation or unionization in its efforts to advance the standards, ideals, and welfare of the profession.

Yet the balance was an uneasy one. Large numbers of members were sufficiently uncomfortable with the 1971–1972 collective bargaining decisions that they left the organization, and the AAUP was unable to reattract them or to replace them with collective bargaining advocates. At the end of 1976 the association had 60,592 active members (and the ratio of staff members to active members was approximately 4,000 to 1), substantially below the 78,000 active members of 1969.[200] In fiscal terms the association willingly used increasingly scarce resources to fund representation rather than reform. In leadership terms General Secretary Davis chose to champion the causes of both academic freedom and collective bargaining in 1974, and only two years later a highly visible opponent of collective bargaining weighted his presidential remarks toward successes in collective bargaining. The association was now balanced between professionalism and unionism, balance with tremendous costs as well as some benefits. Attempts to address the bureaucratization of higher education had some successes in traditional areas of AAUP activity, and some successes in a new method, unionism. The AAUP had also begun to recognize changes in the professoriate, in terms of women and blacks, as well as institutional affiliations such as the increasing number of two-year college professors. The next two decades, for the AAUP and for the professoriate, would highlight the changes of the post–World War II era and confirm them in some unusual ways.

Chapter 6

"More"

1976 to the Early 1990s

B y the mid-1970s the halcyon days of exceptional enrollment growth and public support were gone. While certain types of institutions would experience enrollment growth in the mid-1970s to the late 1980s, others would not fare as well. Regardless of enrollment growth the financial picture for most colleges and universities was foreboding. Already by the middle of the 1970s many institutions, most of them private, had declared financial exigency, and there was no relief in sight. In fact the 1980s brought another version of financial exigency, program extinction. These conditions exacerbated the tension between professionalism and bureaucratization.

In many ways the AAUP changed little in terms of goals, policies, and operations after the balance of 1976 although it managed to recover to some degree from the serious membership losses of the early 1970s. The association continued to address issues of academic freedom, economic status, and faculty participation in governance while serving as a union representative for various faculties.[1] In addition the questions of a more diverse professoriate, especially in terms of gender, race and ethnicity, and eventually sexual orientation, would arise for the AAUP.[2]

For example, in 1984, then 1990, and then again in 1995, the association issued a report on sexual harassment, a report initiated by Committee W on the Status of Women in the Academic Profession. The report, approved as policy in 1995, argues that sexual harassment is a violation of academic freedom. The report also details recommended procedures for addressing complaints.[3] As with other reports on academic freedom, professional ideals existed in concert with suggested bureaucratic procedures.

While the association's Statement on Collective Bargaining developed more direct phrasing in its revisions of 1984 and 1993, the balance between professional ideals and welfare was not just evident, it was more explicit. The 1993 statement begins:

> The basic purposes of the American Association of University Professors are to protect academic freedom, to establish and strengthen institutions of faculty governance, to provide fair procedures for resolving grievances, to promote the economic well-being of faculty and other academic professionals, and to advance the interests of higher education. Collective bargaining is an effective instrument for achieving these objectives.[4]

Thus by the early 1990s the association's purposes had changed substantially, not only from 1915 but also from the mid-1950s when it began to focus on the material welfare of professors. The specificity of goals as well as the inclusion of academic professionals indicated the degree to which the AAUP responded to professionalism and bureaucratization.

In 1995 General Secretary Mary Burgan was also willing to acknowledge that AAUP collective bargaining activities often resembled "union activities in the industrial world of work." She also reminded *Academe* readers (the association changed the name of its major publication from the *AAUP Bulletin* to *Academe* in 1978) that nearly half of the association members were in faculty unions. As of 1995 the association represented over 61,000 faculty in 61 bargaining units. But traditional ideals remain in the association, evidenced by the general secretary's fervent, even emotionally charged response to Richard Chait on the topic of reexamining the need for tenure at the 1997 annual meeting of the Association for the Study of Higher Education.[5]

Both the traditional ideals and the welfare of the profession are vitally important to the AAUP.

Professionalization since the Mid-1970s

While there are important comparisons between the professoriate as a profession and such traditional professions as law and medicine, especially in such areas as the importance of expertise, one point of contrast remains as a fundamental difference. Professors have always been employees of institutions, and thus the history of the development of the occupation has always necessarily included institutional relations. Both attorneys and physicians, even in the heavily corporatized world of the late 1990s, can and do operate as individuals. It is, of course, far more difficult for them to do so than even just twenty years ago. Nevertheless professors in this country have never survived as independent professionals.[6] The very nature of the expertise they offer, either in terms of research or teaching, requires other professors, for colleges and universities do not offer degrees (at least, at the vast majority of institutions) in a single subject, with no other course work. Furthermore colleges and universities certify students in awarding degrees; we do not receive a certificate for having visited a physician or an attorney. In this sense, then, attorneys and physicians have had to come to terms with formal organization and bureaucracy while professors are continuously learning to live within that context.

One problematic condition that attorneys, physicians, and professors share in regard to the confines of the bureaucracy is the reduction of autonomy.[7] Yet Paul Starr marshals autonomy arguments solely in terms of the relative economic efficiency of individual entrepreneurs (physicians) versus corporations (insurance companies), which misses a central point about the inherent inefficiency of professionals.[8] They require reflection in order to pass judgment.

As Starr points out, the institutionalized setting reifies the authority of the professional although in the case of professors, who do not enjoy the hegemony of physicians, there is an intersection of organization and occupation that creates ambiguity of authority.[9] The college president, after all, is an academic and an administrative authority. It seems that almost as quickly as we embraced HMOs, we just as quickly have begun to hear politicians call for limits on HMO authority to make medical judgments. As of yet there are no political advertisements to limit presidential or governing board authority in terms of academic judgments.

Nor, as in the case of medicine, is there limited access to higher education; people who want a degree in this country can get one, and historically that has always been true. Since the early years of higher education in the colonies, colleges have provided not only higher learning but also preparatory education, and while that function has become more specialized, both in the form of community colleges and remedial study programs, it is an enduring function. Physicians and attorneys have earned some of their authority through the exclusion of others while professors have not enforced such a thorough exclusion.[10]

Starr argues that clients are dependent on physicians for a variety of reasons.[11] Students are dependent on professors for certification, the award of a degree, an outcome with specific economic ramifications. Since the beginning of the 1900s, higher education has taken increasing importance as the means to economic success in this country. For all the examples of successes without college educations, from the captains of industry in the early 1900s to the cybergenerals of the late 1990s, higher education is the main sorter of opportunity for most people. In this sense the analysis needs to return to Kimball's argument that professions represent episodic shifts. For the academic profession the bureaucratic setting has, especially in the post–World War II era, given meaning in terms of economic certification rather than learned activity.

Nevertheless professors and physicians share professional characteristics, particularly around the issue of expert knowledge. As Starr documented, the medical profession has increasingly required its members to be specialized, to achieve higher levels of specific expert knowledge.[12] This is an obvious manifestation of the profession itself effecting higher demands, and in a like manner the academic profession has increased its expectations regarding expert knowledge. These expectations evidence themselves in several questions asked in the years 1969, 1975, 1984, and 1989 by the Carnegie Foundation for the Advancement of Teaching (some of the 1975 data and 1984 data are not available by institutional types, and thus some of the following tables have different years for comparison).

Beginning in the mid-1970s, the labor market for professors shifted from one of supply problems to one of demand problems. No longer could aspiring professors leave their graduate programs with master's degrees or without finishing their doctorates, as was the case during the 1950s and 1960s. All colleges and universities, both as institutions and as faculties, could and did increasingly require that applicants have the doctorate. In 1969, 41.4 percent of all professors held the Ph.D. or Ed.D, and in 1975 55.9 percent held the doctorate; by 1989 67.7 percent held one of those degrees.[13]

Furthermore the increased presence of the doctorate permeated all institutional settings, as table 3 shows. Although faculties at two-year colleges showed the fastest growth rate in the percentage of doctorates, even among faculties at four-year colleges the percentage nearly doubled from 1969 to 1989, and among faculties at universities, the rate of increase was over 50 percent.

176

TABLE 3
PERCENTAGE OF PROFESSORS HOLDING THE DOCTORATE*

	Two-Year Colleges	Four-Year Colleges	Universities
1969	5.1	38.6	52.7
1989	17.3	60.3	84.4

SOURCE: All data are from the surveys by the Carnegie Foundation for the Advancement of Teaching. 1975 and 1984 data are not available for the institutional groups.

*Data include only the Ph.D. and Ed.D. degrees.

In addition, professors became more likely to publish articles, a key indicator of the expert knowledge central to the arguments offered by Wilson, Light, and Clark. Of all professors, in 1969, 56.4 percent had published at least one article; in 1975, 69.5 percent had published at least one article, and in 1989, 79.2 percent had published at least one article. As table 4 shows, professors at all types of institutions increased their level of publication from 1969 to 1989. This commitment to research is also part of the reward system for professors, as James S. Fairweather has found; his analysis of faculty salaries and time spent on teaching, from the 1987 National Study of Postsecondary Faculty, indicates that for full-time tenure-track faculty, the more time spent on teaching, the lower the salary, while the more time spent on research, the higher the salary.

TABLE 4
PERCENTAGE OF PROFESSORS WHO HAVE PUBLISHED
AT LEAST ONE ARTICLE

	Two-Year Colleges	Four-Year Colleges	Universities
1969	23.7	48.9	70.5
1989	46.7	73	90.9

Only professors at liberal arts colleges do not exhibit these trends. Furthermore by the late 1980s, for assistant professors across all four-year institutions, time on research and producing publications were "the dominant factors" in their compensation.[14] Nor is this simply a professorial problem, in that both institutions and professors seem to agree on the importance of teaching. In a replication of Caplow and McGee's 1958 study, Dolores L. Burke found in 1985–1986, "Prestige remains the oxygen of higher education—it permeates the atmosphere of the research university."[15] Finally, this appears to be an occupational, i.e., a professional decision and not simply an institutional pressure to produce. Dorothy E. Finnegan showed that new professors at two comprehensive universities increasingly favored research activities from the 1960s to the 1990s.[16]

The pressure to publish focused on new faculty for much of the 1970s and 1980s albeit specifically the increased pressure has occurred among professors at four-year colleges and universities. In view of the unionized status of many public two-year college faculties, many of whom unionized in the late 1960s or early 1970s, it may well be that the union contracts speak to tenure in very different terms from the norms evident at four-year colleges and universities. Overall 43.9 percent of the professors in 1969, 55.2 percent of the professors in 1975, 57.5 percent of the professors in 1984, and 58 percent in 1989 agreed with the statement that it was difficult to get tenure without publishing. (In 1989 the response alternatives for the question included "Neutral," although all previous years' surveys had not allowed for such a response. Thus in this case 1989 data as seen in table 5 are only roughly comparable.)

TABLE 5

IN MY DEPARTMENT IT IS VERY DIFFICULT FOR A PROFESSOR TO ACHIEVE TENURE IF HE OR SHE DOES NOT PUBLISH: AGREE STRONLY OR WITH RESERVATIONS

	Two-Year Colleges	Four-Year Colleges	Universities
1969	8.1	28.7	64.0
1984	6.9	46.3	87.8
1989	7.1	50.1	90. 5

It is remarkable that such a tremendous increase in publication pressure occurred not only at four-year colleges but also universities in the period from 1969 to 1989. The professionalization of professors at all baccalaureate institutions (regardless of advanced degrees offered) appears to have been thorough.

Yet how might this lead to a sense that professors have to do more? Interestingly a question on research interests highlights the problem of increased research within the context of the academic profession. Although professors have substantially increased their emphasis on publications, both for themselves and for colleagues in the tenure process, their identification with research has not increased substantially in balance with their teaching interests. Since 1969 the Carnegie surveys have asked professors to indicate to what degree they identify with research or teaching. As table 6 shows, other than a strong jump in the research interests of professors at universities, there has been little change in the balance between research and teaching interests while at the same time professors have increasingly conducted research leading to publication in academic or professional journals.

TABLE 6

PERCENTAGE OF PROFESSORS WHOSE INTERESTS LIE IN RESEARCH OR TEACHING

| | TWO-YEAR COLLEGES | | FOUR-YEAR COLLEGES | | UNIVERSITIES | |
	RESEARCH	TEACHING	RESEARCH	TEACHING	RESEARCH	TEACHING
1969	4.4	95.5	15.1	84.8	35.2	64.7
1984	7.7	92.3	19.6	80.4	49.9	50.1
1989	7.1	92.9	18.9	81.1	51.7	48.3

This enduring balance between research and teaching, exhibiting only small changes among professors at two-year and four-years institutions, indicates a consequences of academic professionalization. This balance among two-year colleges professors also suggests an area of professionalization for those faculty members, as they further the development of a "discipline of instruction."[17] Increasingly professors at four-year colleges and universities are publishing while at the same time they maintain their interest in teaching, an extension of professionalism.

Bureaucratization: The Drive toward Efficiency and Accountability

In 1980 the U.S. Supreme Court ruled, in what is commonly known as the *Yeshiva* decision, that faculty members often held managerial positions at private colleges and universities such as Yeshiva University. This decision slowed unionization among private institutions, and at some private colleges and universities already unionized, the administrations were able to argue for decertification of the union.[18] While many public faculties had already organized, the 1980s and early 1990s saw some further elections among public colleges and universities. As of 1981 there were 422 bargaining agents, 136 at four-year institutions and 286 at two-year colleges. By 1995 there were 504 agents (much of the increase occurred because of the addition of the Minnesota technical colleges, which included 34 campuses).[19] The growth in unionization slowed, but not the growth in the challenge of bureaucratization.

Arguments for the development of administrative efficiency are long-standing traditions in higher education, and many of those arguments began to develop in the late 1800s and early 1900s. Yet it was the post–World War II period when institutions began to act in earnest upon such suggestions. A federal report on the education professions observed in the late 1960s, "Many colleges are finding it difficult to continue to operate as they have in the past and are struggling with new organizational and managerial systems to encourage the intelligent and responsive allocation of limited resources among seemingly unlimited tasks."[20] The report's solution was managerial:

> If the future management of higher education is to remain in the hands of educators, then we must have planning officers in colleges and universities trained to understand and work with this network of new alliances. These men and women must understand the academic and economic needs of higher education and use this understanding to make comprehensive plans for the future.[21]

For the authors of this report, the specific staffing needs were for more vice-presidents and more student services personnel. To a very real degree staffing of higher education in the 1970s and 1980s reflected such goals. Although federal data are not continuous or consistent on this matter, it is clear from federal reports that two mammoth changes occurred in regard to the staffing of colleges and universities.

First, the sheer numbers represent important changes. In 1967–1968 the number of projected faculty and staff was 753,470; in 1993 the number was 2,602,612. In addition the proportion of administrative and executive staff changed substantially. In 1967–1968 the expected percentage of staff was 10.6, and in 1993 the percentage had doubled to 21.9.[22] Also the level of professionalization of college and university administrators has changed. Programs such as the American Council on Education Fellows and the Harvard Institute for Educational Management are means of educating administrators in their work, rather than the amateur approach that elicited concern in the 1960s. Not only summer programs, but also degree programs and professional associations further the professionalization of administrators, including those at middle-management levels.[23]

By the mid-1970s institutions faced increasing pressure, externally and internally, to be more efficient. Dollars no longer went to budgets in anticipation of more dollars, but rather institutions allocated monies in order to improve already strong programs or to assist potentially strong programs. Furthermore, the requirements of accountability, to describe in detail where dollars went and how departments spent them, increased.[24] The massive enrollment growth of the 1960s led to massive bureaucracies; those bureaucracies now led to bureaucratic efficiency.

Despite the increasing professionalization of the professoriate in the area of research and publications, there is little indication that professors have made any progress in their attempts to participate in college and university governance. Research on the effectiveness of campus senates and on the dismissal of professors indicates that administrations continue to control institutions of higher education.

For example, Barbara A. Lee found that even among effective campus senates, the administration response to the senate had a great deal to do with the level of effectiveness. While administrative deference to faculty decisions regarding academic issues was most important in this area, another important area was the administration's willingness to explain its decisions to the faculty.[25] Another example of the tension between professionalism and bureaucratization rests with AAUP academic freedom cases in the 1980s. As Sheila Slaughter documented, the due process issue received the most attention during that decade.[26] Issues of academic freedom would still arise, as in the case of Rev. Charles Curran. Yet even the Curran case may represent more an issue of bureaucratization rather than academic freedom, as it is clear that the Roman Catholic Church simply waited twenty years, when times appeared more auspicious for the dismissal of a "liberal" professor, to dismiss Curran for a second and final time.[27] Slaughter argues that despite "a deep reservoir of creative energy and institutional commitment," professors were unable to halt administrative attempts to control long-range planning even in such areas as curriculum. She notes, "The alternative strategies for retrenchment devised by the faculty were politely received by the various administrations and largely ignored." Even in the typical faculty arena of tenure review, administrations would choose to make the final decision and had the "bureaucratic and legal authority to do so."[28]

Slaughter in fact argued that tenure, widely recognized in the 1960s and respected first in the 1970s financial exigency cuts, was seriously undermined in the 1980s cases of program changes and cuts. Assumptions about faculty rights and privileges, such as tenure and participation in governance, derive from studies of elite institutions, which themselves have complex histories of professionalization, although such studies are often centered in the late 1800s.[29] The bureaucratic growth of the twentieth century, and especially of the post–World War II era, offered little opportunity for professors' professional control of higher education.

Works on managing the institution and the faculty are now common. For example, the point of *Managing Faculty Disputes* is not how faculty as professionals handle disputes but how "those who have managerial responsibility in universities and colleges—trustees, presidents, deans, division and department heads, and other administrators and faculty leaders who participate in governance and academic affairs" should handle these disputes. The authors emphasize process, using a study of a small college as an example of an entire faculty establishing a grievance against a president, while two large institutions provide a contrast for bureaucratic procedures with decision making in the hands of the administration.[30] Earlier works also suggest the management of the faculty as an institutional goal, furthering educational efficiency.[31] The press toward efficiency appears to be relentless, as the biographer of Frederick Winslow Taylor noted. It is not at all clear that it is meaningful, and it is important to ask how we might make higher education meaningful in terms of the profession and the institution.

Conclusion: The Past as Prologue

The post–World War II era is a time when much of the literature on change in higher education examines the remarkable shifts in enrollments and student behaviors. For example, the late 1960s to the early mid-1970s form a period commonly understood in terms of student movements. Much of the discussion regarding curricular reform cites the 1960s as a period when students gained control of the curriculum (in both political and vocational terms). Examinations focusing on professors, such as the work by Jencks and Riesman (who substantially defined the discussions of professors in the 1960s), address issues of faculty hegemony. Yet much more subtle and powerful forces were at work, forces that reshaped U.S. higher education and continue to exercise predominant influence.

At the core of these forces is the tension between professionalism and bureaucratization. At first glance this tension might seem to be the result of enrollment growth as much as anything else. Yet further careful consideration indicates that regardless of enrollment growth, bureaucracies in higher education continue to grow. In fact part of the growth is directly attributable to faculty actions (such as unionization or the development of faculty senates) as faculties themselves call for greater administrative accountability or at least responsiveness. Much more of it, of course, is obvious in the staffing responses to enrollment growths and to the changing nature of students and to the changing definition of the professoriate, less focused on the student outside the classroom in any form and more focused on the scholarly characteristics of academic life. More students do indeed mean more staff members in the United States-in the registrar's office, in the financial aid office, in the budget offices, in the residence halls. And as students with different backgrounds began to enter colleges and universities in greater numbers, institutions responded—slowly, often inadequately—with staff. Few if any institutions had an office of minority affairs in 1946; now it is difficult to imagine that all but a handful of institutions do not have at least a staff member, if not an office, with such a commitment. Similarly commuting students elicited such a response, as have students with disabilities. And since professors have evidenced decreasing interest in such arenas of college and university life, they have ceded this growth.

The tension was also accentuated by labor market changes of the 1970s. Although the percentage of new professors holding the Ph.D. declined during the mid-1960s, that condition changed substantially by the mid-1970s. The increase in the number and size of doctoral-level and baccalaureate institutions during the 1960s led to an increase in the demand for professors with the doctorate in hand. Furthermore the slow but persistent shift of two-year institutions in the late 1960s to the mid-1970s, as they increasingly moved away from the secondary schools and into either independent postsecondary status or affiliation with public four-year systems, also increased the demand for professors with doctorates.

Ironically the student enrollment pressures of the mid-1970s to the late 1990s have accentuated institutional drives toward recognition, a recognition often earned in the realm of research. Institutions seek visibility among students, and apparently big-time athletics and big-time research are two prominent ways of achieving visibility.

The last several decades do not represent a deprofessionalization of the professoriate, as might appear from the increased bureaucratization of colleges and universities. In fact professors have shown a strong sense of their professionalism, sustained in traditional quarters such as the types of institutions that Logan

Wilson examined in the 1940s and developed further among professors at two-year and particularly four-year institutions. The drive toward more research and even more participation in governance, albeit at administrative discretion, remains strong. Others too have argued that deprofessionalization is not occurring, but rather that "the academic profession mirrors the diversity of the institutions in which it resides."[32]

Furthermore professionalization remains powerful despite demographic changes in the composition of the academic profession. Several books have appeared in the 1990s identifying important perspectives of various participants in the academy such as working-class women, black women, and lesbians. Yet these books share a theme of narratives of people once on the edges of the academy, although able to develop a sense of agency.[33] As Lois Benjamin argues in the opening of *Black Women in the Academy,* despite the increases in the numbers of black women, they "still remain largely invisible."[34]

More important, even among those newly recogized in the academic profession, expert knowledge remains a paramount goal. Fairweather's argument about the rewards for research rather than teaching is a telling one, and other examinations have reaffirmed his conclusions. Finkelstein, Seal, and Schuster analyzed the 1992 federal survey of faculty and found that although the proportion of white male professors was shrinking, the professional ideal of research sustained. They concluded, "But the view afforded by this survey is of a faculty more richly diverse in their origins yet, at this stage, still closely allied with the traditional ways of conducting higher education."[35]

All of these recent studies confirm a major theme of this book. Professionalization and professionalism are major forces in the professoriate, ones that will not likely weaken even as the profession experiences demographic changes. The problem of bureaucratization remains. Professors can not operate outside institutions, as lawyers and physicians still can. Internal and external pressures to be accountable, regardless of expectations of autonomy, are insistent. Regardless of any claims about the development of the flexible organization, evident in the literature on business and higher education, these organizations expect their employees, including their professional employees, to operate within the boundaries of organizational expectations and according to organizational rules (flat or hierarchical, organizations have rules). Strategic planning, for example, has taken a new level of specificity in higher education, as those engaged in planning establish action plans for components of the strategic plans, defining in precise terms the types of activities and support necessary to achieve college or university goals.

The AAUP movement into unionization highlights the problem of the tension between professionalism and bureaucratization, and it illustrates how we got where we are today. Professors aspired to professional status yet wrestled with the challenge of the bureaucratic institution. Although unionization is not as powerful a force as it once was, events at the University of Minnesota in 1996 and 1997 are reminders that unions can and will attract faculty interest in the face of bureaucratic conceptions of the professoriate. Prior to the University of Minnesota Board of Regents' attempt to specify professors' responsibilities and narrow tenure, few observers of higher education, if any, would have predicted that a major research university faculty would come within a few votes of beginning the unionization process.[36]

In fact the consequences of the unionized faculty contracts of the past several years highlights the bureaucratized nature of the university. In an extensive analysis of faculty union contracts, Gary Rhoades concludes that professors are "managed professionals" and administrations have successfully stratified unionized faculties with specified domains of activity.[37] The sense of faculty doing more pervades many reports of the 1980s and 1990s, sometimes purposefully, other times in unanticipated ways. For example, R. Eugene Rice reported on the "Heeding New Voices" project of the American Association for Higher Education and indicated that "new faculty are, on the local level, being encouraged to engage in the very gratifying work of curriculum development and outreach to the broader community through newly initiated service-learning programs" at the same time that research interests must remain their top priority.[38] As Rice also reports, a 1992 report on new professors in the sciences, engineering, and mathematics indicates that their first principle should be achieve excellence in teaching, instructional scholarship, service, and research.[39]

What then, are indicators of how higher education is now responding to this tension? Three characteristics appear to be most informative: the increasing use of part-time faculty; the development and increasing implementation of posttenure review; and the rise of computer technology. All three of these speak to the professional issues of expertise and autonomy and the bureaucratic issues of accountability and efficiency.

Part-time faculty numbers are rising as a result of two pressures: increased faculty release time and administrative uneasiness about appointing full-time (much less full-time tenure-track) faculty.[40] The first pressure is obviously the result of professorial professionalization, the focus on expertise in the area of research as an indicator of professional success. As professors earn release time for their research, the institutions must hire someone to teach their courses. The second is just as obviously a bureaucratic focus on efficiency: part-time faculty members entail less direct costs in terms of salaries and benefits; they are much easier to hire at the last moment and to fire at the last moment.

Posttenure review also reflects both professionalization and bureaucratization. To take the latter, and perhaps more obvious, first, administrations prove institutional accountability to governing boards, legislatures, donors, and the public by requiring that all tenured professors have to prove that they are productive. Reports on the posttenure review process inevitably note the number of professors who completed the process and the number who are following some sort of further evaluative or summative process.[41] In not as visible terms, at least not to professors without some reflection, posttenure review also represents the emphasis on research. Posttenure review committees composed of professors search the records of associate professors for research; service or teaching excellence does not suffice. Although those peer review committees typically learn to restrain their emphasis on research, the message is troublesome.[42] In the land of posttenure review, we must all be full professors.

Finally, there is computer technology: Web access allows instant information (which professors typically know how to sift into worthwhile and worthless information), computer-aided analysis of language, and links among different types of research. It appears to make research efficient, and certainly searching the Web for a correct article title—as was done repeatedly for this book—seems preferable to browsing library stacks. Yet such efficiency also compels us to be efficient in research, to lose the art of reflection for the sake of the craft of research. And colleges and universities grasp at the Web daily to deliver large classes to distant students. Seemingly cost-efficient upgrades of hardware and software are given scant attention in regard to their repetitive, tremendous costs in the drive to the cyberuniversity. In more problematic terms the idea of the professor and the student as two people who need to exchange questions and answers in a direct and even personal way seems to be dissipating into a virtual reality.

The literature about higher education in the late 1990s is replete with suggestions for improvements, such as redefining scholarship, reconsidering tenure, reconfiguring the institutions. Our past, however, is prologue. Professors carry traditions through as many as forty or fifty years of service, and administrators pass traditions even though they may not stay as long at one institution as professors. Both professionalization and bureaucratization continue to grow. Rather than redoing any part of higher education, it may well serve us better to apply Occam's razor, to understand that less can be more. In neither knowledge nor efficiency have we appeared to achieve the level of success that we could expect the increased efforts to show.

Less scholarship done better, avoiding the bureaucratic counting of publications at promotion time, is a solution. Producing presentations and publications as seemingly an act of scholarship, perhaps in itself oxymoronic, does not make professors more knowledgeable, just more expert. Furthermore we inform how we teach within narrow confines, struggling *against* the broader interpretations that college graduates are far more likely to remember.[43] If professors were to emphasize inquiry in scholarship *and* teaching, to ask themselves and their students to think and reflect, and if faculties and administrations were to reward such activity rather than counting publications, then professors, students, and institutions of higher education would achieve higher learning.

Less committee time would acknowledge that representation, of any group of professors, is now impossible in the bureaucratized and importantly diverse college or university.[44] At times committee and ad hoc committee and subcommittee and task force reports seem nothing more than a cacophony, and not one of social diversity—not of gender, race, ethnicity, sexual orientation, and abilities. More often, the cacophony resonates with departmental voices, of college voices, as chemistry pits its demands against music or the college of business maneuvers around the college of arts and sciences, or the administration, temporarily unified, argues against the faculty, temporarily unified. Thus specific academic political activity or bureaucratic participation seems to have only one definite result, the sort of maneuvering that results in more maneuvering. If academic citizenship, responsible participation in major decisions, were the institutional goals, how would we implement such citizenship while not using committees or task forces? In view of the increasingly professionalized administration, it may be time to call upon administrators to write the reports and give faculties the authority to pass judgment—not simply to edit line by line and then vote unanimously to approve, but to modify substantially or to reject.

These are no doubt scandalous suggestions in the eyes of many. The only response here is that as a result of the emphasis on research productivity and bureaucratic procedures, professors find themselves rushing from manuscript to manuscript and from meeting to meeting. Neither our ideals nor our welfare are well met in this process. In the early 1990s professors began to complain about students whose cellular phones rang in the middle of class. Without an adamant resistance to our own inertia as well as that of the bureaucracy, we may face a future in which our own cellular phones are ringing in the middle of class.

NOTES

Introduction

1. Arthur O. Lovejoy, "Discussion and Correspondence: The Association of University Professors," *Science* 60 (November 20, 1914): 744.

2. "General Recommendations and Projections," *AAUP Bulletin* 51 (May 1965): 191n. 1, on addition of "economic welfare."

3. "General Recommendations and Projections," 191n. 1.

4. Logan Wilson, *The Academic Man: A Study in the Sociology of a Profession* (New York: Oxford University Press, 1942), 5 on framing the study of professions within the university setting, 6 on specific research universities.

5. Ibid., 114.

6. Max Weber, *The Theory of Social and Economic Organization,* trans. by A. M. Henderson and Talcott Parsons (New York: Oxford University Press, 1947), 333–334, 337.

7. Wilson, *The Academic Man,* 19–20.

8. Harold L. Wilensky, "The Professionalization of Everyone?" *American Journal of Sociology* 70 (September 1964): 150; Marie R. Haug, "The Deprofessionalization of Everyone?" *Sociological Focus* 8 (August 1975): 199 on Western concept, 212 on client as consumer.

9. Donald Light, Jr., "Introduction: The Structure of the Academic Professions," *Sociology of Education* 47(Winter 1974), 4–10 on Parsons, 10–11 on the three components of professoriate and the characteristics of a profession.

10. Ibid., 10–11.

11. Logan Wilson, *American Academics: Then and Now* (New York: Oxford University Press, 1979), 5–6 on dispersed research, 23–24 on social backgrounds, and 7 on problems.

12. Burton R. Clark, *The Academic Life: Small Worlds, Different Worlds* (Princeton: Carnegie Foundation for the Advancement of Teaching, 1987), 25–44.

13. Martin Finkelstein, "From Tutor to Specialized Scholar: Academic Professionalization in Eighteenth and Nineteenth Century America," *History of Higher Education Annual* 3 (1983): 99–121; and John D. Burton, "The Harvard

Tutors: The Beginning of an Academic Profession, 1690–1825," *History of Higher Education Annual* 16 (1996): 5–20.

14. James D. Anderson, "Race, Meritocracy, and the American Academy during the Immediate Post–World War II Era," *History of Education Quarterly* 33 (Summer 1993): 151–175. Although not framed in terms of race, another work delineates the class structure of professionalism. See Burton J. Bledstein, *The Culture of Professionalism: The Middle Class and the Development of Higher Education in America* (New York: W. W. Norton, 1976).

15. Joseph W. Garbarino and Bill Aussieker, *Faculty Bargaining: Change and Conflict* (New York: McGraw-Hill, 1975), 251.

16. Wilson, *American Academics,* 166; and Clark, *The Academic Life,* 16 and 174–183.

17. Richard Hofstadter and Walter P. Metzger, *The Development of Academic Freedom in the United States* (New York: Columbia University Press, 1955), 126–144; on enrollments at universities, see Laurence Veysey, *The Emergence of the American University* (Chicago: University of Chicago Press, 1965), 339.

18. Thorstein Veblen, *The Higher Learning in America: A Memorandum on the Conduct of Universities by Business Men* (New York: B. W. Huebsch, 1918); Charles Franklin Thwing, *College Administration* (New York: Century Company, 1900); Charles W. Eliot, *University Administration* (New York: Houghton Mifflin, 1908).

19. Weber, *The Theory of Social and Economic Organization,* 329–335.

20. Robert Kanigel, *The One Best Way,* 7. Taylor first learned about principles of efficiency while in prep school where he observed his mathematics instructor at Phillips Exeter Academy timing students' work on problems. The instructor would time the students and then halt them when about half had completed the problems, 215.

21. A[rthur]. O. Lovejoy, "Proceedings of New York Meeting," *Bulletin of the A.A.U.P.* 2 (March 1916): 11. On the search for professional identity, see Hofstadter and Metzger, *The Development of Academic Freedom in the United States,* 478.

22. A[rthur]. O. Lovejoy, "Meeting for Organization of the Association," *Bulletin of the A.A.U.P.* 2 (March 1916): 14; and "Call for the Meeting for Organization of a National Association of University Professors," *Bulletin of the A.A.U.P.* 2 (March 1916): 11.

23. Lovejoy, "Meeting for Organization of the Association," 15–16; "Constitution," *Bulletin of the A.A.U.P.* 2 (March 1916): 20–21; "Council Business from January to April, 1916," *Bulletin of the A.A.U.P.* 2 (April 1916): 15–17; [John H. Wigmore and H. W. Tyler], "Letter on Formation of Local Chapters," *Bulletin of the A.A.U.P.* 2 (April 1916): 18–19.

24. "Report of the Committee of Inquiry on Conditions at the University of Utah" (American Association of University Professors: July 1915).

25. Walter P. Metzger, "The First Investigation," *AAUP Bulletin* 48 (September 1961): 207. (The *Bulletin* of the association was named the *Bulletin of the A.A.U.P.* until 1943, when its name became the *A.A.U.P. Bulletin*. In 1956 the name changed to the *AAUP Bulletin,* and in 1975 the association changed the name to *Academe.* In all cases the journal was the official bulletin of the AAUP; for general ease of reading it is called either the *Bulletin* or the *AAUP Bulletin* in the text of this work.)

26. Walter Metzger, "The First Investigation," 207. "Report of the Committee of Inquiry on Conditions at the University of Utah" was published July 1915, and the first issue of the association's *Bulletin* appeared in December 1915.

27. "Report of the Committee of Inquiry on Conditions at the University of Utah," 13 for Associate Professor G. C. Wise (qualified), 9 for Instructors C. W. Snow and P. C. Bing (as instructors, probably not qualified), and 29–30 for Associate Professor A. A. Knowlton (not qualified). For the conclusion, which did not urge reinstatement, see 34–35.

28. "Report of the Committee of Inquiry Concerning Charges of Violation of Academic Freedom at the University of Colorado," *Bulletin of the A.A.U.P.* 2, part 2 (April 1916): 34–35.

29. "General Report of the Committee on Academic Freedom and Academic Tenure," *Bulletin of the A.A.U.P.* 1, part 1 (December 1915): 40.

30. Prefatory Note, *Bulletin of the A.A.U.P.* 1, part 1 (December 1915): 17.

31. Hofstadter and Metzger, *The Development of Academic Freedom in the United States,* 480–490.

32. Ibid., 492 on redress not being a goal, 494 on the development of the list of censured institutions.

33. [Ralph E. Himstead], "Academic Freedom and Tenure at the University of Texas," *A.A.U.P. Bulletin* 30 (Winter 1944): 627–634; "Concerning the University of Texas," *A.A.U.P. Bulletin* 31 (Autumn 1945): 462–465; [Edward C. Kirkland], "Academic Freedom and Tenure, the University of Texas," *A.A.U.P. Bulletin* 32 (Summer 1946): 374–385 and 384–385 on censure by the council.

34. [Kirkland], "Academic Freedom and Tenure, the University of Texas," 382 on Rainey's protection of academic freedom and tenure for professors at the University of Texas. The AAUP report noted that Rainey's appointment as president included a professorship in education, thus sustaining association involvement in the situation.

35. J[ohn]. H. Wigmore, "President's Report for 1916" and "Report of Committee P on Pensions and Insurance," *Bulletin of the A.A.U.P.* 2 (November 1916): 41–46 and 57–80, respectively.

36. Committee Y, *Depression, Recovery and Higher Education: A Report of Committee Y of the American Association of University Professors,* as prepared by Malcolm M. Willey (New York: McGraw-Hill, 1937), 492–495.

37. J. A. Leighton, "Report of Committee T on Place and Function of Faculties in University Government and Administration," *Bulletin of the A.A.U.P.* 6 (March 1920): 17–47. "Committee T (Place and Function of Faculties in University Government)," *Bulletin of the A.A.U.P.* 10 (May 1924): 23–42. [G. H. Sabine], "Place and Function of Faculties in University Government, Progress Report of Committee T," *Bulletin of the A.A.U.P.* 22 (March 1936): 183–190. [G. H. Sabine], "The Place and Function of Faculties in University and College Government, Report of Committee T," *Bulletin of the A.A.U.P.* 24 (February 1938): 141–150. Paul W. Ward, "Place and Function of Faculties in College and University Government, Report of Committee T," *Bulletin of the A.A.U.P.* 26 (April 1940): 171–189.

38. "Constitution," *Bulletin of the A.A.U.P.* 6 (January 1920): 4.

39. On the relationship between length of service and scientific productivity, see "Report of Membership Committee: Report of Committee E on Qualifications for Membership," *Bulletin of the A.A.U.P.* 2 (October 1916): 16. On widening the membership base, see A[rthur]. O. Lovejoy, "Annual Message of the President," *Bulletin of the A.A.U.P.* 5 (November–December 1919): 28.

40. On the negotiations leading to the 1940 statement, see Hofstadter and Metzger, *The Development of Academic Freedom in the United States,* 487.

41. Loya Metzger, "Professors in Trouble: A Quantitative Analysis of Academic Freedom and Tenure Cases," Ph.D. dissertation, Columbia University, 1978, 58–59 on appointment, 65–66 on revision of the 1925 Conference Statement, 71 on support of faculty government.

42. "Report of Committee O on Organization and Policy," *Bulletin of the A.A.U.P.* 25 (October 1939): 430; and "1939 Annual Meeting Record," *Bulletin of the A.A.U.P.* 26 (April 1940): 286. On admission of junior college professors, see Glenn R. Morrow, "Report of the Self-Survey Committee of the AAUP: Minority Report and Recommendation Regarding Membership Policy," *AAUP Bulletin* 51 (May 1965): 203. See also "Distribution of Membership and Record of Chapter Officers," *Bulletin of the A.A.U.P.* 27 (February 1941): 116–132.

43. Some AAUP members had moved from four-year to two-year institutions prior to the 1939 decision and retained their membership. See Edward

Donald Jackson, Jr., "The American Association of University Professors and Community/Junior Colleges," Ph.D. dissertation, Florida State University, 1974, 56–63.

44. Christopher Jencks and David Riesman, *The Academic Revolution* (Garden City, N.Y.: Doubleday, 1968, Anchor Books, 1969), 13–14, 21, 481–483.

45. *Statistics of Higher Education 1945–46* (Washington, D.C.: United States Government Printing Office, 1949), table VII, 7.

46. Reliable data on the United States professoriate are generally not available, and those data available are not continuous in form. Logan Wilson states that of the 3,088 doctorates awarded in 1939, thirty of the ninety doctorate-granting universities granted 80 percent of the degrees, and ten of those ninety institutions granted 40 percent. Logan Wilson, *The Academic Man,* 34.

47. Hofstadter and Metzger, *The Development of Academic Freedom in the United States,* 478.

48. H. W. Tyler, "Some Problems of the Association," *Bulletin of the A.A.U.P.* 24 (February 1938): 203.

49. "What the American Association of University Professors Is and What It Is Not," *Bulletin of the A.A.U.P.* 24 (March 1938): 235, remarks by Dinsmore Alter; Arthur O. Lovejoy, "Professional Association or Trade Union?" *Bulletin of the A.A.U.P.* 24 (May 1938): 412.

50. Commission on Educational Reconstruction, *Organizing the Teaching Profession: The Story of the American Federation of Teachers* (Glencoe, Ill.: Free Press, 1955, 10.

51. As reported by William Edward Eaton, *The American Federation of Teachers, 1916–1961: A History of the Movement* (Carbondale: Southern Illinois University Press, 1975), 31.

52. Jeannette Ann Lester, "The American Federation of Teachers in Higher Education: A History of Union Organization of Faculty Members in Colleges and Universities," Ph.D. dissertation, University of Toledo, 1968, 91, 249–250.

53. On the initial approval of AAUP involvement in collective bargaining, see "Representation of Economic Interests," *AAUP Bulletin* 52 (June 1966): 229–234. On the strike, see Bertram H. Davis, "Report of the General Secretary," *AAUP Bulletin* 53 (June 1967): 112.

54. Edward Donald Jackson, Jr., "The American Association of University Professors and Community/Junior Colleges," Ph.D. dissertation, Florida State University, 1974, 199.

55. George Strauss, "The AAUP as a Professional Occupation Association," *Industrial Relations* 5 (October 1965): 134–137 and 139.

56. Lionel S. Lewis and Michael N. Ryan, "Professionalization and the Professoriate," *Social Problems* 24 (December 1976): 282–297; and Lionel S. Lewis and Michael N. Ryan, "The American Professoriate and the Movement toward Unionization" in *Comparative Perspectives on the Academic Profession,* ed. Philip G. Altbach (New York: Praeger, 1977), 191–214.

57. David Riesman, *On Higher Education: The Academic Enterprise in an Era of Rising Student Consumerism* (San Francisco: Jossey-Bass, 1980), xx.

58. Veysey, *The Emergence of the American University,* 306.

59. Veysey, *The Emergence of the American University,* 317. Also on professionalization, see Hofstadter and Metzger, *The Development of Academic Freedom in the United States,* especially 369–407 on the influence of the German university and academic research.

60. Bruce A. Kimball, *The "True Professional Ideal" in America: A History* (Cambridge: Blackwell, 1992), 16. Kimball agrees with such authors as Burton Bledstein that the middle class contributed to the rise of professions in the late 1800s, but he also emphasizes the shifting nature of professions. See Burton J. Bledstein, *The Culture of Professionalism: The Middle Class and the Development of Higher Education in America* (New York: W. W. Norton, 1976), 105–128.

61. Kimball, *The "True Professional Ideal" in America,* 199, 214–230.

62. George W. Angell, "Two-Year College Experience" in *Faculty Unions and Collective Bargaining,* ed. E. D. Duryea and Robert S. Fisk (San Francisco: Jossey-Bass, 1973), 92–94; David L. Graham and Donald E. Walters, "Bargaining Process" in *Faculty Unions and Collective Bargaining,* ed. Duryea and Fisk, 45, 48–49. See also Everett Carll Ladd, Jr., and Seymour Martin Lipset, *Professors, Unions and American Higher Education* (Berkeley: Carnegie Foundation for the Advancement of Teaching and Carnegie Commission on Higher Education, 1973), 41–42.

63. James S. Fairweather, *Faculty Work and Public Trust: Restoring the Value of Teaching and Public Service in American Academic Life* (Boston: Allyn and Bacon, 1996), 6.

64. William G. Tierney and Estela Mara Bensimon, *Promotion and Tenure: Community and Socialization in Academe* (Albany: State University of New York Press, 1996).

65. John R. Thelin, "Beyond Background Music: Historical Research on Admissions and Access in Higher Education," in *Higher Education: Handbook of Theory and Research,* ed. John C. Smart, vol. 6 (New York: Agathon Press, 1990), 357.

66. On the former, see for example Patricia J. Gumport and Brian Pusser, "A Case of Bureaucratic Accretion: Context and Consequences," *Journal of Higher Education* 66(September/October) 1995: 493–520 for a discussion of bureaucratization at the University of California. Regarding the latter, see George B. Vaughan, "Scholarship and Community Colleges: The Path to Respect," *Educational Record* 1988 69(2): 26–31.

67. See, for example, Fairweather, *Faculty Work and Public Trust;* and Robert T. Blackburn and Janet T. Lawrence, *Faculty at Work: Motivation, Expectation, Satisfaction* (Baltimore: Johns Hopkins University Press, 1995).

68. On the federal surveys, see Ralph E. Dunham and Patricia S. Wright, *Faculty and Other Professional Staff in Institutions of Higher Education: First Term 1963–64* (Washington, D.C.: United States Government Printing Office, 1966); Richard M. Beazley, *Salaries and Tenure of Instructional Faculty in Institutions of Higher Education 1974–75* (Washington, D.C.: United States Government Printing Office, 1976); *Faculty in Higher Education Institutions, 1988* (Washington, D.C.: United States Government Printing Office, 1990); *National Study of Postsecondary Faculty,* National Center for Education Statistics, 1993.

69. See David W. Leslie and Elaine C. Fygetakis, "A Comparison of Carnegie and NCES Data on Postsecondary Faculty: Ambiguities and Disjunctures," *Research in Higher Education* 33 (August 1993): 447–465 for a discussion of the problems of national databases. In addition to those methodological issues, the Carnegie databases are not complete, with apparent coding errors for some questions.

70. President's Commission on Higher Education, *Higher Education for American Democracy* (New York: Harper & Brothers, 1947); Paul F. Lazarsfeld and Wagner Thielens, Jr., *The Academic Mind: Social Scientists in a Time of Crisis* (Glencoe, Ill.: Free Press, 1958).

71. For a detailed look at this aspect of unionization and the AAUP, see Philo A. Hutcheson, "Reform and Representation: The Uncertain Development of Collective Bargaining in the AAUP, 1946 to 1976, "University of Chicago Ph.D. dissertation, 1991. Local activity within the AAUP, as well as local pressures outside the association, had a major impact on the organization's movement into collective bargaining.

Chapter One: The AAUP from 1946 to 1958

1. Bradford Morse, "The Veteran and His Education," *Higher Education* (1960): 16–19 as cited by Frederick Rudolph, *The American College and University: A History* (New York: Vintage Books, 1965), 486n. 6. See also *Keith*

W. Olson, The G.I. Bill, The Veterans, and The Colleges (Lexington: University Press of Kentucky, 1974).

2. *Higher Education for American Democracy: A Report of the President's Commission on Higher Education*, 2 vols. (Washington, D.C.: United States Government Printing Office, 1947), I: 36 and II: 7.

3. Vannevar Bush, *Science, the Endless Frontier* (Washington, D.C.: United States Government Printing Office, 1945), 31–40. See John T. Wilson, *Academic Science, Higher Education, and the Federal Government, 1950–1983* (Chicago: University of Chicago Press, 1983), 2–3 on Bush and the development of the National Science Foundation. See also Dael Wolfle, *The Home of Science: The Role of the University* (New York: McGraw-Hill, 1972), 107.

4. *Digest of Educational Statistics: 1969 Edition* (Washington, D.C.: United States Government Printing Office, September 1969), table 85, 65.

5. *Digest of Educational Statistics: 1973 Edition* (Washington, D.C.: United States Government Printing Office, 1974), table 91, 76.

6. Federal data collection efforts concerning the number and type of professors (full-time, part-time, senior or junior staff, etc.) are erratic. Not only is information only available for occasional years but also the methods of reporting data vary. Readers should treat any longitudinal comparisons of faculty members in this work with care. *Statistics of Higher Education 1945–46,* table IV, 6 for 1945–1946 data; *Digest of Educational Statistics, 1971 Edition* (Washington, D.C.: United States Government Printing Office, 1971), table 104, 78 for November 1955 data.

7. Allan M. Cartter, *The Ph.D. and the Academic Labor Market* (New York: McGraw-Hill, 1976), 155.

8. Theodore Caplow and Reece McGee, *The Academic Marketplace* (Garden City, N.Y.: Basic Books, 1958), 93–166.

9. Loya Metzger, "Professors in Trouble," 75.

10. H. Bentley Glass, interview in Stony Brook, New York, on 4 March 1986. Glass was chair of the Special Committee that reviewed several alleged violations of academic freedom that the association had *not* addressed during the McCarthy era. See also Loya Metzger, "Professors in Trouble," 77; and Ellen Schrecker, *No Ivory Tower: McCarthyism and the Universities* (New York: Oxford University Press, 1986), 327–328.

11. "Thirty-third Annual Meeting," 5.

12. Frederick S. Deibler, AAUP president from 1940 to 1942, was the last president who was a charter member. "Report of the Nominating Committee," *Bulletin of the A.A.U.P.* 25 (October 1939): 437.

13. Loya Metzger, "Professors in Trouble," 72.

14. Ibid., 74–76. Loya Metzger emphasizes Himstead's concerns about details and power. As will be shown in the case of General Secretary William P. Fidler, the burden of running the association was excessive. Himstead complained in the *Bulletin* about the burden of his office, and the membership and chapters grew considerably during this period, increasing the workload. On Himstead's complaints, see [Ralph E. Himstead], "A Letter to the Membership," *A.A.U.P. Bulletin* 32 (Spring 1946): 163–165; and [Ralph E. Himstead], "A Letter to the Membership," *A.A.U.P. Bulletin* 33 (Autumn 1947): 579–585. The latter documents organizational growth, 584.

15. [Himstead], "A Letter to the Membership" (Autumn 1947), 583–584 on resignation of staff member Robert Ludlum and number of members, 581–583 on Shannon appointment.

16. Ibid., 584–585 on move and 585 on request for patience.

17. Ibid., 585.

18. [Ralph E. Himstead], "The State of the Association, 1936–1950," *A.A.U.P. Bulletin* 36 (Winter 1950): 758 on membership growth, 762 on reserve fund.

19. Ibid., 762–763.

20. [Ralph E. Himstead], "The Association's New Officers," *A.A.U.P. Bulletin* 38 (Spring 1952): 8–9.

21. "Record of Membership for 1951," *A.A.U.P. Bulletin* 38 (Spring 1952): 159 indicates a total of 41,238 Active Members as of 1 January 1952, a month before Middleton's appointment.

22. [Himstead], "Academic Freedom and Tenure at the University of Texas," 629, 632, and 633. This report is also interesting because Himstead quotes the University of Texas regents as accusing the AAUP of being "a 'CIO-like Union' that is attempting to control education in Texas." See 632. External observers continued to apply the union label.

23. Ralph E. Himstead, "Economic Status, Professional Standards and the General Welfare," *A.A.U.P. Bulletin* 33 (Winter 1947): 771–772.

24. Paul W. Ward, "Report of Committee T on the Place and Function of Faculties in College and University Government," *A.A.U.P. Bulletin* 34 (Spring 1948): 61.

25. "Academic Retirement, Statement of Principles," *A.A.U.P. Bulletin* 37 (Spring 1951): 90.

26. "Academic Freedom and Tenure, Evansville College," *A.A.U.P. Bulletin* 35 (Spring 1949): 74–111. The next reports on an investigation occurred in 1956; "Academic Freedom and Tenure: Saint Louis University" and "Academic Freedom and Tenure: North Dakota State Agricultural College,"

AAUP Bulletin 42 (Spring 1956): 108–129 and 130–160, respectively. See the index for the *A.A.U.P. Bulletin* for the intervening years. See also "Disposition of Committee A Cases: January 1, 1950–September 15, 1956," *AAUP Bulletin* 42 (Winter 1956): 706–708.

27. Paul Lazarsfeld and Wagner Thielens, Jr., *The Academic Mind: Social Scientists in a Time of Crisis* (Glencoe, Ill.: Free Press, 1958), table 2–6, 50. Forty-six percent of the reported attacks on professors were based on issues other than political ones. Lazarsfeld and Thielens also address the virulent anti-Communism, 35–39, 47, 49–58.

28. Schrecker, *No Ivory Tower,* 77, 95, 113, 116, 279–280.

29. The AAUP's belated examination of these attacks provides a comprehensive description (and attempted evaluation) of the widespread nature of the problem. "Academic Freedom and Tenure in the Quest for National Security," *AAUP Bulletin* 42 (Spring 1956): 49–107 and particularly 96–100 on the widespread nature of the controversies. In general the reported attacks were more likely to occur at institutions other than the elite colleges and universities, although those institutions also faced serious problems. See Philo A. Hutcheson, "McCarthyism and the Professoriate: A Historiographic Nightmare?" *Higher Education: The Handbook of Theory and Research,* ed. John C. Smart, vol. 12, (New York: Agathon Press, 1997), 435–460.

30. Lazarsfeld and Thielens, *The Academic Mind,* chapter 3, "A Measure of Apprehension," 72–91; Theodore Caplow and Reece J. McGee, *The Academic Marketplace,* 137; Jencks and Riesman, *The Academic Revolution,* 202–204; Schrecker, *No Ivory Tower,* 171–181.

31. On faculties' and professors' support, George R. Stewart, *The Year of the Oath* (Garden City, N.Y.: Doubleday, 1950), 38–41. On the eventual AAUP report (a brief one), see "Academic Freedom and Tenure in the Quest for National Security" (Spring 1956), 64–66.

32. David P. Gardner, *The California Oath Controversy* (Berkeley: University of California Press, 1967), 208–209. Gardner reports that the AAUP delay in action did not help the faculties when they needed assistance. On AAUP quiescence, see Max Radin, "The Loyalty Oath at the University of California," *A.A.U.P. Bulletin* 36 (Summer 1950): 237–248 (including addenda for updates by the author and *Bulletin* editor, the latter based on information from media reports); Ralph E. Himstead, "Two Chapter Letters," *A.A.U.P. Bulletin* 36 (Autumn 1950): 585–587 (includes request for Committee A investigation); "The University of California Loyalty Oath Situation," *A.A.U.P. Bulletin* 37 (Spring 1951): 92–101 (report on the District Court of Appeal decision that the loyalty oath was invalid); [Ralph E. Himstead], "Editor's Note," *A.A.U.P.*

Bulletin 37 (Autumn 1951): 441 (publication of Himstead telegram to university president on reinstatement of professors who did not sign the oath and president's response that the regents had not yet made a decision). On the eventual AAUP censure of the Board of Regents, see "The Forty-second Annual Meeting," *AAUP Bulletin* 42 (Summer 1956): 341.

33. Lazarsfeld and Thielens, *The Academic Mind,* 72–91. Himstead and the AAUP as an organization were not the only ones excruciatingly slow to respond to the attacks, and with strong reason.

34. H. Bentley Glass, interview in Stony Brook, New York, on 4 March 1986.

35. "Twenty-sixth Annual Meeting," *Bulletin of the A.A.U.P.* 26 (February 1940): 7; and "List of Members," *Bulletin of the A.A.U.P.* 2 (March 1916): 36.

36. First years of AAUP membership and Committee A experience are from "Report of the 1945 Nominating Committee," *A.A.U.P. Bulletin* 31 (Autumn 1945): 510 for Edward Kirkland; "Report of the 1947 Nominating Committee," *A.A.U.P. Bulletin* 33 (Autumn 1947): 574 for the 1948–1950 president, Ralph Lutz; "Report of the 1949 Nominating Committee," *A.A.U.P. Bulletin* 35 (Autumn 1949): 561 for the 1950–1952 president, Richard Shryock; "Report of the 1951 Nominating Committee," *A.A.U.P. Bulletin* 37 (Autumn 1951): 590 for the 1952–1954 president, Fred Millett; "Report of the 1953 Nominating Committee and Proposed Constitutional Amendment," *A.A.U.P. Bulletin* 39 (Autumn 1953): 516 for William Britton.

37. George Pope Shannon, "Academic Freedom and Tenure, Report of Committee A for 1946," *A.A.U.P. Bulletin* 33 (Spring 1947): 70; George Pope Shannon, "Academic Freedom and Tenure, Report of Committee A for 1947," *A.A.U.P. Bulletin* 34 (Spring 1948): 132.

38. William T. Laprade, "Academic Freedom and Tenure, Report of Committee A for 1948," *A.A.U.P. Bulletin* 35 (Spring 1949): 65 and 49 on his statement that he was chair in 1941. William T. Laprade, "Academic Freedom and Tenure, Report of Committee A for 1949," *A.A.U.P. Bulletin* 36 (Spring 1950): 44. William T. Laprade, "Academic Freedom and Tenure, Report of Committee A for 1950," *A.A.U.P. Bulletin* 37 (Spring 1951): 82. William T. Laprade, "Academic Freedom and Tenure, Report of Committee A for 1951," *A.A.U.P. Bulletin* 38 (Spring 1952): 114. William T. Laprade, "Academic Freedom and Tenure, Report of Committee A for 1952," *A.A.U.P. Bulletin* 39 (Spring 1953): 120. William T. Laprade, "Academic Freedom and Tenure, Report of Committee A for 1953," *A.A.U.P. Bulletin* 40 (Spring 1954): 79. William T. Laprade, "Academic Freedom and Tenure, Report of Committee A for 1954," *A.A.U.P. Bulletin* 41 (Spring 1955): 31.

39. As selected, representative samples: Shannon, "Academic Freedom and Tenure, Report of Committee A for 1946," 70; Laprade, "Academic Freedom and Tenure, Report of Committee A for 1950," 82. Laprade, "Academic Freedom and Tenure, Report of Committee A for 1954," 31–33.

40. See, for example, Laprade, "Academic Freedom and Tenure, Report of Committee A for 1954," 27.

41. Loya Metzger, "Professors in Trouble," 73; Ellen Schrecker, *No Ivory Tower,* 336, where she identifies Himstead as suffering from a "strange pathology" that caused his inaction.

42. Laprade, "Academic Freedom and Tenure, Report of Committee A for 1954," 29–31, in defense of Himstead.

43. On the 1946 censure, see [Edward C. Kirkland], "Academic Freedom and Tenure, The University of Texas," 384–385. On the lack of reports on council activity, see "Index for 1946," *A.A.U.P. Bulletin* 32 (Winter 1946): 782; "Index for 1947," *A.A.U.P. Bulletin* 33 (Winter 1947): 229–233; "Index for 1948," *A.A.U.P. Bulletin* 35 (Spring 1949): 180; "Index for 1949," *A.A.U.P. Bulletin* 36 (Spring 1950): 194; "Index for 1950," *A.A.U.P. Bulletin* 36 (Winter 1950): 230; "Index for 1951," *A.A.U.P. Bulletin* 37 (Winter 1951–1952): 838; "Index for 1952," *A.A.U.P. Bulletin* 38 (Winter 1952–1953): 675; "Index for 1953," *A.A.U.P. Bulletin* 39 (Winter 1953–1954): 720; "Index for 1954," *A.A.U.P. Bulletin* 40 (Winter 1954–1955): 689. The report of the March 1955 council meeting began a continuing series of *Bulletin* reports on council activity. The spring 1955 meeting focused on reviving Committee A investigations and strengthening the organization—assigning the new president the authority to appoint new committees, for example. [George Pope Shannon], "Record of Council Meetings of American Association of University Professors," *A.A.U.P. Bulletin* 41 (Spring 1955): 104–109. The next section details local leaders' push to action.

44. "Report of the 1945 Nominating Committee," 510–514; and "Officers and Council," *A.A.U.P. Bulletin* 32 (Summer 1946): 232; "Report of the 1946 Nominating Committee," *A.A.U.P. Bulletin* 32 (Autumn 1946): 576–580; and "Thirty-third Annual Meeting," 8; "Report of the 1947 Nominating Committee," 574–578; and "Thirty-Fourth Annual Meeting," *A.A.U.P. Bulletin* 34 (Spring 1948): 11; "Report of the 1948 Nominating Committee," *A.A.U.P. Bulletin* 34 (Autumn 1948): 613–617; and "Thirty-fifth Annual Meeting," *A.A.U.P. Bulletin* 35 (Spring 1949): 11; "Report of the 1949 Nominating Committee," 561–565; and "Thirty-sixth Annual Meeting," *A.A.U.P. Bulletin* 36 (Spring 1950): 17; "Report of the 1950 Nominating Committee," *A.A.U.P. Bulletin* 36 (Autumn 1950): 592–596; and "Thirty-seventh Annual Meeting,"

A.A.U.P. Bulletin 37 (Spring 1951): 70–71; "Report of the 1951 Nominating Committee," 590–595; and "The Thirty-eighth Annual Meeting," *A.A.U.P. Bulletin* 38 (Spring 1952): 104; "Report of the 1952 Nominating Committee," *A.A.U.P. Bulletin* 38 (Autumn 1952): 473–478; and "Thirty-ninth Annual Meeting," *A.A.U.P. Bulletin* 39 (Spring 1953): 101; "Report of the 1953 Nominating Committee and Proposed Constitutional Amendment," 516–521; and "The Fortieth Annual Meeting," *A.A.U.P. Bulletin* 40 (Spring 1954): 123; "Report of the 1954 Nominating Committee," *A.A.U.P. Bulletin* 40 (Autumn 1954): 484–488; and "The Forty-first Annual Meeting," *A.A.U.P. Bulletin* 41 (Spring 1955): 103.

45. Ralph E. Himstead et al., "A Symposium on the Economic Status of the Profession," *A.A.U.P. Bulletin* 32 (Autumn 1946): 428–442 on report, 428 on Himstead's comments.

46. "Thirty-third Annual Meeting," 8–9.

47. Seymour E. Harris, "Professorial Salaries and Tuition, 1947–48: Background and Proposals," *A.A.U.P. Bulletin* 34 (Spring 1948): 98 on survey, 108 on rises of cost of living, salaries, and tuition.

48. Ralph E. Himstead, "The Association and the Economic Status of the Profession," *A.A.U.P. Bulletin* 34 (Summer 1948): 420 and 424.

49. Henry G. Badger, "Constitution of College Teachers' Salary Schedules," *A.A.U.P. Bulletin* 34 (Summer 1948): 407.

50. "Instructional Salaries in 41 Selected Colleges and Universities for the Academic Year 1953–54," *A.A.U.P. Bulletin* 39 (Winter 1953–54): 633.

51. Ibid., 632.

52. Paul W. Ward, "Report of Committee T on the Place and Function of Faculties in College and University Government," *A.A.U.P. Bulletin* 34 (Spring 1948): 61 on previous rates of faculty participation; 61–62 on lack of trend; 58–59 on report's suggestion.

53. "The R"le of Faculties of Colleges and Universities in the Determination of Institutional Policies," *A.A.U.P. Bulletin* 38 (Winter 1952–53): 637–644 for Himstead's announcement of a survey of faculty participation and a copy of the survey and see [Paul W. Ward and Ralph E. Himstead], "The Place and Function of Faculties in College and University Government, Report of Progress," *A.A.U.P. Bulletin* 39 (Summer 1953): 300–318. See 311 on administrations' consultations with faculties.

54. Paul W. Ward, "The Place and Function of Faculties in College and University Government, Report of Committee T," *A.A.U.P. Bulletin* 41 (Spring 1955): 77.

55. Ibid., 74–75 on small colleges, 72–75 on other institutions.

56. Ibid., 78 on joint statement, 80–81 on continuous service.

57. James Holladay, "The R"le and Activities of Region VII of the Association," *A.A.U.P. Bulletin* 41 (Spring 1955): 84–87.

58. Warren Taylor, "The Ohio Conference of Chapters of the American Association of University Professors," *A.A.U.P. Bulletin* 41 (Winter 1955): 677–679.

59. Ibid., II: 354–355.

60. Loya Metzger, "Professors in Trouble," p. 78.

61. R. Beck, "Chapter Minutes, 26 May 1953," AAUP Files, as quoted by Wiberg, "A History of the University of Minnesota Chapter of the American Association of University Professors, 1916–1960," 2 vols., Ph.D. dissertation, University of Minnesota, II: 355.

62. Loya Metzger, "Professors in Trouble," p. 78.

63. [Ralph E. Himstead], "The Thirty-ninth Annual Meeting," *A.A.U.P. Bulletin* 39 (Spring 1953): 102–103 on lack of communication and chapter invitations; 103 on academic freedom violations; 103–104 on chapter involvement.

64. Ibid., 104–105. Loya Metzger writes that Himstead's numbers are "pure fabrications" and that mail was never counted. Metzger, "Professors in Trouble," 73 and 73n. 1, on mail not counted. Simple division, however, indicates that Himstead's numbers would mean 398 communications for each day of the year, using 251 working days. Given the intensity of the McCarthy attacks, their widespread publicity, and the level of chapter activity (as documented in this work), it is reasonable to guess that Himstead took a busy day's communications and exaggerated, but not extraordinarily so. In further support of this assessment of the level of communications, see [George Pope Shannon], "Central Office Notes," *A.A.U.P. Bulletin* 41 (Summer 1955): 366, in which he states that in three months the AAUP staff members wrote 2,500 letters. Assuming 66 working days in three months, the staff members wrote 38 letters per day. Himstead's claim of 20,000 communications best handled by professional staff members would mean 80 per day (using again 251 working days) and would include telephone calls as well as letters.

65. [Himstead], "The Thirty-ninth Annual Meeting," 105.

66. Loya Metzger, "Professors in Trouble," 78–79 on avoiding Committee O, 79–80 on Committee report and Council response, 80 on subcommittee's report, 80–81 on resignation.

67. Wiberg, "A History of the University of Minnesota Chapter," II: 354 on regional meeting; II: 356–357 on attendance and suggestions.

68. Ibid., II: 356 on first section; II: 356 on second and third sections; II: 357–358 on recommendations and delivery to the Central Office.

69. Ibid., II: 358 on second meeting; II: 358 and 359 on discussion; II: 358, 358–359 on annual meeting and instructions to Levi.

70. Werner Levi, "Report on the Annual Meeting of the AAUP, 1954," AAUP Files, as quoted by Wiberg, "A History of the University of Minnesota Chapter," II: 361n. 33.

71. Ibid., II: 361.

72. Ibid.

73. Loya Metzger, "Professors in Trouble," 81. See Wiberg, "A History of the University of Minnesota Chapter," II: 359 on effective date of resignation.

74. Loya Metzger, "Professors in Trouble," 81–82 on fighting Council action, 82 on retirement.

75. Ibid., 82–83.

76. Ibid., 83. See also Ralph F. Fuchs, "A Letter From the General Secretary," *A.A.U.P. Bulletin* 41 (Autumn 1955): 423–424.

77. Ralph F. Fuchs, "Report, 1955–57, by the Retiring General Secretary," *AAUP Bulletin* 43 (September 1957): 415; [William E. Britton], "The General Secretaryship," *A.A.U.P. Bulletin* 41 (Spring 1955): 6. He had been the president of the Washington University chapter (elected to the position two years after joining the AAUP in 1931) and vice-president of the Indiana University chapter in 1949–1950. He had national leadership experience as a member of the council from 1945 to 1947, first vice-president from 1950 to 1951, and chair of the Resolutions Committee for the 1951 and 1952 Annual Meetings. Fuchs had also been a member of the staff of the U.S. solicitor general and active in the Indiana Civil Liberties Union as well as the Association of American Law Schools (serving as chair of that organization's Committee on Academic Freedom and Tenure in 1953). He published widely in the field of administrative law and was reported to be "one of the twelve people who shaped the most important piece of administrative law legislation in our country's history, the Administrative Procedure Act." See [George Pope Shannon], "The General Secretaryship of the American Association of University Professors," *A.A.U.P. Bulletin* 41 (Summer 1955): 212; and "Special Commemorative Meeting of the Indiana University School of Law Faculty in Honor of the Memory of Professor Ralph Follen Fuchs: Transcript of Proceedings" (Bloomington, Ind.: 4 March 1985), 11 and 17.

78. Fuchs, "Report, 1955–57, by the Retiring General Secretary," 416.

79. [Shannon], "Record of Council Meetings of American Association of University Professors," 104–105. The council made these decisions at the

awkward time when Himstead was fighting to stay in the office but Fuchs was to assume the general secretaryship. Thus, although Himstead was at the time general secretary, the decisions appear to respond to Fuchs's anticipated arrival. Elected leadership activity continued beyond committing funds for staff members and urging quick investigations into alleged academic freedom violations. As requested by the council, President William E. Britton began to scrutinize committee membership, and he appointed three new committees, on annual meeting programs, AAUP publications, and eligibility for membership. See [George Pope Shannon], "Central Office Notes," *A.A.U.P. Bulletin* 41 (Summer 1955): 367.

80. [Shannon], "Central Office Notes," 366.

81. Fuchs, "A Letter from the General Secretary," 423 and [Shannon], "Central Office Notes," 366. Although the AAUP president was responsible for appointments, Fuchs assembled the Special Committee according to its chair, H. Bentley Glass. H. Bentley Glass, interview in Stonybrook, New York, on 4 March 1986.

82. [Ralph F. Fuchs], "Central Office Notes," *A.A.U.P. Bulletin* 41 (Autumn 1955): 592–593 on committee membership and requested reports; 592 on contacts.

83. "Academic Freedom and Tenure in the Quest for National Security," 52.

84. Ibid., 50 on Communist infiltration and 56 on needed safeguards.

85. "Academic Freedom and Tenure in the Quest for National Security," 58 on conspiracy; "Academic Freedom and Tenure: Statements of Principles," *AAUP Bulletin,* 42 (Spring 1956): 41–44, and 43–44 on incompetence and moral turpitude; "Academic Freedom and Tenure in the Quest for National Security," 60 on personal freedom. One scholar's examination of the AAUP during World War I suggested that even in those early years the association was willing to sacrifice values of scholarship to the service of the nation; see Carol S. Gruber, *Mars and Minerva: World War I and the Uses of Higher Learning in America* (Baton Rouge: Louisiana State University Press, 1975), 115–117. Another author offered a stronger statement on AAUP activity in defense of academic freedom and tenure principles, stating that the association "sacrificed individuals and substantive principles in order to gain compliance for procedural safeguards from university officials for the profession as a whole." That author also called the Special Committee's report "a massive and pathetic equivocation." See Sheila Slaughter, "The Danger Zone: Academic Freedom and Civil Liberties," *Annals of the American Academy of Political and Social Science* 448 (March 1980): 47–48. Slaughter softened her stance in a more recent article, suggesting that "the degree of academ-

ic freedom varies with historical circumstance." See Sheila Slaughter, "Academic Freedom in the Modern University," in *Higher Education in American Society,* ed. Philip G. Altbach and Robert O. Berdahl, rev. ed. (Buffalo: Prometheus Books, 1987), 84.

86. "Academic Freedom and Tenure in the Quest for National Security," 71.

87. [Ralph F. Fuchs], "Outside Reaction to Last Spring's Special Committee Report and Censure Actions," *AAUP Bulletin* 42 (Autumn 1956): 566–570. See also R. H. Eckleberry, "Editorial Comments: A Double Standard," *Journal of Higher Education* 47 (April 1956): 223–225.

88. "Organization and Policy—Report of Committee O," *AAUP Bulletin* 42 (Spring 1956): 166–167.

89. "Committees of the Association," *AAUP Bulletin* 43 (Spring 1957): 93–99.

90. Ibid., 93–95 on A, T, and Z; 98–99 on district panels.

91. H. W. Tyler, "What the Association Is and Is Not," *AAUP Bulletin* 42 (Spring 1956): 163–165.

92. Ibid., 163.

93. "Organization and Policy—Report of Committee O," 170.

94. Ibid.

95. "General Recommendations and Projections," *AAUP Bulletin* 51 (May 1965): 191n. 1, on addition of "economic welfare." See "Proposed Revision of the Constitution," *AAUP Bulletin* 43 (Spring 1957): 85 on the version to be amended as approved by the council. The original phrase dates back to the 1914 call to organize the association; see the brief history of the association's early years in the first chapter.

96. "The Forty-third Annual Meeting," *AAUP Bulletin* 43 (June 1957): 364.

97. American University chapter delegates to council, 26 April 1957, in "Council Meeting—November 15–16, 1957 Washington, D. C.," file in AAUP Archives, Washington, D.C.

98. "Recommendations of the District of Columbia Regional Conference to the Council" (1 September 1957), 2, in "Council Meeting—November 15–16," file in AAUP Archives, Washington, D.C.

99. "Resolution Adopted at the Annual Meeting of the Illinois Conference of the American Association of University Professors, October 26–7, 1957" in "Council Meeting—November 15–16, 1957," file in AAUP Archives, Washington, D.C.

100. "Recommendations of the District of Columbia Regional Conference to the Council," 1 on symptoms, 1 and 4 on staffing recommendations, 3 on professions.

101. John Wilson, *Academic Science, Higher Education, and the Federal Government,* 45. The National Defense Education Act was also an indication of concern about loyalty in education having subsided rather than ended as it included a required loyalty oath that was not rescinded until 1961. See Wilson, 46–47.

102. President's Commission on Education Beyond the High School, *Second Report to the President* (Washington, D.C.: United States Government Printing Office, July 1957), 4.

103. Fritz Machlup, "Grading of Academic Salary Scales," *AAUP Bulletin* 44 (March 1958): 219. "Report of the Subcommittee on Standards of the Committee on the Economic Status of the Profession," *AAUP Bulletin* 44 (March 1958): 217–218.

104. Machlup, "Grading of Academic Salary Scales," 219–220.

105. Ibid., 219 on purposes of survey, 220 on proposals, 225–226 on construction of scale, 226 on timing of report.

106. Ibid., 225, 231.

107. Ibid., 226 on top grade; See "Report of the Subcommittee on Standards of the Committee on the Economic Status of the Profession," 217 on acceleration.

108. Helen C. White, "The Association in 1958," *AAUP Bulletin* 44 (June 1958): 395–396. White also notes the recent strong change in public attitudes about higher education, 394.

109. "Forty-fourth Annual Meeting," 503.

110. "Record of Council Meeting," *AAUP Bulletin* 43 (September 1957), 538. See also H. Bentley Glass, interview in Stonybrook, New York, on 4 March 1986.

111. "Statement on Procedural Standards in Faculty Dismissal Proceedings," *AAUP Bulletin* 44 (March 1958): 271–274; "Record of Council Meeting," 281 on council approval; "Forty-fourth Annual Meeting [Completed Report]," *AAUP Bulletin* 44 (September 1958): 652–653.

112. "Statement on Procedural Standards in Faculty Dismissal Proceedings," 272.

113. "Record of Council Meeting," *AAUP Bulletin* 44 (September 1958): 658.

114. Bertram H. Davis, interview in Tallahassee, Florida, on 7 March 1986.

115. "Distribution of Membership and Record of Chapter Officers: Record of Membership for 1954," *AAUP Bulletin* 41 (Spring 1955): 170.

116. Ibid., 135–169. The remaining active members at colleges and universities were at professional and technical institutions or foreign colleges and universities.

117. "Membership: Record for 1958," *AAUP Bulletin* 45 (March 1959): 135.

118. *Digest of Educational Statistics: 1971 Edition,* table 104, 78.

119. Staff size was temporarily down to four members at the end of 1958 because General Secretary Carr had resigned, but a new staff member was to be appointed shortly. See "Record of Council Meeting," *AAUP Bulletin* 45 (March 1959): 90 on Fidler's proposal for another member. Staff size of four noted in "Officers and the Council," *AAUP Bulletin* 45 (March 1959): 229 [unnumbered] and active members in "Membership: Record for 1958," 135.

120. "Committees of the Association," *AAUP Bulletin* 44 (December 1958): 792–796 and "Index for 1955," *A.A.U.P. Bulletin* 41 (Winter 1955): 822–823 on committee reports in 1955. There are no published lists of more committees in 1955, although more may have been operating at the time.

121. Ralph F. Fuchs, "Council Election, and Appointment of New General Secretary," *AAUP Bulletin* 43 (June 1957): 247.

122. Clark Byse, interview in Cambridge, Massachusetts, on 2 March 1986. Ralph S. Brown, Jr., interview in New Haven, Connecticut, on 3 March 1986.

123. Fuchs, "Council Election and Appointment of New General Secretary," 248. Carr was the author of books on civil rights and civil liberties, and since 1937 he had been a professor of law and political science at Dartmouth College. His AAUP activities included council membership and service on Committee A and the Special Committee on Academic Freedom and Tenure in the Quest for National Security. See [Ralph F. Fuchs], "The New General Secretary," *AAUP Bulletin* 43 (September 1957): 411.

124. Fuchs, "Council Election and Appointment of New General Secretary," 248.

125. Robert K. Carr, "The Association's New Officers, Council Members, and General Secretary," *AAUP Bulletin* 44 (June 1958): 390–391 on Carr's announcement, 391 on Fidler's appointment.

126. *Statistics of Higher Education: 1955–56, Faculty, Students, and Degrees* (Washington, D.C.: United States Government Printing Office, 1957), table V, 14.

127. Leland Medsker, *The Junior College: Progress and Prospect* (New York: McGraw-Hill, 1960), 172.

128. Logan Wilson, "A President's Perspective," *Faculty-Administration Relationships* ed. Frank C. Abbott (Washington, D.C.: American Council on Education, 1958), 3.

Chapter Two: A Revitalized AAUP, 1958 to 1964

1. Robert K. Carr, "The Association's New Officers and General Secretary," *AAUP Bulletin* 44 (September 1958): 551.

2. Bertram H. Davis, interview in Tallahassee, Florida, on 7 March 1986.

3. [William P. Fidler], "Report by the General Secretary," *AAUP Bulletin* 45 (March 1959): 85 on growth and surplus, 86–87 on new staff,; 87 on committee expansion.

4. "Constitution of the Association," *AAUP Bulletin* 50 (September 1964): 281.

5. "Statement on Academic Freedom of Students," *AAUP Bulletin* 51 (December 1965): 447. "Joint Statement on Rights and Freedoms of Students," 53 *AAUP Bulletin* (December 1967): 365 and "The Fifty-fourth Annual Meeting," *AAUP Bulletin* 54 (June 1968): 242–243.

6. "Academic Salaries, 1958–59: Report of Committee Z on the Economic Status of the Profession," *AAUP Bulletin* 45 (June 1959): 157.

7. Ibid., 167.

8. Ibid., Table 3, 167. No specific national comparison obtains for the response rate because chapters' responses represent a variety of forms, including salary scales for professors at affiliated institutions and chapters at branches or divisions of institutions. Ibid., 167. A rough comparison, treating all chapters as representative of individual institutions, indicates that 14 percent of all colleges and universities submitted reports. See David W. Breneman and Chester E. Finn, Jr., eds., *Public Policy and Private Higher Education* (Washington, D.C.: Brookings Institution, 1978), table 1–3, 20 on number of institutions nationally.

9. Breneman and Finn, Jr., eds., *Public Policy and Private Higher Education*, Appendix I, 177.

10. Ibid., 183, 185, and 179; 183, 186, 189, 178, and 184.

11. [Fritz Machlup], "Progress Report on the Salary Grading Program," *AAUP Bulletin* 45 (December 1959): 493–494.

12. "The Economic Status of the Profession, 1959–60: Annual Report by Committee Z," *AAUP Bulletin* 46 (June 1960): 156.

13. Ibid., 157. As chapter responses, the 1959–1960 participation rate is 55.1 percent; as a national institutional response, the participation rate was 16.4 percent. For the number of the nation's colleges and universities, see

Breneman and Finn, Jr., eds., *Public Policy and Private Higher Education,* table 1–3, 20.

14. Ibid., 170–171. See also "Revised Salary Grading Tables for 1960–61," *AAUP Bulletin* 46 (June 1960): 194–197.

15. Machlup, "Grading of Academic Salary Scales," 226.

16. "Revised Salary Grading Tables for 1960–61," 194; President's Committee on Education Beyond the High School, *Second Report to the President,* 4 on doubling salaries.

17. "Revised Salary Grading Tables for 1960–61," 194.

18. "The Economic Status of the Profession, 1960–61: Annual Report By Committee Z," *AAUP Bulletin* 47 (June 1961): 101.

19. Ibid.

20. Ibid. On the one hand, the level of some administrators' cooperation with the survey, and continued AAUP negotiation with administrators, went beyond the collection of data. In February 1961 representatives of Committee Z and some unidentified higher education associations met to discuss possible improvements in the salary survey. Committee members felt that the discussion was productive and that the committee would incorporate several of the recommendations (102 and 103–104 on planned changes in the program). The committee members looked forward to another such meeting in the fall of 1961 with representatives from the AAC. See "The Economic Status of the Profession, 1960-61," 103; and "Record of Council Meeting," *AAUP Bulletin* 47 (September 1961): 263 for identification of the "leading association" as the AAC. On the other hand, some administrators were sufficiently concerned about the salary survey to urge a partial boycott. In October 1960 the Pennsylvania Association of Colleges and Universities, a college presidents' organization, passed a resolution urging its member institutions to refuse permission for publication of their salary data. "Record of Council Meeting," 263. Yet Committee Z reported that "even within its own group the boycott has been of limited effectiveness." See "The Economic Status of the Profession," 103. The Committee Z and council reports in the *Bulletin* discuss a boycott based on submission but not publication of the salary data; it appears that the Pennsylvania group is the one mentioned—although not by name—in the Committee Z report, 102–103.

21. "The Economic Status of the Profession, 1960-61," 105.

22. "The Economic Status of the Profession, 1961–62: Annual Report by Committee Z," *AAUP Bulletin* 48 (June 1962): 117. The committee continued its initiative in the area of salary surveys in 1963 when it called a conference of representatives from the United States Office of Education, the

Statistical Office of the American Council on Education, the National Education Association, and the AAUP to discuss the "multiplicity of questionnaires." The United States Office of Education was uncertain about its salary survey, but the AAUP and the NEA representatives agreed upon common survey procedures and mailed their two questionnaires together. Only the mailing was cooperative, as both organizations planned to "continue to publish their data in the same manner as before" even though the specific conference impetus was a suggestion to reduce the number of questionnaires. The AAUP and the NEA each saw its salary reports as meeting needs of the professoriate. See "Record of Council Meeting," *AAUP Bulletin* 50 (March 1964): 67–68.

23. "The Economic Status of the Profession, 1961–62," 118 and 117.

24. "The Economic Status of the Profession: Report on the Self-Grading Compensation Survey," *AAUP Bulletin* 48 (June 1962): 120; and "The Economic Status of the Profession, June 1961-62," table 4, 105.

25. See Breneman and Finn, Jr., eds., *Public Policy and Private Higher Education,* table 1–3, 20, for number of colleges and universities. The number of institutions for 1961–1962 is not available, so the calculation uses the average of the 1960–1961 and fall 1962 data.

26. "The Economic Status of the Profession, 1961-62," 120.

27. "The Economic Status of the Profession, 1962–63: Report on the Self-Grading Compensation Survey," *AAUP Bulletin* 49 (June 1963): 141. See Breneman and Finn, Jr., eds., *Public Policy and Private Higher Education,* table 1–3, 20 for national data.

28. "The Economic Status of the Profession, 1962–63," 141.

29. Ibid.

30. "Record of Council Meeting" (March 1964), 68.

31. "The Economic Status of the Profession, 1963–64: Annual Report on The Self-Grading Compensation Survey," *AAUP Bulletin* 50 (June 1964): 136.

32. "The Economic Status of the Profession, 1963–64," 139. Seven hundred fifty-six institutions participated in the 1963–1964 survey, representing 35 percent of the nation's colleges and universities. See "The Economic Status of the Profession, 1963–64," table 19, 148; and Breneman and Finn, Jr., eds., *Public Policy and Private Higher Education,* table 1–3, 20.

33. "The Economic Status of the Profession, 1963–64," 139.

34. Ibid.

35. Ibid., 141.

36. "Interim Report of Committee T on Faculty-Administration Relationships," *AAUP Bulletin* 44 (December 1958): 786.

37. Ibid.

38. Ibid., 787 and 788–790.

39. "Faculty-Administration Relationships: Monmouth College (New Jersey)," *AAUP Bulletin* 47 (March 1961): 5. On the report's development, see "Report of Committee T on Faculty-Administration Relationships," 787 and 789–790.

40. "Faculty-Administration Relationships: Monmouth College (New Jersey)," 5.

41. Ibid.

42. "Record of Council Meeting" *AAUP Bulletin* 46 (March 1960): 109.

43. "Record of Council Meeting," *AAUP Bulletin* 46 (September 1960): 301.

44. "Faculty Participation in College and University Government," *AAUP Bulletin* 46 (June 1960): 203 on request for comment and preamble; 204 on shared power, proposed principles, and institutional relations.

45. "Faculty-Administration Relationships: Monmouth College (New Jersey)," 5–23 and "Faculty-Administration Relationships: The School of Medicine at The University of Miami

(Florida)," *AAUP Bulletin* 47 (March 1961): 24–39.

46. "Forty-seventh Annual Meeting," *AAUP Bulletin* 47 (June 1961): 166. Chapter response to the draft statement on college and university government was mostly favorable. One hundred and fifty chapters submitted comments as of the April 1961 Council meeting, and 110 of those chapters essentially approved the statement in its current version. See "Record of Council Meeting" (September 1961), 264.

47. "Record of Council Meeting," *AAUP Bulletin* 48 (March 1962): 53.

48. Ibid., 55. The other two areas were distinctions between principles and procedures and avoiding "complicating ambiguity."

49. On spring 1962 publication of the draft statement, see "Faculty Participation in College and University Government," *AAUP Bulletin* 48 (March 1962): 16–17. For a report of the meeting with selected administrators, "Record of Council Meeting" (September 1962), 277.

50. [John P. Dawson], "Report of Committee T, 1961–62," *AAUP Bulletin* 48 (June 1962): 164–165 on Monmouth and Miami; 165–166 on Fairleigh Dickinson; 165 on censure and published reports; 166 on chapters' role and shared authority reports.

51. Ralph F. Fuchs, "A Profession in Quest of Itself," *AAUP Bulletin* 48 (June 1962): 104–105 on complexities, 105 on gains.

52. Ward, "The Place and Function of Faculties in College and University Government," 71.

53. Fuchs, "A Profession in Quest of Itself," 107 on solution and conception, 109 on cooperation.

54. "Forty-ninth Annual Meeting," *AAUP Bulletin* 49 (June 1963): 191.

55. "Record of Council Meeting," *AAUP Bulletin* 49 (September 1963): 264.

56. "Faculty Participation in College and University Government," *AAUP Bulletin* 49 (September 1963): 253 on circulation of Syracuse alternatives; 258 on focus of Syracuse draft; 258–259 on budgetary matters; 259 on hostile administrators and role of faculty.

57. "Fiftieth Annual Meeting," 191.

58. Ibid.

59. Ibid.

60. "Disclaimer Affidavit Requirement of the National Defense Education Act of 1958," *AAUP Bulletin* 44 (December 1958): 769–772; Record of Council Meeting," *AAUP Bulletin* 45 (September 1959): 400; [L. J. (Louis Joughin)], "Repealing the Disclaimer Affidavit," *AAUP Bulletin* 46 (March 1960): 57–61; "Protesting the Disclaimer Affidavit: The Association, the Colleges and the Universities," *AAUP Bulletin* 46 (June 1960): 205–206; "Disclaimer Affidavit: Non-Participating and Disapproving Colleges and Universities," *AAUP Bulletin* 47 (March 1961): 52; "Disclaimer Affidavit: Non-Participating and Disapproving Colleges and Universities," *AAUP Bulletin* 47 (June 1961): 164; "Disclaimer Affidavit: Non-Participating and Disapproving Colleges and Universities," *AAUP Bulletin* 47 (September 1961): 267; "Disclaimer Affidavit: Non-Participating and Disapproving Colleges and Universities," *AAUP Bulletin* 47 (December 1961): 343; "Disclaimer Affidavit: Non-Participating and Disapproving Colleges and Universities," *AAUP Bulletin* 48 (March 1962): 49; "Disclaimer Affidavit: Non-Participating and Disapproving Colleges and Universities," *AAUP Bulletin* 48 (June 1962): 180; "Disclaimer Affidavit: Non-Participating and Disapproving Colleges and Universities," *AAUP Bulletin* 48 (September 1962): 282; "Disclaimer Affidavit: Non-Participating and Disapproving Colleges and Universities," *AAUP Bulletin* 48 (December 1962): 331; [Herman I. Orentlicher], "The Disclaimer Affidavit: A Valediction," *AAUP Bulletin* 48 (December 1962): 324–330.

61. [William P. Fidler], "Aid to the Arkansas Professors," *AAUP Bulletin* 46 (March 1960): 19 on Arkansas law and AAUP financial support of the professors; 19–20 on appointment assistance.

62. "The Forty-third Annual Meeting," 363; "Forty-fourth Annual Meeting," 505; Bertram H. Davis, "Academic *Apartheid:* The Association and the South African Professors," *AAUP Bulletin* 46 (March 1960): 63–65. Money

for the fellowship came from the association and an individual association member, 63; Bertram H. Davis, "Academic *Apartheid:* The Association and the South African Professors," *AAUP Bulletin* 46 (March 1960): 63–65. [Bertram H. Davis], "The South African Professors," *AAUP Bulletin* 46 (June 1960): 207–208.

63. "Forty-sixth Annual Meeting" *AAUP Bulletin* 46 (June 1960): 219–220.

64. "The Association and the Desegregation Controversy," *AAUP Bulletin* 48 (June 1962): 167–169. On Woodward's work, see "Record of Council Meeting," *AAUP Bulletin* 48 (September 1962): 277 and "Record of Council Meeting," *AAUP Bulletin* 49 (March 1963): 59. See also C. Vann Woodward, "The Unreported Crisis in the Southern Colleges," *Harper's Magazine* 225 (October 1962): 82–84, 86–89. Woodward noted AAUP effectiveness only within limits and suggested that it could not act against the influential individuals and groups causing the trouble at southern colleges. See 89.

65. "Report of Committee A, 1964–65," *AAUP Bulletin* 51 (June 1965): 239.

66. Carr, "The Association's New Officers and General Secretary," 552.

67. [William P. Fidler], "From the General Secretary," *AAUP Bulletin* 50 (March 1964): 62.

68. "Record of Council Meeting," *AAUP Bulletin* 46 (March 1960): 110. Eventually the association appointed a staff member to work directly with Committee R on Relationships of Higher Education to Federal and State Governments; "Record of Council Meeting," *AAUP Bulletin* 47 (March 1961): 66.

69. Robert K. Carr, "Academic Freedom, the American Association of University Professors, and the United States Supreme Court," *AAUP Bulletin* 45 (March 1959): 24.

70. Ralph F. Fuchs, "The Barenblatt Decision of the Supreme Court and the Academic Profession," *AAUP Bulletin* 45 (September 1959): 333. Ralph S. Brown, Jr., interview in New Haven, Connecticut, on 2 March 1986 on Pyrrhic victory.

71. Fuchs, "The Barenblatt Decision," 338.

72. Bertram H. Davis to author, 16 October 1989.

73. [Bertram H. Davis], "Academic Freedom and Tenure: Four Cases of Late Notice," *AAUP Bulletin* 45 (March 1959): 58–61. On Davis's statement concerning publication of names, see 59.

74. [David Fellman], "Report of Committee A, 1959–60," *AAUP Bulletin* 46 (June 1960): 223.

75. "Record of Council Meeting," *AAUP Bulletin* 48 (March 1962): 53–54.

76. [Bertram H. Davis], "Academic Freedom and Tenure: Late Notice Cases, 1961 and 1962," *AAUP Bulletin* 48 (December 1962): 368.

77. "Advisory Letters from the Washington Office," *AAUP Bulletin* 48 (December 1962): 394–396.

78. "Report of Committee A, 1963–64," *AAUP Bulletin* 50 (June 1964): 128–129.

79. "Report of Committee A, 1963-64," 129; and "Fiftieth Annual Meeting," *AAUP Bulletin* 50 (June 1964): 188.

80. "Forty-fifth Annual Meeting," *AAUP Bulletin* 45 (March 1959): 100 for proposed changes; "Constitution," *AAUP Bulletin* 45 (March 1959) for nomination procedures; "Forty-fifth Annual Meeting," *AAUP Bulletin* 45 (June 1959): 274 on approval at the annual meeting.

81. "Organizational Notes," *AAUP Bulletin* 46 (December 1960): 425.

82. "Record of Council Meeting" (March 1961), 63.

83. "Organizational Notes," *AAUP Bulletin* 49 (September 1963): 293.

84. "Membership: Record for 1958," *AAUP Bulletin* 45 (March 1959): 135; "Membership Record for 1964," *AAUP Bulletin* 51 (March 1965): 54.

85. *Digest of Educational Statistics, 1971 Edition,* table 104, 78.

86. "Institutional Distribution and Chapter Officers," *AAUP Bulletin* 46 (September 1960): 328–346. Thus nearly 8 percent of the institutions represented by AAUP membership were public two-year colleges; nationally just over 15.5 percent of the institutions were public two-year colleges. For number of public two-year colleges, see *Digest of Educational Statistics: 1973 Edition* (Washington, D.C.: United States Government Printing Office, 1974), table 99, 83; and for number of all institutions, see *Education Directory 1960–1961, Part 3: Higher Education* (Washington, D.C.: United States Government Printing Office, 1960), table 4, 12.

87. "Distribution of Membership and Record of Chapter Officers" (February 1941): 116–132; "Institutional Distribution and Chapter Officers," The number of public four-year colleges does not include state flagship and public research universities. Those institutions were comparatively stable in number and were traditional sources of AAUP members and leaders. Table I, 2–3. [Because of the war the Office of Education did not collect data for 1940–41; see cover of volume 1.] *Education Directory 1961–62 Part 3, Higher Education* (Washington, D.C.: United States Government Printing Office, 1962), table 4, 13.

89. "Sun. a.m. Apr. 12" in "Council Meeting April 9–10, 1964 St. Louis, Missouri," file in AAUP Archives, Washington, D.C., remarks by Eveline Burns, 5.

90. "Minutes (Council meeting April 12, morning session)" in "Council Meeting April 9–10, 1964," file in AAUP Archives, Washington, D.C., remarks by Bertram H. Davis, 3.

91. [Bertram H. Davis], "The Editor's Page," *AAUP Bulletin* 50 (June 1964): 107.

92. Melvin Lurie, "Professors, Physicians, and Unionism," *AAUP Bulletin* 48 (September 1962): 272–276.

93. Ibid., 276.

94. Ibid., 272n. 3.

95. Israel Kugler, "Letters: Professors, Physicians, and Unionism," *AAUP Bulletin* 49 (March 1963): 74 on his position, the local's achievements, the AAUP inadequacy, and physicians; 75 on general reality and professional craft; 76 on AAUP transformation and power in higher education.

96. V. Edwin Bixenstine and James Karge Olsen, "Letters: Must AAUP Change Its Image? An Open Letter to the Ad Hoc Self-Survey Committee," *AAUP Bulletin* 50 (September 1964): 285 on local and national AAUP; 286 on genteel national AAUP, view of administrators and governing boards, and national control of investigations; 287 on national control of chapters.

97. Ibid., 287. The authors underlined their statement.

98. Ibid., 287–288.

99. Ibid., 286.

100. "Officers and the Council," *AAUP Bulletin* 44 (December 1958): 706. "Association Officers and Council," *AAUP Bulletin* 50 (December 1964): 308.

101. Active member figures of 1 January 1959 and 1 January 1965 were used to calculate these ratios. See 164.

102. Schrecker, *No Ivory Tower,* 336; and Loya Metzger, "Professors in Trouble," 78.

103. "Proceedings of the American Association of University Professors, Council Meeting, April 26, 1962, Morrison Hotel, Chicago, Illinois," file in AAUP Archives, Washington, D.C., remarks by Ralph Fuchs, 6.

104. Ibid., 5.

105. Ibid., 5–6.

106. "Record of Council Meeting" (March 1962), 55.

107. Bertram H. Davis, interview in Tallahassee, Florida, on 7 March 1986.

Chapter Three: Custodians of the Interests of Higher Education, or Employees?

1. [Bertram H. Davis], "The Editor's Page," *AAUP Bulletin* 47 (March 1961): 69.

2. Ibid.

3. Clark Kerr, *The Uses of the University* (Cambridge: Harvard University Press, 1963), 43, 44, and 109.

4. Spencer Klaw, "The Affluent Professors," *Reporter,* 22 (23 June 1960): pp. 16–25; and Richard Hofstadter, *Anti-Intellectualism in American Life* (New York: Alfred A. Knopf, 1963), 228–29. See also Howard R. Bowen and Jack A. Schuster, *American Professors: A National Resource Imperiled* (New York: Oxford University Press, 1986), 5.

5. *The States and Higher Education* (San Francisco: Jossey-Bass, 1976), 38–39 and table 3, 30. Published as a commentary of the Carnegie Foundation for the Advancement of Teaching.

6. David G. Brown, *The Mobile Professors* (Washington, D.C.: American Council on Education, 1967), 37–38, 58, 62.

7. Joseph W. Garbarino and Bill Aussieker, *Faculty Bargaining: Change and Conflict* (New York: McGraw-Hill, 1975), 27. These authors are adamant on this subject. See also E. D. Duryea and Robert S. Fisk, Epilogue, in *Faculty Unions and Collective Bargaining,* ed. E. D. Duryea and Robert S. Fisk (San Francisco: Jossey-Bass, 1973), 197–199. Duryea and Fisk emphasize professional and shared authority at the informal level of bargaining. See also Everett Carll Ladd, Jr., and Seymour Martin Lipset, *The Divided Academy: Professors and Politics* (New York: McGraw-Hill, 1975), 245–246 on the AAUP specifically (until 1972).

8. Charles P. Dennison, *Faculty Rights and Obligations in Eight Liberal Arts Colleges* (New York: Teachers College, Columbia University Press, 1955); and John J. Corson, *Governance of Colleges and Universities* (New York: McGraw-Hill, 1960). Corson notes the tension between faculties and administrations, 113–116, but nevertheless his observations are based on the informal nature of administration and governance.

9. Wilson, *Academic Man,* 119.

10. Robert W. Ozanne, *The Labor Movement in Wisconsin: A History* (Madison, Wisc.: State Historical Society of Wisconsin, 1984), 75. Ozanne notes that in 1961 the Wisconsin legislature passed another law requiring municipalities to bargain with public employees if a majority of the employees indicated that they wanted a union.

11. Garbarino and Aussieker, *Faculty Bargaining,* 17–18; Robert K. Carr and Daniel Van Eyck, *Collective Bargaining Comes to the Campus* (Washington, D.C.: American Council on Education, 1973), 19; Ladd and Lipset, *The Divided Academy,* 293.

12. Robert O. Berdahl, *Statewide Coordination of Higher Education* (Washington, D.C.: American Council on Education, 1971), 26 on changes

from 1940 to 1969, 10–19 on expectations about the boards' influence and control.

13. Joseph W. Garbarino, "Emergence of Collective Bargaining," in *Faculty Unions and Collective Bargaining,* ed. Duryea and Fisk, 2.

14. Garbarino and Aussieker, *Faculty Bargaining,* 83–84, 92 on the AFT; Carr and Van Eyck, *Collective Bargaining Comes to the Campus,* 20; Ladd and Lipset, *The Divided Academy,* 245–250.

15. George W. Angell, "Two-Year College Experience" in *Faculty Unions and Collective Bargaining,* ed. Duryea and Fisk, 92–94; David L. Graham and Donald E. Walters, "Bargaining Process" in *Faculty Unions and Collective Bargaining,* ed. Duryea and Fisk, 45, 48–49.

16. "At Henry Ford: Four-Day Walkout Brings First College Contract," *American Teacher Magazine* 51 (September 1966): 19.

17. Eaton, *The American Federation of Teachers,* 163–165; and Stephen Cole, *The Unionization of Teachers: A Case Study of the UFT* (New York: Praeger, 1969), 20–22. See Victor G. Reuther, *The Brothers Reuther and the Story of the UAW* (Boston: Houghton Mifflin, 1976), 365 and 367; Myron Lieberman and Michael H. Moskow, *Collective Negotiations for Teachers: An Approach to School Administration* (Chicago: Rand McNally, 1966), 17n., 38–39n., for descriptions of the AFL-CIO support of the AFT unionization of New York City schoolteachers.

18. "NEA Unit Claims Legal Labor Status under Wisconsin Law," *American Teacher* 9 (November 1962): 1–2. As indicated by the article's title, the National Education Association also sought representation status at the school.

19. "Union Election for Vocational Teachers Set," *Milwaukee Journal,* 15 May 1963, part 1: 10.

20. "Milwaukee Vocational Union Elected Bargaining Agent," *American Teacher* 10 (September 1963): 1, 11; "Union Wins Teacher Vote," *Milwaukee Journal,* 4 June 1963, part 2: 14.

21. "Collective Bargaining Elections," *American Teacher* 12 (January 1966): 4.

22. West, *The National Education Association,* 28–31, 33–34, 36; and Lorraine M. McDonnell, "The Internal Politics of the NEA," *Phi Delta Kappan* 18 (October 1976): 185.

23. West, *The National Education Association,* 38 and 46–47; McDonnell, "The Internal Politics of the NEA," 185; and *Addresses and Proceedings of the Ninety-ninth Annual Meeting Held at Atlantic City, New Jersey, June 25–June 30, 1961* 99 (Washington, D.C.: National Education Association, 1961), 216–218 on resolution promoting the representation of teachers by professional associations.

24. James A. Carey, Address, in National Education Association, *Addresses and Proceedings of the One-Hundredth Annual Meeting Held at Denver, Colorado, July 1–July 6, 1962* 100 (Washington, D.C.: National Education Association, 1962), 52.

25. West, *The National Education Association,* 56–57 and 65–67.

26. Ibid., 66–67.

27. *Addresses and Proceedings of the One-Hundredth Annual Meeting:* "NEA Membership by States," 6, "Financial Report," 341, "Headquarters Staff," 404–405; McDonnell, "The Internal Politics of the NEA," 186 on state staff.

28. "Agenda for Meeting of the Executive Committee," in "Council Meeting—October 30, 31 1964" file, AAUP Archives, 1.

29. "Record of Council Meeting," *AAUP Bulletin* 51 (March 1965): 50. Fellman requested that Davis plan the conference because Fidler was on sabbatical leave, customary among AAUP staff members. See 48.

30. Bertram H. Davis, interview in Tallahassee, Florida, on 7 March 1986.

31. "Committees of the Association," *AAUP Bulletin* 50 (September 1964): 276. The committee members were AAUP President David Fellman (political science, University of Wisconsin), Frances C. Brown (chemistry, Duke University), James M. Darlington (biology, Franklin and Marshall College), John P. Dawson (law, Harvard University), Ralph Fuchs (law, Indiana University), and Fritz Machlup (economics, Princeton University).

32. Bertram H. Davis, interview in Tallahassee, Florida, on 7 March 1986.

33. "Draft—Council Minutes, Sunday afternoon, April 11, 1965—Barbara Davie," file in AAUP Archives, remarks by David Fellman, 4.

34. Ralph S. Brown, Jr., "Representation of Economic Interests: Report of a Conference," *AAUP Bulletin* 51 (September 1965): 374–375n. 3.

35. See, as examples, the preceding descriptions of the Committee Z conferences with representatives of the AAC and with other organizations requesting salary data and see the Committee T conferences with representatives of ACE.

36. "Summary of Conference on Representation of Economic Interests," Document #52–26–65, in "Council & Annual Meeting—April 9–11, 1965 Washington, D.C.," file, AAUP Archives, Washington, D.C., 2. On McPherson's position in the AAUP, see "Committees of the Association" (September 1964), 276.

37. "Summary Of Conference," 4–5 on dues systems, 6 on New York situation.

38. Ibid., 13–14 on exclusive representation, 12 on the strike. On Barbash and Summers, see Brown, "Representation of Economic Interests" (September 1965), 374–375n. 3.

39. Ibid., 19–21 on Fellman's statements, 21–22 on statements by Brown and Barbash.

40. Ibid., 22 on Byse's question and Barbash's response, 23 on Summers's disagreement. On Byse's position, see "Committees of the Association" (September 1964), 276.

41. Ibid., 24.

42. Ibid., 24–25 on Fidler's comments, 26 on Joughin's question and responses by Barbash and Summers.

43. "Record of Council Meeting," *AAUP Bulletin* 51 (September 1965): 386.

44. Ibid.

45. "Draft-Council Minutes, Sunday afternoon, April 11, 1965," file in AAUP Archives, Washington, D.C., remarks by David Fellman, 5 and 12; Bertram H. Davis, interview in Tallahassee, Florida, on 7 March 1986.

46. Ralph S. Brown, Jr., "Representation of Economic Interests" (September 1965), 374–375n. 3. Clyde Summers, Jack Barbash, and J. Bailey Harvey (speech, City College of New York), and William McPherson were eventual members of the Special Committee; see "Committees of the Association," *AAUP Bulletin* 51 (December 1965): 452.

47. "Council Meeting, April 8, 1965 (evening session)," in "Council Meeting, April 8 and 11, 1965, Washington, D.C.," file in AAUP Archives, Washington, D. C., remarks by Bertram H. Davis, 6–7.

48. "Notes Taken at Council Meeting Sunday, April 11, 1965, 9:30 a.m.," in "Council Meeting, April 8 and 11, 1965, Washington, D.C.," file in AAUP Archives, Washington, D.C., remarks by David Fellman, 2–3.

49. Ibid., remarks by Clark Byse, 10, and Louis Joughin, 6.

50. Ibid., remarks by Clark Byse, 8.

51. Ibid., remarks by William P. Fidler, 8.

52. Ibid., remarks by William McPherson, John Dawson, Robert Bierstedt, and unnamed council members, 7–8.

53. Ibid., remarks by David Fellman, 9.

54. Ibid., 9–10.

55. Ibid., remarks by Ralph Fuchs, David Fellman, Clark Byse, 10.

56. Ibid., remarks by William McPherson and David Fellman, 10–11.

57. [William P. Fidler], "From the General Secretary," *AAUP Bulletin* 52 (March 1966): 5.

58. Ibid., 5. The AAUP had no such experience with a single institution from 1946 to 1965.

59. [Fidler], "From the General Secretary" (March 1966), 5.

60. Ibid.

61. "Academic Freedom and Tenure: St. John's University (N.Y.)," *AAUP Bulletin* 52 (March 1966): 15. The quoted remarks are from university documents provided to the AAUP.

62. [Fidler], "From the General Secretary" (March 1966), 5–6.

63. Ibid., 6 on activities from December 15 to 21, 6–7 on board telegram.

64. Ibid., 8.

65. Ibid.

66. Ibid.

67. Ibid.

68. Ibid., 9 on irreversible dismissals and meeting on strikes, 9–10 on strike and press release.

69. Ibid., 9.

70. Ibid., 10.

71. Ibid., 10. The rapidity of the appointment and visit of the investigating committee was in direct contrast to the length of time typically spent on Committee A investigations. See "Report by the Special Committee on Procedures for the Disposition of Complaints under the Principles of Academic Freedom and Tenure," *AAUP Bulletin* 51 (May 1965), 211, on the average seventeen-month time lapse between receipt of a complaint and an investigating committee's visit to the campus in question.

72. "Academic Freedom and Tenure: St. John's University" (March 1966), 12 on duration of visit, 19 on violation of standards, 17–18 on violation of 1940 statement.

73. [Ralph S. Brown, Jr.], "Report of Committee T, 1965–66," *AAUP Bulletin* 52 (June 1966): 221.

74. [Joseph M. Conant], "Report from Committee D: St. John's University and the Middle States Association of Colleges and Secondary Schools," *AAUP Bulletin* 52 (September 1966): 302–303 on letters to presidents; 303 on acting responsibly and in good faith.

75. Ibid., 304.

76. Ibid.

77. [William P. Fidler], "Report of the General Secretary," *AAUP Bulletin* 52 (June 1966): 111 on contributions; 111–112 on uses of contributions.

78. Ibid., 112; and "Budget of the Association for 1966," *AAUP Bulletin* 52 (June 1966): 272.

79. [Fidler], "From the General Secretary" (March 1966), 10 on the governing board's support for the 1940 statement in the spring of 1966.

80. "Record of Council Meeting" (March 1965), 48.

81. Ibid.

82. [Bertram H. Davis], "The Editor's Page," *AAUP Bulletin* 51 (March 1965): 3.

83. [Bertram H. Davis], "Academic Freedom and Tenure: A Report on Late Notice Cases," *AAUP Bulletin* 51 (March 1965): 23–24.

84. "Report of Committee A, 1964–65," 240.

85. "Academic Freedom and Tenure: Two Cases of Excessive Probation," *AAUP Bulletin* 52 (March 1966): 32–45; 44 on the Princeton faculty approval of an extended probationary period; and 41 on the administration and governing board of American University of Beirut as responsible for nonrenewal of the professor's appointment.

86. "The Economic Status of the Academic Profession: Taking Stock, 1964–65," *AAUP Bulletin* 51 (June 1965): 248 on review of accomplishments; 249 on poverty; table 4, 251; 252 and table 4, 251, on professors' relative position; 253 on disappointing rate of growth.

87. "Fifty-first Annual Meeting," *AAUP Bulletin* 51 (June 1965): 318–319 on another draft of the statement; 320 on institutional investigations and problems at St. John's.

88. "Record of Council Meeting" (March 1966), 63–64 on negotiations, 64 on visits.

89. "Report of the Self-Survey Committee of the AAUP," 99–209. The remaining fifteen pages of the issue presented the related report of the Special Committee concerning the processing of academic freedom and tenure complaints. See "Report by the Special Committee on Procedures for the Disposition of Complaints under the Principles of Academic Freedom and Tenure," *AAUP Bulletin* 51 (May 1965): 210–224. For members of the Self-Survey Committee, Glenn Morrow was in philosophy at the University of Pennsylvania, and the other two members were professors at Indiana University and Franklin and Marshall College; see [William P. Fidler], "From the General Secretary," *AAUP Bulletin* 50 (March 1964): 62.

90. "Report of the Self-Survey Committee," 104 on A and 106 on T.

91. Ibid., 107 on economics, 108 on Committee Z reports.

92. Ibid., 109.

93. Ibid., 165.

94. Ibid., 153–154.

95. Ibid., 176.

96. Ibid., 176 and 177 on industrial model, 177 on preference for AAUP unit and unit responsibilities.

97. Ibid., 191.

98. Ibid.

99. "Record of Council Meeting" (March 1966), 61. As early as the 1965 Annual Meeting Association leaders were citing the recommendations of the Self-Survey Committee. See Ralph S. Brown, Jr.'s report as chair of Committee T and the suggestion of increased support for that committee's work, "Fifty-first Annual Meeting," 320.

100. Walter P. Metzger, "Origins of the Association: An Anniversary Address," *AAUP Bulletin* 51 (June 1965): 237.

101. "Membership," *AAUP Bulletin* 43 (Spring 1947): 190 and "Membership Record for 1965," *AAUP Bulletin* 52 (March 1966): 72.

102. Brown, *The Mobile Professors,* 5 on year of survey and table 68, 162 on reasons for departures. Thirty-five percent of the respondents indicated administrations and administrators as reasons for leaving. The survey data are only for professors at four-year institutions, 5.

103. "Collective Bargaining Elections," 4.

104. James Brann, "Unionizing the Academies," *New Republic* 25 February 1967, 10.

105. Ibid., 10. See also Geoffrey Wagner, "Local 1640," *Universities Quarterly* 19 (December 1964): 78–80, for a member's description of the activities of the New York City AFT affiliate for professors, the United Federation of College Teachers.

106. *Los Angeles Times* 5 February 1965, part 2: 1, as reported in John R. Van de Water, "Union-Management Relations in Public and Private Education," *CUPA Journal* 17 (November 1965): 1.

107. Brann, "Unionizing the Academies," 10.

108. Sidney Ingerman, "Employed Graduate Students Organize at Berkeley," *Industrial Relations* 5 (October 1965): 141.

109. Ibid., 147.

110. Ibid., 145.

111. "AFT Schedules National Conference for College Teachers," *American Teacher* 12 (March 1966): 5.

112. "AFT and the Colleges," *American Teacher* 12 (May 1966): 8. One of those leaders, Israel Kugler, was also active at AAUP annual meetings in the middle and late 1960s. See, for example, his resolution at the 1966 Annual Meeting as described later in this chapter.

113. Allan M. Cartter, "A New Look at the Supply of College Teachers," *Educational Record* 46 (Summer 1965): 276–277.

114. Cartter, *The Ph.D. and the Academic Labor Market,* 155.

115. *Digest of Educational Statistics, 1965 Edition* (Washington, D.C.: United States Government Printing Office, 1965), table 65, 87; and *Digest of Educational Statistics, 1970 Edition* (Washington, D.C.: United States Government Printing Office, 1970), table 105, 79.

116. Ralph S. Brown, Jr., "Representation of Economic Interests" (September 1965), 374 on AAUP opposition to unions, 375–377 on major issues and possible bargaining methods, 377 on rival groups and unnecessary exclusive representation.

117. "Record of Council Meeting," *AAUP Bulletin* 52 (March 1966): 61–62; Bertram H. Davis, interview in Tallahassee, Florida, on 7 March 1986.

118. Clyde Summers, interview in Philadelphia, Pennsylvania, on 5 March 1986.

119. On Paul Fenlon's assignment, "Record of Council Meeting" (March 1966), 62. On Summers' letter, see Paul Fenlon, Memorandum to Members of the Council, 25 October 1965, in "Council Meeting—October 29–30, 1965, Washington, D.C.," file in AAUP Archives, Washington, D.C., 1.

120. Summers, as cited by Paul Fenlon, Memorandum to Members of the Council, 25 October 1965, 1.

121. Ibid.

122. Ibid.

123. "Committees of the Association" (December 1965), 452.

124. Barbash was pictured on the front cover of *American Teacher Magazine* 45 (February 1961); his book was advertised on the back cover of *American Teacher Magazine* 44 (October 1959).

125. "Report of the 1962 Nominating Committee," *AAUP Bulletin* 48 (September 1962): 285; "Record of Council Meeting" (September 1963), p. 264; and "Committees of the Association," *AAUP Bulletin* 51 (December 1965): 451.

126. Ralph S. Brown, Jr., "Representation of Economic Interests" (September 1965), 375n. 3.

127. "Committees of the Association" (December 1965), 451.

128. "Report of the 1960 Nominating Committee," *AAUP Bulletin* 46 (September 1960): 306; "Association Officers and Council," *AAUP Bulletin* 47 (June 1961): 98; Ralph S. Brown, Jr., "Representation of Economic Interests" (September 1965), 375n. 3; "Committees of the Association" (December 1965), 450.

129. "Report of the 1964 Nominating Committee," *AAUP Bulletin* 50 (September 1964): 259–260; "New Council Members," *AAUP Bulletin* 51 (June 1965): 303 on Daniel Adler, Patty's opponent, as new member of the council.

130. "Record of Council Meeting," *AAUP Bulletin* 52 (March 1966): 64.

131. Clyde W. Summers, interview in Philadelphia, Pennsylvania, on 5 March 1986. Despite Fenlon's report to the council that the Special Committee would meet in November, there is no indication in the *AAUP Bulletin* or in the AAUP Archives (as available) that the committee met. Nor does Clyde Summers recall such a meeting. Given the events of the fall of 1965 in the AAUP, the meeting might have been canceled due to the more pressing issue of the situation at St. John's University.

132. Ibid.

133. Ibid. Unfortunately but not surprisingly the events of a committee meeting so many years ago are not clear for Summers. He does not recall how he succeeded in convincing the committee members to stay with the draft developed on March 11, just that he did so.

134. "Representation of Economic Interests," *AAUP Bulletin* 52 (June 1966): 229–234.

135. Clark Byse, interview in Cambridge, Massachusetts, on 2 March 1986. Ralph S. Brown, Jr., interview in New Haven, Connecticut, on 3 March 1986. Clyde W. Summers, interview in Philadelphia, Pennsylvania, on 5 March 1986. Summers especially emphasizes the bitterness of the debate. Bertram H. Davis, interview in Tallahassee, Florida, on 7 March 1986. For a fuller examination of the 1966 decision, see Hutcheson, "From Reform to Representation."

136. "Representation of Economic Interests" (June 1966): 229. Exclusive representation is a common collective bargaining regulation or law, restricting representation of the collectivity or individuals to only the elected collective bargaining agent. See 231 for the AAUP assessment of this condition.

137. Ibid., 230.

138. Ibid., 229–230.

139. "Report of the Self-Survey Committee" (May 1965), 130.

140. Brann, "Unionizing the Academies," 10. See also, "Local News Notes" from San Jose State College, AFT Local 1362, in "Annual Meeting—April 28–29, 1966 Atlanta, Ga.," file in AAUP Archives, Washington, D.C., 1–3. According to that newsletter, the local had 201 members. The San Jose State College AAUP chapter had 68 members—see Paul Fenlon, Memorandum to Representation of Economic Interests Committee, 1, in "Annual Meeting—April 28–29, 1966 Atlanta, Ga.," file in AAUP Archives, Washington, D.C.

141. Charles M. Larsen to Robert Van Waes [AAUP Staff Associate], 18 April 1966 (copy). See also Charles M. Larsen to David Fellman at University of Wisconsin-Madison, 17 April 1966 (on San Jose State College AAUP chapter letterhead, copy); Charles M. Larsen to Paul Fenlon, 15 April 1966 (on San Jose State College AAUP chapter letterhead, copy) with copies to Fidler, Fellman, Van Waes, and Daniel Adler (council member and professor of psychology at San Francisco State College). All copies of letters in "Annual Meeting—April 28–29, 1966," file in AAUP Archives, Washington, D.C.

142. Paul Fenlon, Memorandum to Representation of Economic Interests Committee, 13 April 1966, #114–3–66, in "Council Meeting—April 28–29, 1966, Atlanta, Ga.," file in AAUP Archives, Washington, D.C., 1 on San Jose vote, 1–2 on position of the council of the California association.

143. "Proposals from the Floor on Association Organization and Activities," in "Annual Meeting—April 28–29, 1966," file in AAUP Archives, 1; "Fifty-second Annual Meeting," *AAUP Bulletin* 52 (June 1966): 206; and "Substitute for Resolution Presented by Mr. Israel Kugler," separate page, in "Annual Meeting—April 28–29, 1966," file in AAUP Archives.

144. Allen Weaver, Resolution, in "Proposals from the Floor on Association Organization and Activities" in "Council Meeting—April 28–29, 1966," file in AAUP Archives, Washington, D.C., 1. See "Fifty-second Annual Meeting," 205–206 on resolutions from the floor approved by the members.

145. For the council members' employing institutions during the McCarthy era, see "Report of the 1963 Nominating Committee," *AAUP Bulletin* 49 (September 1963): 261–263; "Report of the 1964 Nominating Committee," 259–262; "Report of the 1965 Nominating Committee," *AAUP Bulletin* 51 (September 1965): 380–382. Some of the council members had been at institutions reviewed by the AAUP in the 1956 Special Committee report, such as the University of California–Berkeley, the University of California–Los Angeles, and the University of Oklahoma.

146. Clark Byse, interview in Cambridge, Massachusetts, on 2 March 1986; Ralph S. Brown, Jr., interview in New Haven, Connecticut, on 4 March 1986; Bertram H. Davis, interview in Tallahassee, Florida, on 7 March 1986.

147. Bertram H. Davis, interview in Tallahassee, Florida, on 7 March 1986.

148. Philip W. Semas, "Davis, A.A.U.P. [*sic*] Head, to Resign in a Year," *Chronicle of Higher Education* (24 September 1973): 3.

149. Bertram H. Davis, interview in Tallahassee, Florida, on 7 March 1986. Given that the earliest scholarly evaluations of faculties' collective bargaining

appeared in 1968 as articles, AAUP leaders were not alone. See Joseph W. Garbarino, "Professional Negotiations in Education," *Industrial Relations* 7 (February 1968): 93–106. This is the earliest scholarly work found in the literature review for this study.

150. Tracy H. Ferguson, "Collective Bargaining in Universities," *Labor Law Journal* 19 (December 1968): 779, 797, and 804.

151. Garbarino and Aussieker, *Faculty Bargaining,* table 5, 56.

152. "Representation of Economic Interests" (June 1966), 231 and Leonard Meizlish, "Letters: The Collective Bargaining Agent at Flint Community Junior College," *AAUP Bulletin* 52 (September 1966): 351.

153. "Representation of Economic Interests" (June 1966), 231.

154. Ibid., 230.

155. Ibid., 233.

156. "Fifty-first Annual Meeting," 313. This was, of course, shortly after the UFCT strike at St. John's University in New York.

157. Ibid., 314.

158. Winston W. Ehrmann Memorandum to William P. Fidler, "Unionization" of the AAUP?, #104–3–4/66 in "Annual Meeting—April 28–29, 1966," file in AAUP Archives, Washington, D.C., 1. on Fidler's concern and Ehrmann's agreement, 1 and 2 on exceptional circumstances.

159. David Fellman, "The Association's Agenda," *AAUP Bulletin* 52 (June 1966): 106.

160. Clark Byse, "Collective Bargaining and Unionism in American Higher Education: Some Preliminary Comments," address delivered at the Danforth Foundation Workshop on Liberal Arts Education, Colorado Springs, Colorado, in "Council 1967 File" in AAUP Archives, Washington, D.C., 13.

161. Ibid.

162. "Transcript of Proceedings: American Association of University Professors, Fifty-fifth Annual Meeting, Council Meeting, 1 and 4 May 1969," 2 vols. In AAUP Archives, Washington, D.C., remarks by Ralph S. Brown, Jr., I: 108.

163. "The Economic Status of the Profession, Report of the Self-Grading Compensation Survey, 1965–66," *AAUP Bulletin* 52 (June 1966): 141 on doubling rate; 145 on increase of participation. See Breneman and Finn, *Public Policy and Private Higher Education,* table 1–3, 20, for national information.

164. Ibid., 149.

165. Peggy Heim and William Baumol, "Salary Structures in Public Junior Colleges Which Do Not Have the Usual Academic Ranks, 1965–66," *AAUP Bulletin* 52 (December 1966): 401–407.

166. [Ralph S. Brown, Jr.], "Report of Committee T, 1965–66," *AAUP Bulletin* 52 (June 1966): 220 on statement, 220–222 on individual institutions, 221 and 222 on assistance to faculty men and women.

167. "Statement on Government of Colleges and Universities," *AAUP Bulletin* 52 (December 1966): 375. At the top of the page, even above the title of the statement, are listed the names of the three sponsoring organizations—the AAUP, ACE, and AGB.

168. Ibid., 375. Thereafter the statement is known as the 1966 statement, paralleling the short term for the Statement on Principles of Academic Freedom and Tenure, which is also known as the 1940 statement.

169. Philip Denenfeld, "Western Michigan University, Faculty Participation in the Government of the University: The Faculty Senate," *AAUP Bulletin* 52 (December 1966): 396.

170. Howard Vallance Jones, "The State College of Iowa: Faculty Participation in the Government of the College," *AAUP Bulletin* 52 (December 1966): 440–441.

171. William P. Fidler, Statement Read to the Council, October 28, 1966, in "Council—1966," file of Jordan Kurland, associate general secretary of the AAUP, Washington, D.C., p. 1. Fidler's phrase, "one of the toughest assignments in higher education," coming from such a "thoroughly Southern gentleman," reinforce the earlier argument that Himstead was not simply pathological in his final years as general secretary.

172. "Statement Read to the Council," 1; and "Record of Council Meeting" *AAUP Bulletin* 53 (March 1967), 55.

Chapter Four: The AAUP and Unionization, 1966 to 1971

1. "Transport News: Flight Insurance," *New York Times,* 29 September 1966, 93.

2. James Brann, "Unionizing the Academies," 25 February 1967, 11.

3. Joel M. Douglas and Elizabeth Kotch, "Faculty Contracts and Bargaining Agents in Public and Private Institutions," in *Directory of Faculty Contracts and Bargaining Agents in Institutions of Higher Education* (New York: National Center for the STudy of Collective bargaining in Higher Education and the Professions–Baruch College, City University of New York, 1985), 3–68. The number of AFT agents includes twenty-one serving in affiliation with locally formed groups such as the Professional Staff Congress at the City University of New York.

4. "Teaching Aides Organize, Seek a Wider Role," *Chronicle of Higher Education* (17 May 1967): 1, 3.

5. Ibid., 3. It is not clear from this report whether the University of California–Berkeley local was an extension or a renewal of Local 1570, or a new AFT local. Graduate assistants at two other public universities also organized into bargaining units according to this *Chronicle of Higher Education* report. The group of assistants at the University of Minnesota refused an offer of affiliation from the American Federation of Teachers and gained recognition from the AAUP chapter. The fifth group of assistants was at the University of Oklahoma, and the report does not indicate that the group sought affiliation with any national organization.

6. Richard A. Hixon in Maurice R. Duperre, "Faculty Organizations as an Aid to Employment Relations in Junior Colleges," *Employment Relations in Higher Education,* ed. Stanley Elam and Michael H. Moscow (Bloomington, Ind.: Phi Delta Kappa, 1969), 191.

7. Douglas and Kotch, *Directory of Faculty Contracts and Bargaining Agents in Institutions of Higher Education,* 3–68.

8. American Association for Higher Education, *Faculty Participation in Academic Governance* (Washington, D.C.: American Association for Higher Education, 1967), 1. The task force studied thirty-four colleges and universities in a sample of presumed representative institutions, 6.

9. Ibid., 9.

10. Ibid., 1 and 17 on centers of discontent and administrative dominance, 2–4 on collective bargaining and strike.

11. Clyde E. Blocker, Robert H. Plummer, and Richard C. Richardson, Jr., *The Two-Year College: A Social Synthesis* (Englewood, New Jersey: Prentice Hall, 1965): 141–147.

12. Ibid., 147.

13. Leland Medsker and Dale Tillery, *Breaking the Access Barriers: A Profile of the American Junior College* (New York: McGraw-Hill, 1971), 89.

14. E. Alden Dunham, *Colleges of the Forgotten Americans: A Profile of State Colleges and Regional Universities* (New York: McGraw-Hill, 1969), 103–104.

15. Jencks and Riesman, 541 on academic imperium, 8–27 on universities and university colleges. Many years later Riesman withdrew from the suggestion of an imperium, indicating that in those years the professoriate had in fact probably reached the height of faculty control. See David Riesman, *On Higher Education: The Academic Enterprise in an Era of Rising Student Consumerism,* xx.

16. Allan M. Cartter, *The Ph.D. and the Academic Labor Market,* 194–204 on prestige, 204–220 on gender, and 224–237 on disciplines.

17. Alan E. Bayer, *College and University Faculty: A Statistical Description* (Washington, D.C.: American Council on Education), table 4, 16. Just over

51 percent of the professors approved of their administrations, suggesting continued disapproval by a sizable minority of professors as in the case of David Brown's 1965 survey data.

18. "Record of Council Meeting" *AAUP Bulletin* 53 (March 1967), 57; and Louis Joughin, "Three Problems of the California State Colleges," *AAUP Bulletin* 53 (June 1967): 228n. 2.

19. Louis Joughin, associate secretary of the AAUP, spent two weeks in California in the fall of 1966; William Fidler spent nearly all of February 1967 in California. In addition Clyde Summers, chair of the Special REI Committee, spent two days in California in September 1966, and Professor Charles Larsen was an AAUP Consultant from 10 August to 31 October 1966. See Joughin, "Three Problems of the California State Colleges," 228n. 2.

20. "Result of Collective Bargaining Poll in the California State Colleges," *AAUP Bulletin* 53 (September 1967): 350; and "California State College Trustees Approve 1966 Statement on Government," *AAUP Bulletin* 53 (December 1967): 403–404.

21. Byse, "Collective Bargaining and Unionism in American Higher Education: Some Preliminary Comments," 10 on election, 11 on interpretation.

22. Bertram H. Davis, interview in Tallahassee, Florida, on 7 March 1986 on chapter members' uncertainty about their next step. See also Peggy Heim, "Growing Tensions in Academic Administration," *North Central Association Quarterly* 42 (Winter 1968): 247n. 3 on the postelection contact.

23. Byse, "Collective Bargaining and Unionism in American Higher Education: Some Preliminary Comments," 11.

24. Ibid.

25. "Record of Council Meeting," *AAUP Bulletin* 56 (September 1970): 318. Association leaders of the 1960s have to this day kind, even humorous memories of the election and ensuing negotiations; see Ralph S. Brown, Jr., interview in New Haven, Connecticut, on 3 March 1986. Bertram H. Davis, interview in Tallahassee, Florida, on 7 March 1986.

26. "Organizational Notes," *AAUP Bulletin* 54 (March 1968): 114; and Bertram H. Davis, interview in Tallahassee, Florida, on 7 March 1986. Davis later reported that Ralph Fuchs suggested that the AAUP should not discourage the chapter but rather should guide it. Bertram H. Davis to author, 16 October 1989.

27. Byse, "Collective Bargaining and Unionism in American Higher Education: Some Preliminary Comments," 15.

28. Clark Byse, Some Notes Re AAUP and Collective Bargaining, Document #271–2–67, in "Council 1967," file in AAUP Archives, Washington,

D.C., 1. Bertram H. Davis distributed this memorandum as well as his Danforth address to the council with a 6 October 1967 memorandum from Davis.

29. Ibid., 2.

30. Byse, "Collective Bargaining and Unionism In American Higher Education: Some Preliminary Comments," 2–5 and 5 on extreme approaches, 9–10 on developments, 16–17 and 17 on inevitable bargaining and recalcitrant administrations, 16 and 17 on Byse's stance.

31. "Record of Council Meeting" *AAUP Bulletin* 54 (June 1968), 94. See "Association Officers and Council," *AAUP Bulletin* 54 (March 1968): 2 on Adler's position.

32. C[harles]. M. Larsen, "'Collective Bargaining' Issues in the California State Colleges," *AAUP Bulletin* 53 (June 1967): 222–223; Joughin, "Three Problems of the California State Colleges," 230, 233, and 235; "A New Publication on the Collective Bargaining Issue," *AAUP Bulletin* 53 (September 1967): 336; "Result of Collective Bargaining Poll in the California State Colleges," 350; "California State College Trustees Approve 1966 Statement on Government," 403–404.

33. "Catholic University Hit by Strike," *New York Times,* 20 April 1967, 45.

34. "Catholic Students in Capital Score Ouster of Priest," *New York Times,* 19 April 1967, 23; and "Catholic University Hit by Strike," 45. The Catholic University of America is the only Catholic institution of higher education in the United States (except for a few seminaries) with faculties—including the theology faculty—chartered by the Vatican. Hence heretical views at the university are extremely disturbing to church officials. See Edward J. Power, *Catholic Higher Education in America: A History* (New York: Appleton-Century-Crofts, 1972), 356–359 on the university's role in the United States and "Vatican Orders Curran, Catholic U. Theologian, to Retract His Views," *Chronicle of Higher Education* (19 March 1986): 30 on the Vatican charter.

35. "Catholic University Hit by Strike," 45; and "Catholic U. Strike Backed By Rector," *New York Times,* 1 October 1967, 51.

36. "Catholic U. Classes Stopped as Protest Spreads in Faculty," *New York Times,* 21 April 1967, 1 and 50.

37. "Catholic University Hit by Strike," 45.

38. "Catholic U. Classes Stopped as Protest Spreads in Faculty," 50; and "Catholic U. Strike Backed by Rector," 51.

39. William P. Fidler, "From the Retiring General Secretary," *AAUP Bulletin* 53 (June 1967): 114. On revision of his statement, see Robert Jacobson,

"AAUP to Reconsider Stand against Strikes by Faculties," *Chronicle of Higher Education* (3 May 1967): 5.

40. Bertram H. Davis, "Report of the General Secretary," *AAUP Bulletin* 53 (June 1967): 112.

41. Fidler, "From the Retiring General Secretary," 115–116 on support for shared authority, 116 on opposition to outside bargaining representatives. Fidler spoke at a banquet in his honor, so he was not giving an organizational speech and may have chosen to be less circumspect on the issue of association policy. "Fifty-third Annual Meeting," *AAUP Bulletin* 53 (June 1967): 133.

42. Bertram H. Davis, "Report of the General Secretary" (June 1967), 110–112. Davis spoke to the members at a general session. See "Fifty-third Annual Meeting," 133.

43. In an interview with the *Chronicle of Higher Education* following the March 1967 announcement of his appointment, Davis said that academic freedom and tenure would continue as the major focus of the AAUP. He added, however, that the association would also expand its staff to address further the economic status of the profession, faculty participation in governance, and ethics. The sense of expansion included membership, as "one staff estimate had projected a total membership of more than 150,000 within six years." "Bertram H. Davis to Be AAUP's Chief Executive" *Chronicle of Higher Education* (22 March 1967): 1.

44. Bertram H. Davis, interview in Tallahassee, Florida, on 7 March 1986. Nor could the association find a suitable recipient for the Alexander Meiklejohn Award for the first time since the award's inception in 1958. The annual meeting also rejected a proposal to consider a merger with the AFT despite a "spirited" debate on the motion, suggesting that neither association leadership nor membership at the moment was committed to one form or another of AAUP activity. There is no mention of the Meiklejohn award in the report on the 1967 Annual Meeting: see "Fifty-third Annual Meeting," 133–135. For the description of the award as an annual event, see "The Ninth Annual Alexander Meiklejohn Award," *AAUP Bulletin* 52 (June 1966): 211. On the AFT vote, see Jacobson, "AAUP to Reconsider Stand against Strikes by Faculties" 3 May 1967, 5. About two-thirds of the voters opposed the motion.

45. Arnold Berleant, "Letters: The AAUP and the 'Right to Strike,'" *AAUP Bulletin* 53 (September 1967): 345. Berleant identifies the presenter of the motion as the president of the United Federation of Teachers, who was Israel Kugler.

46. Sanford H. Kadish, "Letters: Professor Kadish Replies," *AAUP Bulletin* 53 (September 1967): 346.

47. Berleant, "Letters: The AAUP and the 'Right to Strike,'" 346.

48. Jacobson, "AAUP to Reconsider Stand against Strikes by Faculties," 1.

49. "Record of Council Meeting," *AAUP Bulletin* 53 (September 1967): 335. Although *Bulletin* reports do not typically designate which spring council actions precede the annual meeting, in this case the Committee A report, including its recommendation concerning sanctions, indicates Kadish's motion occurred at the meeting prior to the annual meeting.

50. "Record of Council Meeting," 335. On the committee's membership, see "Committees of the Association," *AAUP Bulletin* 53 (December 1967): 426 for list of members and 424–426 for members' AAUP positions, disciplines, and institutions.

51. "AAUP to Reconsider Stand against Strikes by Faculties," 5.

52. "Catholic U. Classes Stopped as Protest Spreads in Faculty," 1 and 50, and "Catholic U. Strike Backed by Rector," 51, are in Ralph Brown's personal file on the Special Joint Committee. (Copy in author's possession.) See "Faculty Participation in Strikes," *AAUP Bulletin* 54 (June 1968): 155 for reference to the strike at the Catholic University.

53. "At Henry Ford: Four-Day Walkout Brings First College Contract," 19; on the strikes at Chicago State and Northeastern Illinois Colleges, see "Teacher Strike Hits 2 Colleges in Illinois," 8.

54. Ralph S. Brown, Jr., Memorandum for Special Joint Committee on Bargaining, Sanctions, and Representation to the Council, 18 October 1967, Document 286–3–67, in "Council 1967," file in AAUP Archives, Washington, D.C., 1.

55. "Faculty Participation in Strikes," in "Council 1967," file in AAUP Archives, Washington, D.C., 1–2; and Brown, Memorandum for Special Joint Committee, 1 on "never" and "hardly ever," key words in the eventual transition to approval of the faculty strike.

56. "Faculty Participation in Strikes," 1–2.

57. Brown, Memorandum for Special Joint Committee, 1.

58. "Record of Council Meeting," *AAUP Bulletin* 54 (March 1968): 94. Ralph S. Brown, Jr., Memorandum of Transmittal Draft, 23 February 1968, to the Council, in Ralph S. Brown, Jr., Personal File on Special Joint Committee on Representation, Bargaining, and Sanctions, 1. Copy in author's possession.

59. Ralph S. Brown, Jr., Personal File on Special Joint Committee on Representation, Bargaining, and Sanctions. Copies in author's possession.

60. Ralph S. Brown, Jr., Memorandum to Special Committee, 23 February 1968, Ralph S. Brown, Jr., Personal File on Special Joint

Committee on Representation, Bargaining, and Sanctions, 1. Copy in author's possession.

61. Sanford H. Kadish to Ralph S. Brown, Jr., 1 February 1968, Ralph S. Brown, Jr., Personal File on Special Joint Committee on Representation, Bargaining, and Sanctions, 1. Copy in author's possession.

62. "Faculty Participation in Strikes," 23 February 1968 Draft, Ralph S. Brown, Jr., Personal File on Special Joint Committee on Representation, Bargaining, and Sanctions, 1–2. Copy in author's possession.

63. Ibid., 1.

64. Ralph S. Brown, Jr., Memorandum to AAUP Special Joint Committee, 12 March 1968; William J. Baumol to Ralph S. Brown, Jr., 11 March 1968; Clark Byse to Ralph S. Brown, Jr., 11 March 1968; Bertram H. Davis to Ralph S. Brown, Jr., 13 March 1968, 1. Memorandum and letters in Ralph S. Brown, Jr., Personal File on Special Joint Committee on Representation, Bargaining, and Sanctions. Copies in author's possession.

65. Ralph S. Brown, Jr., Memorandum to Special Joint Committee, 23 February 1968, Ralph S. Brown, Jr., Personal File on Special Joint Committee on Representation, Bargaining, and Sanctions, 1. Copy in author's possession.

66. "Transcript of Proceedings, Fifty-fourth Annual Meeting," 26 and 27 April 1968, 3 vols., in AAUP Archives, Washington, D.C., remarks by Ralph S. Brown, Jr., 3: 299.

67. Ibid., 3: 299–300.

68. Ibid., 3: 303.

69. Ibid., 3: 303–316.

70. Ibid., 3: 316.

71. "Statement on Faculty Participation in Strikes," *AAUP Bulletin* 54 (June 1968): 157; "Faculty Participation in Strikes," 155–159; Sanford H. Kadish, "The Strike and the Professoriate," *AAUP Bulletin* 54 (June 1968): 160–168.

72. Kadish, "The Strike and the Professoriate," 167 and 161–167.

73. Ibid., 167. Some authors have misread this paper as well as Kadish's 1972 AAUP presidential address and suggest that he opposed faculty participation in strikes. See Sanford H. Kadish, "The Theory of the Profession and Its Predicament," *AAUP Bulletin* 58 (June 1972): 122 for reference to the University of Illinois paper, 125 on acceptance of the *economic* strike in the "most extraordinary circumstances"; and Lionel S. Lewis and Michael N. Ryan, "The American Professoriate and the Movement toward Unionization," in *Comparative Perspectives on the Academic Profession,* 208 on Kadish's supposed opposition.

74. "Report of Committee T, 1966–67," *AAUP Bulletin* 53 (June 1967): 214.

75. Ibid., 214.

76. Ibid., 214 on Ralph S. Brown's report; see "Fifty-third Annual Meeting," 133 for approval.

77. On the date of the meeting, see "Record of Council Meeting" (September 1967), 333.

78. "Report of Committee T, 1966–67," 215.

79. "The Fifty-fifth Annual Meeting," *AAUP Bulletin* 55 (June 1969): 151.

80. [Otway Pardee], "Report of the Survey Subcommittee of Committee T," *AAUP Bulletin* 55 (June 1969): 184.

81. "The Fifty-fifth Annual Meeting," 151.

82. Ibid., 152.

83. Ibid., 151.

84. Edward Jackson reported a general increase in AAUP activity concern - ing two-year college faculties during the 1960s. See Jackson, "The American Association of University Professors and Community/Junior Colleges," 133–145.

85. "Record of Council Meeting" *AAUP Bulletin* 56 (March 1970), 44.

86. [William J. Baumol and Peggy Heim], "Further Progress: The Economic Status of the Profession, Report on the Self-Grading Compensation Survey, 1966–67," *AAUP Bulletin* 53 (June 1967): 136 on compensation rise and rate, 140 on caution.

87. [William J. Baumol and Peggy Heim], "On the Financial Prospects for Higher Education: The Annual Report on the Economic Status of the Profession, 1967–68," *AAUP Bulletin* 54 (June 1968): 182.

88. Ibid.

89. Ibid., 185 and 186. The 1967–1968 analyses were based on approxi - mately 1,040 reports received, representing 42 percent of the nation's col- leges and universities. 182n. 1 on the number of participating institutions. See Breneman and Finn, *Public Policy and Private Higher Education,* table 1–3, 20, for the number of institutions in the nation.

90. Ibid., 196.

91. John W. Lloyd, "Productivity, Compensation, and Institutional Excellence: A Commentary on the Report on the Economic Status of the Profession, 1967–68," *AAUP Bulletin* 54 (December 1968): 445–447 on anal- ysis, 447 on conclusion.

92. [William J. Baumol], "The Threat of Inflationary Erosion: The Annual Report on the Economic Status of the Profession, 1968–69," *AAUP Bulletin* 55 (June 1969), 193 on inflation and decline in rate of increase, 194 on pri- vate universities, 196 on underpaid teachers.

93. "The Association's New Officers," *AAUP Bulletin* 54 (June 1968): 141.

94. "The Association's New Officers," 141; and Ralph S. Brown, Jr., interview in New Haven, Connecticut, 3 March 1986.

95. "Transcript of Proceedings: American Association of University Professors, National Council Meeting, Friday, October 25, and October 26, 1968," 2 vols., in AAUP Archives, Washington, D.C., remarks by Ralph S. Brown, Jr., I: 7–8 on defensive AAUP, I: 8–10 on obstacles, I: 12 on tripartite statement and student demands.

96. Ibid., 12 on industrial unions, 13–14 on ACE survey and push toward industrial model.

97. Ibid., 14.

98. Ibid., 46–50.

99. On the AAUP response to the Chicago demonstrations, see "Change in 1969 Annual Meeting," *AAUP Bulletin* 54 (December 1968): 441; "American Association of University Professors, National Council Meeting, Friday, October 25, 1968," I: 105–167. On the new site, see "Change in Annual Meeting," 441. On the discussion about the annual meeting sessions, see "National Council Meeting, Friday, October 25, 1968," remarks by Henry Mason, I: 210 and remarks by William J. Baumol, I: 230, remarks by William Van Alstyne, I: 271, and council decision, I: 286–287. On the annual meeting sessions themselves, see "Challenge and Change Forum," *AAUP Bulletin* 55 (June 1969): 273–276. Two of the panels, "Student Power" and "The Corporate University," made *brief* mention of the AAUP, while there is no mention of the AAUP in the other three reports. At its fall 1969 council meeting the council reviewed and approved a report of the Special Committee on Challenge and Change. There is essentially no examination of professors and their problems; the statement focuses heavily on students and their discontents. Nor did the council choose to refocus the committee on professors but rather gave the instruction to examine university and general community relationships. See "A Statement of the Association's Special Committee on Challenge and Change," *AAUP Bulletin* 55 (December 1969): 461–462; and "Record of Council," 45.

100. "Academic Freedom and Tenure: A Report on Late Notice Cases," *AAUP Bulletin* 54 (December 1968): 462–465.

101. Ibid., 464 and 465.

102. "1968 Recommended Institutional Regulations on Academic Freedom and Tenure," *AAUP Bulletin* 54 (December 1968): 448–452.

103. [Paul Oberst], "Report of the Special Committee on State Legislation Affecting Academic Freedom," *AAUP Bulletin* 55 (June 1969): 256.

104. "Statement on Professional Ethics," *AAUP Bulletin* 55 (March 1969): 86. The members at the annual meeting also endorsed the "Statement on Professors and Political Activity." Although the statement focused on professors' involvement in campaigns, it also continued association ambiguity on the professor as professional in its request that a professor engage in political activity consistent "with his obligations as a teacher and scholar." See "Statement on Professors and Political Activity," *AAUP Bulletin* 55 (September 1969): 388 on annual meeting endorsement, 389 on obligations.

105. "Policy on Representation of Economic Interests," *AAUP Bulletin* 54 (June 1968): 152. Clark Byse also supported this revision. See Clark Byse to Ralph S. Brown, Jr., 11 March 1968. In Ralph S. Brown, Jr., Personal File on Special Joint Committee on Representation, Bargaining, and Sanctions. Copy in author's possession.

106. "Representation of Economic Interests" (June 1966), 230.

107. "Policy on Representation of Economic Interests," 153.

108. "Representation of Economic Interests" (June 1966), 229; and "Representation of Economic Interests" (June 1968), 153.

109. "Representation of Economic Interests" (June 1966), 230; and "Representation of Economic Interests" (June 1968), 154.

110. "Policy on Representation of Economic Interests," 152.

111. [Bertram H. Davis], "Report of the General Secretary," *AAUP Bulletin* 54 (June 1968): 151.

112. "American Association of University Professors, National Council Meeting, October 26, 1968," remarks by Alfred Sumberg and Matthew Finkin, II: 354–386. General Secretary Davis also announced at this meeting that the AAUP hoped to open a Northeastern Regional Office by 1 November 1968. See "Record of Council Meeting," *AAUP Bulletin* 55 (March 1969): 95.

113. "National Council Meeting," in AAUP Archives, remarks by Alfred Sumberg and Matthew Finkin, II: 354–356, 356A-356B, and 355 on the New York issues.

114. Ibid., II: 356B-357.

115. "National Council Meeting," remarks by Bertram H. Davis and Ralph S. Brown, Jr., II: 375 and II: 376, respectively.

116. Ibid., remarks by Bertram H. Davis, II: 374–375.

117. Ibid., remarks by Alfred Sumberg, 373. Emphasis added.

118. Ibid., 383–385.

119. Ibid., remarks by Ralph S. Brown, Jr., 383 on current problem, 386 on Davis' article.

120. Harry A. Marmion, "Unions and Higher Education," *Educational Record* 49 (Winter 1968): 41 and 47. Marmion was referring to the 1967 Annual Meeting in his comments on "union-oriented" members.

121. Bertram H. Davis, "Unions and Higher Education: Another View," *Educational Record* 49 (Spring 1968): 139. See Bertram H. Davis, "Unions and Higher Education: Another View," *AAUP Bulletin* 54 (September 1968): 317–320 for the reprinting of his article.

122. Bertram H. Davis, "Unions and Higher Education: Another View," 139.

123. Ibid., 143 on "seductive" exclusive bargaining agreements and 144 on the importance of the goal of shared responsibility.

124. "American Association of University Professors, Fifty-fifth Annual Meeting, Council Meeting, May 1 and 4, 1969," remarks by William Leonard, I: 62.

125. "American Association of University Professors, Fifty-fifth Annual Meeting, Council Meeting, May 1 and 4, 1969," remarks by Alfred Sumberg, I: 66 on New Jersey ruling; I: 67 and 68 on public and private institutions and representing AAUP members.

126. Ibid., 68.

127. Ibid., 69.

128. Ibid., remarks by Ralph S. Brown, Jr., 71 on drift, 76 on fall presentation and dilemma of drift.

129. Ibid, remarks by William Murphy, Alfred Sumberg, and Matthew Finkin, 73–74.

130. Ibid., remarks by Alfred Sumberg, 76–77. Excluding 1969, since reports do not indicate which month a faculty elected a representative, fifty-six colleges and universities had faculties that selected collective bargaining agents by the end of 1968. Douglas and Kotch, *Directory of Faculty Contracts and Bargaining Agents in Institutions of Higher Education,* 3–68. Sumberg's honest estimate appears to have been inaccurate.

131. "American Association of University Professors, Fifty-fifth Annual Meeting, Council Meeting, May 1 and 4, 1969," remarks by Ralph S. Brown, Jr., I: 105.

132. Ibid., I: 107.

133. Ibid., I: 107, and Brown's agreement with Byse, I: 108–111 on quorum and recommendation, I: 111 on council approval.

134. "Transcript of Proceedings: American Association of University Professors, Fifty-fifth Annual Meeting, Convention, May 3, 1969," 2 vols., in AAUP Archives, Washington, D.C., remarks by Ralph S. Brown, Jr., II: 281.

135. Ibid., II: 280–282.

136. Ibid., remarks by Ralph Kaminsky, II: 287–288.

137. Ibid., remarks by William Leonard, II: 289.

138. [William N. Leonard], "Report of Committee T, 1968–69," *AAUP Bulletin* 55 (June 1969): 179.

139. Ibid.

140. Ibid.

141. "Record of Council Meeting" (March 1970), 44.

142. "Transcript of Proceedings, American Association of University Professors, Council Meeting, October 31 and November 1, 1969," 2 vols., in AAUP Archives, Washington, D.C., remarks by Alfred Sumberg, I: 253–254.

143. Ibid., I: 257.

144. Ibid., I: 252.

145. "Policy on Representation of Economic and Professional Interests," *AAUP Bulletin* 55 (December 1969): 490. There is no discussion in the records of the council meeting discussion, either in the AAUP Archives or in the *AAUP Bulletin,* on the addition of "Professional" to the title. Given the broader scope of the revised statement, perhaps council members assumed the change to be natural.

146. Transcript of Proceedings, American Association of University Professors, Council Meeting, October 31 and November 1, 1969," remarks by William A. Baumol, I: 269–270.

147. Ibid., remarks by Bertram H. Davis and Daniel Adler, I: 273.

148. Ibid., remarks by Donald Koster, I: 275–276.

149. Ibid., remarks by Carl Stevens, I: 276–277.

150. Ibid., remarks by Matthew Finkin, I: 278.

151. Ibid., I: 275 on clause stating AAUP preference for shared authority, 279–280 on vote, and 280, remarks by Ralph S. Brown, Jr., 282 on vote.

152. "Policy on Representation of Economic and Professional Interests," 490.

153. "American Association of University Professors, Council Meeting, October 31 and November 1, 1969," remarks by Ralph S. Brown, Jr., I: 273–274; remarks by Alfred Sumberg, I: 274. See "Policy on Representation of Economic and Professional Interests," 490 on need for "alert" chapters and conferences. The caution that chapters and conferences should be "alert" to inappropriate legislation was also in the 1968 version of the REI Statement but apparently did not elicit any comment at the time of its review. See "Policy on Representation of Economic Interests," 153.

154. "Record of Council Meeting" (March 1970), 44.

155. "American Association of University Professors, Council Meeting, October 31 and November 1, 1969," remarks by Bertram H. Davis, I: 283.

156. Ibid., I: 283, remarks by Bertram H. Davis, and 285 for council approval. See also "Record of Council Meeting" (March 1970), 44 for the committee letter and name.

157. "Report on the National Leadership Conference for Conference Officers" *AAUP Bulletin* 55 (December 1969): 494.

158. Ibid., 495.

159. Ibid.

160. Ibid.

161. "Record of Council Meeting" (September 1970), 317 on date of meeting, 317–318 on committee discussion.

162. Ibid., 318.

163. "Transcript of Proceedings: American Association of University Professors, Council Meeting, Chairman: Ralph S. Brown, Jr., President," 23 and 26 April 1970, 2 vols., in AAUP Archives, Washington, D.C., remarks by Ralph S. Brown, Jr., II: 222. Finkin had been discussing multicampus systems where the NEA would have five thousand members paying one hundred dollars for annual dues.

164. "Record of Council Meeting," *AAUP Bulletin* 56 (September 1970): 318.

165. "Transcript of Proceedings: American Association of University Professors, Council Meeting, Chairman: Ralph S. Brown, Jr., President," 23 and 26 April 1970, remarks by Alfred Sumberg, II: 238 on controversy, 238–239 on committee consideration.

166. Ibid., remarks by Sanford H. Kadish, II: 255.

167. Ibid., remarks by Ned Bowler and Alfred Sumberg, II: 242–243.

168. Ibid., remarks by Matthew Finkin and Ralph S. Brown, Jr., II: 248.

169. Ibid., remarks by Richard Peairs, II: 250.

170. Ibid., remarks by Patterson and Bertram H. Davis, II: 244–245. The transcript does not identify Patterson as a member of the council or as a staff member; perhaps the stenographer misheard his or her name. Nor does the *Bulletin* identify a Paterson. See "Association Officers, Staff and Council," *AAUP Bulletin* 56 (March 1970): 2; "Association Officers, Staff and Council," *AAUP Bulletin* 56 (June 1970): 114. As concerns the SUNY election, the AAUP attempted to secure representative status in the 1969–1970 campaign and election among SUNY faculties. It placed third behind the AFT and NEA affiliates. See Robert S. Fisk and William C. Puffer, "Public University System: State University of New York," in *Faculty Unions and Collective Bargaining,* ed. Duryea and Fisk, 134–140.

171. Ibid., remarks by Matthew Finkin, II: 251–252.

172. "American Association of University Professors, Council Meeting, Chairman: Ralph S. Brown, Jr., President," remarks by Carl Stevens, II: 253.

173. Ibid., remarks by Ralph S. Brown, Jr., II: 253. Brown was interrupted in his explanation of the St. John's approach, yet the direction of his statement appears clear, a continuation of the emphasis on the faculty senate.

174. "Proposed Constitutional Amendments," *AAUP Bulletin* 56 (December 1970): 440.

175. As quoted by [Ralph A. Loomis], "Report on Developments Relating to State and Regional Conferences," *AAUP Bulletin* 56 (December 1970): 381. The assembly also passed a resolution thanking the national AAUP for its financial assistance to the conferences. See 381.

176. "Record of the Council Meeting," *AAUP Bulletin* 57 (March 1971): 127. Hickman served as a member of the AAHE Task Force that published the 1967 report on faculty participation in governance. On his participation in the AAHE Task Force, see "Report of the 1969 Nominating Committee," *AAUP Bulletin* 55 (September 1969): 392.

177. Ibid., 127. Finkin reported on activities in the Northeast. See 127.

178. [Bertram H. Davis], "From the General Secretary," *AAUP Bulletin* 56 (December 1970): 357.

179. Matthew W. Finkin, "Collective Bargaining and University Government," *AAUP Bulletin* 57 (June 1971): 149.

180. Ibid., 161. The institutions were Central Michigan University (unit affiliated with the NEA) and Southeastern Massachusetts University (unit affiliated with the AFT), 155, the New Jersey State Colleges (NEA unit) and St. John's University of New York (an AAUP unit in affiliation with an independent local faculty association), 156, and the City University of New York, (unit affiliated with the United Federation of College Teachers), 160.

181. Ibid., 162.

182. "A Report from Committee D: The Question of Accreditation by Faculty," *AAUP Bulletin* 56 (December 1970): 377 on annual meeting instruction; 377–379 on the review and analysis, 380 on faculty monopoly.

183. Ibid.

184. [Bertram H. Davis], "Report of the General Secretary," *AAUP Bulletin* 56 (June 1970): 145 on myths and quick resolutions; 146 on timeliness.

185. Ibid., 146.

186. Bertram H. Davis, "Principles and Cases: The Mediative Work of the AAUP," *AAUP Bulletin* 56 (June 1970): 169 on censure; 170–173 on staff efforts; 172–173 on conclusion.

187. [Bertram H. Davis], "Report of the General Secretary," *AAUP Bulletin* 57 (June 1971): 181.

188. Ibid., 182. It is also likely that the pressures to recognize women in the professoriate, as symbolized by the reestablishment of the standing committee, W, caused Davis to look for gender discrepancies in these cases.

189. "Rising Costs and the Public Institutions: The Annual Report on the Economic Status of the Profession, 1969–70," *AAUP Bulletin* 56 (June 1970): 240 on public institutions; 174 and 175 on compensation changes; 175 on trends at public institutions; 185 on the next decade and effort required.

190. "Report of the General Secretary" (June 1970), 146.

191. "College and University Government: Long Island University," *AAUP Bulletin* 57 (March 1971): 59 and 58.

192. Ibid., 67. Many faculty members were heavily involved in an earlier campus confrontation between a chancellor and provost that included all campus constituencies and was marked by "interrupted classes, strikes, and pickets." See 67.

193. Ibid., 64 and 65 on university structure, 66 on trustees' legal right.

194. "Report of the Survey Subcommittee of Committee T," *AAUP Bulletin* 57 (March 1971): 68.

195. Ibid., table 1, 69. Surprisingly only 85.9 percent of the faculties indicated determination of students' academic performance; 0.7 percent indicated no faculty participation in such decisions.

196. Ibid., 73.

197. Ibid.

198. "Report of the General Secretary" (June 1971), 182. Although the AAUP continued to expand its activities, its membership (and hence revenue) was virtually stable in 1969 and 1970. See "Membership Record for 1969," *AAUP Bulletin* 56 (March 1970): 40 and "Membership Record for 1970," *AAUP Bulletin* 57 (March 1971): 57.

199. "Report of the General Secretary" (June 1971), 182.

200. Bertram H. Davis to Council, "Council Letter No. 2, 1971," in "Council Letters 1971," file in AAUP Archives, 1 on mail ballot, 2 on N and Executive Committee, 1 on reasons for study, 3 on enclosures.

201. Joseph Garbarino, "Precarious Professors: New Patterns of Representation," *Industrial Relations* 10 (February 1971): 15. Dexter L. Hanley, "Issues and Models for Collective Bargaining in Higher Education," 8 and 12–13 in "Council Letters 1971," file in AAUP Archives.

202. "Report of the General Secretary" (June 1971), 182–183.

203. "Record of Council Meeting," *AAUP Bulletin* 57 (September 1971): 447 on demands, 447 on financial exigency and academic freedom, 447–448 on deficit.

204. Ibid., 448 on NLRB decision, 448–449 on unit determination, 448 on agency shops.

205. Ibid., 448.

206. [Walter Adams], "Report of Committee T, 1970–71," *AAUP Bulletin* 57 (June 1971): 184.

207. [Ralph S. Brown, Jr.], "Forging Better Tools: Report of Committee N, 1970–71," *AAUP Bulletin* 57 (June 1971): 211. Note that Brown chose to quote a trade unionist.

208. Ibid., 212.

209. Ibid.

210. Ibid.

211. Ibid., 212–213 on unit determination, 212 on AAUP membership criteria, 212–213 on name change, 213 on principle.

212. Ibid., 213. Readers should bear in mind that in the late 1960s and early 1970s the phrase "conscientious objection" was a highly charged statement, more typically referring to those people who chose to refuse to serve in the military because of the conflict in Viet Nam.

213. Ibid.

214. Ibid., 213–214 on investigation, 214 on AAUP functions and summer study.

215. Ibid., 214.

216. Ibid.

217. Ibid.

218. Ralph S. Brown, Jr., interview in New Haven, Connecticut, on 3 March 1986.

219. [Davis], "Report of the General Secretary" (June 1971), 183.

220. "At the Brink: Report on the Economic Status of the Profession, 1970–71," *AAUP Bulletin* 57 (June 1971): 223. A total of 1345 institutions submitted data, representing 52 percent of all colleges and universities. See table 10, 240; and Breneman and Finn, *Public Policy and Private Higher Education,* table 1–3, 20.

221. "At the Brink: Report on the Economic Status of the Profession, 1970–71" (June 1971), 178 on Wage-Price Freeze, 225–226 on crisis, 227 on faculties, 229 on decade ahead, 229–230 on hard choices. See also Earl F. Cheit, *The New Depression in Higher Education: A Study of Financial Conditions at 41 Colleges and Universities* (New York: McGraw-Hill, 1971).

222. Ibid., 230 on modes, 231 on choices.

223. [Ralph S. Brown, Jr.], "The National Labor Relations Board and Faculty Representation Cases: A Report from Committee N," *AAUP Bulletin* 57 (September 1971): 433.

224. Ibid, 437 on Merton C. Bernstein (law, Ohio State University) and Clyde Summers' assistance in the development of the AAUP statement on unit determination, and 434n. 6 on AAUP chapters' petitions from Manhattan College and the University of Detroit. See 437 on NLRB response.

Chapter Five: To Hedge Our Bets

1. *Statistics of Higher Education 1945–46,* table VI, 7; and *The Condition of Education, 1978 Edition* (Washington, D.C.: United States Government Printing Office, 1978), table 4.12, 79.

2. *Digest of Educational Statistics 1976* (Washington, D.C.: United States Government Printing Office, 1977), table 101, 98 on 1972 data; *Digest of Educational Statistics 1982* (Washington, D.C.: United States Government Printing Office, 1982), table 96, 106 on 1976 data. On faculty of color, see *Digest of Educational Statistics 1974* (Washington, D.C.: United States Government Printing Office, 1975), table 103, 88.

3. Douglas and Kotch, *Directory of Faculty Contracts and Bargaining Agents in Institutions of Higher Education,* 3–68. From 1970 to 1972 one AFT agent was elected in affiliation with a local group.

4. McDonnell, "The Internal Politics of the NEA," 185. Curiously, however, as late as 1972–1973 administrators were influential in the NEA. See West, *The National Education Association,* 242–243.

5. McDonnell, "The Internal Politics of the NEA," 201; West, *The National Education Association,* 85 and 87.

6. Douglas and Kotch, *Directory of Faculty Contracts and Bargaining Agents in Institutions of Higher Education,* 3–68. Three of the NEA agents at two-year colleges served in affiliation with local agents.

7. Martha A. Brown, "Collective Bargaining on Campus: Professors, Associations and Unions," *Labor Law Journal* 21 (March 1970): 173–180.

8. Everett Carll Ladd, Jr. and Seymour Martin Lipset, *Professors, Unions and American Higher Education,* 41–42 on members' employing institutions, table 16, 44 on publications and age, 42–43 and table 16, 45 on political views, 43 and 46 on local surveys.

9. V. L. Lussier, "National Faculty Associations in Collective Bargaining: A Comparative Discussion," *Journal of Higher Education* (Summer 1975): 507–518.

10. Bertram H. Davis, Memorandum to Council Members, 2 October 1971 in "Council Meetings, October 29–30, 1971," file in AAUP Archives, 1 and Sanford H. Kadish (Chairman) et al., "Collective Bargaining and the Structure and Functioning of the Association," #97–59–71, in "Council Meetings, October 29–30," 1971 file in AAUP Archives, Washington, D.C., cover page on confidential nature.

11. "Collective Bargaining and the Structure and Functioning of the Association," iv. Kadish was elected AAUP president in 1970; his predominant AAUP experience was as chair of Committee A from 1966 to 1970. See "The Association's New Officers," *AAUP Bulletin* 56 (June 1970): 137.

12. Ibid., 1–4.

13. Ibid., 2–3.

14. Ibid., 2–3.

15. Ibid., 2–3 on past elections, 4 on upcoming elections and state flagship universities, 3–4 on institutes and private universities.

16. Ibid., 3.

17. Ibid., 4–5.

18. Ibid., 6 on specialized bargaining, 6–7 on traditional goals, 7 on chapter resentment and potential contribution.

19. Ibid., 18–19 on the need for choice, 19 on vigorous pursuit.

20. Ibid., 8–17 on legal review, 19 on budget and staffing, 19–20 on funding.

21. Ibid., 25–26 on Landrum-Griffin Act, 22 on AAUP traditions and external affiliate.

22. Ibid., 27.

23. Ibid., 27.

24. Ibid., 28 on combined activities, 29 on tensions, 30 on relations, 31 on membership and adversarial relationships.

25. Ibid., 33. There is no indication of a sharp division in the available AAUP records. There was the bitter debate at the May 1966 council meeting.

26. Ibid., 49–50, 52.

27. Ibid., 53.

28. Alfred Sumberg, Memorandum to Members of Council, 26 October 1971, in "Council Meetings, October 29–30, 1971," file in AAUP Archives, 1 on vigorous pursuit, 3 on unique form.

29. LJ [Louis Joughin], Memorandum to Council, 18 October 1971, in "Council Meetings, October 29–30, 1971," in AAUP Archives, 1–3.

30. TJT [Tom J. Truss], Memorandum to BHD [Bertram H. Davis], 15 October 1971, #109–3–71 in "Council Meetings, October 29–30, 1971," in AAUP Archives, 1–2 on clubby AAUP, 3 on vague support.

31. Bertram H. Davis et al. Memorandum to Members of Council, 21 October 1971, in "Council Meetings, October 29–30, 1971," in AAUP Archives, 4. The other staff members were William P. Fidler, Herman I. Orentlicher, Jordan E. Kurland, Richard H. Peairs, Matthew W. Finkin, William B. Woolf, Joseph E. Schwartz, Daniel L. Adler, Margaret L. Rumbarger, Martin Lapidus.

32. Ibid., 1–2 on economic benefits, 4–5 on chapters, 2 and 5 on traditional methods and receptive approach, 5 on judicial function.

33. Ralph Loomis and Wilfred Kaplan, Memorandum to Council Members, 28 October 1971, in "Council Meetings, October 29–30, 1971," in AAUP Archives, 1. On Adams' nomination see "Report of the 1971 Nominating Committee," *AAUP Bulletin* 57 (September 1971): 443.

34. Meeting of Committee N, September 24 and 25 1971, Actions Taken, in "Council Meetings, October 29–30, 1971," in AAUP Archives, 1.

35. Untitled statement, 4, in "Council Meetings, October 29–30, 1971," in AAUP Archives.

36. "Successive Votes on Policy Positions Suggested in Committee A Discussion of Collective Bargaining," 28 October 1971, in "Council Meetings, October 29–30, 1971," in AAUP Archives, single page document.

37. [Bertram H. Davis], "Council Position on Collective Bargaining," *AAUP Bulletin* 57 (December 1971): 511.

38. "Association Officers, Staff and Council," *AAUP Bulletin* 57 (December 1971): 466

39. "Transcript of Sanford H. Kadish's Remarks—Council, Friday Evening, 10/29/71" in "Council Meetings, October 29–30, 1971," in AAUP Archives, 2 on AAUP function, 3 on his balance.

40. Ibid., 7.

41. "Council Position on Collective Bargaining," *AAUP Bulletin* 58 (March 1972): 51. Neither *Bulletin* reports nor the available AAUP archives name the members of the committee.

42. Ibid., 51–52.

43. Ibid., 52 on votes, 46 on *Bulletin* publication.

44. [Davis], "Council Position on Collective Bargaining" (December 1971), 511–512 on council, 511 on committees, 512 on limits of policy.

45. Ibid., 512.

46. "Council Position on Collective Bargaining" (March 1972), 46. See Prefatory Note (December 1915), 17–19 and "General Report of the Committee on Academic Freedom and Academic Tenure" (December 1915), 15–43. See also "Representation of Economic Interests" (June 1966), 230–234.

47. Ibid., 46 on review, 46–47 on policy development, 47 on policy issues, California state colleges, and 1940 and 1966 s.

48. Ibid., 47.

49. Ibid., 48.

50. Ibid., 49.

51. Ibid., 49–50.

52. Ibid., 50–51.

53. Ibid., 51.

54. Ibid.

55. Ibid., 52.

56. Ibid., 52–53.

57. Ibid., 53–54 on decades of victories, 54 on unique potential, 53–54 on need to participate.

58. Ibid., 54.

59. Ibid. Curiously Stevens missed the significant point of collective bargaining, its power to afford de jure rather than to allow de facto recognition of faculties' rights to governance.

60. Ibid., 54–55.

61. Ibid., 57 on brief history, 58 on Committee A alternative, 58–59 on academic freedom investigations.

62. Ibid., 59 on membership losses.

63. Ibid., 60–61.

64. Ibid., 61.

65. Robert L. Jacobson, "AAUP Votes Overwhelmingly to Pursue Bargaining; Some See Sacrifice of Association's Character," *Chronicle of Higher Education* (15 May 1972): 1 on debate, 1–2 on opposition.

66. Ibid., 1.

67. Robert L. Jacobson, "Collective Bargaining Is Expected to Get Formal Endorsement of Professors' Association," *Chronicle of Higher Education* (1 May 1972): 5 on Keck's statement, 1 on vote.

68. "The Fifty-eighth Annual Meeting," *AAUP Bulletin* 58 (June 1972): 135–36 on budget; 136 on membership. Although the annual meeting report does not state that the motion passed, see "Constitution of the Association," *AAUP Bulletin* 58 (June 1972): 175 on the revised Article II of the Constitution and 175n. 1, that the Constitution was amended at the 1972 Annual Meeting.

69. [Bertram H. Davis], "1973 Dues Schedule,"*AAUP Bulletin* 58 (June 1972): 144.

70. "Coping with Adversity: Report on the Economic Status of the Profession, 1971–72," *AAUP Bulletin* 58 (June 1972): 178. See "The Fifty-

eighth Annual Meeting," 136 on delivery of the report at that annual meeting.

71. Ibid., 178–179.

72. [Walter Adams], "Report of Committee T, 1971–72," *AAUP Bulletin* 58 (June 1972): 168 on report at annual meeting; 169 on questions and Committee N.

73. Ibid.

74. "The Role of the Faculty in Budgetary and Salary Matters," *AAUP Bulletin* 58 (June 1972): 170 on elected representatives; 171 on exigency; 172 on salaries.

75. "Faculty Participation in the Selection and Retention of Administrators: A Report by Committee T," *AAUP Bulletin* 58 (June 1972): 173 on joint determination in selection and 174 on joint determination in deciding about retention.

76. Ibid., 165 on elections, 164 on the "parade," and 165 on the mergers and vigor.

77. Ibid., 165.

78. "Record of Council Meeting," *AAUP Bulletin* 59 (March 1973): 12.

79. Ibid., 13.

80. "Statement on Collective Bargaining," *AAUP Bulletin* 58 (December 1972): 423–424 and 423 on the previous statements. See "Policy on Representation of Economic and Professional Interests," 489–490 on statements on shared authority and enabling legislation.

81. Ibid., 423.

82. "The Fifty-ninth Annual Meeting," *AAUP Bulletin* 59 (June 1973): 139, 140.

83. "Record of Council Meeting," *AAUP Bulletin* 59 (September 1973): 364.

84. Ibid.

85. "Record of Council Meeting," *AAUP Bulletin* 60 (March 1974): 35.

86. "Record of Council Meeting" (March 1973), 13.

87. "Record of Council Meeting" (March 1974), 39.

88. Ibid., 38–39.

89. Ibid., 39.

90. "Record of Council Meeting," *AAUP Bulletin* 60 (September 1974): 342.

91. "Distribution of Expenditures, 1971" *AAUP Bulletin* 58 (June 1972): 250; "Distribution of Expenditures, 1974," *AAUP Bulletin* 61 (August 1975): 218.

92. [Donald J. Cameron], "Report of Committee F, 1973–74," *AAUP Bulletin* 60 (June 1974): 250. The size of the professoriate was not an issue because the number of professors continued to grow, albeit more slowly than in previous years. There were 380,000 full-time instructors in 1972 and 389,000 in 1973. See *Digest of Educational Statistics* (Washington, D.C.: United States Government Printing Office, 1979), table 99, 104.

93. "Record of Council Meeting" (September 1973), 364.

94. "Council Position on Collective Bargaining" (March 1972): 47; Carl Stevens, "Report of Committee N, 1973–74," *AAUP Bulletin* 60 (June 1974): 156.

95. Stevens, "Report of Committee N" (June 1974), 156–157.

96. Bertram H. Davis, "Report of General Secretary," *AAUP Bulletin* 59 (June 1973): 148.

97. "Report of the Auditors, 1971," *AAUP Bulletin* 58 (June 1972): 247; "Report of the Auditors, 1973," *AAUP Bulletin* 60 (June 1974): 274; "Report of the Auditors, 1974," *AAUP Bulletin* 61 (August 1975): 213.

98. The approximate expenditures for collective bargaining were calculated by multiplying the annual expenditures (n. 25) by the percentages of expenditures on collective bargaining (n. 19).

99. "Record of Council Meeting" (September 1973), 367.

100. "Record of Council Meeting" (March 1974), 36.

101. Ibid., 37.

102. Ibid., 37.

103. "Record of Council Meeting" (September 1974), 343. See also Philip W. Semas, "AAUP Reaffirms Its Reluctance to Merge or Collaborate with Rival Organizations," *Chronicle of Higher Education* (6 May 1974): 6.

104. [Cameron], "Report of Committee F, 1973–74," 250. See "The Sixtieth Annual Meeting," *AAUP Bulletin* 60 (June 1974): 140 for notice of Cameron's report at the annual meeting.

105. [Cameron], "Report of Committee F, 1973–74," 250.

106. Ibid., 251.

107. [Russell E. Miller], "Integrated Dues: A Report from Committee F," *AAUP Bulletin* 59 (March 1973): 17–19; "The Fifty-ninth Annual Meeting," 139–140; [Cameron], "Report of Committee F, 1973–74," 250 on affiliate membership (the committee recommended that the association use the mailing lists of state bar associations and the ACLU, with no indication of whether those groups would share such information), 250–251 on fiscal year.

108. [Matthew Finkin] "Report of Committee A, 1983–84," *Academe* 70 (September–October 1984): 25a and 26a; and "Institutional Distribution and

Chapter Officers," 328–346. Finkin presented 1965 data only for the research universities. Given the substantial growth in AAUP membership from 1960 to 1965, it is likely that the decline in members at selective colleges from 1965 to 1975 is greater than the decline from 1960 to 1975.

109. "Annual Meeting," *Bulletin of the A.A.U.P.* 22 (January 1936): 5–6.

110. "Report of the 1973 Nominating Committee," 370.

111. Ibid.

112. "Three Vie for Presidency of AAUP; First Real Contest in 59 Years," *Chronicle of Higher Education* (19 February 1974): 5.

113. Ibid.

114. Ibid.

115. Ibid.

116. "The Sixtieth Annual Meeting," 139. AAUP members cast between 15,819 and 16,270 votes in the elections for the other three national offices (first vice-president, second vice-president, secretary-treasurer), while casting 16,696 votes in the presidential election. See 139.

117. Walter Adams, "The State of Higher Education: Myths and Realities," *AAUP Bulletin* 60 (June 1974): 119–125.

118. "AAUP Intensifies Its Interest in Politics, College Finance," *Chronicle of Higher Education* (13 May 1974): 3. The *AAUP Bulletin* report indicated that Adams received a "standing ovation" at the end of his speech. "The Sixtieth Annual Meeting," 141.

119. Adams, "The State of Higher Education," 119.

120. Ibid. See, for example, his introductory remarks, 119–122.

121. Ibid., 125.

122. "Dr. Davis to Resign," *Academe* 8 (September 1973): 1.

123. [Bertram H. Davis], "Report of the General Secretary," *AAUP Bulletin* 60 (June 1974): 145.

124. Ibid.

125. Ibid.

126. Ibid. There were 1,523 participating institutions, representing 51 per-cent of the nation's colleges and universities. See "Hard Times: Report on the Economic Status of the Profession," *AAUP Bulletin* 60 (June 1974), 172 for the number of participating institutions; and Breneman and Finn, *Public Policy and Private Higher Education,* table 1–3, 20, for national information.

127. [Davis], "Report of the General Secretary" (June 1974), 145.

128. Ibid.

129. [William Van Alstyne], "The Association's New General Secretary," *AAUP Bulletin* 60 (September 1974): 287; and [William Van Alstyne], "The

Retirement of Bertram H. Davis as General Secretary," *AAUP Bulletin* 60 (September 1974): 286.

130. [William Van Alstyne], "The Retirement of Bertram H. Davis as General Secretary," 287.

131. [Joseph Duffey], "From the General Secretary," *AAUP Bulletin* 60 (December 1974): 365. Douglas, later U.S. senator from Illinois, reviewed *Depression, Recovery and Higher Education* in a 1938 issue of the *Bulletin*. See Paul H. Douglas, "Review," *AAUP Bulletin* 24 (October 1938): 541–543.

132. [Duffey], "From the General Secretary" (December 1974), 365–366.

133. "Record of Council Meeting" (March 1974), 39.

134. Ralph S. Brown, Jr., interview in New Haven Connecticut, 3 March 1986.

135. "Record of Council Meeting" (March 1974), 36.

136. [Alice S. Rossi], "Report of Committee W, 1972–73," *AAUP Bulletin* 59 (June 1973): 172 on "he" and "man," 174 on women in collective bargaining. Members at the 1970 Annual Meeting evidenced the first post–World War II association concern about representation of women on AAUP committees and on the staff. They adopted a proposal that "the AAUP provide for equitable representation of women in committees, offices, and staff positions and on other activities and programs of the association." See "The Fifty-sixth Annual Meeting," 141. Rossi herself identifies the 1970 actions as a sign of the times, as women began to struggle for professional identity in a number of associations. See Alice S. Rossi and Ann Calderwood, eds., *Academic Women on the Move* (New York: Russell Sage Foundation, 1973), xi-xii.

137. Georgina M. Smith, ""Faculty Women at the Bargaining Table," *AAUP Bulletin* 59 (December 1973): 403.

138. Ibid., 406.

139. "Hard Times," 171

140. Ibid., 184.

141. "The Beatrice G. Konheim Award for Outstanding Chapter Achievement," *AAUP Bulletin* 60 (June 1974): 163. On council approval of the award, see [Davis], "Report of the General Secretary" (1974), 147.

142. "Hard Times," 181–182.

143. "Sixtieth Annual Meeting," 142.

144. [Donald L. Pierce], "Report of Committee L, 1973–74," *AAUP Bulletin* 60 (June 1974): 244 on AAUP interest; 245 on conference.

145. Ibid.

146. "Sixtieth Annual Meeting," 142.

147. "Record of Council Meeting," *AAUP Bulletin* 61 (October 1975): 281.

148. "The Sixty-first Annual Meeting," *AAUP Bulletin* 61 (August 1975): 101–102 on collective bargaining and state conference committees; 102 on tensions and AAUP principles.

149. On militancy, see Lipset, *Rebellion in the University,* 195. On faculty attitudes, see Walter P. Metzger, "The American Academic Profession in 'Hard Times,'" *Daedalus* 104 (Winter 1975): 25–44.

150. Bowen and Schuster, *American Professors: A National Resource Imperiled,* 6. On the extent of financial exigencies, see Merle F. Allshouse, "The New Academic Slalom: Mission—Personnel Planning—Financial Exigency—Due Process," *Liberal Education* 61 (October 1975): 349–368.

151. "Termination of Faculty Appointments Because of Financial Exigency, Discontinuance of a Program or Department, or Medical Reasons," *AAUP Bulletin* 61 (December 1975): 329.

152. "Termination of Faculty Appointments Because of Financial Exigency, Discontinuance of a Program or Department, or Medical Reasons," *AAUP Bulletin* 60 (December 1974): 411.

153. Ibid., 411–413.

154. "Termination of Faculty Appointments Because of Financial Exigency" (December 1975), 329.

155. Ibid., 329–331; and "1972 Recommended Institutional Regulations on Academic Freedom and Tenure," *AAUP Bulletin* 58 (December 1972): 429–430.

156. "Faculty Participation in the Selection and Retention of Administrators," *AAUP Bulletin* 60 (December 1974): 414–415 on faculty participation; 414 on Council approval.

157. "Record of Council Meeting" *AAUP Bulletin* 61 (April 1975), 15.

158. Ibid., 16–17.

159. Ibid., 16–17 on membership, 18 on issues and committee examinations.

160. Ibid., 16.

161. "Record of Council Meeting" (October 1975), 279.

162. Ibid.

163. Ibid., 282.

164. Ibid., 282.

165. "The Sixty-first Annual Meeting," (August 1975): 99.

166. Ibid., 99. The AAUP collective bargaining unit at the University of Washington had to await voluntary recognition by the governing board because the state of Washington did not have enabling legislation.

167. Ibid.

168. Ibid.

169. Ibid.

170. "Record of Council Meeting," *AAUP Bulletin* 62 (April 1976): 115–116.

171. Ibid., 100.

172. "Sixty-first Annual Meeting," *Academe* 9 (June 1975): 1.

173. "Sixty-first Annual Meeting" (August 1975), 100; and [Robert Dorfman], "Two Steps Backward: Report on the Economic Status of the Profession, 1974–75," *AAUP Bulletin* 61 (August 1975): 118.

174. [Dorfman], "Two Steps Backward," 118.

175. Philip W. Semas, "Faculty Unions Talking Cooperation—Gingerly," *Chronicle of Higher Education* (9 June 1975): 4. It is interesting that the reporter chose to call all three organizations "unions."

176. Ibid.

177. "Record of Council Meeting," *AAUP Bulletin* 62 (October 1976): 333.

178. John A. Crowl, "AAUP Censures Five, Takes Another from List," *Chronicle of Higher Education* (6 July 1976): 5.

179. Philip W. Semas, "NEA Reaffirms Interest in Merger," *Chronicle of Higher Education* (6 July 1976): 4.

180. "The Sixty-second Annual Meeting," *AAUP Bulletin* 62 (August 1976): 165.

181. [Robert Dorfman], "Nearly Keeping Up: Report on the Economic Status of the Profession," *AAUP Bulletin* 62 (August 1976): 195–284.

182. Ibid.

183. Ibid., 197.

184. Ibid., 201–206.

185. Douglas and Kotch, *Directory of Faculty Contracts and Bargaining Agents in Institutions of Higher Education,* 3–68, and table 9, "Summary of Decertifications," 100. Two of the agents selected from 1972 to 1976 were affiliated with other groups, one with the AAUP at Eastern Montana College and one with the National Education Association at Somerset County College in New Jersey.

186. Ibid., 3–68 and table 9, "Summary of Decertifications," 100. Ten of the NEA agents were affiliated with local organizations, and three were affiliated with the AAUP—at the University of Hawaii, Kent State University, and the University of Northern Iowa.

187. Ibid., 3–68.

188. Howard B. Means and Philip W. Semas, eds., *Faculty Collective Bargaining* (Washington, D.C.: Editorial Projects Education, Inc., 1976), 98–101.

189. Van Alstyne, "The Strengths of the AAUP" *AAUP Bulletin* 62 (August 1976): 136. By the end of 1975 there were 60,942 active members, and in

the previous year there were 60,966. See "Membership Record of 1975," *AAUP Bulletin* 62 (April 1976): 69 and "Membership Record for 1974," *AAUP Bulletin* 61 (April 1975): 83.

190. Van Alstyne, "The Strengths of the AAUP," 136.

191. Ibid. The reader can only wonder if Van Alstyne was aware that John Dewey was for a period an enthusiastic member of the AFT.

192. Ibid., 136–137.

193. Ibid., 137.

194. Ibid., 137–138. Van Alstyne's optimism about union membership increases ignored the tremendous membership losses of the early 1970s among professors not in AAUP bargaining units.

195. Ibid. Italics in the original *Bulletin* publication.

196. Ibid.

197. Ibid., 139.

198. Ibid.

199. Ibid., 140.

200. "Membership Record for 1976," *AAUP Bulletin* 63 (February 1977): 31; see "Association Officers, Staff and Council," *AAUP Bulletin* 62 (August 1976): 130 for the number of staff members; "Membership Record for 1969," *AAUP Bulletin* 55 (March 1970): 40.

Chapter Six: "More"

1. See *Policy Documents and Reports* (Washington, D.C.: Association of American University Professors, 1990). The AAUP issues this collection on a regular basis, and it contains the variety of policy reports (including those on academic freedom and governance). The annual report on the economic status of the profession continues, with still revealing titles. See, for example, "Not So Bad: The Annual Report on the Economic Status of the Profession," *Academe* (March-April 1996), 14–108.

2. Issues of diversity have presented the AAUP with substantial challenges in the past several years. For example, in 1991, a special AAUP committee issued a statement on political correctness that elicited a strongly worded resolution of opposition from the California Conference. See "Record of Council Meeting," *Academe* 78 (January–February 1992), 37. Although not directly part of this book's examination, the "principled" nature of academic freedom, that is, the association stance that colleges and universities should not restrain speech becomes highly problematic in the critical eyes of multiculturalism or postmodernism. It is also problematic given the AAUP's restrictions on speech in the 1956 Report on Academic Freedom and Tenure in the Quest for

National Security. How the AAUP, or any group in higher education, constructs academic freedom is a challenging and intriguing question.

3. "Sexual Harassment: Suggested Policy and Procedures for Handling Complaints," *Academe* 81 (July-August 1995), 62–64.

4. "Statement on Collective Bargaining," *Academe* 80 (September-October 1994), 86.

5. [Mary Burgan], "From the General Secretary: AAUP and the Labor Movement," *Academe* 81 (November-December 1995), 2; and Mary Burgan, "A Conversation about Tenure," Association for the Study of Higher Education Annual Meeting, November 6, 1997, Albuquerque, New Mexico. On AAUP representation, see "Unionization among College Faculty: 1996," *National Center for the Study of Collective Bargaining in Higher Education and the Professions Newsletter* 24 (April–May 1996), 4.

6. Paul Starr, *The Social Transformation of American Medicine* (New York: Basic Books, 1982), 11.

7. Ibid., 24.

8. Ibid., 26.

9. Ibid., 20.

10. Ibid., 21.

11. Ibid., 9–17.

12. Ibid., 358–59, see also 382 on concerns about overspecialization.

13. On the changing labor market, see Howard R. Bowen and Jack H. Schuster, *American Professors: A National Resource Imperiled* (New York: Oxford University Press, 1986), figure 9.1, 176. Percentages of doctorates are from the reports of the Carnegie Foundation for the Advancement of Teaching. For 1968 data, see Alan E. Bayer, *College and University Faculty: A Statistical Description*, vol. 5, no. 5 (Washington, D.C.: American Council on Education, 1970). The data from 1989 are from the Carnegie 1989 "Survey among College and University Faculty," available from the Roper Center.

14. James S. Fairweather, "Academic Values and Faculty Rewards," *Review of Higher Education* 17 (Fall 1993), 43 and 53 for time spent on teaching and research, 64 on assistant professors.

15. Dolores L. Burke, *A New Academic Marketplace* (New York: Greenwood Press, 1988), 114.

16. Dorothy E. Finnegan, "Segmentation in the Academic Labor Market: Hiring Cohorts in Comprehensive Universities," *Journal of Higher Education* 64 (November/December 1993): 621–656.

17. Alan E. Bayer and John M. Braxton, "The Normative Structure of Community College Teaching: A Marker of Professionalism, *Journal of Higher*

Education 69 (March/April 1998): 202. Robert Blackburn and Janet Lawrence argued that it is in fact preferable for the community college professor to hold a doctorate, in view of both the demand for higher student transfer rates to the four-year institutions and the ability of community colleges to provide some support for research interests, either on campus or at neighboring institutions. See Blackburn and Lawrence, *Faculty at Work,* 217–218.

18. Barbara A. Lee, "The Yeshiva Decision: An Ultimatum for Professionals?" *New York University Education Quarterly* 13 (Spring 1982): 21–28. On effects on private and eventually public institutions, see "Joel M. Douglas, ed., "'Yeshivawatch'—Year Seven," *Newsletter of the National Center for the Study of Collective Bargaining in Higher Education and the Professions* (September-October 1986); Scott Heller, "Boston U. Professors Not Entitled by Law to Bargain Collectively, Labor Board Says," *Chronicle of Higher Education* (October 8, 1986): 13, 18; Scott Heller, "Professors at U. of Pittsburgh Called Managers, Ruled Ineligible to Bargain," *Chronicle of Higher Education* (March 25,1987): 13 and 15; Katherine S. Mangan, "High Court's 'Yeshiva' Ruling on Faculty Unions Is Starting to Affect Public Campuses," *Chronicle of Higher Education* (May 13, 1987): 16, 17, 25; Patrick Nagle, "Yeshiva's Impact on Collective Bargaining in Public-Sector Higher Education," *Journal of College and University Law* 20 (Winter 1994): 383–403.

19. On 1981 figures, see Joel M. Douglas and Steve Kramer, *Directory of Faculty Contracts and Bargaining Agents in Institutions of Higher Education* (New York: Baruch College, City of New York, National Center for the Study of Collective Bargaining in Higher Education and the Professions, 1982). For 1995 data, see "Unionization among College Faculty: 1996," 3.

20. *The Education Professions: A Report on the People Who Serve Our Schools and Colleges-1968* (Washington, D.C.: United States Government Printing Office, June 1969), 11–12.

21. Ibid., 12.

22. For 1967–68 projections, see *The Education Professions,* table 42a, 327. For 1993 data, see *Digest of Educational Statistics 1996* (Washington, D.C.: United States Government Printing Office, November 1996), table 218, 229.

23. Thomas R. Chibucos and Madeleine F. Green, "Leadership Development in Higher Education," *Journal of Higher Education* 60 (January/February 1989): 21–42.

24. Howard R. Bowen, *Investment in Learning: The Individual and Social Value of American Higher Education* (San Francisco: Jossey-Bass, 1980), 3–30. Bowen highlights public expectations for efficiency in higher education.

25. Barbara A. Lee, "Campus Leaders and Campus Senates," in *Faculty in Governance: The Role of Senates and Joint Committees in Academic Decision Making*, New Directions for Higher Education, vol. 19, no. 75 (San Francisco: Jossey-Bass, 1991), 41–61.

26. Sheila Slaughter, "Academic Freedom at the End of the Century: Professional Labor, Gender, and Professionalism," in *Higher Education in American Society*, eds. Philip G. Altbach, Robert O. Berdahl, and Patricia J. Gumport, 3d ed. (Buffalo: Prometheus Books, 1994), 73–100.

27. "Academic Freedom and Tenure: The Catholic University of America," *Academe* 36 (October 1989): 27–40.

28. Slaughter, "Academic Freedom at the End of the Century," 79 on long-range planning and 92 on tenure.

29. Ibid., 95–96 on undermining tenure, 95 on governance.

30. Jane McCarthy, Irving Ladimer, and Josef P. Sirefman, *Managing Faculty Disputes: A Guide to Issues, Procedures, and Practices* (San Francisco: Jossey-Bass, 1984), ix on audience and topic of book, 108–125 on three institutions.

31. See, for example, George Keller, *Academic Strategy: The Management Revolution in American Higher Education* (Baltimore: Johns Hopkins University Press, 1983).

32. Kenneth P. Ruscio, "The Distinctive Scholarship of the Selective Liberal Arts College," *Journal of Higher Education* 58 (March–April 1987): 222.

33. See Lynne B. Welch, ed., *Women in Higher Education: Changes and Challenges* (New York: Praeger, 1990); Michelle M. Tokarczk and Elizabeth A. Fay, *Working Class Women in the Academy: Laborers in the Knowledge Factory* (Amherst: University of Massachusetts Press, 1993); Beth Mintz and Esther Rothblum, *Lesbians in Academia: Degrees of Freedom* (New York: Routledge, 1997); Lois Benjamin, ed., *Black Women in the Academy: Promises and Perils* (Gainesville: University Press of Florida, 1997).

34. Benjamin, *Black Women in the Academy*, 9.

35. Martin J. Finkelstein, Robert K. Seal, and Jack H. Schuster, *The New Academic Generation: A Profession in Transformation* (Baltimore: Johns Hopkins University Press, 1998), 109 on research orientation, 111 on traditional ways. See also Lionel S. Lewis, *Marginal Worth: Teaching and the Academic Labor Market* (New Brunswick: Transaction, 1996) for an examination of the faculty reward system and the limited value placed on teaching.

36. Denise K. Magner, "Minnesota Regents Change Tenure Policy for Their Law School," *Chronicle of Higher Education* (November 15, 1995): A13; Denise K. Magner, "Minnesota Professors Irate over Plans They Say Threaten Tenure," *Chronicle of Higher Education* (May 17, 1996): A21; Governor Enters Fray over

Tenure at U. Of Minnesota," *Chronicle of Higher Education* (October 11, 1996): A10; Denise K. Magner, "Fierce Battle over Tenure at U. of Minnesota Ends Quietly," *Chronicle of Higher Education* (June 20, 1997): A14.

37. Gary Rhoades, *Managed Professionals: Unionized Faculty and Restructuring Academic Labor* (Albany: State University of New York Press, 1998), 5 and 257.

38. R. Eugene Rice, "Making a Place for the New American Scholar," New Pathways Working Paper Series, Inquiry #1 (Washington, D.C.: American Association for Higher Education, 1996), 10.

39. Ibid., 21.

40. On faculty developing course releases, resulting in the appointment of part-time faculty, see William F. Massy and Robert Zemsky, "Faculty Discretionary Time: Departments and the Academic Ratchet," *Journal of Higher Education* 65 (January–February 1994), 1–22. On administrative, cost-saving considerations of part-time faculty, see Judith M. Gappa and David W. Leslie, *The Invisible Faculty: Improving the Status of Part-Timers in Higher Education* (San Francisco: Jossey-Bass, 1993). Gappa and Leslie documented the economic considerations in the use of part-time professors, while highlighting the false economies of such decisions, 92–109.

41. Christine M. Licata, "Post-Tenure Review: Policies, Practices, and Precautions," New Pathways Working Paper Series, Inquiry #12 (Washington, D.C.: American Association for Higher Education, 1996).

42. Philo Hutcheson, Lisa Beck, and H. Parker Blount, "Voices in the Wilderness? Faculty Responses to Post-Tenure Review," National Education Association Higher Education Conference, Savannah, Georgia, March 1998.

43. There is a vast literature on the impact of higher education on students, and two conclusions in the academic area appear to be consistent. First, students learn the most in a specific content area—a gratifying outcome, given the predominance of majors. Second, students tend to forget the specifics of courses but retain the principles and themes of their courses. See Howard Bowen, *Investment in Learning: The Individual and Social Value of American Higher Education* (Baltimore: Johns Hopkins University Press, 1996), 97–100; and Ernest T. Pascarella and Patrick T. Terenzini, *How College Affects Students: Findings and Insights from Twenty Years of Research* (San Francisco: Jossey-Bass, 1991), 107–108 and 155.

44. On reducing committee service, see William G. Tierney, *Building Communities of Difference: Higher Education in the Twenty-first Century* (Westport, Conn.: Bergin & Garvey, 1993), 102–103. Tierney frames this argument within a postmodernist critical theory, an approach substantially different from this book's. Nevertheless the issue sustains: what do we accomplish with stand-

ing committees? As I have argued in a review of two recent works on tenure, in some important ways committees particularly enervate women and faculty of color, as institutions rush to assure representation. See Philo A. Hutcheson, "Essay Review: Tenure: Traditions, Policies, and Practices," *Review of Higher Education* 21 (Spring 1998): 303–313.

BIBLIOGRAPHY

AAUP Archival Materials

Washington, D.C. AAUP Archives. "Council & Annual Meeting—April 9–11, 1965 Washington, D.C." file.

———. "Council 1967" file.

———. "Council—1966" files of Jordan Kurland, associate general secretary of the AAUP.

———. "Council Letters 1971" file.

———. "Council Meeting, April 8 and 11, 1965, Washington, D.C." file.

———. "Council Meeting April 9–10, 1964, St. Louis, Missouri" file.

———. "Council Meeting—April 28–29, 1966, Atlanta, Ga." file.

———. "Council Meeting—November 15–16, 1957, Washington, D.C." file.

———. "Council Meeting—October 29–30, 1965, Washington, D.C." file.

———. "Council Meetings, October 29–30, 1971" file.

———. "Proceedings of the American Association of University Professors, Council Meeting, April 26, 1962, Morrison Hotel, Chicago, Illinois." 3 vols.

———. "Transcript of Proceedings, American Association of University Professors, Council Meeting, October 31 and November 1, 1969," 2 vols.

———. "Transcript of Proceedings: American Association of University Professors, Fifty-Fifth Annual Meeting, Convention, May 2 and 3, 1969," 2 vols.

———. Transcript of Proceedings: American Association of University Professors, Fifty-Fifth Annual Meeting, Council Meeting, 1 and 4 May 1969," 3 vols.

———. "Transcript of Proceedings: American Association of University Professors, Fifty-Fourth Annual Meeting," 26 and 27 April 1968, Washington, D.C. 3 vols.

———. "Transcript of Proceedings: American Association of University Professors, National Council Meeting," October 25 and 26, 1968." 2 vols.

258

———. "Transcript of Proceedings: American Association of University Professors, Council Meeting, Chairman: Ralph S. Brown, Jr., President," 23 and 26 April 1970, 2 vols.

Other AAUP Materials

"Academic Freedom and Tenure: A Report on Late Notice Cases," *AAUP Bulletin* 54 (December 1968): 462–465.

"Academic Freedom and Tenure: The Catholic University of America," *Academe* 36 (October 1989): 27–40.

"Academic Freedom and Tenure, Evansville College," *A.A.U.P. Bulletin* 35 (Spring 1949): 74–111.

"Academic Freedom and Tenure in the Quest for National Security," *AAUP Bulletin* 42 (Spring 1956): 49–107.

"Academic Freedom and Tenure, 1940 Statement of Principles, Proposed Interpretive Comments," *AAUP Bulletin* 56 (March 1970): 28–29.

"Academic Freedom and Tenure: North Dakota State Agricultural College," *AAUP Bulletin* 42 (Spring 1956): 130–150.

"Academic Freedom and Tenure: Saint Louis University," *AAUP Bulletin* 42 (Spring 1956): 108–129.

"Academic Freedom and Tenure: St. John's University (N.Y.)," *AAUP Bulletin* 52 (March 1966): 12–19.

"Academic Freedom and Tenure: Statements of Principles," *AAUP Bulletin,* 42 (Spring 1956): 41–44.

"Academic Freedom and Tenure: Two Cases of Excessive Probation," *AAUP Bulletin* 52 (March 1966): 32–45.

"Academic Retirement, Statement of Principles," *A.A.U.P. Bulletin* 37 (Spring 1951): 90–91.

"Academic Salaries, 1958–59: Report of Committee Z on the Economic Status of the Profession," *AAUP Bulletin* 45 (June 1959): 157–194.

Adams, Walter. "A Letter from the President," *AAUP Bulletin* 58 (June 1972): 117.

———. "Report of Committee T, 1970–71," *AAUP Bulletin* 57 (June 1971): 184–186.

———. "Report of Committee T, 1971–72," *AAUP Bulletin* 58 (June 1972): 168–169.

———. "The State of Higher Education: Myths and Realities," *AAUP Bulletin* 60 (June 1974): 119–125.

"Advisory Letters from the Washington Office," *AAUP Bulletin* 48 December 1962): 394–396.

"Annual Meeting," *Bulletin of the A.A.U.P.* 22 (January 1936): 5–6.

"Announcements and Reminders," *AAUP Bulletin* 60 (March 1974): inside front cover.

"The Association and the Desegregation Controversy," *AAUP Bulletin* 48 (June 1962): 167–169.

"Association News," *A.A.U.P. Bulletin* 32 (Spring 1946): 157–162.

"Association Officers and Council," *AAUP Bulletin* 47 (June 1961): 98.

"Association Officers and Council," *AAUP Bulletin* 50 (December 1964): 308.

"Association Officers and Council," *AAUP Bulletin* 51 (March 1965): 2.

"Association Officers and Council," *AAUP Bulletin* 54 (March 1968): 2.

"Association Officers, Staff and Council," *AAUP Bulletin* 56 (March 1970): 2.

"Association Officers, Staff and Council," *AAUP Bulletin* 56 (June 1970): 114.

"Association Officers, Staff and Council," *AAUP Bulletin* 57 (December 1971): 466

"Association Officers, Staff and Council," *AAUP Bulletin* 62 (August 1976): 130.

"The Association's New Officers," *AAUP Bulletin* 52 (June 1966): 101–102.

"The Association's New Officers," *AAUP Bulletin* 54 (June 1968): 141–142.

"The Association's New Officers," *AAUP Bulletin* 56 (June 1970): 137–138.

"The Association's New Officers," *AAUP Bulletin* 60 (June 1974): 117–118.

"At the Brink: Report on the Economic Status of the Profession, 1970–71," *AAUP Bulletin* 57 (June 1971): 223–285.

Badger, Henry G. "Constitution of College Teachers' Salary Schedules," *A.A.U.P. Bulletin* 34 (Summer 1948): 406–418.

Barth, Alan "Universities and Political Authority," *A.A.U.P. Bulletin* 39 (Spring 1953): 5–15.

Baumol, William J. "The Threat of Inflationary Erosion: The Annual Report on the Economic Status of the Profession, 1968–69," *AAUP Bulletin* 55 (June 1969): 192–153.

Baumol, William J., and Heim, Peggy. "On the Financial Prospects for Higher Education: The Annual Report on the Economic Status of the Profession, 1967–68," *AAUP Bulletin* 54 (June 1968): 182–241.

"The Beatrice G. Konheim Award for Outstanding Chapter Achievement," *AAUP Bulletin* 60 (June 1974): 163.

Berleant, Arnold. "Letters: The AAUP and the 'Right to Strike,'" *AAUP Bulletin* 53 (September 1967): 345–346.

Bixenstine, V. Edwin, and James Karge Olsen. "Letters: Must AAUP Change Its Image? An Open Letter to the Ad Hoc Self-Survey Committee," *AAUP Bulletin* 50 (September 1964): 285–288.

Bowman, Claude C. "Letters: New Orientation . . . New Tactics," *AAUP Bulletin* 51 (March 1965): 58.

Britton, William E. "The General Secretaryship," *A.A.U.P. Bulletin* 41 (Spring 1955): 6.

Brown, Ralph S., Jr. "Forging Better Tools: Report of Committee N, 1970–71," *AAUP Bulletin* 57 (June 1971): 211–214.

———. "Increasing Vigor, Increasing Success: Report of Committee N, 1971–72," *AAUP Bulletin* 58 (June 1972): 164–165.

———. New Haven, Connecticut. Interview, 4 March 1986.

———. Personal File on Special Joint Committee on Representation, Bargaining, and Sanctions. Copy in author's possession.

———. "Report of Committee T, 1965–66," *AAUP Bulletin* 52 (June 1966): 220–222.

———. "Representation of Economic Interests: Report of a Conference," *AAUP Bulletin* 51 (September 1965): 374–377.

———. "The National Labor Relations Board and Faculty Representation Cases: A Report from Committee N," *AAUP Bulletin* 57 (September 1971): 433–438.

"Budget of the Association for 1966," *AAUP Bulletin* 52 (June 1966): 272.

[Burgan, Mary]. "From the General Secretary: AAUP and the Labor Movement," *Academe* 81 (November–December 1995): 2.

———. "A Conversation about Tenure," Association for the Study of Higher Education annual meeting, November 6, 1997, Albuquerque, New Mexico.

Byse, Clark. Cambridge, Massachusetts. Interview, 2 March 1986.

———. "Letters: The University of Illinois–Koch Case," *AAUP Bulletin* 49 (September 1963): 284–285.

"California State College Trustees Approve 1966 Statement on Government," *AAUP Bulletin* 53 (December 1967): 403–404.

"Call for the Meeting for Organization of a National Association of University Professors," *Bulletin of the A.A.U.P.* 2 (March 1916): 11–13.

Cameron, Donald J. "Report of Committee F, 1973–74," *AAUP Bulletin* 60 (June 1974): 250–251.

Carr, Robert K. "A Letter from the General Secretary," *AAUP Bulletin* 43 (September 1957): 413–414.

———. "Academic Freedom, the American Association of University Professors, and the United States Supreme Court," *AAUP Bulletin* 45 (March 1959): 5–24.

———. "The Association's New Officers and General Secretary," *AAUP Bulletin* 44 (September 1958): 549–552.

————. "The Association's New Officers, Council Members, and General Secretary," *AAUP Bulletin* 44 (June 1958): 389–391.

"Central Office Notes," *AAUP Bulletin* 42 (Winter 1956): 741–745.

"Challenge and Change Forum," *AAUP Bulletin* 55 (June 1969): 273–276.

"Change in 1969 Annual Meeting," *AAUP Bulletin* 54 (December 1968): 441.

"College and University Government: Long Island University," *AAUP Bulletin* 57 (March 1971): 58–67.

"Committee A Statement on Extramural Utterances," *AAUP Bulletin* 51 (March 1965): 29.

Committee Y. *Depression, Recovery and Higher Education: A Report of Committee Y of the American Association of University Professors.* As prepared by Malcolm M. Willey. New York: McGraw-Hill, 1937.

"Committee T (Place and Function of Faculties in University Government)," *Bulletin of the A.A.U.P.* 10 (May 1924): 23–104.

"Committees for 1940," *Bulletin of the A.A.U.P.* 26 (February 1940): 126–132.

"Committees for 1943," *A.A.U.P. Bulletin* 29 (April 1943): 306–311.

"Committees of the Association," *AAUP Bulletin* 42 (Spring 1956): 188–190.

"Committees of the Association," *AAUP Bulletin* 43 (June 1957): 93–99.

"Committees of the Association," *AAUP Bulletin* 44 (December 1958): 792–796.

"Committees of the Association," *AAUP Bulletin* 50 (September 1964): 276–278.

"Committees of the Association," *AAUP Bulletin* 51 (December 1965): 450–452.

"Committees of the Association," *AAUP Bulletin* 53 (December 1967): 424–427.

Conant, Joseph M. "Report from Committee D: St. John's University and the Middle States Association of Colleges and Secondary Schools," *AAUP Bulletin* 52 (September 1966): 302–304.

"Concerning the University of Texas," *A.A.U.P. Bulletin* 31 (Autumn 1945): 462–465.

"Constitution," *Bulletin of the A.A.U.P.* 2 (March 1916): 20–23.

"Constitution," *Bulletin of the A.A.U.P.* 6 (January 1920): 3–6.

"Constitution," *A.A.U.P. Bulletin* 41 (Spring 1955): 125–134.

"Constitution," *AAUP Bulletin* 43 (June 1957): 367–372.

"Constitution," *AAUP Bulletin* 45 (March 1959): 101–106.

"Constitution of the Association," *AAUP Bulletin* 50 (September 1964): 280–282.

"Constitution of the Association," *AAUP Bulletin* 58 (June 1972): 175–178.

"Contributors to This Issue," *A.A.U.P. Bulletin* 39 (Summer 1953): 208 (un-paginated).

"Coping with Adversity: Report on the Economic Status of the Profession, 1971–72," *AAUP Bulletin* 58 (June 1972): 178–243.

"Council Business from January to April, 1916," *Bulletin of the A.A.U.P.* 2 (April 1916): 14–17.

"Council Position on Collective Bargaining," *AAUP Bulletin* 58 (March 1972): 46–61.

Cummins, Earl E., and Harold A. Larrabee. "Individual *Versus* Collective Bargaining for Professors," *Bulletin of the A.A.U.P.* 24 (October 1938): 487–496.

"Current Constitutional Considerations: National or District Elections to the Council," *AAUP Bulletin* 52 (June 1966): 239–248.

Davis, Bertram H. "Academic *Apartheid:* The Association and the South African Professors," *AAUP Bulletin* 46 (March 1960): 62–65.

———. "Academic Freedom and Tenure: A Report on Late Notice Cases," *AAUP Bulletin* 51 (March 1965): 21–24.

———. "Academic Freedom and Tenure: Four Cases of Late Notice," *AAUP Bulletin* 45 (March 1959): 58–61.

———. "Academic Freedom and Tenure: Late Notice Cases, 1961 and 1962," *AAUP Bulletin* 48 (December 1962): 368–371.

———. "Council Position on Collective Bargaining," *AAUP Bulletin* 57 (December 1971): 511–512.

———. "The Editor's Page," *AAUP Bulletin* 47 (March 1961): 69.

———. "The Editor's Page," *AAUP Bulletin* 48 (June 1962): 99.

———. "The Editor's Page," *AAUP Bulletin* 49 (September 1963): 219.

———. "The Editor's Page," *AAUP Bulletin* 50 (June 1964): 107.

———. "The Editor's Page," *AAUP Bulletin* 51 (March 1965): 3.

———. "From the General Secretary," *AAUP Bulletin* 56 (December 1970): 357.

———. "1972 Dues Levels," *AAUP Bulletin* 57 (September 1971): 327.

———. "1973 Dues Schedule," *AAUP Bulletin* 58 (June 1972): 144.

———. Note to author 16 October 1989.

———. "Principles and Cases: The Mediative Work of the AAUP," *AAUP Bulletin* 56 (June 1970): 169–173.

———. "Report of the General Secretary," *AAUP Bulletin* 53 (June 1967): 112.

———. "Report of the General Secretary," *AAUP Bulletin* 54 (June 1968): 151.

————. "Report of the General Secretary," *AAUP Bulletin* 56 (June 1970): 145–147.

————. "Report of the General Secretary," *AAUP Bulletin* 57 (June 1971): 181–183.

————. "Report of the General Secretary," *AAUP Bulletin* 58 (June 1972): 140–144.

————. "Report of General Secretary," *AAUP Bulletin* 59 (June 1973): 146–149.

————. "Report of the General Secretary," *AAUP Bulletin* 60 (June 1974): 145–147.

————. "The South African Professors," *AAUP Bulletin* 46 (June 1960): 207–208.

————. Tallahassee, Florida. Interview, 7 March 1986.

————. "Unions and Higher Education: Another View," *AAUP Bulletin* 54 (September 1968): 317–320.

————. "Unions and Higher Education: Another View," *Educational Record* 49 (Spring 1968): 139–145.

Dawson, John P. "Report of Committee T, 1961–62," *AAUP Bulletin* 48 (June 1962): 164–166.

Denenfeld, Philip. "Western Michigan University, Faculty Participation in the Government of the University: The Faculty Senate," *AAUP Bulletin* 52 (December 1966): 390–397.

Dewey, John. "Presidential Address," *Bulletin of the A.A.U.P.* 1, Part 1 (December 1915): 9–13.

"Disclaimer Affidavit: Non-Participating and Disapproving Colleges and Universities," *AAUP Bulletin* 47 (March 1961): 52.

"Disclaimer Affidavit: Non-Participating and Disapproving Colleges and Universities," *AAUP Bulletin* 47 (June 1961): 164.

"Disclaimer Affidavit: Non-Participating and Disapproving Colleges and Universities," *AAUP Bulletin* 47 (September 1961): 267.

"Disclaimer Affidavit: Non-Participating and Disapproving Colleges and Universities," *AAUP Bulletin* 47 (December 1961): 343.

"Disclaimer Affidavit: Non-Participating and Disapproving Colleges and Universities," AAUP Bulletin 48 (March 1962): 49.

"Disclaimer Affidavit: Non-Participating and Disapproving Colleges and Universities," AAUP Bulletin 48 (June 1962): 180.

"Disclaimer Affidavit: Non-Participating and Disapproving Colleges and Universities," *AAUP Bulletin* 48 (September 1962): 282.

"Disclaimer Affidavit: Non-Participating and Disapproving Colleges and Universities," *AAUP Bulletin* 48 (December 1962): 331.

"Disclaimer Affidavit Requirement of the National Defense Education Act of 1958," *AAUP Bulletin* 44 (December 1958): 769–772.

"Disposition of Committee A Cases: January 1, 1950–September 15, 1956," *AAUP Bulletin* 42 (Winter 1956): 706–708.

"Distribution of Expenditures, 1971," *AAUP Bulletin* 58 (June 1972): 250.

"Distribution of Expenditures, 1974," *AAUP Bulletin* 61 (August 1975): 277.

"Distribution of Membership and Record of Chapter Officers," *Bulletin of the A.A.U.P.* 27 (February 1941): 116–132.

"Distribution of Membership and Record of Chapter Officers," *A.A.U.P. Bulletin* 33 (Spring 1947): 171–189.

"Distribution of Membership and Record of Chapter Officers," *A.A.U.P. Bulletin* 36 (Spring 1950): 159–188.

"Distribution of Membership and Record of Chapter Officers: Record of Membership for 1954," *AAUP Bulletin* 41 (Spring 1955): 135–169.

Dorfman, Robert. "Nearly Keeping Up: Report on the Economic Status of the Profession," *AAUP Bulletin* 62 (August 1976): 195–284.

―――――. "Two Steps Backward: Report on the Economic Status of the Profession, 1974–75," *AAUP Bulletin* 61 (August 1975): 118–199.

Douglas, Paul H. "Review," *AAUP Bulletin* 24 (October 1938): 541–543.

"Dr. Davis to Resign," *Academe* 8 (September 1973): 1–7.

Duffey, Joseph. "From the General Secretary," *AAUP Bulletin* 60 (December 1974): 365–366.

"The Economic Status of the Profession," *A.A.U.P. Bulletin* 33 (Spring 1947): 79–101.

"The Economic Status of the Profession, 1959–60: Annual Report by Committee Z," *AAUP Bulletin* 46 (June 1960): 156–193.

"The Economic Status of the Profession, 1960–61: Annual Report By Committee Z," *AAUP Bulletin* 47 (June 1961): 101–134.

"The Economic Status of the Profession, 1961–62: Annual Report by Committee Z," *AAUP Bulletin* 48 (June 1962): 116–119.

"The Economic Status of the Profession, 1963–64: Annual Report by Committee Z," *AAUP Bulletin* 50 (June 1964): 136–138.

"The Economic Status of the Profession: Report on the Self-Grading Compensation Survey," *AAUP Bulletin* 48 (June 1962): 120–154.

"The Economic Status of the Profession, 1962–63: Report on the Self-Grading Compensation Survey," *AAUP Bulletin* 49 (June 1963): 141–187.

"The Economic Status of the Profession, Report of the Self-Grading Compensation Survey, 1965–66," *AAUP Bulletin* 52 (June 1966): 141–195.

"The Economic Status of the Academic Profession: Taking Stock, 1964–65," *AAUP Bulletin* 51 (June 1965): 248–301.

"Editor's Notes," *AAUP Bulletin* 43 (June 1957): 381–384.

"Educational Developments," *AAUP Bulletin* 43 (Spring 1957): 110–112.

"Educational Developments," *AAUP Bulletin* 44 (March 1958): 299–307.

"Educational Developments," *AAUP Bulletin* 49 (March 1963): 80–85.

"Educational Developments," *AAUP Bulletin* 49 (September 1963): 289–292.

"Endorsers of the 1940 'Statement of Principles on Academic Freedom and Tenure.'" *AAUP Bulletin* 56 (December 1970): 360.

"Faculty Participation in College and University Government," *AAUP Bulletin* 46 (June 1960): 203–204.

"Faculty Participation in College and University Government," *AAUP Bulletin* 48 (March 1962): 16–17.

"Faculty Participation in College and University Government," *AAUP Bulletin* 49 (September 1963): 253–259.

"Faculty Participation in Strikes," *AAUP Bulletin* 54 (June 1968): 155–159.

"Faculty Participation in the Selection and Retention of Administrators," *AAUP Bulletin* 60 (December 1974): 414–415.

"Faculty Participation in the Selection and Retention of Administrators: A Report by Committee T," *AAUP Bulletin* 58 (June 1972): 173–174.

"Faculty-Administration Relationships: Monmouth College (New Jersey)," *AAUP Bulletin* 47 (March 1961): 5–23.

"Faculty-Administration Relationships: The School of Medicine at the University of Miami (Florida)" *AAUP Bulletin* 47 (March 1961): 24–39.

Fellman, David. "The Association's Agenda," *AAUP Bulletin* 52 (June 1966): 110.

———."Report of Committee A, 1959–60," *AAUP Bulletin* 46 (June 1960): 222–230.

Fidler, William P. "Aid to the Arkansas Professors," *AAUP Bulletin* 46 (March 1960): 19–20.

———. "From the General Secretary," *AAUP Bulletin* 50 (March 1964): 62.

———. "From the General Secretary," *AAUP Bulletin* 52 (March 1966): 5–11.

———. "From the Retiring General Secretary," *AAUP Bulletin* 53 (June 1967): 113–117.

———. "Report by the General Secretary," *AAUP Bulletin* 45 (March 1959): 85–87.

————. "Report of the General Secretary," *AAUP Bulletin* 52 (June 1966): 111–114.

"Fiftieth Annual Meeting," *AAUP Bulletin* 50 (June 1964): 188–192.

"Fifty-First Annual Meeting," *AAUP Bulletin* 51 (June 1965): 313–322.

"Fifty-Second Annual Meeting," *AAUP Bulletin* 52 (June 1966): 205–208.

"Fifty-Third Annual Meeting," *AAUP Bulletin* 53 (June 1967): 133–135.

"The Fifty-Fourth Annual Meeting," *AAUP Bulletin* 54 (June 1968): 242–245.

"The Fifty-Fifth Annual Meeting," *AAUP Bulletin* 55 (June 1969): 150–154.

"The Fifty-Sixth Annual Meeting," *AAUP Bulletin* 56 (June 1970): 139–144.

"The Fifty-Eighth Annual Meeting," *AAUP Bulletin* 58 (June 1972): 135–39.

"The Fifty-Ninth Annual Meeting," *AAUP Bulletin* 59 (June 1973): 139–144.

"Financial Report for 1968 and Budget for 1969," *AAUP Bulletin* 55 (June 1969): 282.

"Financial Report For 1969 and Budget for 1970," *AAUP Bulletin* 56 (June 1970): 248.

Finkin, Matthew. "Report of Committee A, 1983–84," *Academe* 70 (September–October 1984): 21a–28a.

————. "Collective Bargaining and University Government," *AAUP Bulletin* 57 (June 1971): 149–162.

"Foreword," *AAUP Bulletin* 44 (March 1958): 3.

"The Fortieth Annual Meeting," *A.A.U.P. Bulletin* 40 (Spring 1954): 113–124.

"The Forty-First Annual Meeting," *A.A.U.P. Bulletin* 41 (Spring 1955): 90–103.

"The Forty-Second Annual Meeting," *AAUP Bulletin* 42 (Summer 1956): 338–351.

"The Forty-Third Annual Meeting," *AAUP Bulletin* 43 (June 1957): 359–365.

"Forty-Third Annual Meeting: Completed Report," *AAUP Bulletin* 43 (September 1957): 532–536.

"Forty-Fourth Annual Meeting," *AAUP Bulletin* 44 (June 1958): 501–507.

"Forty-Fourth Annual Meeting [Completed Report]," *AAUP Bulletin* 44 (September 1958): 652–653.

"Forty-Fifth Annual Meeting," *AAUP Bulletin* 45 (March 1959): 98–100.

"Forty-Fifth Annual Meeting," *AAUP Bulletin* 45 (June 1959): 272–278.

"Forty-Fifth Annual Meeting (Completed Report)," *AAUP Bulletin* 45 (September 1959): 406–414.

"Forty-Sixth Annual Meeting," *AAUP Bulletin* 46 (June 1960): 218–221.

"Forty-Sixth Annual Meeting [Completed Report]," *AAUP Bulletin* 46 (September 1960): 292–293.

"Forty-Seventh Annual Meeting," *AAUP Bulletin* 47 (June 1961): 165–168.

"Forty-Ninth Annual Meeting," *AAUP Bulletin* 49 (June 1963): 188–191.

Fuchs, Ralph F. "The Barenblatt Decision of the Supreme Court and the Academic Profession," *AAUP Bulletin* 45 (September 1959): 333–338.

————."Central Office Notes," *A.A.U.P. Bulletin* 41 (Autumn 1955): 592–597.

————. "Council Election, and Appointment of New General Secretary," *AAUP Bulletin* 43 (June 1957): 247–248.

————."A Letter from the General Secretary," *A.A.U.P. Bulletin* 41 (Autumn 1955): 423–424.

————. "The New General Secretary," *AAUP Bulletin* 43 (September 1957): 411–412.

————. "Outside Reaction to Last Spring's Special Committee Report and Censure Actions," *AAUP Bulletin* 42 (Autumn 1956): 566–571.

————. "A Profession in Quest of Itself," *AAUP Bulletin* 48 (June 1962): 104–109.

————. "Report, 1955–57, by the Retiring General Secretary," *AAUP Bulletin* 43 (September 1957): 415–429.

"Further Progress: The Economic Status of the Profession, Report on the Self-Grading Compensation Survey, 1966–67," *AAUP Bulletin* 53 (June 1967): 136–195.

"General Recommendations and Projections," *AAUP Bulletin* 51 (May 1965): 190–201.

"General Report of the Committee on Academic Freedom and Academic Tenure," *Bulletin of the A.A.U.P.* 1, Part 1 (December 1915): 15–43.

Glass, H. Bentley. Stony Brook, New York. Interview, 4 March 1986.

"Hard Times: Report on the Economic Status of the Profession, 1973–74," *AAUP Bulletin* 60 (June 1974): 171–243.

Harris, Seymour E. "Professorial Salaries and Tuition, 1947–48: Background and Proposals," *A.A.U.P. Bulletin* 34 (Spring 1948): 97–109.

Heim, Peggy, and Baumol, William. "Salary Structures in Public Junior Colleges Which Do Not Have the Usual Academic Ranks, 1965–66," *AAUP Bulletin* 52 (December 1966): 401–407.

Himstead, Ralph E. "Academic Freedom and Tenure at the University of Texas," *A.A.U.P. Bulletin* 30 (Winter 1944): 627–634.

————. "The Association and the Economic Status of the Profession," *A.A.U.P. Bulletin* 34 (Summer 1948): 419–424.

————. "The Association's New Officers," *A.A.U.P. Bulletin* 38 (Spring 1952): 5–9.

————. "Economic Status, Professional Standards and the General Welfare," *A.A.U.P. Bulletin* 33 (Winter 1947): 766–773.

————. "Editor's Note," *A.A.U.P. Bulletin* 37 (Autumn 1951): 441.

————."A Letter to the Membership," *A.A.U.P. Bulletin* 32 (Spring 1946): 163–165.

————. "A Letter to the Membership," *A.A.U.P. Bulletin* 33 (Autumn 1947): 579–585.

————. "The State of the Association, 1936–1950," *A.A.U.P. Bulletin* 36 (Winter 1950): 758–763.

————. "Thirty-Sixth Annual Meeting," *A.A.U.P. Bulletin* 36 (Spring 1950): 10–17.

————. "The Thirty-Ninth Annual Meeting," *A.A.U.P. Bulletin* 39 (Spring 1953): 102–104.

————. "Two Chapter Letters," *A.A.U.P. Bulletin* 36 (Autumn 1950): 577–589.

————, Maurice Visscher, August C. Krey, and Sumner Slichter. "A Symposium on the Economic Status of the Profession," *A.A.U.P. Bulletin* 32 (Autumn 1946): 425–442.

Holladay, James. "The Role and Activities of Region VII of the Association," *A.A.U.P. Bulletin* 41 (Spring 1955): 82–89.

Holt, W. Stull. "Letters: The University of Illinois–Koch Case," *AAUP Bulletin* 49 (September 1963): 284.

"Index for 1946," *A.A.U.P. Bulletin* 32 (Winter 1946): 781–785.

"Index for 1947," *A.A.U.P. Bulletin* 33 (Winter 1947): 229–233.

"Index for 1948," *A.A.U.P. Bulletin* 35 (Spring 1949): 180–183.

"Index for 1949," *A.A.U.P. Bulletin* 36 (Spring 1950): 193=196.

"Index for 1950," *A.A.U.P. Bulletin* 36 (Winter 1950): 229–233.

"Index for 1951," *A.A.U.P. Bulletin* 37 (Winter 1951–1952): 837–841.

"Index for 1952," *A.A.U.P. Bulletin* 38 (Winter 1952–1953): 675–677.

"Index for 1953," *A.A.U.P. Bulletin* 39 (Winter 1953–1954): 719–722.

"Index for 1954," *A.A.U.P. Bulletin* 40 (Winter 1954–1955): 689–692.

"Index for 1955," *A.A.U.P. Bulletin* 41 (Winter 1955): 822–826.

"Institutional Distribution and Chapter Officers," *AAUP Bulletin* 46 (September 1960): 328–346.

"Instructional Salaries in 41 Selected Colleges and Universities for the Academic Year 1953–54," *A.A.U.P. Bulletin* 39 (Winter 1953–1954): 632–681.

"Interim Report of Committee T on Faculty-Administration Relationships," *AAUP Bulletin* 44 (December 1958): 785–790.

"Joint Statement on Rights and Freedoms of Students," *AAUP Bulletin* 53 (December 1967): 365–368.

Jones, Howard Vallance. "The State College of Iowa: Faculty Participation in the Government of the College," *AAUP Bulletin* 52 (December 1966): 437–441.

Joughin, Louis. "Repealing the Disclaimer Affidavit," *AAUP Bulletin* 46 (March 1960): 55–61.

———. "Three Problems of the California State Colleges," *AAUP Bulletin* 53 (June 1967): 228–235.

Kadish, Sanford H. "Letters: Professor Kadish Replies," *AAUP Bulletin* 53 (September 1967): 346.

———. "The Strike and the Professoriate," *AAUP Bulletin* 54 (June 1968): 160–168.

———. "The Theory of the Profession and Its Predicament," *AAUP Bulletin* 58 (June 1972): 120–125.

Kirkland, Edward C. "Academic Freedom and Tenure, The University of Texas," *A.A.U.P. Bulletin* 32 (Summer 1946): 374–385.

Kugler, Israel. "Letters: Professors, Physicians, and Unionism," *AAUP Bulletin* 49 (March 1963): 74–76.

Kurland, Jordan E. "Critical Events at Bloomfield College," *AAUP Bulletin* 59 (September 1973): 285.

Laprade, William T. "Academic Freedom and Tenure, Report of Committee A for 1948," *A.A.U.P. Bulletin* 35 (Spring 1949): 49–65.

———. "Academic Freedom and Tenure, Report of Committee A for 1949," *A.A.U.P. Bulletin* 36 (Spring 1950): 44.

———. "Academic Freedom and Tenure, Report of Committee A for 1950," *A.A.U.P. Bulletin* 37 (Spring 1951): 72–82.

———. "Academic Freedom and Tenure, Report of Committee A for 1951," *A.A.U.P. Bulletin* 38 (Spring 1952): 105–115.

———. "Academic Freedom and Tenure, Report of Committee A for 1952," *A.A.U.P. Bulletin* 39 (Spring 1953): 107–120.

———. "Academic Freedom and Tenure, Report of Committee A for 1953," *A.A.U.P. Bulletin* 40 (Spring 1954): 62–79.

———. "Academic Freedom and Tenure, Report of Committee A for 1954," *A.A.U.P. Bulletin* 41 (Spring 1955): 19–32.

Larsen, C[harles]. M. "'Collective Bargaining' Issues in the California State Colleges," *AAUP Bulletin* 53 (June 1967): 217–227.

Leighton, J. A. "Report of Committee T on Place and Function of Faculties in University Government and Administration," *Bulletin of the A.A.U.P.* 6 (March 1920): 17–47.

Leonard, William N. "Report of Committee T, 1968–69," *AAUP Bulletin* 55 (June 1969): 178–180.

Lewaski, Kenneth F. "Rhode Island Report: Teacher's Pledge of Loyalty Abolished," *AAUP Bulletin* 51 (March 1965): 34–37.

"List of Members," *Bulletin of the A.A.U.P.* 2 (March 1916): 24–47.

Lloyd, John W. "Productivity, Compensation, and Institutional Excellence: A Commentary on the Report on the Economic Status of the Profession, 1967–68," *AAUP Bulletin* 54 (December 1968): 445–447.

Loomis, Ralph A. "Report on Developments Relating to State and Regional Conferences," *AAUP Bulletin* 55 (December 1969): 492–493.

———. "Report of the Special Committee on Grants to State and Regional Conferences," *AAUP Bulletin* 56 (June 1970): 246–247.

———. "Report of the Special Committee on Grants to State and Regional Conferences," *AAUP Bulletin* 57 (June 1971): 286–287.

———. "Report of the Special Committee on State and Regional Conferences," *AAUP Bulletin* 55 (June 1969): 277–278.

———. "Report on Developments Relating to State and Regional Conferences," *AAUP Bulletin* 56 (December 1970): 381–382.

Lovejoy, A[rthur]. O. "Annual Message of the President," *Bulletin of the A.A.U.P.* 5 (November–December 1919): 10–40.

———. "Meeting for Organization of the Association," *Bulletin of the A.A.U.P.* 2 (March 1916): 14.

———. "Proceedings of New York Meeting," *Bulletin of the A.A.U.P.* 2 (March 1916): 15–19.

———. "Professional Association or Trade Union?" *Bulletin of the A.A.U.P.* 24 (May 1938): 409–417.

Lurie, Melvin. "Professors, Physicians, and Unionism," *AAUP Bulletin* 48 (September 1962): 272–276.

Machlup, Fritz. "Grading of Academic Salary Scales," *AAUP Bulletin* 44 (March 1958): 219–236.

———. "Progress Report on the Salary Grading Program," *AAUP Bulletin* 45 (December 1959): 493–495.

Martin, George W. "Report of Committee O on Organization and Policy," *A.A.U.P. Bulletin* 41 (Spring 1955): 110–118.

"Meeting for Organization of the Association," *Bulletin of the A.A.U.P.* 2 (March 1916): 14–19.

Meizlish, Leonard. "Letters: The Collective Bargaining Agent at Flint Community Junior College," *AAUP Bulletin* 52 (September 1966): 351.

"Membership," *AAUP Bulletin* 43 (Spring 1947): 171–190.

"Membership," *A.A.U.P. Bulletin* 42 (Spring 1956): 200–230.

"Membership Record for 1964," *AAUP Bulletin* 51 (March 1965): 54.

"Membership Record for 1965," *AAUP Bulletin* 52 (March 1966): 72.

"Membership Record for 1966," *AAUP Bulletin* 53 (March 1967): 84.

"Membership Record for 1969," *AAUP Bulletin* 55 (March 1970): 40.

"Membership Record for 1970," *AAUP Bulletin* 57 (March 1971): 57.

"Membership Record for 1974," *AAUP Bulletin* 61 (April 1975): 83.

"Membership Record of 1975," *AAUP Bulletin* 62 (April 1976): 69.

"Membership Record for 1976," *AAUP Bulletin* 63 (February 1977): 31.

"Membership: Record for 1958," *AAUP Bulletin* 45 (March 1959): 135–137.

"National Advisory Referendum," *AAUP Bulletin* 52 (June 1966): 249–250.

Miller, Russell E. "Integrated Dues: A Report from Committee F," *AAUP Bulletin* 59 (March 1973): 17–19.

Morrow, Glenn R. "Report of the Self-Survey Committee of the AAUP: Minority Report and Recommendation Regarding Membership Policy," *AAUP Bulletin* 51 (May 1965): 202–204.

"New Council Members," *AAUP Bulletin* 51 (June 1965): 303.

"The New General Secretary," *AAUP Bulletin* 53 (June 1967): 109.

"A New Publication on the Collective Bargaining Issue," *AAUP Bulletin* 53 (September 1967): 336.

"New York University," *AAUP Bulletin* 44 (March 1958): 21–52.

"1939 Annual Meeting Record," *Bulletin of the A.A.U.P.* 26 (April 1940): 285–294.

"1966 Standards for Committee T Investigations," *AAUP Bulletin* 52 (June 1966): 224.

"1968 Recommended Institutional Regulations on Academic Freedom and Tenure," *AAUP Bulletin* 54 (December 1968): 448–452.

"1972 Recommended Institutional Regulations on Academic Freedom and Tenure," *AAUP Bulletin* 58 (December 1972): 429–433.

"The Ninth Annual Alexander Meiklejohn Award," *AAUP Bulletin* 52 (June 1966): 211–213.

"Not So Bad: The Annual Report on the Economic Status of the Profession," *Academe* (March–April 1996): 14–108.

Oberst, Paul. "Report of the Special Committee on State Legislation Affecting Academic Freedom," *AAUP Bulletin* 55 (June 1969): 254–256.

"Officers and Council," *A.A.U.P. Bulletin* 32 (Summer 1946): 229 [unpaginated].

"Officers and the Council," *AAUP Bulletin* 44 (December 1958): 706 [unpaginated].

"Officers and the Council," *AAUP Bulletin* 45 (March 1959): 2 [unpaginated].

Orentlicher, Herman I. "The Disclaimer Affidavit: A Valediction," *AAUP Bulletin* 48 (December 1962): 324–330.

"Organization and Policy—Report of Committee O," *AAUP Bulletin* 42 (Spring 1956): 166–171.

"Organizational Notes," *AAUP Bulletin* 43 (Spring 1957): 100–104.

"Organizational Notes," *AAUP Bulletin* 43 (June 1957): 373–375.

"Organizational Notes," *AAUP Bulletin* 45 (December 1959): 586–589.

"Organizational Notes," *AAUP Bulletin* 46 (December 1960): 425–427.

"Organizational Notes," *AAUP Bulletin* 49 (March 1963): 86–88.

"Organizational Notes," *AAUP Bulletin* 49 (June 1963): 203–207.

"Organizational Notes," *AAUP Bulletin* 49 (September 1963): 293–294.

"Organizational Notes," *AAUP Bulletin* 50 (December 1964): 365–368.

"Organizational Notes," *AAUP Bulletin* 51 (December 1965): 462–465.

"Organizational Notes," *AAUP Bulletin* 53 (March 1967): 85–87.

"Organizational Notes," *AAUP Bulletin* 54 (March 1968): 113–115.

Pardee, Otway. "Report of the Survey Subcommittee of Committee T," *AAUP Bulletin* 55 (June 1969): 180–185.

Pierce, Donald L. "Report of Committee L, 1973–74," *AAUP Bulletin* 60 (June 1974): 244–245.

Policy Documents and Reports. Washington, D.C.: The Association of American University Professors, 1990.

"Policy on Representation of Economic and Professional Interests," *AAUP Bulletin* 55 (December 1969): 489–491.

"Policy on Representation of Economic Interests," *AAUP Bulletin* 54 (June 1968): 152–154.

"Prefatory Note," *Bulletin of the A.A.U.P.* 1, Part 1 (December 1915): 17–19.

"Proposed Constitutional Amendments," *AAUP Bulletin* 53 (March 1967): 27–29.

"Proposed Constitutional Amendments," *AAUP Bulletin* 56 (December 1970): 440–442.

"Proposed Revision of the Constitution," *AAUP Bulletin* 43 (Spring 1957): 85–90.

"Protesting the Disclaimer Affidavit: The Association, the Colleges and the Universities," *AAUP Bulletin* 46 (June 1960): 205–206.

Radin, Max. "The Loyalty Oath at the University of California," *A.A.U.P. Bulletin* 36 (Summer 1950): 237–248.

"Record of Council Meeting," *AAUP Bulletin* 43 (September 1957): 537–542.

"Record of Council Meeting," *AAUP Bulletin* 44 (March 1958): 275–281.

"Record of Council Meeting," *AAUP Bulletin* 44 (September 1958): 654–658.

"Record of Council Meeting," *AAUP Bulletin* 45 (March 1959): 90–97.

"Record of Council Meeting," *AAUP Bulletin* 45 (September 1959): 400–405.

"Record of Council Meeting," *AAUP Bulletin* 46 (March 1960): 106–110.
"Record of Council Meeting," *AAUP Bulletin* 46 (September 1960): 300–303.
"Record of Council Meeting," *AAUP Bulletin* 47 (March 1961): 63–68.
"Record of Council Meeting," *AAUP Bulletin* 47 (September 1961): 262–266.
"Record of Council Meeting," *AAUP Bulletin* 48 (March 1962): 52–57.
"Record of Council Meeting," *AAUP Bulletin* 48 (September 1962): 277–281.
"Record of Council Meeting," *AAUP Bulletin* 49 (March 1963): 56–60.
"Record of Council Meeting," *AAUP Bulletin* 49 (September 1963): 264–269.
"Record of Council Meeting," *AAUP Bulletin* 50 (March 1964): 65–68.
"Record of Council Meeting," *AAUP Bulletin* 50 (September 1964): 273–276.
"Record of Council Meeting," *AAUP Bulletin* 51 (March 1965): 48–52.
"Record of Council Meeting," *AAUP Bulletin* 51 (September 1965): 383–387.
"Record of Council Meeting," *AAUP Bulletin* 52 (March 1966): 61–65.
"Record of Council Meeting," *AAUP Bulletin* 52 (September 1966): 326–329.
"Record of Council Meeting," *AAUP Bulletin* 53 (March 1967): 55–58.
"Record of Council Meeting," *AAUP Bulletin* 53 (September 1967): 333–336.
"Record of Council Meeting," *AAUP Bulletin* 54 (March 1968): 90–94.
"Record of Council Meeting," *AAUP Bulletin* 55 (March 1969): 94–98.
"Record of Council Meeting," *AAUP Bulletin* 56 (March 1970): 43–45.
"Record of Council Meeting," *AAUP Bulletin* 56 (September 1970): 315–318.
"Record of the Council Meeting," *AAUP Bulletin* 57 (March 1971): 125–128.
"Record of Council Meeting," *AAUP Bulletin* 57 (September 1971): 447–451.
"Record of Council Meeting," *AAUP Bulletin* 59 (March 1973): 12–16.
"Record of Council Meeting," *AAUP Bulletin* 59 (September 1973): 363–369.
"Record of Council Meeting," *AAUP Bulletin* 60 (March 1974): 35–40.
"Record of Council Meeting," *AAUP Bulletin* 60 (September 1974): 341–345.
"Record of Council Meeting," *AAUP Bulletin* 61 (April 1975): 15–21.
"Record of Council Meeting," *AAUP Bulletin* 61 (October 1975): 279–284.
"Record of Council Meeting," *AAUP Bulletin* 62 (April 1976): 112–119.
"Record of Council Meeting," *AAUP Bulletin* 62 (October 1976): 333–338.
"Record of Council Meeting," *Academe* 78 (January-February 1992), 37.
"Record of Council Meeting of American Association of University Professors," *AAUP Bulletin* 42 (Spring 1956): 176–184.
"Record of Council Meetings of American Association of University Professors," *A.A.U.P. Bulletin* 41 (Spring 1955): 104–109.
"Record of Membership for 1951," *A.A.U.P. Bulletin* 38 (Spring 1952): 159.
"Reed College," *AAUP Bulletin* 44 (March 1958): 102–136.
"A Report from Committee D: The Question of Accreditation by Faculty," *AAUP Bulletin* 56 (December 1970): 377–380.

"Report of Committee A, 1963–64," *AAUP Bulletin* 50 (June 1964): 125–135.

"Report of Committee A, 1964–65," *AAUP Bulletin* 51 (June 1965): 238–247.

"Report of Committee O on Organization and Policy," *Bulletin of the A.A.U.P.* 25 (October 1939): 429–436.

"Report of Committee T, 1966–67," *AAUP Bulletin* 53 (June 1967): 213–216.

"Report of Membership Committee: Report of Committee E on Qualifications for Membership," *Bulletin of the A.A.U.P.* 2 (October 1916): 14–19.

"Report of the Annual Meeting," *A.A.U.P. Bulletin* 33 (Spring 1947): 5.

"Report of the Auditors, 1971," *AAUP Bulletin* 58 (June 1972): 246–249.

"Report of the Auditors, 1973," *AAUP Bulletin* 60 (June 1974): 273–277.

"Report of the Auditors, 1974," *AAUP Bulletin* 61 (August 1975): 212–216.

"Report of the Committee of Inquiry Concerning Charges of Violation of Academic Freedom at the University of Colorado," *Bulletin of the A.A.U.P.* 2, Part 2 (April 1916): 1–72.

"Report of the Committee of Inquiry on Conditions at the University of Utah," American Association of University Professors: July 1915.

"Report of the 1945 Nominating Committee," *A.A.U.P. Bulletin* 31 (Autumn 1945): 510–514.

"Report of the 1946 Nominating Committee," *A.A.U.P. Bulletin* 32 (Autumn 1946): 576–580.

"Report of the 1947 Nominating Committee," *A.A.U.P. Bulletin* 33 (Autumn 1947): 573–578.

"Report of the 1948 Nominating Committee," *A.A.U.P. Bulletin* 34 (Autumn 1948): 613–617.

"Report of the 1949 Nominating Committee," *A.A.U.P. Bulletin* 35 (Autumn 1949): 559–565.

"Report of the 1950 Nominating Committee," *A.A.U.P. Bulletin* 36 (Autumn 1950): 592–596/

"Report of the 1951 Nominating Committee," *A.A.U.P. Bulletin* 37 (Autumn 1951): 588–595.

"Report of the 1952 Nominating Committee," *A.A.U.P. Bulletin* 38 (Autumn 1952): 473–478

"Report of the 1954 Nominating Committee," *A.A.U.P. Bulletin* 40 (Autumn 1954): 482–488.

"Report of the 1960 Nominating Committee," *AAUP Bulletin* 46 (September 1960): 304–307.

"Report of the 1962 Nominating Committee," *AAUP Bulletin* 48 (September 1962): 283–286.

"Report of the 1963 Nominating Committee," *AAUP Bulletin* 49 (September 1963): 260–263.

"Report of the 1964 Nominating Committee," *AAUP Bulletin* 50 (September 1964): 259–262.

"Report of the 1965 Nominating Committee," *AAUP Bulletin* 51 (September 1965): 378–382.

"Report of the 1967 Nominating Committee," *AAUP Bulletin* 53 (September 1967): 325–329.

"Report of the 1969 Nominating Committee," *AAUP Bulletin* 55 (September 1969): 390–394.

"Report of the 1971 Nominating Committee," *AAUP Bulletin* 57 (September 1971): 442–446.

"Report of the 1973 Nominating Committee," *AAUP Bulletin* 59 (September 1973): 370–375.

"Report of the 1953 Nominating Committee and Proposed Constitutional Amendment," *A.A.U.P. Bulletin* 39 (Autumn 1953): 514–521.

"Report of the Nominating Committee," *Bulletin of the A.A.U.P.* 25 (October 1939): 437–439.

"Report of the Self-Survey Committee of the AAUP," *AAUP Bulletin* 51 (May 1965): 99–209.

"Report of the Special Committee on Procedures for the Disposition of Complaints under the Principles of Academic Freedom and Tenure," *AAUP Bulletin* 51 (May 1965), 210–224.

"Report of the Special Committee on Publications," *AAUP Bulletin* 42 (Spring 1956): 172–175.

"Report of the Subcommittee on Standards of the Committee on the Economic Status of the Profession," *AAUP Bulletin* 44 (March 1958): 217–218.

"Report of the Survey Subcommittee of Committee T," *AAUP Bulletin* 57 (March 1971): 68–124.

"Report of the Task Force of the Assembly of State Conferences," *AAUP Bulletin* 60 (June 1974): 252–266.

"Report on the National Leadership Conference for Conference Officers" *AAUP Bulletin* 55 (December 1969): 494–497.

"Representation of Economic Interests," *AAUP Bulletin* 52 (June 1966): 229–234.

"Result of Collective Bargaining Poll in the California State Colleges," *AAUP Bulletin* 53 (September 1967): 350.

"Revised Salary Grading Tables for 1960–61," *AAUP Bulletin* 46 (June 1960): 194–197.

"Rising Costs and the Public Institutions: The Annual Report on the Economic Status of the Profession, 1969–70," *AAUP Bulletin* 56 (June 1970): 174–239.

Rossi, Alice S. "Report of Committee W, 1972–73," *AAUP Bulletin* 59 (June 1973): 172–175.

"The Role of Faculties of Colleges and Universities in the Determination of Institutional Policies," *A.A.U.P. Bulletin* 38 (Winter 1952–53): 637–644.

"The Role of the Faculty in Budgetary and Salary Matters," *AAUP Bulletin* 58 (June 1972): 170–172.

Sabine, G. H. "The Place and Function of Faculties in University and College Government, Report of Committee T," *Bulletin of the A.A.U.P.* 24 (February 1938): 141–150.

————."Place and Function of Faculties in University Government, Progress Report of Committee T," *Bulletin of the A.A.U.P.* 22 (March 1936): 183–190.

"The Self-Grading Compensation Survey," *AAUP Bulletin* 50 (June 1964): 139–184.

Shannon, George Pope. "Academic Freedom and Tenure, Report of Committee A for 1946," *A.A.U.P. Bulletin* 33 (Spring 1947): 55–70.

————. "Academic Freedom and Tenure, Report of Committee A for 1947," *A.A.U.P. Bulletin* 34 (Spring 1948): 110–133.

————. "Central Office Notes," *A.A.U.P. Bulletin* 41 (Spring 1955): 120–124.

————. "Central Office Notes," *A.A.U.P. Bulletin* 41 (Summer 1955): 366–372.

————. "The General Secretaryship of the American Association of University Professors," *A.A.U.P. Bulletin* 41 (Summer 1955): 209–213.

————. "Record of Council Meetings of American Association of University Professors," *A.A.U.P. Bulletin* 41 (Spring 1955): 104–109.

"Sexual Harassment: Suggested Policy and Procedures for Handling Complaints," *Academe* 81 (July–August 1995): 62–64.

"The Sixtieth Annual Meeting," *AAUP Bulletin* 60 (June 1974): 139.

"Sixty-First Annual Meeting," *Academe* 9 (June 1975): 1.

"The Sixty-First Annual Meeting," *AAUP Bulletin* 61 (August 1975): 97–103.

"The Sixty-Second Annual Meeting," *AAUP Bulletin* 62 (August 1976): 160–168.

Smith, Georgina M. "Faculty Women at the Bargaining Table," *AAUP Bulletin* 59 (December 1973): 403.

"A Statement of the Association's Special Committee on Challenge and Change," *AAUP Bulletin* 55 (December 1969): 461–462.

"A Statement of the Committee on Academic Freedom and Tenure," *AAUP Bulletin* 44 (March 1958): 5–10.

"Statement on Academic Freedom of Students," *AAUP Bulletin* 51 (December 1965): 447–449.

"Statement on Collective Bargaining," *AAUP Bulletin* 58 (December 1972): 423–424.

"Statement on Collective Bargaining," *Academe* 80 (September–October 1994): 86.

"Statement on Faculty Participation in Strikes," *AAUP Bulletin* 54 (June 1968): 157.

"Statement on Faculty Workload," *AAUP Bulletin* 56 (March 1970): 30–32.

"Statement on Government of Colleges and Universities," *AAUP Bulletin* 52 (December 1966): 375–379.

"Statement on Procedural Standards in Faculty Dismissal Proceedings," *AAUP Bulletin* 44 (March 1958): 270–274.

"Statement on Professional Ethics," *AAUP Bulletin* 55 (March 1969): 86–87.

"Statement on Professors and Political Activity," *AAUP Bulletin* 55 (September 1969): 388–389.

"Status of Department Chairmen," *AAUP Bulletin* 59 (March 1973): 20–21.

Stevens, Carl "Report of Committee N, 1973–74," *AAUP Bulletin* 60 (June 1974): 156.

"The Structure of the Association—Report from Committee O," *AAUP Bulletin* 43 (Spring 1957): 81–84.

Summers, Clyde. Philadelphia, Pennsylvania. Interview, 5 March 1986.

Taylor, Warren. "The Ohio Conference of Chapters of the American Association of University Professors," *A.A.U.P. Bulletin* 41 (Winter 1955): 677–683.

"Termination of Faculty Appointments because of Financial Exigency, Discontinuance of a Program or Department, or Medical Reasons," *AAUP Bulletin* 60 (December 1974): 411–413.

"Termination of Faculty Appointments because of Financial Exigency, Discontinuance of a Program or Department, or Medical Reasons," *AAUP Bulletin* 61 (December 1975): 329–331.

"Thirty-Third Annual Meeting," *A.A.U.P. Bulletin* 33 (Spring 1947): 5–9.

"Thirty-Fourth Annual Meeting," *A.A.U.P. Bulletin* 34 (Spring 1948): 8–14.

"Thirty-Fifth Annual Meeting," *A.A.U.P. Bulletin* 35 (Spring 1949): 5–11.

"Thirty-Sixth Annual Meeting," *A.A.U.P. Bulletin* 36 (Spring 1950): 10–17.

"Thirty-Seventh Annual Meeting," *A.A.U.P. Bulletin* 37 (Spring 1951): 65–71.

"The Thirty-Eighth Annual Meeting," *A.A.U.P. Bulletin* 38 (Spring 1952): 96–104.

"Thirty-Ninth Annual Meeting," *A.A.U.P. Bulletin* 39 (Spring 1953): 90–105.

Tschan, Francis J. "The Organization and Functions of Chapters of the American Association of University Professors," *A.A.U.P. Bulletin* 39 (Summer 1953): 319–341.

"Twenty-Sixth Annual Meeting," *Bulletin of the A.A.U.P.* 26 (February 1940): 7 .

Tyler, H. W. "The Defense of Freedom by Educational Organizations" in *Educational Freedom and Democracy* (Second Yearbook of the John Dewey Society, New York, 1938), pp. 229–239. Cited in Walter P. Metzger, *Academic Freedom in the Age of the University.* New York: Columbia University Press, 1955, paperback edition, 1969, p. 212n. 54.

———. "Some Problems of the Association," *Bulletin of the A.A.U.P.* 24 (February 1938): 201–204.

———. "What the Association Is and Is Not," *AAUP Bulletin* 42 (Spring 1956): 163–165.

"The University of California Loyalty Oath Situation," *A.A.U.P. Bulletin* 37 (Spring 1951): 92–101.

"The University of Michigan," *AAUP Bulletin* 44 (March 1958): 53–101.

"The University of Vermont," *AAUP Bulletin* 44 (March 1958): 11–21.

Van Alstyne, William. "The Association's New General Secretary," *AAUP Bulletin* 60 (September 1974): 287.

———. "The Retirement of Bertram H. Davis as General Secretary," *AAUP Bulletin* 60 (September 1974): 286.

———. "The Strengths of the AAUP: A Bicentennial Report," *AAUP Bulletin* 62 (August 1976): 135–140.

———. "The Supreme Court Speaks to the Untenured: A Comment on 'Board of Regents *v.* Roth' and 'Perry *v.* Sinderman.'" *AAUP Bulletin* 58 (September 1972): 267–278.

Ward, Paul W. "Place and Function of Faculties in College and University Government, Report of Committee T," *Bulletin of the A.A.U.P.* 26 (April 1940): 171–189.

———. "Report of Committee T on the Place and Function of Faculties in College and University Government," *A.A.U.P. Bulletin* 34 (Spring 1948): 55–66.

———. "The Place and Function of Faculties in College and University Government, Report of Committee T," *A.A.U.P. Bulletin* 41 (Spring 1955): 62–81.

———, and Ralph E. Himstead. "The Place and Function of Faculties in College and University Government, Report of Progress," *A.A.U.P. Bulletin* 39 (Summer 1953): 300–318.

"What the American Association of University Professors Is and What It Is Not," *Bulletin of the A.A.U.P.* 24 (March 1938): 230–248.

White, Helen C. "The Association in 1958," *AAUP Bulletin* 44 (June 1958): 392–400.

Wigmore, J[ohn]. H. "President's Report for 1916," *Bulletin of the A.A.U.P.* 2 (November 1916): 9–52.

———. "Report of Committee P on Pensions and Insurance," *Bulletin of the A.A.U.P.* 2 (November 1916): 57–80.

———, and H. W. Tyler. "Letter on Formation of Local Chapters," *Bulletin of the A.A.U.P.* 2 (April 1916): 18–19.

Wilde, Edwin F. "Letters: Letter of Appreciation," *AAUP Bulletin* 50 (December 1964): 360.

Other Materials

"AAUP Intensifies Its Interest in Politics, College Finance," *Chronicle of Higher Education* (13 May 1974): 3.

"AFT and the Colleges," *American Teacher* 12 (May 1966): 8–9.

"AFT Schedules National Conference for College Teachers," *American Teacher* 12 (March 1966): 5.

Allshouse, Merle F. "The New Academic Slalom: Mission—Personnel Planning—Financial Exigency—Due Process," *Liberal Education* 61 (October 1975): 349–368.

American Association for Higher Education. *Faculty Participation in Academic Governance.* Washington, D.C.: American Association for Higher Education, 1967.

American Teacher Magazine 44 (October 1959): back cover.

American Teacher Magazine 45 (February 1961): front cover.

Anderson, James D. "Race, Meritocracy, and the American Academy during the Immediate Post–World War II Era," *History of Education Quarterly* 33 (Summer 1993): 151–175.

Angell, George W. "Two-Year College Experience," in *Faculty Unions and Collective Bargaining,* edited by E. D. Duryea and Robert S. Fisk. San Francisco: Jossey-Bass, 1973, pp. 87–107.

"At Henry Ford: Four-Day Walkout Brings First College Contract," *American Teacher Magazine* 51 (September 1966): 19.

Bayer, Alan E. *College and University Faculty: A Statistical Description.* Washington, D.C.: American Council on Education, 1970.

———, and John M. Braxton. "The Normative Structure of Community College Teaching: A Marker of Professionalism," *Journal of Higher Education* 69 (March/April 1998).

Beazley, Richard M. *Salaries and Tenure of Instructional Faculty in Institutions of Higher Education 1974–75.* Washington, D.C.: United States Government Printing Office, 1976.

Benjamin, Lois, ed., *Black Women in the Academy: Promises and Perils.* Gainesville: University Press of Florida, 1997.

Berdahl, Robert O. *Statewide Coordination of Higher Education.* Washington, D.C.: American Council on Education, 1971.

"Bertram Davis To Be AAUP's Chief Executive" *Chronicle of Higher Education* (22 March 1967): 1.

Blackburn, Robert T., and Janet T. Lawrence. *Faculty at Work: Motivation, Expectation, Satisfaction.* Baltimore: Johns Hopkins University Press, 1995.

Bledstein, Burton J. *The Culture of Professionalism: The Middle Class and the Development of Higher Education in America.* New York: W.W. Norton, 1976.

Blocker, Clyde E., Robert H. Plummer, and Richard C. Richardson, Jr. *The Two-Year College: A Social Synthesis.* Englewood, N.J.: Prentice Hall, 1965.

Bowen, Howard R. *Investment in Learning: The Individual and Social Value of American Higher Education.* San Francisco: Jossey-Bass, 1980.

Bowen, Howard R., and Jack A. Schuster. *American Professors: A National Resource Imperiled.* New York: Oxford University Press, 1986.

Brann, James. "Unionizing the Academies," *New Republic* (25 February 1967): 10–11.

Breneman, David W., and Chester E. Finn, Jr., eds. *Public Policy and Private Higher Education.* Washington, D.C.: Brookings Institution, 1978.

Brown, David G. *The Mobile Professors.* Washington, D.C.: American Council on Education, 1967.

Brown, Martha A. "Collective Bargaining on Campus: Professors, Associations and Unions," *Labor Law Journal* 21 (March 1970): 167–181.

Burke, Dolores L. *A New Academic Marketplace.* New York: Greenwood Press, 1988.

Burton, John D. "The Harvard Tutors: The Beginning of an Academic Profession, 1690–1825," *History of Higher Education Annual* 16 (1996): 5–20.

Bush, Vannevar *Science, the Endless Frontier.* Washington, D.C.: United States Government Printing Office, 1945.

Caplow, Theodore, and Reece J. McGee. *The Academic Marketplace.* Garden City, N.Y.: Basic Books, 1958.

Carnegie Foundation for the Advancement of Teaching, "1984 Carnegie Foundation National Surveys of Higher Education, Faculty Sample," Roper Center for Public Opinion Research, Storrs, Connecticut, 1984.

Carnegie Foundation for the Advancement of Teaching, "1975 Carnegie Foundation National Surveys of Higher Education, Faculty Sample," Roper Center for Public Opinion Research, Storrs, Connecticut, 1975.

Carnegie Foundation for the Advancement of Teaching, "Survey among College and University Faculty," Roper Center for Public Opinion Research, Storrs, Connecticut, 1989.

Carr, Robert K., and Daniel Van Eyck. *Collective Bargaining Comes to the Campus.* Washington, D.C.: American Council on Education, 1973.

Cartter, Allan M. "A New Look at the Supply of College Teachers," *Educational Record* 46 (Summer 1965): 267–277.

———. *The Ph.D. and The Academic Labor Market.* New York: McGraw-Hill, 1976.

"Catholic Students in Capital Score Ouster of Priest," *New York Times,* 19 April 1967, p. 23.

"Catholic U. Classes Stopped as Protest Spreads in Faculty," *New York Times,* 21 April 1967, pp. 1, 50.

"Catholic U. Strike Backed by Rector," *New York Times,* 1 October 1967, sec. 1, p. 51.

"Catholic University Hit by Strike," *New York Times,* 20 April 1967, p. 45.

Cheit, Earl F. *The New Depression in Higher Education: A Study of Financial Conditions at 41 Colleges and Universities* (New York: McGraw-Hill, 1971).

Chibucos, Thomas R., and Madeleine F. Green,"Leadership Development in Higher Education," *Journal of Higher Education* 60 (January/February 1989): 21–42.

Clark, Burton R. *The Academic Life: Small Worlds, Different Worlds.* Princeton: Carnegie Foundation for the Advancement of Teaching, 1987.

Cole, Stephen. *The Unionization of Teachers: A Case Study of the UFT.* New York: Praeger, 1969.

"Collective Bargaining Elections," *American Teacher* 12 (January 1966): 4.

Commission on Educational Reconstruction. *Organizing the Teaching Profession: The Story of the American Federation of Teachers.* Glencoe, Ill.: Free Press, 1955.

The Condition of Education, 1978 Edition. Washington, D.C.: United States Government Printing Office, 1978.

Corson, John J. *Governance of Colleges and Universities.* New York: McGraw-Hill, 1960.

Crowl, John A. "AAUP Censures Five, Takes Another from List," *Chronicle of Higher Education* 6 July 1976, p. 5.

Dennison, Charles P. *Faculty Rights and Obligations in Eight Liberal Arts Colleges.* New York: Teachers College, Columbia University Press, 1955.

Digest of Educational Statistics. Washington, D.C.: United States Government Printing Office, 1979.

Digest of Educational Statistics, 1965 Edition. Washington, D.C.: United States Government Printing Office, 1965.

Digest of Educational Statistics, 1969 Edition. Washington, D.C.: United States Government Printing Office, September 1969.

Digest of Educational Statistics, 1970 Edition. Washington, D.C.: United States Government Printing Office, 1970.

Digest of Educational Statistics, 1971 Edition. Washington, D.C.: United States Government Printing Office, 1971.

Digest of Educational Statistics: 1973 Edition. Washington, D.C.: United States Government Printing Office, 1974.

Digest of Educational Statistics: 1974. Washington, D.C.: United States Government Printing Office, 1975.

Digest of Educational Statistics: 1976. Washington, D.C.: United States Government Printing Office, 1977.

Digest of Educational Statistics: 1982. Washington, D.C.: United States Government Printing Office, 1982.

Digest of Educational Statistics 1996. Washington, D.C.: United States Government Printing Office, 1996.

Douglas, Joel M., ed., "'Yeshivawatch'—Year Seven," *Newsletter of the National Center for the Study of Collective Bargaining in Higher Education and the Professions* (September–October 1986).

————, and Elizabeth Kotch. *Directory of Faculty Contracts and Bargaining Agents in Institutions of Higher Education.* New York: National Center for the Study of Collective Bargaining in Higher Education and the Professions—Baruch College, City University of New York, 1985.

————, and Steve Kramer. *Directory of Faculty Contracts and Bargaining Agents in Institutions of Higher Education.* New York: Baruch College, City of New York, National Center for the Study of Collective Bargaining in Higher Education and the Professions, 1982.

Dunham, E. Alden. *Colleges of the Forgotten Americans: A Profile of State Colleges and Regional Universities.* New York: McGraw-Hill, 1969.

Dunham, Ralph E., and Patricia S. Wright. *Faculty and Other Professional Staff in Institutions of Higher Education: First Term 1963–64.* Washington, D.C.: United States Government Printing Office, 1966.

Duryea, E. D. and Robert S. Fisk. "Epilogue," in *Faculty Unions and Collective Bargaining,* edited by E.D. Duryea and Robert S. Fisk. San Francisco: Jossey-Bass, 1973, pp. 195–216..

Eaton, William Edward. *The American Federation of Teachers, 1916–1961: A History of the Movement.* Carbondale, Illinois: Southern Illinois University Press, 1975.

Eckleberry, R. H. "Editorial Comments: A Double Standard," *Journal of Higher Education* 47 (April 1956): 223–225.

Education Directory 1960–1961, Part 3 Higher Education. Washington, D.C.; United States Government Printing Office, 1960.

Education Directory 1961–62, Part 3 Higher Education. Washington, D.C.: United States Government Printing Office, 1962.

The Education Professions: A Report on the People Who Serve Our Schools and Colleges-1968. Washington, D.C.: United States Government Printing Office, June 1969.

Eliot, Charles W. *University Administration.* New York: Houghton Mifflin, 1908.

Faculty in Higher Education Institutions, 1988. Washington, D.C.: United States Government Printing Office, 1990.

Fairweather, James S. "Academic Values and Faculty Rewards," *Review of Higher Education* 17 (Fall 1993): 43–68.

Fairweather, James S. *Faculty Work and Public Trust: Restoring the Value of Teaching and Public Service in American Academic Life.* Boston: Allyn and Bacon, 1996.

Ferguson, Tracy H. "Private Institutions and the NLRB," in *Faculty Power: Collective Bargaining on Campus,* edited by Terrence N. Tice. Ann Arbor, Mich.: Institute of Continuing Legal Education, 1972, pp. 59–66.

———. "Collective Bargaining in Universities," *Labor Law Journal* 19 (December 1968): 778–804.

Finnegan, Dorothy E. "Segmentation in the Academic Labor Market: Hiring Cohorts in Comprehensive Universities," *Journal of Higher Education* 64 (November/December 1993): 621–656.

Finkelstein, Martin. "From Tutor to Specialized Scholar: Academic Professionalization in Eighteenth and Nineteenth Century America," *History of Higher Education Annual* 3 (1983): 99–121.

———, Robert K. Seal, and Jack H. Schuster. *The New Academic Generation: A Profession in Transformation.* Baltimore: Johns Hopkins University Press, 1998.

Fisk, Robert S., and William C. Puffer. "Public University System: State University of New York. " in *Faculty Unions and Collective Bargaining,* edited by E. D. Duryea and Robert S. Fisk. San Francisco: Jossey-Bass, 1973, pp. 130–155.

Gappa, Judith M., and David W. Leslie. *The Invisible Faculty: Improving the Status of Part- Timers in Higher Education.* San Francisco: Jossey-Bass, 1993.

Garbarino, Joseph W. "Emergence of Collective Bargaining," in *Faculty Unions and Collective Bargaining,* edited by E. D. Duryea and Robert S. Fisk. San Francisco: Jossey-Bass, 1973, pp. 1–19.

————. "Precarious Professors: New Patterns of Representation," *Industrial Relations* 10 (February 1971): 1–20.

————. "Professional Negotiations in Education," *Industrial Relations* 7 (February 1968): 93–106.

————, and Bill Aussieker. *Faculty Bargaining: Change and Conflict.* New York: McGraw-Hill, 1975.

Gardner, David P. *The California Oath Controversy.* Berkeley: University of California Press, 1967.

Goodchild, Lester P., and Jonathan D. Fife. *Administration as a Profession,* New Directions for Higher Education No. 76, v19. San Francisco: Jossey-Bass, 1991.

"Governor Enters Fray over Tenure at U. of Minnesota," *Chronicle of Higher Education* (October 11, 1996): A10.

Graham, David L., and Donald E. Walters. "Bargaining Process," in *Faculty Unions and Collective Bargaining,* edited by E.D. Duryea and Robert S. Fisk. San Francisco: Jossey-Bass, 1973, pp. 44–65.

Gruber, Carol S. *Mars and Minerva: World War I and the Uses of Higher Learning in America.* Baton Rouge: Louisiana State University Press, 1975.

Gumport, Patricia J., and Brian Pusser. "A Case of Bureaucratic Accretion: Context and Consequences," *Journal of Higher Education* 66 (September/October 1995): 493–520.

Haug, Marie R. "The Deprofessionalization of Everyone?" *Sociological Focus* 8(August 1975): 197–213.

Heller, Scott. "Boston U. Professors Not Entitled by Law to Bargain Collectively, Labor Board Says," *Chronicle of Higher Education* (October 8, 1986): 13, 18.

Heller, Scott. "Professors at U. of Pittsburgh Called Managers, Ruled Ineligible to Bargain," *Chronicle of Higher Education* (March 25,1987): 13 and 15.

Heim, Peggy. "Growing Tensions in Academic Administration," *North Central Association Quarterly* 42 (Winter 1968): 244–251.

Higher Education for American Democracy: A Report of the President's Commission on Higher Education. 2 vols. Washington, D.C.: United States Government Printing Office, 1947.

Hixon, Richard A., and Maurice R. Duperre, "Faculty Organizations as an Aid to Employment Relations in Junior Colleges," in *Employment Relations in Higher Education,* edited by Stanley Elam and Michael H. Moscow. Bloomington, Ind.: Phi Delta Kappa, 1969, pp. 181–215.

Hofstadter, Richard. *Anti-Intellectualism in American Life.* New York: Knopf, 1963.

————, and Walter P. Metzger, *The Development of Academic Freedom in the United States.* New York: Columbia University Press, 1955.

Hutcheson, Philo A. "Essay Review: Tenure: Traditions, Policies, and Practices," *Review of Higher Education* 21 (Spring 1998): 303–313.

————. "McCarthyism and the Professoriate: A Historiographic Nightmare?" *Higher Education: The Handbook of Theory and Research,* v. 12, edited by John C. Smart (New York: Agathon Press, 1997), pp. 435–460.

————. "Reform and Representation: The Uncertain Development of Collective Bargaining in the AAUP, 1946 to 1976," University of Chicago Ph.D. dissertation, 1991.

————, Lisa Beck, and H. Parker Blount, "Voices in the Wilderness? Faculty Responses to Post-Tenure Review," National Education Association Higher Education Conference, Savannah, Georgia, March 1998.

Ingerman, Sidney. "Employed Graduate Students Organize at Berkeley," *Industrial Relations* 5 (October 1965): 141–150.

Jackson, Edward Donald, Jr. "The American Association of University Professors and Community/Junior Colleges," Ph.D. dissertation, Florida State University, 1974.

Jacobson, Robert [L]. "AAUP to Reconsider Stand Against Strikes by Faculties," *Chronicle of Higher Education* (3 May 1967): 1 and 5.

————. "AAUP Votes Overwhelmingly to Pursue Bargaining; Some See Sacrifice of Association's Character," *Chronicle of Higher Education* (15 May 1972): 1–2.

————. "Bertram Davis to Be AAUP's Chief Executive," *Chronicle of Higher Education* (22 March 1967): 1 and 4.

————. "Collective Bargaining Is Expected to Get Formal Endorsement of Professors' Association," *Chronicle of Higher Education* (1 May 1972): 1 and 5.

Jencks, Christopher, and David Riesman. *The Academic Revolution.* Garden City, N.Y.: Doubleday, 1968 & Anchor Books, 1969.

Kanigel, Robert. *The One Best Way: Frederick Winslow Taylor and the Enigma of Efficiency.* New York: Viking Penguin, 1997.

Keller, George. *Academic Strategy: The Management Revolution in American Higher Education.* Baltimore: Johns Hopkins University Press, 1983.

Kerr, Clark. *The Uses of the University.* Cambridge: Harvard University Press, 1963.

Klaw, Spencer. "The Affluent Professors," *Reporter,* 23 June 1960, pp. 16–25.

Kimball, Bruce A. *The "True Professional Ideal" in America: A History.* Cambridge: Blackwell, 1992).

Ladd, Everett Carll, Jr., and Seymor Martin Lipset. *Professors, Unions and American Higher Education.* Berkeley: Carnegie Foundation for the Advancement of Teaching and Carnegie Commission on Higher Education, 1973.

————. *The Divided Academy: Professors and Politics.* New York: McGraw-Hill, 1975.

Lazarsfeld, Paul, and Wagner Thielens, Jr. *The Academic Mind: Social Scientists in a Time of Crisis.* Glencoe, Ill.: Free Press, 1958.

Lee, Barbara A., "Campus Leaders and Campus Senates," in *Faculty in Governance: The Role of Senates and Joint Committees in Academic Decision Making.* New Directions for Higher Education, No. 75, v. 19. San Francisco: Jossey-Bass, 1991: 41–61.

————. "The Yeshiva Decision: An Ultimatum for Professionals?" *New York University Education Quarterly* 13 (Spring 1982): 21–28.

Leslie, David W., and Elaine C. Fygetakis. "A Comparison of Carnegie and NCES Data on Postsecondary Faculty: Ambiguities and Disjunctures," *Research in Higher Education* 33 (August 1993): 447–465.

Lester, Jeannette Ann. "The American Federation of Teachers in Higher Education: A History of Union Organization of Faculty Members in Colleges and Universities," Ph.D. dissertation, University of Toledo, 1968.

Lewis, Lionel S. *Marginal Worth: Teaching and the Academic Labor Market.* New Brunswick: Transaction, 1996.

————, and Michael N. Ryan. "Professionalization and the Professoriate," *Social Problems* 24 (December 1976): 282–297.

————. "The American Professoriate and the Movement toward Unionization" in *Comparative Perspectives on the Academic Profession,* edited by Philip G. Altbach. New York: Praeger, 1977, pp. 191–214.

Licata, Christine M. "Post-Tenure Review: Policies, Practices, and Precautions," New Pathways Working Paper Series, Inquiry #12. Washington, D.C.: American Association for Higher Education, 1996.

Lieberman, Myron, and Michael H. Moskow. *Collective Negotiations for Teachers: An Approach to School Administration.* Chicago: Rand McNally, 1966.

Light, Jr., Donald. "Introduction: The Structure of the Academic Professions,"*Sociology of Education* 47 (Winter 1974): 2–28.

Lussier, V.L. "National Faculty Associations in Collective Bargaining: A Comparative Discussion," *Journal of Higher Education* (Summer 1975): 507–518.

Magner, Denise K. "Fierce Battle over Tenure at U. of Minnesota Ends Quietly," *Chronicle of Higher Education* (June 20, 1997): A14.

————. "Minnesota Professors Irate over Plans They Say Threaten Tenure," *Chronicle of Higher Education* (May 17, 1996): A21.

————. "Minnesota Regents Change Tenure Policy for Their Law School," *Chronicle of Higher Education* (November 15, 1995): A13.

Mangan, Katherine S. "High Court's 'Yeshiva' Ruling on Faculty Unions Is Starting to Affect Public Campuses," *Chronicle of Higher Education* (May 13, 1987): 16, 17, 25.

Marmion, Harry A. "Unions and Higher Education," *Educational Record* 49 (Winter 1968): 41–47.

Massy, William F., and Robert Zemsky. "Faculty Discretionary Time: Departments and the Academic Ratchet," *Journal of Higher Education* 65 (January–February 1994): 1–22.

McCarthy, Jane, Irving Ladimer, and Josef P. Sirefman. *Managing Faculty Disputes: A Guide to Issues, Procedures, and Practices.* San Francisco: Jossey-Bass, 1984.

McDonnell, Lorraine M. "The Internal Politics of the NEA," *Phi Delta Kappan* 18 (October 1976): 185–186, 201.

Means, Howard B., and Philip W. Semas. eds. *Faculty Collective Bargaining.* Washington, D.C.: Editorial Projects for Education, Inc., 1976.

Medsker, Leland. *The Junior College: Progress and Prospect* New York: McGraw-Hill, 1960.

————, and Dale Tillery. *Breaking the Access Barriers: A Profile of the American Junior College.* New York: McGraw-Hill, 1971.

Metzger, Loya. "Professors in Trouble: A Quantitative Analysis of Academic Freedom and Tenure Cases," Ph.D. dissertation, Columbia University, 1978.

Metzger, Walter P. "The American Academic Profession in 'Hard Times.'" *Daedalus* 104 (Winter 1975): 25–44.

————. "The First Investigation," *AAUP Bulletin* 48 (September 1961): 206–210.

————. "Origins of the Association: An Anniversary Address," *AAUP Bulletin* 51 (June 1965): 229–237.

"Milwaukee Vocational Union Elected Bargaining Agent," *American Teacher* 10 (September 1963): 1, 11.

Mintz, Beth, and Esther Rothblum. *Lesbians in Academia: Degrees of Freedom.* New York: Routledge, 1997.

Morse, Bradford. "The Veteran and His Education," *Higher Education* (1960): 16–19. Cited by Frederick Rudolph, *The American College and University: A History,* New York: Vintage, 1965, p. 486n. 6.

Nagle, Patrick. "Yeshiva's Impact on Collective Bargaining in Public-Sector Higher Education," *Journal of College and University Law* 20 (Winter 1994): 383–403.

National Education Association. *Addresses and Proceedings of the Ninety-Ninth Annual Meeting Held at Atlantic City, New Jersey, June 25–June 30, 1961.* 99. Washington, D.C.: National Education Association, 1961.

National Education Association. *Addresses and Proceedings of the One-Hundredth Annual Meeting Held at Denver, Colorado, July 1–July 6, 1962.* Washington, D.C.: National Education Association, 1962.

National Study of Postsecondary Faculty, National Center for Education Statistics, 1993.

"NEA Unit Claims Legal Labor Status under Wisconsin Law," *American Teacher* 9 (November 1962): 1–2.

Olson, Keith W. *The G.I. Bill, the Veterans, and the Colleges.* Lexington: University Press of Kentucky, 1974.

Ozanne, Robert W. *The Labor Movement in Wisconsin: A History.* Madison, Wisc.: State Historical Society of Wisconsin, 1984.

Pascarella, Ernest T., and Patrick T. Terenzini. *How College Affects Students: Findings and Insights from Twenty Years of Research.* San Francisco: Jossey-Bass, 1991.

Power, Edward J. *Catholic Higher Education in America: A History* New York: Appleton- Century-Crofts, 1972.

President's Commission on Education Beyond the High School. *Second Report to the President.* Washington, D.C.: United States Government Printing Office, July 1957.

President's Commission on Higher Education, *Higher Education for American Democracy.* New York: Harper & Brothers, 1947.

Reuther, Victor G. *The Brothers Reuther and the Story of the UAW.* Boston: Houghton- Mifflin, 1976.

Rhoades, Gary. *Managed Professionals: Unionized Faculty and Restructuring Academic Labor.* Albany: State University of New York Press, 1998.

Rice, R. Eugene. "Making a Place for the New American Scholar," New Pathways Working Paper Series, Inquiry #1. Washington, D.C.: American Association for Higher Education, 1996.

Riesman, David. *On Higher Education: The Academic Enterprise in an Era of Rising Student Consumerism.* San Francisco: Jossey-Bass, 1980.

Rossi, Alice S., and Ann Calderwood, eds., *Academic Women on the Move.* New York: Russell Sage Foundation, 1973.

Ruscio, Kenneth P. "The Distinctive Scholarship of the Selective Liberal Arts College," *Journal of Higher Education* 58 (March–April 1987): 205–222.

Schrecker, Ellen W. *No Ivory Tower: McCarthyism and the Universities.* New York: Oxford University Press, 1986.

Semas, Philip W. "AAUP Reaffirms Its Reluctance to Merge or Collaborate with Rival Organizations," *Chronicle of Higher Education* (6 May 1974): 6.

————. "Davis, A.A.U.P. Head, to Resign in a Year," *Chronicle of Higher Education* (24 September 1973): 3.

————. "Faculty Unions Talking Cooperation—Gingerly," *Chronicle of Higher Education* (9 June 1975): 4.

————. "NEA Reaffirms Interest in Merger," *Chronicle of Higher Education* (6 July 1976): 4.

Slaughter, Sheila. "Academic Freedom at the End of the Century: Professional Labor, Gender, and Professionalism," in *Higher Education in American Society,* edited by Philip G. Altbach, Robert O. Berdahl, and Patricia J. Gumport. 3d edition. Buffalo: Prometheus, 1994, pp. 73–100.

————. "Academic Freedom in the Modern University," in *Higher Education in American Society,* edited by Philip G. Altbach and Robert O. Berdahl. Revised ed. Buffalo: Prometheus Books, 1987, pp. 77–105.

————. "The Danger Zone: Academic Freedom and Civil Liberties," *Annals of the American Academy of Political and Social Science* 448 (March 1980): 46–61.

"Special Commemorative Meeting of the Indiana University School of Law Faculty in Honor of the Memory of Professor Ralph Follen Fuchs: Transcript of Proceedings," Bloomington, Ind., 4 March 1985, pp. 1– 24.

Statistics of Higher Education 1945–46. Washington, D.C.: United States Government Printing Office, 1949.

Statistics of Higher Education: 1955–56, Faculty, Students, and Degrees. Washington, D.C.: United States Government Printing Office, 1957.

Starr, Paul *The Social Transformation of American Medicine.* New York: Basic, 1982.

Stewart, George R. *The Year of the Oath.* Garden City, New York: Doubleday, 1950.

The States and Higher Education. San Francisco: Jossey-Bass Publishers, 1976. Published as a commentary of the Carnegie Foundation for the Advancement of Teaching.

Strauss, George. "The AAUP as a Professional Occupation Association," *Industrial Relations* 5 (October 1965): 128–140.

"Teaching Aides Organize, Seek A Wider Role," *Chronicle of Higher Education* (17 May 1967): 1, 3.

Tierney, William G. *Building Communities of Difference: Higher Education in the Twenty-First Century.* Westport, Conn.: Bergin & Garvey, 1993.

————, and Estela Mara Bensimon. *Promotion and Tenure: Community and Socialization in Academe.* Albany: State University of New York Press, 1996.

Thelin, John R. "Beyond Background Music: Historical Research on Admissions and Access in Higher Education," in *Higher Education: Handbook of Theory and Research,* ed. John C. Smart, vol. 6. New York: Agathon, 1990, pp. 349–380.

"Three Vie for Presidency of AAUP; First Real Contest in 59 Years," *Chronicle of Higher Education* (19 February 1974): 5.

Thwing, Charles Franklin. *College Administration.* New York: Century, 1900.

Tokarczk, Michelle M., and Elizabeth A. Fay. *Working Class Women in the Academy: Laborers in the Knowledge Factory.* Amherst: University of Massachusetts Press, 1993.

"Transport News: Flight Insurance," *New York Times,* 29 September 1966, p. 93.

"Union Election for Vocational Teachers Set," *Milwaukee Journal,* 15 May 1963, part 1, p. 10.

"Union Wins Teacher Vote," *Milwaukee Journal,* 4 June 1963, part 2, p. 14.

"Unionization among College Faculty: 1996," *National Center for the Study of Collective Bargaining in Higher Education and the Professions Newsletter* 24 (April–May 1996).

Van de Water, John R., "Union- Management Relations in Public and Private Education," *CUPA Journal* 17 (November 1965): 1–30. Some cited material first published in *Los Angeles Times* 5 February 1965, part 2, p. 1

"Vatican Orders Curran, Catholic U. Theologian, to Retract His Views," *Chronicle of Higher Education* (19 March 1986): 30.

Vaughan, George B. "Scholarship and Community Colleges: The Path to Respect," *Educational Record* 69, no. 2 (1988): 26–31.

Veblen, Thorstein. *The Higher Learning in America: A Memorandum on the Conduct of Universities by Business Men.* New York: B. W. Huebsch, 1918.

Veysey, Laurence. *The Emergence of the American University* (Chicago: University of Chicago Press, 1965).

Wagner, Geoffrey. "Local 1640," *Universities Quarterly* 19 (December 1964): 78–80.

Weber, Max. *The Theory of Social and Economic Organization,* trans. by A. M. Henderson and Talcott Parsons. New York: Oxford University Press, 1947.

Welch, Lynne B., ed., *Women in Higher Education: Changes and Challenges.* New York: Praeger, 1990.

West, Allan M. *The National Education Association: The Power Base for Education.* New York: Free Press, 1980.

Wiberg, Charles E. "A History of the University of Minnesota Chapter of the American Association of University Professors, 1916–1960," 2 vols. Ph.D. dissertation, University of Minnesota, 1964.

Wilensky, Harold L. "The Professionalization of Everyone?" *American Journal of Sociology* 70 (September 1964): 137–158.

Wilson, John T. *Academic Science, Higher Education, and the Federal Government, 1950–1983.* Chicago: University of Chicago Press, 1983.

Wilson, Logan. "A President's Perspective," in *Faculty-Administration Relationships,* Edited by Frank C. Abbott. Washington, D.C.: American Council on Education, 1958, pp. 1–12.

————. *American Academics: Then and Now.* New York: Oxford University Press, 1979.

————. *The Academic Man: A Study in the Sociology of a Profession.* New York: Oxford University Press, 1942.

Wolfle, Dael. *The Home of Science: The Role of the University.* New York: McGraw-Hill, 1972.

Woodward, C. Vann. "The Unreported Crisis in the Southern Colleges," *Harper's Magazine* October 1962, pp. 82–84, 86–89.

INDEX

academic labor market, 23, 66, 84, 85, 99, 176, 183
Adams, Walter, 131, 142, 157
Adler, Daniel, 102, 119
Alexander Meiklejohn Award, 39
American Association for Higher Education, 98
American Association of University Professors
  academic freedom, 8–10, 25–28, 31–35, 39, 56, 82, 83, 112, 114, 121, 123, 127–128, 147, 148, 160, 162–163, 165. *See also* Alexander Meiklejohn Award; Committee A; Special Committee on Academic Freedom in the Quest for National Security
  administrative intransigience, 131. *See also* Catholic University; St. John's University (NY)
agency shop. *See* membership
annual meeting
  1953, 30
  1954, 32
  1958, 55
  1960, 55
  1961, 51
  1965, 73
  1966, 91
  1967, 104–105
  1968, 113
  1969, 117
  1971, 148–149
  1973, 152
  1975, 162–163
  1976, 168
apartheid, 55
black professors, 161, 162
chapters, 31–32, 153
  Belleville College, 100–101, 114, 123
  Collective Bargaining Caucus, 160, 165–166, 167, 168
  Indiana University, 101
  Oakland University, 132, 145–146, 169
  Rider College, 169
  Rutgers University, 123, 132
  St. John's University (N.Y.), 75–79, 123, 131, 132, 145–146. *See also* St. John's University (N.Y.)
  Syracuse University, 53–54, 124
  University of Bridgeport, 169
  University of Minnesota, 30, 32
civil liberties, 55–56, 171
civil rights, 55–56
collective bargaining. *See* unionization
council meetings, 28, 31, 33, 40
  April 1965, 73–74
  May 1966, 89–92
  October 1967, 102
  April 1968, 112

October 1968, 114–115
May 1969, 115–116
October 1969, 118–120
April 1970, 123–125
April 1971, 131
October 1971, 143–144
April 1974, 155
November 1974, 164–165
June 1975, 165–166
November 1975, 167
June 1976, 168
faculty dismissals, 39–40, 56–57, 80, 112, 127–128, 158. *See also* St. John's University (N.Y.)
faculty strikes, 15, 62, 77–78, 103–108, 113, 145, 169
federal unionization laws and regulations, 130, 132, 139, 166–167. *See also* National Labor Relations Board
female professors, 128, 160–161, 164–165, 167. *See also* Committee W
financial affairs, 79, 124, 129–130, 138–139, 145, 146, 147, 148, 153, 154–155, 164–166, 165–166, 170–171
financial exigency, 149–150, 158, 163–164, 170
legal issues, 56, 57, 139, 170
loyalty oaths
Arkansas, 55
University of California, 26
National Defense Education Act, 55
membership, 11, 13, 25, 40–41, 58–59, 84, 122–123, 125, 131, 134, 138–139, 140–141, 145–146, 148, 152–153, 153–154, 155–156, 164–165,

168, 170, 172. *See also* Committee F
distribution by institutional type, 59
dues, 148, 170
policy approval procedures, 44, 89–90
presidents, 12, 59, 156
professionalism, 7, 60–61, 93, 113, 115, 126, 133, 148, 158–159
and bureacratization, 146–147
professorial ethics, 82. *See also* Committee B
professors and college or university governance, 11, 40, 51, 65, 95–96, 129, 131, 150, 160, 168. *See also* Committe T
professors at two-year colleges, 16, 109, 121, 163
professors' political attitudes, 111, 157
professors' salaries and benefits, 10–11, 28–29, 36–38, 81. *See also* Committee Z
representation of economic interests, 73, 87–95
self-study
1965 Self-Study Committee, 81–84
1971 report, 130–131, 137–144
1973 report, 152–153
staff, 25, 31, 35, 41, 63, 139, 142, 172
state and regional conferences, 30, 61–62, 121–122, 125
Michigan Conference, 142
state unionization laws and regulations, 114, 116, 118, 120, 125, 146, 166–167

tenure, 157, 158, 160, 174

unionization, 14, 16, 36, 60–62, 69–75, 82–83, 86, 100–102, 111, 114–118, 120, 121–122, 124–125, 129–130, 133–135, 137–149, 151–152, 158, 160, 161, 162, 163, 164–167, 170–171, 174. *See also* representation of economic interests

unit determination. *See* membership

American Council on Education, 9, 25, 53, 54–55, 81, 95

American Federation of Teachers, 14–15, 61, 67, 68, 69, 84–85, 86, 91, 97–98, 105, 116, 124, 136–137, 139, 150, 167, 170, 169

United Federation of College Teachers, 75, 77–78

Association of American Colleges, 13, 25, 29, 46–47, 52, 140, 151

Association of Governing Boards, 81, 95

Barbash, Jack, 71–72, 87

Baumol, William, 105, 119

Bierstadt, Robert, 74, 93

Brown, Jr., Ralph S., 41, 54–55, 71–73, 77, 86, 91, 94, 96, 105–107, 108, 110–111, 114–115, 116– 117, 122, 123–125, 131–134, 134–135, 137, 150

bureaucratization, 6
in higher education, 67, 85, 98, 180–182

Byse, Clark, 41, 71–73, 74, 76–77, 80, 91, 94, 96, 100–102, 105, 117

California State Colleges, 91, 92, 100, 145

Carr, Robert, 42

Catholic University, 103–104

City University of New York, 92, 114, 122, 124, 150

collective bargaining. *See* unionization

committees, 187

Committee A, 27–28, 35, 53, 56, 57–58, 76, 78, 123–124, 127–128, 140, 143, 148, 151, 153, 163–164, 170. *See also* Special Committee on Academic Freedom in the Quest for National Security

American University of Beirut, 80

censure, 9–10, 80, 153, 165

General Declaration of Principles and Practical Proposals, 9

1940 Statement of Principles on Academic Freedom and Tenure, 13

1925 Conference Statement on Academic Freedom and Tenure

Princeton University, 80

Statement on the Standards for Notice of Nonreappointment, 57

grievance procedures, 80

Committee B, 112

Committee D, 78, 126–127

Committee F, 40, 155–156, 168

Committee L, 162

Committee N, 120–121, 122–123, 130–134, 142, 149, 153, 154–155, 164–165, 166, 168

Committee O, 30, 31, 35, 36, 40

Committee S, 44

Committee T, 29–30, 31, 35, 53, 78, 108–109, 128–129, 142, 149–150, 154, 163–164

investigations, 49, 50, 51, 52, 54, 81, 128–129

1958 report, 49

Committee T *(continued)*
  Statement on College and University
    Government, 50–51, 51–52,
    53–55, 81, 95, 108, 114, 164
Committee V, 163
Committee W, 128, 160, 165, 173–174
Committee Z, 28–29, 35, 38, 81–82,
    140, 151, 164–165
  1959 report, 44–45
  1960 report, 45–46
  1961 report, 46–47
  1962 report, 47
  1963 report, 47
  1964 report, 48
  1965 report, 81
  1966 report, 95
  1967 report, 109
Committee Z *(continued)*
  1968 report, 109–110
  1969 report, 110
  1970 report, 128
  1972 report, 149
  1974 report, 161
  1975 report, 167
  1976 report, 168–169
  public and private institutions, 110
computer technology, 186
Curran, Reverend Charles, 103

Davis, Bertram H., 15, 56–57, 60,
    63–64, 65, 69–70, 73, 74, 79–80,
    91–92, 101, 103–104, 113–114,
    114–115, 119, 124, 126, 127–128,
    129–130, 138, 144–145, 152, 154,
    158–159
Duffey, Joseph, 159–160, 167

Executive Committee, 69–70, 72, 130,
    137–139

faculty strikes, 68, 98, 105, 169
Fellman, David, 57, 69–72, 73–74,
    93–94, 148
Fenlon, Paul, 77, 87–89
Fidler, William S., 42, 43–44, 51, 53,
    55, 56, 61–62, 63, 72, 74, 75–79,
    83, 86, 93, 96, 100, 103–104, 134,
    142
Finkin, Matthew, 114, 116, 119, 120,
    121–122, 124, 126, 166
Fuchs, Ralph F., 33–34, 41, 52–53,
    55–56, 63, 74

G.I. Bill, 22
graduate student unions, 85, 97–98,
    136

Hickman, C. Addison, 125, 148
Himstead, Ralph E., 13, 24–28, 30–33
Joughin, Louis, 56, 72–74, 100, 102,
    142

Kadish, Sanford H., 104–105, 106–108,
    123–124, 138, 143–144, 147–148
Kugler, Israel, 61, 91, 104, 107, 120

Larsen, Charles M., 90–91, 100, 101
Leonard, William, 115, 116, 117–118
Levi, Werner, 30, 31–32

Machlup, Fritz, 38, 93
McCarthyism, 23–24, 26–28, 34
McPherson, William, 70–72, 74, 87
Metzger, Walter P., 83–84
Milwaukee Vocational School, 68

National Education Association, 15, 67,
    68–69, 116, 124, 136–137, 139,
    142, 149, 150, 167, 168, 169, 170

National Labor Relations Board, 125–126, 131, 134–135, 150
National Science Foundation, 22
New Jersey State Colleges, 124, 138

Pennsylvania State Colleges, 124, 138, 148
posttenure review, 186
President's Commission on Education beyond High School, 38, 46
President's Commission on Higher Education for American Democracy, 22
professionalism, 5, 174–176
and bureaucratization, 16–18, 98–99, 182–187
professionalism and the professoriate, 2–5, 98, 174–179
professionalization, 5
professors
distribution at public and private institutions, 13, 85
distribution at four-year and two-year institutions, 42, 85, 136
female professors, 136
lesbian professors, 184
number of, 23, 41, 58
part-time professors, 185–186
political attitudes, 111, 163
preparation, 13, 42, 85, 176–177
preparation at two-year institutions, 99
professors of color, 136, 184
publications and research, 177–178
salaries, 177
working-class female professors, 184
professors and college or university governance, 98–99

Recommended Institutional Regulations on Academic Freedom and Tenure, 112, 163–164

St. John's University (N.Y.), 75–79, 122
scholarship and teaching, 187
Shannon, George Pope, 32–33
Special Committee on Academic Freedom in the Quest for National Security, 34–35
Special Committee on Representation of Economic Interests, 83, 86–90, 114. See also Committee N
Special Joint Committee on Bargaining, Sanctions, and Representation, 105–107, 117
State University of New York, 114, 122, 124, 132, 138, 150
Statement on Collective Bargaining, 151–152
and professional ideals, 174
Statement on Faculty Participation in Strikes, 107–108, 117
Statement on Representation of Economic Interests, 89–90, 112–113, 117–120. See also Statement on Representation of Professional and Economic Interests
Statement on Representation of Professional and Economic Interests, 120, 146. See also Statement on Collective Bargaining
Stevens, Carl, 120, 124, 147, 152, 156–157, 164, 165, 166
student enrollment, 23
Subcommittee on Taxes, 48
Sumberg, Alfred, 114, 115–116, 117, 118–119, 123–124, 125, 141–142

Summers, Clyde W., 71–72, 77, 86–89, 92, 100, 105

tenure, 182

United Federation of Teachers, 68
United States Merchant Marine Academy, 85, 97
unionization, 66–69, 180
    Wisconsin state legislature, 67
    National Labor Relations Board, 67
untenured professors, 10, 60, 127–128

Van Alstyne, William, 141, 147–148, 151, 152, 156–157, 159, 165–166, 170–172

Wartofsky, Marx, 156–157
Webb, Robert, 139, 141, 147–148
White, Helen, 39
Woodcock, Leonard, 167

Yeshiva decision, 179–180

PHILO A. HUTCHESON is assistant professor of educational policy studies at Georgia State University. He is well known for his research and writings on historical and contemporary issues concerning the faculties of U.S. colleges and universities and has also worked in the field of college admissions and in other administrative roles.